THINKING CRITICALLY
TECHNIQUES FOR LOGICAL REASONING

THINKING CRITICALLY

Techniques for Logical Reasoning

James H. Kiersky

Georgia State University

Nicholas J. Caste

University of North Carolina-Charlotte

WEST PUBLISHING COMPANY

Minneapolis/St. Paul   New York   Los Angeles   San Francisco

WEST'S COMMITMENT TO THE ENVIRONMENT

In 1906, West Publishing Company began recycling materials left over from the production of books. This began a tradition of efficient and responsible use of resources. Today, up to 95% of our legal books and 70% of our college texts and school texts are printed on recycled, acid-free stock. West also recycles nearly 22 million pounds of scrap paper annually—the equivalent of 181,717 trees. Since the 1960s, West has devised ways to capture and recycle waste inks, solvents, oils, and vapors created in the printing process. We also recycle plastics of all kinds, wood, glass, corrugated cardboard, and batteries, and have eliminated the use of Styrofoam book packaging. We at West are proud of the longevity and the scope of our commitment to the environment.

Cover image: © Zefa-Mueller, W.H./The Stock Market
Copyediting: Loretta Palagi
Text Design: Johnston Design Office
Composition: Parkwood Composition, Inc.
Illustration: Miyake Illustration
Indexing: Schroeder Indexing
Production, Prepress, Printing and Binding by West Publishing Company.

TEXT IS PRINTED ON 10% POST CONSUMER RECYCLED PAPER

PRINTED WITH SOY INK™

British Library Cataloguing-in-Publication Data.
A catalouge record for this book is available from the British Library.

COPYRIGHT © 1995 by   WEST PUBLISHING CO.
                                       610 Opperman Drive
                                       P.O. Box 64526
                                       St. Paul, MN 55164–0526

Printed in the United States of America

02 01 00 99 98 97 96 95   876543210
Library of Congress Cataloging-in-Publication Data

Kiersky, James Hugh.
          Thinking critically: techniques of logical reasoning/James H.
Kiersky, Nicolas J. Caste.
          p. cm
          Includes index.
          ISBN 0–314–04352-7 (pbk.)
          1. Critical thinking. 2. Reasoning. 3. Logic I. Caste, Nicolas
J. II. Title
BC177.K514 1995
160—dc20
                                       94-34797
                                       CIP

To Doris and Hubert

To Joe C.

CONTENTS

Thinking Critically. . . is first and foremost a textbook on critical thinking and informal logic. As such, it encompasses many of the traditional topics that have been associated with these fields since the time of Aristotle, two and a half millenia ago: good and bad thinking, fallacies, definitions, meaning, induction, deduction, syllogisms, enthymemes, sorities, and a host of others. It also covers more recent additions to the field—conditionals, counterfactuals, predicate logic, truth tables, standardized testing, logical writing and organization, to name a few. Rather than simply learn a number of apparently disconnected skills or memorize interesting but out-of-date technical terminology, we have approached the topics of critical thinking and informal logic as if they were themselves *processes* for helping all of us better our lives as well as those of others. Admittedly, this is a fairly tall order.

But if there are good grounds for seeing critical thinking and logical reasoning as *processes* that are (or can be) a part of everyday life, then several beneficial results may occur. First, it becomes a fairly simple task to get an overview of the entire subject matter, which in turn will help us keep in mind where we are and why we are there. Second, by considering reasoning from the perspective of a process, we can then devise a set of strategies and techniques for approaching and resolving problems as they arise. Third, by studying logic and critical thinking from the practical standpoint, it is more likely that the skills learned will be put to use outside of academics, possibly retained beyond the end of a quarter or semester, and even incorporated into one's working set of behavioral dispositions. If this is correct, the notion of critical thinking as a *skills* course begins to take on deeper significance. Those skills are not simply means to an end (i.e., passing another course), nor are they ends in themselves (i.e., exercises that may be intrinsically enjoyable, but which have no apparent applicability). Instead, if they can be both instrumental in helping us improve the quality of our lives and the lives around us, they should also enrich those lives.

No doubt, this is a bold claim. To what extent we can actually make logic and critical thinking work for us will depend as much on those using the book, students, professors, readers, as on those of us who formulated it in the first place. This is not meant to abrogate any responsibility; we hope we have done our part for the text itself. But we also realize there may be no such thing as the perfect text especially in these areas. Indeed, we would like to reduce the number of flaws in the event of a second edition. With that in mind, we would appreciate any and all comments on the text—good, bad, critical, helpful. Please write and let us know. Whatever suggestions we incorporate into the next edition will be so acknowledged.

Organization of the Text   The text has been organized around a central idea—that of "The Critical Technique," one possible way of many for analyzing, evaluating, formulating, and/or writing arguments and lines of reasoning. To that end it has been divided into three distinct parts. Part One focuses on recognizing arguments, analyzing them, breaking them down into their component parts, clarifying the content and meaning where necessary, and then portraying with accuracy the structure of that reasoning. Certain measurable skills should result from a study of this portion of the test: enhanced ability to recognize premises and conclusions, to spot indicator words, to distinguish inductive from deductive reasoning, to identify presuppositions (unstated premises) and implications (including unstated conclusions), plus the ability to assess definitions, clarify meaning, recognize vagueness and ambiguity, among other skills.

Part Two continues the development of the Critical Technique by shifting from the analysis of arguments and disagreements to the assessment or evaluation of those lines of reasoning. There are three distinguishable phases here, although one of them is clearly a blend of the other two. We begin with that phase: recognizing fallacies, mistakes in the reasoning process. Then we move to a second important phase, that of critically evaluating lines of reasoning solely on the basis of their structure or form. Finally, arguments may be critiqued on the basis of their content: how true, relevant, fair, or adequate the evidence is in support of the conclusion. Again, certain very measurable skills should result: for example, the ability to distinguish between validity, truth, and soundness; the ability to distinguish valid argument forms from invalid ones, the ability to draw immediate inferences and to determine what necessarily follows from a line of thinking. A study of fallacious modes of reasoning should also result in enhanced capabilities for determining what evidence is relevant, pertinent, fair, and adequate or sufficient for drawing what conclusions.

Part Three forms the conclusion of the text by showing some of the applications of the Technique, particularly in the fields of non-deductive reasoning, in scientific thinking, causal argumentation, analogical reasoning, explanations, theories, hypotheses, and several parallel forms of reasoning. It also focuses in upon the relevance of many of these critical strategies for standardized test taking. And, it concludes with a discussion of ways in which these strategies may help improve argumentative writing skills. Some of the measurable skills that may be expected to result from this portion of the text should be fairly evident from this description alone: improved writing and organizational skills, enriched test-taking skills, better understanding of scientific reasoning, analogical thinking, theories, hypotheses, explanations, causal reasoning, parallel reasoning, moral argumentation, to name a few.

Different Possible Uses/Applications

If a textbook in the fields of critical thinking and logical reasoning, is to be worth its salt, it will have to be *quite* adaptable. These are arenas covering such a broad spectrum of human cognitive life that almost everyone teaching or using a text of this nature will have their own agenda for doing so. Indeed, even the two authors use the text quite differently. We can only begin to show some of the possible options for using the text to maximum advantage by giving you four quick examples.

(1) The Linear Approach. (fig 1)   The text is organized in such a way that it can actually be followed from start to finish by studying Part One first, then proceeding to Parts Two and Three. Much of the material will turn out to be cumulative in the sense of a building of basic skills that are sharpened and integrated as the text proceeds.

(2) The Critical Thinking Approach. (fig. 2)   For those more interested in developing critical thinking skills, the text can be followed by studying Chapters One through Four first, then continuing with a study of Chapter Five on Fallacies, then moving to Chapters Twelve and Fourteen. Once these portions of the text have been mastered, then attention can be turned to Chapter Thirteen on standardized test questions and Chapters Six and Seven to cover categorical reasoning, syllogisms, and the rudiments of deductive argument forms.

(3) The More Traditional Approach. (fig. 3)   For those who find it more practical or desirable, the study of logical forms may be accomplished first, by beginning with a quick reading of Chapter One and the second half of Chapter Two (Sections 2–2 and 2–3). Chapters Eight through Eleven on Truth Functional Connections and Propositional Logic should be studied next, followed by a return to Chapters Six and Seven on the older categorical forms of reasoning. Once this has been accomplished, the first half of

Part One: Identifying and Analyzing Arguments

Ch 1 → Ch 2 → Ch 3 → Ch 4

▼

Part Two: Evaluating Arguments

Ch 5; Ch 6 & Ch 7 → Ch 8–11

▼

Part Three: Applying the Technique

Ch 12 → Ch → 13 → Ch 14

(fig 1)

Part One: Identifying and Analyzing Arguments

Ch 1 → Ch 2 → Ch 3 → Ch 4

▼

Fallacies (Ch 5)→ Inductive Reasoning (Ch 12)

↓

Argumentative Writing (Ch 14)

▼

Logical Puzzles/Games Ch 13

↓

Categorical Reasoning and Syllogisms (Chh 6–7)

(fig 2)

Chapter Two and Chapters Twelve and Thirteen would round this form of studying logical reasoning processes.

(4) The Standardized Test Approach. (fig. 4)   In order to use the text as an aid for preparing to take a standardized test such as the LSAT, the GRE, the GMAT, or even the MCAT, one of the main considerations is how much time remains until the test date. If you have planned ahead and left yourself five to six months before the test, then you have ample time to read through using Linear Method 1 just described, and you will better understand a lot of the theory behind the test. If you are more like the majority of us and have only limited time at your disposal, you can do the following:

(a) Read and work Chapter Thirteen so that you have a working knowledge of at least some of the kinds of logical puzzles and games likely to come up on the analytical and logical reasoning sections of the text.

(b) Go back and scan Sections 2–2 and 2–3 to understand the nature of arguments and inductive versus deductive reasoning enough to read 3–1 carefully. Then, work the B-Level problems at the end of section 3–1. Once you have mastered the kinds of assumption—implication problems likely to arise, then,

(c) Go to Section 14–2 and read and work the B-Level exercises on parallel reasoning.

(d) Now, go to Chapters Six and Seven and study the *diagramming* techniques for dealing with syllogisms and categorical logic. See how well you do on the exercises in those chapters and, once you are getting 75–80% or better on all of these sections, and are feeling reasonably comfortable about these problems, then

(e) Skim through Chapter Five in order to be able to pick out fallacious forms of reasoning. If any time remains and if the test you are taking contains a writing sample,

(f) Read and work the remaining exercises in Chapter Fourteen in order to be able to anticipate the writing sample portion of these tests.

Exercises

As in perhaps any critical thinking and logical reasoning book, the exercises in the text are one of the most crucial ingredients for understanding, applying, and mastering the skills and techniques. We have placed them at the *end of each section* of *every chapter* so that there would be no long gaps in between testing out what you have been covering. If there is a problem, you will not have to wait to find out what it is. Second, we have tried to keep the exercises as relevant as possible without becoming too tedious or overwhelming. We also attempted to increase the difficulty level gradually. And, most importantly, we have organized the exercises on *three distinct levels:* The *A-Level exercises* are there as a kind of barometer to let you and your instructor know how well you have read and understood the material in that

---

Logic & Critical Thinking (Ch 1)
↓
Inductive/Deductive Arguments Ch 2–2 & 2–3
▼
Propostitional Logic, Truth-Functional Connectives Chh 8, 9, 10, 11
▼
Categorical Logic; Syllogism Immedicate Inference, Enthymemes, Sorites Chh 6 and 7
▼
Reasons & Causes, Analogies, Hypotheses, Theories, Explanations (Ch 12) Logical Puzzles/Games Ch 13

(fig 3)

Logical Puzzles/Games Ch 13
▼
Ch 2-2 and 2-3, Inductive and Deductive Reasoning Then: Ch 3-1 Spotting Assumptions and Implications
▼
Ch 14-2: Parallel Reasoning Exercises in B-Level Ex.
▼
Chh 6 and 7, esp. diagramming techniques. Work exercises
▼
Ch 5- Fallacies and Mistakes in Reasoning, esp. Personal Attack, Begging the Question and Assuming the Cause
▼
Ch 14- Writing Sample Exercises in Chapter

(fig 4)

section. There are immediate tests for feedback. *The B-Level exercises* test your ability to *apply* to a range of problems the distinctions that have been made during that section. *The C-Level exercises* are in a way self-referential tests of how functional those distinctions may be in actuality. They may contain questions at a much deeper level of difficulty. They may contain questions about the limits of applying the distinctions made during that portion of the chapter. Or, they may contain questions relating different portions of the text to material currently being studied. Selected solutions to these exercises appear in an appendix to the text.

Integration with Writing

More and more, a connection, hitherto unseen, between critical thinking and logical reasoning on the one hand and argumentative writing on the other is being recognized and fostered on college campuses. This text is designed with that factor in mind. Over fifty percent of the logic and critical thinking courses we teach have a writing component as one of the major, stated objectives. The exercises at the end of each section as well as the entirety of Chapter Fourteen contain ongoing ideas for improving writing skills at each level of the Technique until they are all reintegrated and reinforced at the conclusion of the text. Indeed, if we were teaching a writing course that contained critical thinking skills as a component, this text could also be utilized quite practically by beginning with Chapter Fourteen. You will notice that virtually every component in that chapter is explained in much greater detail, point by point, earlier in the text.

Whether used in a writing course or a critical thinking course, or even a logic course, the writing component can be integrated to whatever extent is deemed appropriate.

Special Features

We have tried to incorporate a number of features that worked particularly well in our own classes and to eliminate others when student feedback took a negative turn. Generically, some of the major features we retained include

— "A Critical Technique", a masterplan, an overview of the subject matter to be covered with a chapter by chapter roadmap of where we are.
— At the beginning of each chapter, a list of the important terms and concepts occurring in that chapter, a sort of "mini-index and glossary".
— "Reality Checks", which could consist of anything from a comic strip, to a letter to the editor, to a "sound-bite" from a television show, and which functions as an example (or sometimes a counter-example) of the material under discussion. Usually, the "reality checks" are there for the purpose of illustration when they might be disruptive of the flow of the text, if incorporated directly into it.
— Exercises at three distinct levels of difficulty as discussed above and placed at the end of each section of each chapter.
— A concise chapter or sectional summary to highlight the important points discussed in that portion of the text.
— A Case Study at the end of each chapter to exemplify something of importance about that chapter: for example, a way in which the *Technique* may be utilized at this level, or a case in which newly acquired skills may be practiced on a larger scale, or an alternative to the approach we covered in the chapter.
— A Glossary of Terms (and Symbols) at the end of the text.
— A particular slant to some of the exercises in each chapter to show how questions of the sort are used on standardized tests (particularly ones like the LSAT, the GRE, the GMAT, and others); plus an entire Chapter devoted to the logic of puzzles and games and standardized test questions.
— Examples from as many areas of life as we could think of, from business to medicine, law to engineering, computers to art, morals to baseball, culinary skills to world politics.

— Suggested aids for improved writing skills beginning with becoming more culturally sensitive and moving toward greater organizational skills.

Acknowledgments

Unlike many first editions, the text of this particular book has undergone many revisions which are the direct result of excellent student feedback. Add to that the diligence and care that our editors here at West Publishing Company, especially Joan Gill and Becky Stovall, have bestowed upon the text as well as the reviewers they have chosen for their professional expertise, and we find very few persons other than ourselves upon whom we could place the blame for what errors remain in the text itself. There is no way that we could name all the people to whom we owe a considerable debt. There are many who should be named, and for those we may have omitted, we are truly sorry. That being said, we make no pretense of having created a novel work. There are many whose works we have used when we were undergraduate and graduate students, then later when we were young instructors. The debt to such writers and logicians as Salmon, Copi, Fearnside, Carney, Sheer, Toulmin, Scriven, Jeffries, Pospesl, and many, many others is incalculable. Likewise, much is owed to our colleagues, particularly, Milton Snoeyenbos, Don Nilson, and in our younger days, Nick Fotion. Family and friends not only provided a great deal of support both "moral" and as informal editors and source material.

We would be sorely remiss if we did not at least mention Caren, Mary, and Maggie, Carole, Lisa, and Jill—all of whom served as wonderful inspirations, as great listeners, sometimes providing the source of our examples, and supplying rather generous doses of patient when most needed. Also, David Aton provided many humorous and illustrative anecdotes, some of which found their way into these pages.

We would also like to thank the reviewers of this text for their contributions and suggestions:

Andy Young
California State University
Stanislaus, CA

Henry N. Carrier
Brevard Community College
Cocoa, FL

Bill Simpson
University of Colorado—Boulder
Boulder, CO

Lynn Hankinson-Nelson
Rowan College of New Jersey
Glassboro, NJ

David Hitchcock
McMaster University
Hamilton, Ontario

H. S. Moorehead
Northeastern Illinois University
Chicago, IL

Dr. Ronald Hall
Francis Marion University
Florence, SC

Eric Kraemer
University of Wisconsin—LaCrosse
LaCrosse, WI

Jeffrey Berger
Community College of Philadelphia
Philadelphia, PA

Robert Cogan
Edinboro University of Pennsylvania
Edinboro, PA

James Cox
West Georgia College
Carrollton, GA

Daniel Flage
James Madison University
Harrisonburg, VA

Roger Ward
Baylor University
Waco, TX

Albert Lyngzeidetson
University of Miami
Coral Gables, FL

John Humphrey
Mankato State University
Mankato, MN

Phyllis Berger
Diablo Valley College
Pleasant Hill, CA

Robert Mellert
Brookdale Community College
Lincroft, NJ

Lawrence Habermehl
American International College
Springfield, MA

Frank K. Fair
Sam Houston State University
Huntsville, TX

Ronald Burnside
Sinclair Community College
Dayton, OH

W. Mark Cobb
Pensacola, Junior College
Pensacola, FL

William J. Kinnaman
Community College of Rhode Island
Lincoln, RI

Walter G. Scott
Oklahoma State University
Stillwater, OK

Michael A. Principe
Middle Tennessee State University
Murfreesboro, TN

Gordon Steinhoff
Utah State University
Logan, UT

Theodore Gracyk
Moorehead State University
Moorehead, MN

Norris Frederick
Queens College
Charlotte, NC

Jessie Hobbs
Washington University
St. Louis, MO

Dr. Jack Sibley
Texas Women's University
Denton, TX

Russell Wall
Idaho State University
Pocatello, ID

Kevin Stanley
Yavapi College
Prescott, AZ

1

THE ANALYSIS OF ARGUMENTS

Two main parts of the critical technique include (1) analysing arguments and (2) evaluating arguments. The initial analytical phase primarily involves breaking down arguments into their component statements (claims), identifying premises and conclusions, distinguishing deductive from inductive reasoning, spotting assumptions and implications, portraying the structure of the reasoning involved, and clarifying meaning as necessary. This part of phase one is covered in the first four chapters and is preliminary to a fair, adequate, and accurate assessment of the argument, which is a major goal for the critical technique itself.

A TECHNIQUE FOR THINKING CRITICALLY

step one
What is the main claim?

step four
What is the meaning of the terms employed?

step two
Is there an argument?

step three
Are there any assumptions or implications?

step five
Are there any fallacies?

step six
What is the argument's structure?

step seven
What other conclusions can be drawn?

"The ruling passion, be it what it will,
The ruling passion conquers reason still."
—Alexander Pope (1738)

"Irrationally held truths
may be more harmful
than reasoned errors."
—T. H. Huxley (1886)

step eight
Do you agree or disagree with the conclusion?

KEY TERMS

Argument - A set of related claims in which one is said to follow from or be based on the others. The two types of claims in an argument are premises and conclusions.

Argument structure - How the premises of an argument are related to the conclusion.

Claim - An assertion or statement capable of being assessed as true or false.

Conclusion - The claim that is to be established or proven in an argument.

Critical technique - The eight-step method of critical thinking presented in this book.

Critical thinking - The ability to correctly validate or refute claims presented for our belief.

Fallacy - An error of reasoning. Do not confuse it with a false claim.

Hidden assumption - An assumption in an argument that is not explicitly stated, but assumed to be true. A hidden assumption is also known as an *unstated premise*, or *logical presupposition*.

Inductive argument - One in which the truth of the premises merely makes the truth of the conclusion more or less probable. Inductive arguments are considered to be strong or weak according to the degree or probability with which the conclusion is established.

Invalid deductive argument - An argument presented as a valid deductive argument, but due to a flaw in the argument's structure, it is possible for all of the premises to be true while the conclusion is nevertheless false.

Meaning - How a word, phrase, sentence, or gesture is understood, as well as how it is used.

Premise - A claim offered in support of the conclusion.

Valid deductive argument - An argument is deductively valid if and only if it is impossible for all of the premises to be true and the conclusion false.

This is a book about thinking. More specifically, it's a manual for thinking critically. Thinking is certainly a very important part of our lives. Our waking hours are filled with thoughts. We might begin the day with a decision about whether or not to push the snooze alarm and end it with the conclusion that we've watched enough television. But if thinking is something that we all do so often, why would anyone need a manual? And why think "critically"?

Our beliefs influence our emotions and our actions. So it is important that they accurately reflect the real world. This is the purpose of **critical thinking**—*to help answer the question of whether or not to adopt a belief.* Critical thinking is concerned with the justification and validation of our beliefs, *not* their origin. The difference between the questions "Where did you get that idea?" and "How do you know that this idea is true?" is significant. The origins of beliefs are studied by psychologists, sociologists, anthropologists, and to some extent physiologists. Regardless of its origin, however, the claim made by any belief can be evaluated critically. So the critical thinker is interested in whether the evidence presented for a claim is true and accurate. She is also interested in the adequacy of the evidence and even the fairness of the argument.

This book is intended to teach you how to think critically. It will do this in the following ways. *First,* it will increase your awareness of the variety of ways that human beings think, reason, justify, explain, rationalize, and persuade. *Second,* this book will provide the tools for sharpening your skills in both evaluating the claims made by others and organizing, presenting, and putting into writing your own arguments. *Third,* a study of this book will enhance your problem-solving and decision-making skills. A *fourth* objective is to foster an appreciation for problems, conflicts, and disagreements such that they become challenges rather than nuisances. The *fifth* aim of this text is to give you the necessary background to approach the reasoning sections of the standardized tests used to screen applicants to law school, postgraduate business school, medical school, and graduate school. *Sixth,* it will provide a foundation for you to enhance your own sense of self-awareness. By developing strategies for detecting unconsciously held prejudices you will be able to refine your judgments.

This book is organized on the basis of what we call the **Critical Technique.** It is a method concerned with both *analyzing* lines of reasoning and *evaluating* their worth. Only by doing the former can we fairly, accurately, and objectively proceed to the latter. The Technique consists of eight questions to be asked when you are evaluating an argument:

A CRITICAL TECHNIQUE

1   WHAT IS THE MAJOR CLAIM BEING ADVANCED?

The first step in the analysis of an argument or a line of reasoning is to determine which claims are being made or advanced. A **claim** is an assertion or a statement someone advances as being true. What claim is the passage trying to make? If you are constructing the argument yourself, what is the point you are trying to make?

IS THERE AN ARGUMENT?

Claims are not usually made in isolation. When a claim is presented that someone would have you believe is true, it is usually made in the context of other statements. When a set of claims is brought together in a relationship where some of those claims support another, an **argument** results. The major claim being advanced in an argument is known as a **conclusion.** It is the point of the argument. The conclusion of most political speeches, for instance, is that you should vote for that politician. The other type of claim involved in an argument is a **premise.** A premise is a claim that supports the argument's conclusion. The premises of many political speeches consist of claims that the particular candidate would be best for that office.

Before that argument can be evaluated, its structure must first be determined, and the relationships between the premises and the conclusion established. Several arguments might be employed to advance the same claim. These arguments should be distinguished from one another and the relationships between them determined.

 WHAT IS NOT BEING STATED?

Finding **hidden assumptions** leads to a better understanding of an argument's implications. These are assumptions made within an argument but not explicitly stated. Hidden assumptions are also known as *unstated premises.* A person's choice of words and the way an argument is presented often influence one's acceptance of an argument's conclusion. These hidden assumptions should be subject to the same scrutiny as the explicit ones.

 WHAT IS THE MEANING OF THE TERMS BEING EMPLOYED?

Clarifying the **meaning** of words, phrases, and sentences allows one to better understand the meaning of the language being used. It also allows one to construct clearer and less diffuse arguments. An understanding of the meaning of a term or phrase will also help you spot hidden assumptions. In Chapter 4, we present a method for the clarification of the meaning of the words, phrases, sentences, and sometimes even the gestures from which the argument is constructed.

 ARE ANY FALLACIES INVOLVED?

Once the meaning of the terms is ascertained, the next step is to locate any fallacies employed in the argument. **Fallacies** are forms of bad reasoning that are often accepted by *uncritical* thinkers as good evidence for the conclusion. The content of the argument should also be questioned:

Are the premises relevant to the conclusion? To what degree?

Are the premises true? If you disagree with them, is the disagreement factual, evaluative, interpretive, or verbal?

Are the premises fair? Or are they slanted or biased? How so?

Are the premises adequate? Is there a need for more evidence? Are important objections to the argument left out?

6   IS THE ARGUMENT INDUCTIVE OR DEDUCTIVE?

A distinction needs to be made between **deductive arguments** and **inductive arguments.** A good deductive argument is known as a **valid** deductive argument. An argument is deductively valid if and only if it is impossible for all of its premises to be true while the conclusion is false. If an argument is deductively **invalid,** the conclusion is not proven or established even if its premises all turn out to be true. The validity or invalidity of a deductive argument is established by its **argument structure,** not its content.

Inductive arguments are those that only attempt to establish the more or less *probable* truth of their conclusions. Inductive arguments are considered stronger or weaker according to the degree of probability with which the conclusion is established.

7   WHAT CONCLUSIONS CAN BE DRAWN FROM THE ARGUMENT?

Not all arguments are presented with their conclusions. Sometimes the conclusions must be deduced or induced from the premises presented. When a detective examines evidence in a murder case, when a biological researcher attempts to solve a medical mystery, when a student attempts to answer questions on the reasoning portions of standardized tests, and when a puzzle fan attempts to solve logical puzzles, the conclusions are not present in the argument. They must be *discovered* or found.

8   DO YOU AGREE OR DISAGREE WITH THE CONCLUSION

Having analyzed the structure and content of an argument, you must decide whether you agree or disagree with the conclusion. If the argument seems to be a good one and you agree with the conclusion, can you add anything more in support of it? If you disagree with the conclusion, how would you refute it? Would you question the truth of the premises or would you criticize the argument's structure? Finally, taking a step back from the whole critical process, how important is critical analysis in this case? Is the issue being considered one in which rationality serves any real purpose?

These are the eight "steps" of the Technique. By asking and answering these questions, you will be able to analyze and evaluate almost any argument you encounter. Steps 1 through 4 are considered the analytical phase of The Technique. By correctly answering the questions these steps raise, you will be able to discern the various components of an argument. These steps are discussed in Chapters 1 through 4 of this book.

Having discerned the components of an argument, you will then begin to question the quality of an argument: Is it a good argument or a bad one? Steps 5 through 8 of the Technique are concerned with the *evaluation* of arguments. They will be considered in Chapters 5 through 11.

CALVIN AND HOBBES MEET THE TECHNIQUE

"Calvin and Hobbes' provides a clever insight into this *technique for critical thinking*.

Cartoon is reprinted with permission from Universal Press Syndicate, copyright © 1993.

In frame one, Calvin is trying to solve a problem. This figures prominently under Step 1 of the technique, and will show up particularly in Chapter 2 under the topic of "Disagreements." In frame two, Calvin continues by exploring some of the alternatives open to him. (One of the problems may be whether he has considered an adequate range of solutions.) He proceeds in frame three to show that the consequences of each of the alternatives are undesirable. Is this a false dilemma or a real one? In frames four through six, each of the options is reinforced by reasons or rationalizations, depending on how one looks at them. Finally, we see how a decision is reached and justified. Moreover, we get a glimpse at what may be considered a self-referential paradox (i.e., cheating on an ethics test). By using the Technique, we will have a tool for analyzing and ultimately assessing the worth of any line of reasoning in order to see whether or not it is worth believing.

Finally, you will be given a chance to apply some of the methods derived from the critical technique in the third section of this book. Chapter 12 shows applications of the technique in areas of inductive reasoning including analogies, theories, hypotheses, and causal reasoning. Chapter 13 considers some of the Technique's applications to the problems now found in standardized tests, and Chapter 14 sheds light on how to develop your own written arguments.

To accomplish these aims, we must rely on some technical terms. A technical vocabulary provides for simplicity of expression. In many cases it is simpler to characterize a complex state of affairs by a single word or phrase. This will permit a clearer overview of the reasoning being employed. (It would be distracting to have to recapitulate the complex state of affairs every time you referred to it.) To help familiarize you with these terms, a glossary of each chapter's important terms is provided at the beginning of each chapter. This list also alerts you to key concepts within the chapter. A complete glossary of terms is also provided at the end of this book. Although learning these terms may take some effort, doing so will allow more concentrated attention on the topics and techniques being discussed. It is also important to remember that some of the terms employed in this book have meanings in ordinary language that differ significantly from their technical application. The term *fallacy*, for instance, is often used in ordinary language to refer to any false statement. When reading this book, it is important to keep the technical terminology in mind.

Once you have mastered this book, you should avoid the common error of believing that critical thinking is a destructive tool, a "strip-miner" of reasoning that allows you to criticize and destroy the arguments of others. But, as stressed in the later stages of the technique, it can also be used by people to examine, clarify, and express their own thoughts. The ability to construct better arguments is just one of the positive features of learning to think critically. When trying to decide on a course of action, for instance, a careless analysis and sloppy reasoning can easily lead to a misguided response.

The exercises in each chapter are arranged on three levels. Level A consists of questions designed to test your understanding of the concepts explained in the chapter. Level B questions test your ability to apply the concepts in real and imagined cases. Level C provides more challenging exercises. At the end of every chapter, we also provide a *case study*. These passages demonstrate the application of the methods discussed in the chapter.

SUMMARY

This chapter introduced you to some of the basic concepts involved in critical thinking and to the eight steps of the Technique followed in the rest of this book. Critical thinking is not concerned with the origin of beliefs, but with their validation and justification. The analysis of critical thinking presented in this book is organized on the basis of the Technique. It consists of the eight concerns a good critical thinker would have. The Technique involves asking the following questions:

- What claims are being advanced?
- Are any arguments involved?
- Do any logical assumptions or implications exist?
- Does the meaning of the terms involved affect our acceptance or rejection of any of the claims?

- Are any fallacies involved?
- How sound is the argument's structure?
- In what ways can the Technique be applied?
- How can an argument be constructed on the basis of the Technique?

These questions need not be asked in this particular order, but some of the questions naturally lead to others (see the flowchart presented at the beginning of this chapter). Use of the Technique can help in the criticism of the arguments of others, and it can also increase your problem-solving ability on both practical and theoretical levels.

EXERCISES

 A   **LEVEL**

Questions on this level are designed to measure your success in reading and digesting the material in the chapter.

Multiple Choice

* 1. The best description of *critical thinking* is that it is
      A. a method for criticizing the faults of others
   ➤ B. a set of intellectual tools for examining claims to determine whether they are worth believing
      C. a set of rules for determining whether beliefs are true or false
      D. negative thinking
      E. all of the above

* 2. Unlike a psychologist, a critical thinker is concerned with the question
   ➤ A. How do you know that belief is true?
      B. Where did that belief come from?
      C. Are you absolutely certain that belief is true?
      D. How does your mood affect your beliefs?
      E. none of the above

* 3. A *claim* is
      A. evidence presented in an argument
      B. the conclusion of an argument
      C. the structure of an argument
      D. the point of an argument
      E. none of the above

* 4. A *fallacy* is
      A. a trick of reasoning
      B. a false statement

   C. a trick used to help win an argument

→ **D.** an error in reasoning

   E. none of the above

* **5.** The purpose of using technical terminology in critical thinking is to

   A. confuse your opponent with technical jargon

   B. more simply refer to complex states of affairs

   C. increase your vocabulary

   D. frighten your opponent with your verbal ability

   E. all of the above

Fill in the Blanks

* **6.** The evident statements used in an argument are known as _premises_____, whereas the major claim being advanced is called the _conclusion___.

* **7.** A(n) _hidden_____ assumption is one that is not explicitly stated. *(unstated, tacit, or implicit)*

* **8.** Another name for the answer to Exercise 7 is _logical presupposition_

* **9.** A(n) _deductive_____ argument is one in which the truth of the conclusion is guaranteed by the truth of the premises.

***10.** A(n) _inductive_____ arguments one in which the truth of the premises only makes the truth of the conclusion more or less possible.

B   LEVEL

These exercises are designed to test your ability to apply the concepts learned in the chapter. Although most of the terms mentioned here are dealt with more extensively in the rest of the book, your ability to answer these questions will help determine whether or not you really grasp the concepts of this chapter.

  State the *conclusion* (if any) that would most probably be advanced in the following situations. Then state what type of evidence would probably be advanced to support this claim.

  Example: A newspaper cartoon ridiculing a political figure's policy.

  Conclusion: The policy that was adopted was wrong.

 1. A defendant on trial for a crime.

 2. A politician giving a speech a few days before an election.

 3. A television ad for toothpaste,

 4. A student explaining why she didn't turn in an assignment on time.

 5. The warning on a pack of cigarettes that smoking can cause cancer and heart disease.

 6. The explanation a student offers the campus traffic office of why he was illegally parked.

 7. A children's fable (such as one by Aesop, for instance).

 8. The sermon given in a place of worship.

 9. A classical music concert.

 10. A rock concert to raise money for AIDS victims.

Try to name the type of evidence you would offer to support the following conclusions.

Example: That a legislator should vote for lowering taxes.

Answer: The benefits of people having more disposable income.

11. That your client is not guilty of a particular crime.

12. That a friend should vote for a certain politician.

13. That an acquaintance should contribute to a particular charity.

14. That your instructor should allow you to take a make-up exam because of illness.

15. That a friend should/shouldn't cheat on an exam.

16. That God does/doesn't exist.

17. That there is/isn't intelligent life on Mars.

18. That classical music is/is not better than rock music.

C   LEVEL

These are more difficult questions and require more thoughtful answers.

1. Write an essay of one or two pages in length attempting to persuade a friend that a college education helps/doesn't help a person become a more responsible voter and citizen.

2. You have just found the ideal job, but you need one more letter of recommendation. You happen to know a college professor whose reputation will carry much weight and who knows you very well. This professor tells you that she is too busy to write the letter, but that if you will write it yourself she will sign it and mail it for you. Write that letter.

3. Try to find four or five examples of bad reasoning in letters to the editor in your local newspaper. Describe as best you can what is wrong with each.

CASE STUDY

Characterizations of Reasoning

(Quotations reprinted with permission from Laurence J. Peter, *Peter's Quotations: Ideas for Our Time*, New York: Doubleday Dell Publishing Group, 1979, and Edwards *et al.*, *The New Dictionary of Thought: A Cyclopedia of Quotations*, Standard Book Company, 1963.)

Each chapter of this book concludes with a case study. Case studies allow you to apply the lessons learned in the chapter to some real-life situations. To get you started, the case study presented here is a series of quotes by famous (and some not-so-famous) people presenting their ideas on reasoning. Find the quote with which you most agree and the one with which you disagree the most. Then write a brief essay comparing the two.

"Learn to reason forward and backward on both sides of a question."

—Thomas Blandi

"There's a mighty big difference between good, sound reasons and reasons that sound good."

—Burton Hillis

"Alas, reason is not effective against faith, or against searches for miracles by the desperate."

—Dr. Michael B. Shimkin

Since attaining the full use of my reason no one has ever heard me laugh."

—Earl of Chesterfield

"If the work of God could be comprehended by reason, it would be no longer wonderful, and faith would have no merit if reason provided the proof."

—Pope Gregory I (Saint Gregory the Great)

"Most of our so-called reasoning consists in finding arguments for going on believing as we already do."

—James Harvey Robinson

"Emotion has taught mankind to reason."

—Marquis de Vauvenargues

"I do not feel obliged to believe that the same God who has endowed us with sense, reason, and intellect has intended us to forego their use."

—Galileo Galilei

"He who will not reason is a bigot; he who cannot is a fool; and he who dares not is a slave."

—Sir William Drummond

"Question with boldness even the existence of God; because, if there be one, He must more approve of the homage of reason than that of blindfolded fear."

—Thomas Jefferson

"My reason is not framed to bend or stoop; my knees are."

—Michel de Montaigne

"Reason—the Devil's harlot."

—Martin Luther

"The gods plant reason in mankind, of all good gifts, the highest."

—Sophocles

"I believe in instinct, not in reason. When reason is right, nine times out of ten it is impotent, and when it prevails, nine out of ten times it is wrong."

—A. C. Benson

"For here we are not afraid to follow truth wherever it may lead, not to tolerate error so long as reason is free to combat it."

—Thomas Jefferson

"The authority of reason is far more imperious than that of a master; for he who disobeys the one is unhappy, but he who disobeys the other is a fool."

—Blaise Pascal

"We have, on the face of it, loved, honored, and obeyed reason more in the last century and a half than at any other epoch, and yet cumulatively and collectively, in the grand total of all our individual lives, we have produced more unreason, bigger and fiercer wars, than any other age in history."

—Laurens van der Post

"Never reason from what you do not know. If you do you will soon believe what is utterly against reason."

—Ramsay

"'Theirs not to make reply, theirs not to reason why' may be a good enough motto for men who are on their way to be shot. But from such men expect no empires to be builded, no inventions made, no great discoveries brought to light."

—Bruce Barton

"Man is a creature of impulse, emotion, action rather than reason. Reason is a very late development in the world of living creatures, most of whom, as far as we know, get along admirably in daily life without it."

—J. T. Adams

"If we would guide by the light of reason, we must let our minds be bold."

—Justice Louis Brandeis

"To despise the animal basis of life, to seek value only at the level of conscious intelligence, and rational effort, is ultimately to lose one's sense of cosmic relationships."

—Lewis Mumford

"We think so because other people all think so; or because—after all—we do think so; or because we were told so, and think we must think so; or because we once thought so, and think we still think so; or because, having thought so, we think we will think so."

—Henry Sidgewick

"If you make people think they're thinking, they'll love you; but if you really make them think, they'll hate you."

—Don Marquis

"Intelligence isn't all it's cracked up to be; if it were, you wouldn't be so (expletive depleted) stupid."

—Peggy Sullivan

DISAGREEMENTS
AND ARGUMENTS

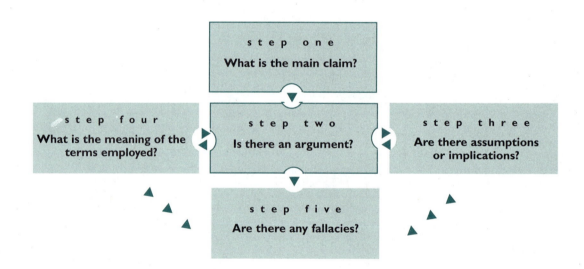

step one
What is the main claim?

step four
What is the meaning of the terms employed?

step two
Is there an argument?

step three
Are there assumptions or implications?

step five
Are there any fallacies?

Couples are wholes and not wholes,

what agrees disagrees,

the concordant is discordant.

From all things one

and from one all things,

—*Heracleitus (ca. 490 B.C.)*

There are three sides

to every dispute: your

side, his side, and to

hell with it.

—*G. D. Strauss (ca. 1951)*

KEY TERMS

Argument - A set of related claims. The two types of claims in an argument are premises and conclusions. Arguments are often used to settle disagreements.

Conclusion - The claim that is to be established or proven in an argument.

Disagreement - A difference of opinion, attitude, or belief between two or more persons. or within one and the same person.

Evaluative disagreement - Difference in the assessment of the moral, aesthetic, or practical value of an event, object, or course of action.

Explanation - Usually a special kind of argument in which the conclusion is more familiar or better known than the premise or premises supporting it.

Extraneous statement - A statement that is neither premise nor conclusion.

Factual disagreement - A dispute about a fact. May be settled by observation or experiment.

Inductive argument - One in which the truth of the premises merely makes the truth of the conclusion more or less probable.

Interpretive disagreement - Conflict between different interpretations of the same set of facts.

Premise - A claim designed to support the conclusion.

Strong inductive argument - One in which the truth of the premises establishes a relatively high degree of probability that the conclusion is also true.

Verbal disagreement - Results from different understandings of the meaning of a word or phrase.

Weak inductive argument - One in which the truth of the premises establishes a relatively low degree of probability that the conclusion is also true.

Steps 1 and 2 of the Critical Technique are concerned with arguments and their basic components, claims. Claims are the subject of study in this chapter. A claim is an assertion or statement advanced as being true. Claims are not usually presented in isolation; more often, claims or statements are presented within the context of an argument, which is a set of related claims. In this chapter we study the nature of claims and their roles and functions within an argument.

While the terms *disagreement* and *argument* are often used interchangeably, they have very different meanings. A **disagreement** is a difference of opinion, attitude, or belief. Disagreements represent conflicts between two or more apparently opposing claims or solutions. They usually occur between two or more individuals and often provide the motivation for defending a position or attacking that of an opponent. But disagreements can also occur within an individual when, for example, she is forced to choose between options.

One instrument for defending or refuting a person's position is an **argument.** Arguments may be thought of as lines of reasoning. They provide the basic unit of study for this text. In everyday language, the term *argument* can mean anything from a heated dispute (e.g., "Jill and Lisa got into an argument over whose turn it was to have the car for the weekend") to a deliberate and thoughtful chain of reasoning (e.g., "Carole argued that a woman's right to choose what happens to her body is a fundamental right for several reasons"). In this book, the term *argument* is used to refer only to those cases where a set of reasons is offered in support of a conclusion. Of course, even in a heated argument a set of reasons may be used to support a claim. Jill, for instance, might remind Lisa that she had driven the car the week before. Such an argument could be analyzed by the methods presented in this book.

2.1 DISAGREEMENTS

Very often the occasion giving rise to the need for an argument is a disagreement of some sort. Disagreements sometimes give rise to disputes or conflicts between individuals (Lisa and Jill's dispute about the car or groups of individuals opposing sides in the abortion debate, for instance). They may even occur within an individual (such as an habitual smoker offering himself reasons to quit while thinking of other reasons not to quit).

Disagreements such as these basically represent differences of beliefs. Lisa and Jill each believes that she, and not the other, should get the car. The Pro-Choice advocates believe that a woman's right to choose what to do with her body is a fundamental right, whereas the Pro-Life proponents believe otherwise. And the wavering smoker believes at different times that he ought/ought not to light that cigarette. An explanation of four different kinds of disagreements follows.

Factual Disagreements

Factual disagreements could also be called *empirical disagreements* because the conflict is, at least in principle, capable of resolution through observation or experimentation. If Joe disagrees with Alison over whether or not the VCR was correctly set to record their favorite show, they can play the tape to see if the program had been recorded. Two homicide detectives disagreeing as to the cause of a victim's death might find the resolution of their disagreement in the coroner's report. In general, factual disagreements are the easiest to resolve.

POSSIBLE FACTUAL DISAGREEMENTS

The following contrived scenarios represent a smattering of the kinds of factual disagreements likely to come up during the normal course of conversation:

Al: He was out at first!

Bo: No way! He was safe. Look at the instant replay!

Cy: Did you know that the word *bit* in computer language originally came from the acronym for *binary digit?*

Di: That's the stupidest thing I ever heard of; it's not true.

Ed: Could there be life on other planets in other galaxies?

Fa: Of course not; what's the chance of there being another planet like ours?

Gi: It should be easy to hang glide from up here.

Hu: Not a chance! Wind conditions would make it impossible for anyone to survive.

Id: Michelangelo's *Last Supper* is one of the greatest paintings I've ever seen.

Jo: The *Last Supper* is an incredible painting, but da Vinci did it, not Michelangelo.

Interpretive Disagreements

When people disagree about the meaning or significance of a situation or event, it may be that each observes the same things and has access to the same set of facts, but still cannot agree on how those facts are to be interpreted or construed. Sometimes this is spoken of as "seeing" things differently. Scientists often give conflicting interpretations to the same set of data. Sometimes **interpretative disagreements** occur because a sufficient number of facts have not yet been determined. These disputes may ultimately be resolved on a factual basis. But some interpretive disagreements are not suited to factual resolution. The resolution of these disputes depends to a great extent on the strength of the arguments offered.

Verbal Disagreements

A **verbal disagreement** occurs when at least one of the disputants is using a critical word or phrase to mean something different than at least one of the other disputants thinks it means. While this may sound like an interpretive disagreement, there is a significant difference between the two. In an interpretive dispute, both parties clearly understand the nature of the disagreement. They are responding in different ways to the same events. A verbal dispute, on the other hand, always involves some critical word or phrase that is used in different senses by the disputants. Verbal disagreements are not often genuine disagreements because the disputants may be "talking past one another."

Interpretive disagreements often seem to have no right or wrong answer; they are merely two different ways of seeing the same phenomena. For example, in the two following cartoons, it would almost be a category mistake to call any one of these views or positions "wrong":

It's a duck!

No, it's a rabbit!

A classic example of a verbal dispute involves the philosophical question: "If a tree fell in the forest and there was no one around to hear it, would it make a sound?" John might respond to this question by saying "Of course it made a sound; a falling tree is going to cause noises whether or not someone is around to hear them." Keri, on the other hand, might reply that, "It can't make a sound because you need a human being for that." The most common difficulty experienced with a verbal dispute is that it is not perceived as such. Arguments and counterarguments constructed in such cases often miss the point. We could just as well call disagreements of this type "pseudo-disagreements," because they are not genuine disputes at all and are more likely to be dissolved than resolved. Once this happens, one of the other types of disagreement may still arise.

Evaluative Disagreements

Evaluative disagreements are conflicts in value judgments or appraisals. When people disagree about the rightness or wrongness of an action or the artistic merit of a painting, they are involved in an evaluative disagreement. There are several types of evaluative disagreements.

Moral disagreements have gained a reputation for inspiring the use of violence and force for their resolution. Many religions attempt to settle moral disputes by appeal to a holy book (such as the Bible or the Koran) thought to reveal the moral decisions of a "higher source." Of course, this tends also to generate a significant number of interpretive disputes. Moral disagreements are one of the types most likely to occur

Still, in some interpretive disagreements, one position is clearly better than another. In those instances, resolving the disagreement will not only depend on factual and empirical evidence, but also on the addition of a theoretical framework that helps to explain the inadequacy of other "views" when compared to the "more scientifically correct" one.

at the intrapersonal level. A person wondering if she is drinking too much might alternatively value her overall health and the relaxing effects of alcohol.

Aesthetic disagreements pertain to disputed judgments about beauty and ugliness. Questions of artistic, literary, or musical merit fall into this category as well as the assessment of natural wonders (such as the Grand Canyon). An old adage has it that "Beauty is in the eye of the beholder." Yet while most people are tolerant of the taste of others, music and film critics still offer arguments for their conclusions.

Practical disagreements involve disputes about what should or should not be done in a certain situation. If Steve and Shirley disagree about whether or not to repaint their kitchen, they are involved in a practical dispute. If they thought critically about the problem, they would resolve the disagreement by discussing the strengths and weaknesses of their arguments for each option.

Not all disagreements can be neatly classified into one of these categories. Often more than one type of disagreement is involved in a dispute. If Dave is a student taking a course with Professor Clinton, he might disagree with the grade of C he received, believing instead that he earned a B. Dave might argue the practical point that his teacher should have assigned him the higher grade. He might also offer an interpretive argument that he had actually met the requirements for the grade of B. A factual disagreement may even arise over whether he had handed in a required assignment.

Most disputes involve several different kinds of disagreement. But different kinds of disagreement require different kinds of arguments to resolve them. Factual disagreements may require only the addition

MAKING FUN OF VERBAL DISAGREEMENTS

In previous sections, we have looked at examples of factual and interpretive disagreements. In the cartoon and characterizations that follow, we see that some liberties have been taken with a well-worn example of a verbal disagreement:

On *Newhart,* when the character "Larry" (of Larry, Darryl, and Darryl) was asked whether the tree would make a sound, he responded by saying that if the tree fell on his brother, Darryl, that Darryl (who normally does not utter a word) would make a sound. (Courtesy of ABC)

On *Cheers,* when Cliff asks the Coach if the tree would make a sound when no one was around, the following dialogue ensues:

Cliff:	Coach, it's clear we've reached a philosophical impasse here. It's much like the question of a tree falling in the woods.
Coach:	A what, Cliff?
Cliff:	A tree falling in the woods.
Coach:	Ah.
Cliff:	The question is, if a tree falls in the woods, and there's no one there to hear it, is there a sound?
Coach:	If there's no one there, how do you know it fell?
Cliff:	Coach, we assume it fell.
Coach:	But you don't know.
Cliff:	Okay, okay. I went into the woods the next day and saw it lying on the ground.
Coach:	That doesn't mean it fell. A bunch of beavers could've chewed through it and gently lowered it to the ground.
Cliff:	You got me there, Coach.
Coach:	You're ususally better prepared than this, Cliff.
Cliff:	Sorry, Coach. I fell asleep last night when I was going over my notes for our conversation.
Coach:	Oh, you do that , too?

(Script Excerpt from Cheers, "Showdown Part II," Glen and Les Charles, courtesy of Paramount Studios.)

of some new empirical evidence. Evaluative disagreements cannot be settled by appeals to facts and observations alone but require the support of normative premises. Verbal disagreements need to be "*dis*solved" more than "*re*solved" by showing that they result from misunderstandings.

CAN YOU NAME THAT DISAGREEMENT?

Garry Trudeau ran a very insightful set of cartoons spanning several months' time and depicting disagreements arising out of a dispute about a student's grade on a test. What sorts of disagreement do you perceive in the interchange between Mr. Slocum and Professor Deadman? (You are right insofar as he will be accused of using the infamous "Deadman's Curve.")

Doonesbury

BY GARRY TRUDEAU

(Reprinted courtesy of Garry Trudeau.)

EXERCISES

A LEVEL

Short Answers

1. What is the main difference between disagreements and arguments?
2. Explain the difference between an interpretive disagreement and a verbal one.
3. If two people disagree as to whether a particular policy is right or wrong, what type of disagreement are they having:?

True or False

* 4. _F_ One kind of disagreement necessarily precludes another kind of disagreement from happening at the same time.
* 5. _F_ One kind of disagreement necessarily involves at least one other kind of disagreement as well. For example, if a dispute is interpretive in nature, it has to be factual as well.

Evaluative

* **6.** __F__ Even though disagreements may differ in nature, they are all basically resolved in the same way.

Name the type of disagreement involved in each of the following situations.

Evaluative
* **7.** A dispute over whether Guns and Roses is a <u>better</u> rock group than U2.

Factual
* **8.** A disagreement about which group in Exercise 7 made more money from the sale of their CDs last year.

Interpretive
* **9.** A political debate about whether or not socialists are really communists.

Interpretive
* **10.** A debate concerning whether or not the Bible permits capital punishment.

Evaluative
* **11.** Two members of congress discussing whether to send monetary aid to the Commonwealth of Independent States.   *"What should we do"—Evaluative*

Evaluative (Moral)
* **12.** A discussion about the rightness or wrongness of the barricading of abortion clinics.

Evaluative (Practical)
* **13.** Someone trying to decide whether to cut down on the amount of cholesterol in his diet.

Evaluative
* **14.** A debate over the limits of news reporters' questioning of political candidates' private lives.

Evaluative (Moral)
* **15.** Assertions by groups of Native Americans that the U.S. government should recompense them for land taken from their reservations.

Evaluative (Practical)
* **16.** A difference of opinion about who was the greatest heavyweight boxing champion of all time.

Evaluative (Factual)
* **17.** Two people with conflicting opinions as to what is wrong with their plumbing system.

Evaluative (Aesthetic)
* **18.** A couple who disagree about which restaurant they would most like to dine at.

Factual
* **19.** An umpire and a manager arguing over whether or not a base runner was tagged out at home plate.

Interpretive
* **20.** A disagreement over the "deeper significance" of a modern drama.

B   LEVEL

Applications.

Take a look at the disputes below, then identify

(a) The main point or points at issue.

(b) The type or types of disagreement involved.

(c) How you would go about trying to resolve the disagreements found.

* **1.** Mary: I just finished reading a great book, *The Outsider,* and I would have to conclude that Franz Fanon is a superb writer.

    Maggie: I agree that Fanon is a great writer, but he didn't write *The Outsider.* Richard Wright wrote it.

    Mary: That can't be right.

2. Cynthia: A woman has the fundamental right to choose what happens to or within her body.

    Daniel: That isn't true any more. The State of Louisiana, for instance, has recently denied that right to women.

Interpretive
Factual
Evaluative
3. Roger: Well, if you ask me, I would say that the best way to get from Lake Nebagamon to Minneapolis by car would be to drive the county roads to Duluth and then take Interstate 35 to 35W and into Minneapolis.

Judy: No, the best way to get there is to take U.S. 53 south to Minong and then Routes 77 and 48 west into Hinkley where you can pick up I-35 into Minneapolis. It's much prettier and doesn't take that much longer.

Factual

4. Ernst: After we finish our audit today of Acme Industries, I am going to recommend that they switch to the ACRS method of depreciation.

Arthur: I considered that too, but I think now that they should remain with the method they have been using. Here, look at the books and I will show you why.

5. George: Well, you're going to have to admit that the United States certainly enjoys much more favorable sentiment at home and abroad due to the patriotic efforts of our soldiers in Operation Desert Storm.

Jimmy: It may look that way, but I know that your motives were much less than pure since this was your way of shoring up your reelection campaign.

*Factual
Interpretive
Evaluative*

6. Alice Rose: Don't you think this is one of the best statues you have ever seen? I would have to say that Fred X is one of the best living Italian artists working in marble today.

Harold: No, this is an excellent copy of a Bernini and Fred X is a fine technician. But I cannot agree with your assessment of his artistic merits. And he is not Italian at all. Remember, he is from Mississippi.

*Interpretive
Evaluative*

7. John: The Upper Gauley is gorgeous and one of the most technically demanding stretches of water, one that only the most experienced open-boat canoeists should attempt to run.

Bill: That is crazy. Anyone who can hold a canoe paddle can negotiate that river.

*Factual
Evaluative*

8. Omar: With the recession coming to a peak and interest rates having bottomed out, now is the perfect time for Michele to buy a new house.

Jomo: I disagree. Lending agencies are going to be much stricter in their financial checks on her sources of income, property appraisals are going to be much lower, and property values may not show much appreciation for a number of years.

Evaluative

9. Ellen: Unless we allocate much more federal funding toward AIDS research, the United States is not going to have much success eradicating this horrible disease during the present decade.

Barbara: That allocation would be a terrible waste of precious government resources, which should be allocated for much more socially worthy goals.

10. Jim: We are better off staying close-hauled with the storms off our leeward beam than risk heading directly into the marina through all that lightning.

Kathy: Nonsense. We are a giant lightning rod as it is, and we might as well make for the slip as quickly as we possibly can.

 LEVEL

Deeper Applications

1. Think back over the past few days and remember any disagreements you have had with other people or any that you witnessed. Perhaps you read about one in the newspapers or saw one on television. Describe what kind of disagreement it was and then be prepared to discuss alternative ways in which it could have been resolved. Which methods seem to work better and why?

2. Take a look at Gary Larson's "*Far Side*" cartoon from March 21, 1992, and at the two "Letters to the Editor." What kind of disagreement or disagreements are occurring between the respondents?

THE FAR SIDE   By GARY LARSON

God as a kid tries to make a chicken in his room.

Charlotte Observer, Saturday, April 11, 1992

"I regret seeing the . . . *Observer* print the March 21 *Far Side* cartoon, "God as a Kid Tries to Make a Chicken in His Room." There are problems here: The *Bible* never says that God was a child. God is eternal; without beginning or end, God could not have been a child. Also, God does not make mistakes. This cartoon is irreverent. It presents God in a manner that makes fun of him."

—Bill Marlin, Charlotte, North Carolina

Charlotte Observer, Monday, April 20, 1992

"In response to Bill Marlin's letter about the *Far Side* depicting God as an experimenting kid. . .:

"If God could not have been a child, where does that leave the infant, Jesus? And if God does not make mistakes, why are there head lice?"

—E. A. Hall, Decatur, Georgia

(Reprinted courtesy of *The Charlotte Observer*)

2.2 ARGUMENTS

When the participants in a disagreement attempt to resolve their dispute, they will have to resort to some method to advance their case. Violence, coercion, warfare, and propaganda are some of the more sinister methods used to settle conflicts. A more rational approach is the use of arguments to defend one's position or to try to convince others of our own beliefs. An *argument* is a line of reasoning made up of two or more related statements. A *statement* is an assertion that something is true. Every argument contains two kinds of statements. The **conclusion** of the argument is the "point" of the argument. It is the statement the arguer most wants us to accept, the claim he is trying to get us to believe. A defense lawyer, for instance, tries to structure her arguments to get the jury to conclude that her client is innocent. An advertiser wants us to conclude that we should buy his product, and a politician that we vote her into office. The statements that support the conclusion are called the **premises**. They provide the evidence, support, or grounds for the conclusion. The defense lawyer produces an alibi, whereas the advertiser and politician promise us a better life.

Some arguments are contained in a single sentence, and others may be long and drawn out. To be considered an argument, however, a line of reasoning must have at least one premise and one conclusion. For instance, one might offer the following argument:

> *People are animals, and animals are basically aggressive,*
> *so people must be basically aggressive.*

Although contained in a single sentence, this argument consists of three distinct statements. The two premises are on the first line and the conclusion on the second.

When displaying the structure of an argument, it is useful to list the premises first and the conclusion last. Be aware, however, that in the ordinary course of communicating and thinking, statement order is not a guaranteed indicator of which statements are premises and which conclusions. You should also note that the entire argument is contained in a single sentence. It is for this reason that arguments were characterized in terms of their component statements rather than their component sentences. So while one sentence may contain an entire argument, there must be at least two component statements.

There are clues, however, that indicate a conclusion or a premise is about to appear. These clues are words that announce a conclusion or a set of premises. The terms that announce a premise are called *premise indicators;* those that announce a conclusion are called *conclusion indicators.* A premise indicator lets you know that a reason or a piece of evidence is about to be produced in support of a conclusion. When a beer commercial suggests you drink a certain brand *because* it contains fewer calories, it is offering a premise. The term *since* is also a common premise indicator. Conclusion indicators are more common. Some conclusion indicators are the terms *therefore, thus, so* and *hence* (see Figures 2.1 and 2.2).

Unfortunately, not all arguments come neatly packaged with built-in indicators. One cannot simply assume that the words one sees or hears are being used correctly. A writer may on occasion throw in a *thus* when she meant to say *and.* This could be the result of poor grammar, but it could also indicate a mistake in the reasoning process. One of the assumptions most people tend to make is that other people are reasoning the same way they are. This leads us to take their indicator words at face value.

Like many other kinds of words, most indicator words have more than one usage. They are often used in sentences that are not part of any argument. The terms *since* and *for,* for instance, may function as prepositions. So if one were asked "How long has it been *since* you've shaved?", he might answer "I haven't shaved *for* a month." In cases like these, the terms function as neither conclusion nor premise indicators.

On occasion an argument will appear with no discernible indicator words at all. Unlike people, when arguments are undressed they are less recognizable. Consider the following passage from B. F. Skinner's book, *About Behaviorism:*

DISAGREEMENTS & ARGUMENTS IN THE "STREET SENSE"

I believe in [the theory of behaviorism's] importance. The major problems facing the world today can be solved only if we improve our understanding of human behavior. Traditional views have been around for centuries, and I think it is fair to say that they have proved to be inadequate. They are largely responsible for the situation in which we now find ourselves. Behaviorism offers a promising alternative, and I have written this book in an effort to make it clear. (Reprinted with permission from B. F. Skinner, *About Behaviorism,* 1974, Alfred A. Knopf, Inc.)

The function of this passage is not immediately evident. Is Skinner describing a science of human behavior? Is he recommending it? Or is he trying to justify it? He doesn't use any conclusion or premise indicators to help us decide.

The So–Because Test

When indicator words are missing from a passage, the conclusion can sometimes be differentiated from the premises by applying the *so–because test.* This test is not foolproof, but it useful in the analysis of many

Figure 2-1

SOME COMMON PREMISE INDICATOR WORDS.

Since	Inasmuch as
Because	Insofar as
For	To the extent that
As	On the basis of
For the reason that	As shown by
As indicated by	As implied by
May be deduced from	Follows from the fact
In view of the fact that	On account of
	Assuming that

Figure 2-2

SOME COMMON CONCLUSION INDICATOR WORDS.

Therefore	As a result
Thus	It follows that
Hence	We may conclude that
So	Which proves that
Consequently	You can see that
Which explains	This shows why
Which provides that	So it has to be the case that
Allows us to infer	I must conclude that
Obviously . . .	Which implies that
Which means that	Points to the fact that
So it must be that	

arguments. To apply the so–because test, first insert a conclusion indicator word (such as *so* or *therefore*) before one of the statements and read it. Then apply the same term to another statement. Compare the two. Based on your understanding of the passage, which makes more sense? If neither of the statements seems to be the conclusion, apply it to another statement and see how that one holds up as a possible conclusion. If you're still not sure, try out some of the statements as premises by applying terms like *because*. If we applied the so–because test to the first two sentences in the Skinner passage we would have as an alternative:

Alternative 1:
I believe in its importance, *because* the major problems facing the world today can be solved only if we improve our understanding of human behavior.

The premise-indicator *because* placed before the second statement indicates that the first statement "I believe in its importance" is the conclusion. Not only does this reading make perfectly good sense, but we are also better able to understand the relationship between the first and second sentences of the original passage. Suppose, however, that we had inserted the conclusion indicator word *therefore*. Then the passage would read:

> **Alternative 2:**
> I believe in its importance, *therefore* the major problems facing the world today can be solved only if we improve our understanding of human behavior.

Now it looks as though the argument has a completely different point. The meaning of the second alternative seems to be that behaviorism is the only hope for solving world problems *because* Skinner believes in its importance. But Skinner's *belief* in behaviorism's importance does not provide very much support (if any) for the truth of the conclusion that "the major problems facing the world today can be solved only if we improve our understanding of human behavior." It is not likely that a scientist trained in analytical methods would make such an assertion. The first alternative, however, does make sense. It concludes that behaviorism is important and offers as evidence the claim that it can solve world problems. Of course, the so–because test does not guarantee that we will choose the correct alternative, but it does give us a way to approach arguments where the structure is not apparent.

   Note that application of the so–because test might leave us with two plausible alternatives. Is Maggie "smiling because she is happy" or is she "happy because she is smiling"? Both of these are reasonable readings. The two statements might also be combined to read that "Maggie is happy *and* she is smiling." In this case, there isn't even an argument. Sometimes the test will not solve the problem. In these cases it is best to examine the passage in its wider context to determine how it fits into the book or article from which it was taken. If the person who made the statement is available, an even better way to determine the passage's meaning is simply to ask her.

Extraneous Statements and Nonstatements

Another common feature of arguments is the presence of unnecessary, irrelevant, or extraneous language. Imagine a situation in which a friend remarks:

> Dr. Boyd is certainly a well-respected psychologist, and I feel sure that her ideas about human motivation have been carefully considered. She's mistaken, however, in believing that failing Hernandez on the test will scare him into working harder, because Hernandez is not afraid of anything.

Your friend's conclusion that Dr. Boyd is making a mistake is supported by the assertion that Hernandez is not afraid of anything. But what about the first sentence? It is not the conclusion of the argument. It provides a bit of background on Dr. Boyd, but it doesn't offer any evidence in support of the conclusion either. So it cannot be a premise. So is it totally irrelevant? Perhaps the remark is meant to convey the speaker's overall respect for Dr. Boyd despite the conclusion. Maybe it was meant sarcastically. In terms of the argument's structure, though, the first sentence is irrelevant and is considered to be an **extraneous statement**.

It is important to remember that only a statement can function as a premise or a conclusion. Like the term *argument,* the term *statement* has a specific meaning for critical thinking that is not exactly the same as its everyday usage. "Totally awesome!" may be an emotional expression of approval. But because the expression is not an assertion that a given claim is true, it is not a statement in the technical sense. Similarly, a command such as "Thou shalt not kill" functions as a directive rather than an assertion and so would not be considered a statement either.

Arguments and "If . . . then" Statements

Arguments, especially simple ones, often resemble "if . . . then" statements. These are also known as "conditional" or "hypothetical" statements, and should not be confused with arguments. Some common types of conditional statements include promises, threats, contracts, hypotheses, suppositions, predictions, guarantees, and warranties. Look closely at two apparently similar sentences:

(A): Because you are paying attention, you will probably get it.

(A′): If you are paying attention, then you will probably get it.

By now you should be able to see that the first sentence, (A), fits the description of an argument. What about (A′)? Looking at (A′) closely, you will see that although it too appears to be composed of two statements, the second part, "then you will probably get it", does not stand by itself independently from the first part. It is only being asserted *conditionally,* that is, depending upon your paying attention. Statements of this variety are called *conditional* or *hypothetical* statements; they seem to be the life blood of logicians and standardized testing institutions. Actually, statements of the "if-then" sort are used in a number of distinctive ways (some of which may even constitute arguments!) but for now, as a rule of thumb which will be refined in time, understand hypothetical or conditional sentences as *statements,* not as arguments. It will be easier to do this if two of their traits are borne in mind. One is that in an argument the conclusion is being asserted *because* the premises are being asserted, whereas in a conditional statement, the "then" part (or consequent) is not being asserted *unless* the "if" part (or antecedent) is also asserted. This is a feature common to conditional statements of any type—threats, promises, contracts, predictions, and counterfactual statements. Take a concrete case:

If these tires wear out in 40,000 miles or less, we will replace them at no cost to you.

You are not being told that your tires will wear out in 40,000 miles or less. Nor are you being guaranteed that we will replace them at no cost to you. Your guarantee is equivalent in meaning to an either-or (or disjunctive) statement: "Either these tires will not wear out in 40,000 miles or less, or we will replace them at no cost to you." In both cases the two parts of the statement are related to each other instead of being independently asserted and hence constitute a statement rather than an argument. Both hypothetical statements and disjunctive statements will be referred to as complex statements, because they are composed of two or more simple statements which could have stood by themselves, but which take on a slightly new meaning when conjoined with each other. It may help to remember that the sign, "If you park here, then your car will be towed away," is not exactly designed to tell you to park there.

Arguments and Explanations

One way of looking at the difference between explanations and arguments is to say that the main point of an *argument,* the conclusion, is reasoned to or reached through the premises. In an **explanation,** however, the main point (the "conclusion") is accepted to begin with and the alleged causes or justifications are then offered.

A common type of explanation is a justification. A *justification* is an explanation for an action that attempts to show that the action taken was the correct one from either a practical or moral point of view. (Unaccepted justifications are sometimes known as *excuses*.) Suppose John is late for an appointment and apologizes: "I'm sorry, but I am late because I had a flat tire." The truth of the statement "John is late" is not in doubt. But there is actually another conclusion being offered here: John is trying to convince his audience that his being late should not count against him. The conclusion of this explanatory argument is not that John is late, but that it's okay that he's late. Whether or not his explanation is acceptable will depend on the strength of the reasons John offers.

Another common type of explanation is a *causal explanation*. A causal explanation offers a chain of related events leading to the event being explained. These often occur in scientific disputes as well as in everyday life. Some scientists today, for instance, believe that mountains are formed by the collision of continental plates pushing against one another. A geologist offering such an explanation would have to support her conclusion with relevant data.

When thinking critically about explanations, you should be aware of the possibility that any explanation may also function as an argument. In many cases the conclusion of the argument is not directly stated, but only implied.

EXERCISES

A   LEVEL

Short Answers

1. What are the component parts of an argument? *Premise & conclusion*
2. What is the difference between a statement and a sentence? *All statements are sentences. Not all*
3. In what ways do arguments differ from explanations?
4. List three conclusion indicators. *Therefore, so, hence*
5. List two premise indicators. *Since, because, for*

True or False

6. __T__ In itself, no statement is a premise or a conclusion but only becomes one or the other by its place in an argument.
7. __F__ No argument can be stated in a single sentence.
8. __F__ Sentences and statements are essentially the same thing.
9. __T__ The purpose of the so–because test is to distinguish arguments from nonarguments.
10. __T__ Some explanations are not arguments.

Shitty Questions!

B   LEVEL

For each of the following passages,

(a) State whether an argument is present.

(b) If an argument is present, identify the premises.

(c) State the conclusion, if any.

(d) Identify irrelevant or extraneous remarks.

(e) Identify any indicator words.

(f) Identify explanations with the letter "e".

a,b,c **1.** Dick and Debbie prefer meals that are low in saturated fats, <u>because</u> they are trying to control their cholesterol intake.

2. Because Dick and Debbie prefer meals that are low in saturated fats, they will probably reduce their risk of coronary heart disease.

3. Since we spent all of our money at the ball game last night, we should just get a rental movie tonight. After all, we only have six dollars between us.

4. Spike Lee's movies are daring and provocative because they deal with subject matter that few other directors would consider putting on film. And they focus on sensitive issues without being superficial.

5. The main reason Clinton won the election was that he won back Democratic voters who had gone for Bush and Reagan in previous elections.

6. Since Mary and Maggie don't like any extra ingredients other than mushrooms on their pizza, we should probably order the plain one, even though Morgan likes anchovies on hers.

7. If global warming is not taking place, then why has the Earth's average temperature risen so sharply since the beginning of the industrial age?

8. It is highly unlikely that the problem is external to our electric range itself. The power is on in the rest of the house and none of the circuit breakers has been tripped. The clock and timer are both still working and so is the oven.

9. We have to be sailing a northerly course. Just look—we are sailing toward the pole star. The last two stars in the Big Dipper point to it. And the wind, which is out of the east tonight, is directly off our starboard beam. Of course, the compass pointing at 360 degrees helps a bit.

10. If timing were not the crucial factor that it is, then it would not matter when you complete your assignment. Since, however, it does matter when you complete this task, timing must indeed be a crucial factor.

Read the following arguments. Identify the premises and the conclusion, circle indicator words, and draw a light line through any extraneous material.

11. "For now, Bill Clinton needs a healthy third force in this campaign. He needs Ross Perot so that he can keep at least a half-dozen Southern states in play, thus keeping President Bush from the traditional Republican lock on the Confederacy's 147 electoral votes."

—(Thomas Oliphant, reprinted courtesy of *The Boston Globe*)

12. "U.S. politicians are still trying to erase Vietnam from their memories. Our political mythology imbues us with the idiocy of 'We're No. 1!' so we aren't very good at handling defeats in war—and no good at all at learning . . . from them."

—Sydney Schranberg, reprinted courtesy of *Newsday*

13. "All of the arguments [urging the U.S. to reduce its military forces in Europe] are flawed. First, two world wars have proved that the United States ignores events in Europe at its own peril . . ."

—Richard Nixon, quoted in *The National Review*, reprinted courtesy of Simon and Schuster

14. "How people feel, deep down, is critical, Dr. Zullow says, because their mood governs how much money they spend. And consumer spending accounts for about two-thirds of all economic activity."

—Bill Hendrick, reprinted with permission from *The Atlanta Journal* and *The Atlanta Constitution*

15. "Home Depot Chairman Bernard Marcus has pledged $1 million to the U.S. Holocaust Memorial Museum in Washington. Why? Because 6 million people were exterminated, he says. 'And there are still people in the world who are savages.'"

—Susan Harte, reprinted with permission from *The Atlanta Journal* and *The Atlanta Constitution*

C   LEVEL

1. Locate four different arguments in newspapers or periodicals. Analyze those arguments the way you did for Level B exercises.
2. Try to think of seven or eight examples of sentences that would *not* qualify as *statements* according to the definition offered in this book.
3. If the following sentences are not statements, what could be their intended function?
   a. What kind of fool do you think I am?
   b. I know that I told you to turn the damn light off, so do it!
   c. Thou shalt not steal.

2.3   INDUCTIVE AND DEDUCTIVE ARGUMENTS

One useful way of distinguishing arguments is by the type of support the premises give the conclusion. In some cases the premises' support for the conclusion is stronger than in other cases. In a *deductive argument* the premises support the conclusion so strongly that if it turns out that the premises are all true, then the conclusion is guaranteed to be true as well. When all of the premises of a valid deductive argument are true, the argument is said to be *sound*. The following is an example of a **sound deductive argument:**

Thomas Jefferson must have been the third president of the United States because I know that the third president was either Thomas Jefferson or Aaron Burr. And since Aaron Burr was never president, that leaves only Jefferson.

There are two premises in this argument. One states that either Jefferson or Burr was the third president of the United States. The other premise asserts that it couldn't be Burr, because he was never president. The argument concludes that the third president must have been Jefferson. If you examine this argument closely, you'll find that it is impossible to *reasonably* believe that the premises are true yet the conclusion is false. If it is true that either Jefferson or Burr was the third president, and if it's also true that Burr was not, then it must be true that Jefferson indeed was the third president.

The truth of the premises of an **inductive argument,** on the other hand, does not guarantee the truth of its conclusion. They only make the truth of the conclusion more or less probable. The more probability with which the conclusion is established by the premises, the stronger the argument is said to be. **Weak inductive arguments** are those that establish the truth of their conclusions with relatively less probability. The following is an example of a **strong inductive argument:**

It hasn't snowed in Miami for the past hundred winters, so it's not likely to snow this year. Besides, the average temperature in the city is two degrees warmer than it was last year.

Even if the two premises of this argument are true, the truth of the conclusion is by no means guaranteed. It would be entirely reasonable in this case to believe the premises to be true and yet to conclude that there is some possibility, however small, of its snowing this winter in Miami.

TABLE 2-1

DISTINGUISHING BETWEEN DEDUCTIVE AND INDUCTIVE REASONING

Deductive Arguments	Inductive Arguments
1. The premises are supposed to guarantee the conclusion beyond any doubt.	1. The premises are supposed to support, but not necessarily guarantee the conclusion.
2. The conclusion is supposed to be contained in the premises already.	2. The conclusion goes beyond what is contained in the premises.
3. The argument is put forth as if it would be an outright contradiction to say that the premises are true but the conclusion is false.	3. The argument is not put forth as if it would be an outright contradiction to say that the premises are true but the conclusion is false.

The reason for the difference between deductive and inductive arguments is that in a sound deductive argument, the conclusion is actually "contained" in the set of premises. The conclusion of an inductive argument gives us information not already contained in the premises. In the Jefferson argument, one of the stated options was the third president. The elimination of Burr as a possibility combined with the first premise to provide the inevitable conclusion. In the snow argument, however, the conclusion that it will not snow in Miami in the coming year is not the inevitable result of the combination of premises. Next winter's snowfall is not even mentioned in the set of premises.

It is important to be able to distinguish between inductive and deductive arguments because the rules for assessing the goodness or badness of each type are different (see Table 2.1). And although they are both very common parts of the reasoning process, they play very different roles. As the philosopher Alfred North Whitehead noted: "There is a tradition of opposition between adherents of induction and deduction. In my view, it would be just as sensible for two ends of a worm to quarrel."

SUMMARY

Chapter 2 discussed the difference between disagreements and arguments. In this chapter, you learned how to identify arguments, and also how to differentiate the premises and the conclusion of an argument. Steps 1 and 2 of the critical technique were addressed.

Claims are often advanced in the context of arguments. The basic nature of arguments and the role and function of claims within arguments were analyzed. To obtain a true picture of the nature of arguments, however, they must first be distinguished from disagreements. Disagreements are disputes and conflicts encountered in everyday life. They are an incentive for thinking about means to resolve them. Thinking about them critically enhances the prospects for their successful resolution. Disagreements may occur between nations, groups, individuals, or even within an individual. There are four types of disagreements. Factual disagreements may be settled by experiment or observation. Interpretive disagreements are not as easy to resolve because they involve different ways of "seeing" things. Verbal disagreements involve different understandings of the meaning of key words or phrases. Evaluative disagreements express a difference in the moral, aesthetic, or practical value of an event, object, or course of action.

An argument is a line of reasoning composed of two types of statement. A statement is an assertion that a certain state of affairs is true. Premise statements provide the grounds or the evidence for the conclusion statement. To determine whether a statement functions as a conclusion or premise, we should consider the use of indicator words, which announce either the premise or the conclusion. The so–because test is useful in those cases where no indicator words exist. The source of the argument may also be consulted in some cases and in others the larger context in which the passage appears can help determine which statements are premises and which is the conclusion. It is also important to watch for extraneous statements within an argument; these types of statements function as neither premise nor conclusion. While explanations can be distinguished from arguments, many explanations also function as arguments.

An argument is deductively valid if and only if it is impossible for all of the premises to be true while the conclusion is false. Invalid arguments are those that appear to be deductive, but in which all the premises may turn out to be true while the conclusion remains false. In inductive arguments, the truth of the premises only makes the truth of the conclusion more or less probable, depending on the strength or weakness of the argument.

EXERCISES

A   LEVEL

Short Answers

1. How can you distinguish a deductive from an inductive argument?
2. Why don't the premises of an inductive argument guarantee the truth of its conclusion?
3. What is meant by the statement that the conclusion of a deductive argument is contained within its premises?

True or False

4. __F__ Inductive arguments never occur with deductive arguments and the two are never mixed in any line of reasoning.
5. __T__ If someone reasons about the way things will be in the future, based on the ways things were in the past, the reasoning is inductive.
6. __F__ An inductive argument is one in which the conclusion is inescapable if the premises are true.

B   LEVEL

Identify arguments stating the premises and conclusion. Also circle indicator words and then state whether the argument is inductive or deductive and why.

Deductive + Inductive 1. Every day the traffic is reported to be congested I always take the subway into town. Since the traffic report is for yet another day of gridlock, I'll take the subway today.

More 2. Every day this year that the traffic has been reported to be congested, Carole has taken the subway into town. It is supposed to be congested again today, so she'll probably take the subway again today.

Inductive 3. Anniece has taken her dry cleaning to three of the twelve Acme Dry Cleaning stores and has been dissatisfied with their work each time. She has concluded that they must not do very high-quality work.

Deductive 4. The bigger the taco is, the better the taco is, and we're here to tell you that Nacho Momma's has the biggest tacos around. So, you can be sure we've got the best tacos anywhere around.

More Deductive 5. Your Honor, I could not have been driving the car at that time because I was on Flight 108 from Salem to San Diego at the time and nobody can be in two places at once.

Inductive 6. The Broncos have won every game that speedster Trak Starr has played in and he is in the starting lineup for tomorrow's game. So, the Broncos are bound to win.

Yet, Inductive – *Also Deductive* **7.** Senator Snort said he would not enter the upcoming gubernatorial race unless the Democrats made him very angry. So far no one has aroused his ire, so I guess he doesn't plan on entering the race.

Inductive **8.** Market conditions have always tended to be cyclical in some appreciable manner. Rising interest rates have always been followed by falling ones. Conversely, falling interest rates have always been succeeded by rising ones. There's no need to worry, the rates will go back up eventually.

Inductive **9.** Mack's is the best bar around. They don't card anyone, they've got the best juke box around and the cheapest beer prices.

10. Coal seams have been discovered in Antarctica. This means that the climate there was once warmer than it is now. Thus, either the geographical location of the continent has shifted or the whole Earth was once warmer than it is now.

C   LEVEL

Find an extended argument in a magazine article. State which parts of the argument are deductive and which are inductive. As best you can, assess the strengths and weaknesses of each part of the argument.

CASE STUDY

National Public Radio's *Weekend Edition*

The case study for this chapter consists of a conversation about the environment aired on National Public Radio's *Weekend Edition*. After reading through the edited transcript, state where disagreements occur. What kind of disagreements are they? Also try to find the arguments offered by two participants in support of their respective positions. Notice whether they are talking about the same issues. Finally, state which person had a more convincing presentation and try to explain why.

The interview begins with an introduction by the host, Scott Simon. The two participants are Dennis Meadows, coauthor of a book entitled *Beyond the Limits,* which claims that we are reaching the Earth's environmental limits. The authors claim that they are much closer than eighty years away. Nevertheless, Mr. Meadows feels that there is still time to save ourselves from environmental disaster. The other participant is Lawrence Summers, vice president of development economics and chief economist for the World Bank. He disagrees with many of the findings of Mr. Meadows.

Simon: Mr. Meadows, if I could, let me begin with you to—to try and state this as explicitly as we can. Environmentalists often use terms like *sustainable* and *unsustainable.* What are some of the activities you think we simply cannot sustain for much longer?

Meadows: The analysis we've just done suggests that right across the board, human activities are above sustainable limits. We're eroding our soils, overcatching the ocean's fish, overcutting the trees and putting too many contaminants into the air and into the water. In the poorer countries, population growth has to be stopped as quickly as possible. And in the rich countries we have to give up our confusion about the difference between social progress and material acquisition.

Simon: Mr. Summers, let me turn to you because you have been outspoken in some of your disagreements. Which disagreements might you offer now to help us understand your counter to this argument?

Summers: I think the kind of extrapolations that say we're going to run out of things—these have been a staple of Malthusian rhetoric since Malthus wrote. In New York City in 1870 they worried that the city would be overrun fifty years hence with horse manure from all the carriages. In 1973, Professor Meadows and his colleagues joined the chorus worrying that we were going to see a desperate oil shortage and very high prices of oil. Those predictions haven't proved to be right in the past, and I think because of what technology's going to bring and because what markets do in raising the price of things that become scarce, this kind of doom and gloom is not a constructive way to approach environmental problems in the future.

Simon: Can the market system operate quickly enough?

                  * * * *

Meadows: Well, I'm sorry; it can't. In this country right today, we see a systematic effort to reduce and weaken environmental control standards, and the justification always put forth is growth. I think it is a disservice to liken horse manure to the scientific consensus which now exists about ozone destruction and the potential for climate change. We're now in a situation where about sixty countries and regions, according to Larry's own bank data, have—are failing to sustain positive growth rates in GNP. Almost 100 countries now have declining food production per capita. I feel that comes from soil erosion and from neglect in the past. If the eighties, which were a wonderfully expansionistic period, haven't solved these problems, Larry, what's going to do it in the nineties?

                  * * * *

Summers: Any one resource is something you run out of, but what we've seen, the reason that all those projections have proven wrong, is because of the capacity of mankind, because of the capacity of markets, to adapt.

* * * *

Simon: If we conserve resources wisely, if we do more with less, doesn't that create the circumstances for increased prosperity without the kind of growth that—that might be harmful?

Summers: There's no question that there's a strong case for environmental protection. There's a strong case for making polluters pay in ways that they're not paying. There's a strong case for supporting women's ability to choose the number of children they want to have. That's where we need to put our emphasis. The fact that air pollution is lower in many major cities, the fact that if you look across countries, you find that the ones with higher standards of living tend to have healthier environments. That's what we need to do, we need to focus on the twin goals of environment and development.

Simon: . . . Mr. Meadows, do you see development as separate from your goals?

Meadows: We are very careful to make an important distinction between development and physical growth. By growth, we mean physical expansions. By development, we mean social progress. If I put my energy-efficient light bulb in my room, the growth actually grows down—I'm using less electricity—but my standard of living may go up. I think there's plenty of opportunity for social progress but it will only come when we focus on the flows of materials and energies through the environment, look at our real resource availability and start making informed choices based on that information.

Simon: Gentlemen, thank you both very much for being with us.

LOGICAL ASSUMPTIONS, IMPLICATONS, AND ARGUMENT DIAGRAMS

step one
What is the main claim?

▼

step two
Is there an argument?

▶ **step three**
Are there any assumptions or implications?

▼

step five
Are there any fallacies?

▲ ▲ ▲

Nonviolence and truth (Satya) are
inseparable and presuppose each other.
There is no higher god than truth.
–Mohandas K. (Mahatma) Ghandi (1939)

Some people say there's a woman to blame,
But I know, it's my own damn fault.
(Jimmy Buffett)

KEY TERMS

Compound argument - One in which two or more premises combine to imply the conclusion, but which do not do so independently.

Convergent argument - One in which two or more independent claims or premises imply the conclusion.

Divergent argument - One in which a statement generates two or more independent conclusions or implications.

Explicit assumption - A claim that is actually stated and functions as the premise of an argument but which *is itself not supported by any further premises.* (An unsupported claim.)

Implication - A claim that follows from another claim such that, if the original claim is true, then the implication must also be true; also called an *unstated conclusion.*

Implicit assumption - An unstated claim functioning as the premise of an argument, sometimes known as an *unstated premise,* or logical presupposition.

Linear argument - An argument in which the premises and conclusions can be arranged such that each claim implies the next.

Principle of fairness - The idea that one should be as fair as possible in assigning unstated premises or implications to the argument advanced by another.

Unstated conclusion - A conclusion not explicitly stated but usually thought to be inevitable given the content and structure of an argument. Also called a *logical implication.*

Unstated premise - A missing link in an inductive argument which connects the content of the premises with the content of the conclusion so as to turn the argument into a deductive one. Unstated premises are sometimes called logical or hidden assumptions or presuppositions.

Unsupported claim - A statement which functions as a premise in an argument but does not have another statement to act as a premise for it.

This chapter is concerned with the questions asked in Step 3 of *the Technique: "What is not being stated?"* In this chapter you will learn how to spot the hidden assumptions lurking within arguments. Hidden assumptions are assumptions made within an argument but not explicitly stated. They often have a very strong bearing on the value of the argument. So in the evaluation of an argument, it is just as important to learn how to identify any hidden assumptions as it is to recognize the explicit ones. You will then learn how to schematize arguments in order to show the relationships between the premises and the conclusion.

Hidden assumptions also function as *unstated premises.* It is often the case that an argument is advanced in which not all of the premises are actually stated. Sometimes this results from the fact that the arguer assumes that her audience already believes the premise or premises to be true. In other cases the unstated premise can result from mere oversight. In still others, assumptions may be intentionally hidden because the arguer wants to manipulate her audience into accepting a conclusion with which they might not otherwise agree. In still other cases, cultural differences might blind one to the assumptions of another. (When then-President George Bush visited Australia, he responded to a cheering crown by holding up his hands in the classic "V for victory" sign. What he didn't realize is that in Australia, the same gesture has a significantly different meaning. The audience became angry when they assumed that the president was showing the same sign of contempt that is often experienced on American roadways.) A critical thinker should be capable of finding and then analyzing the role that hidden assumptions play within an argument. When an assumption is actually stated in an argument, we refer to it as an ***explicit assumption.*** Assumptions that are not actually stated are referred to as ***implicit assumptions.***

Closely related to implicit assumptions are implications. Although the term has a technical meaning, we employ its common meaning. An ***implication*** is a claim that directly follows from another claim in such a way that if the initial claim is true the implication must also be true. For instance, the statement "Mel was just traded to another team by the Giants" implies that Mel was a player with the Giants. Similarly, the statement "Caren enjoyed her trip to Paris" can be construed as implying that Caren visited Paris. As in the case of hidden assumptions, we should be careful to identify and criticize any of the implications of the statements within an argument. Although an implication may not have a direct bearing on the development of an argument, the psychological effects can often influence an uncritical thinker.

Once you have discovered all of the implicit assumptions of an argument, you are then in a position to trace the relationships between the premises—both implicit and explicit—and the argument's conclusion. You will learn to do this through the use of diagrams that will enable you to schematize an entire argument so that you can determine which premises directly support a conclusion, which premises support the conclusion indirectly through support of another premise, which supposed premises have no direct bearing on the conclusion, and which premises are supposed to carry more weight than other premises (or less weight).

3.1 SPOTTING HIDDEN ASSUMPTIONS

Some hidden assumptions are easier to spot than others. When the arguer assumes that his audience shares his beliefs, for instance, spotting an assumption requires us to examine the beliefs that support the claims. Consider the following argument:

Anne: Serge must be pretty tall. After all, he's on the basketball team.

Anne's conclusion is that Serge is pretty tall. The only explicit premise she offers to support it is that Serge is on the basketball team. How is the premise connected to the conclusion? It seems that the premise and the conclusion are simply stating some things about Serge: He's tall and he's on the basketball team. Anne, however, sees a connection between the two facts. The connection she is making in this case is that basketball players are usually, if not always, pretty tall. This is the hidden assumption. If Anne did not make this type of assumption, we would have difficulty seeing how she reached her conclusion. In an argument like this one, the omission of the assumption from the argument would probably be motivated by Anne's desire to state her case in the simplest way. She might simply assume that her audience already accepts the claim that basketball players are usually pretty tall.

Of course, Anne might be wrong. Perhaps Serge is among the shorter players of the game. (And we're not exactly sure what Anne means by the term pretty *tall*. Does she mean taller than herself? Taller than six feet?) But whether she is right or wrong, to reach her conclusion on the basis of her premises, the hidden assumption must be made. If the assumption is not made, the remaining premise simply does not support the conclusion. "Serge must be pretty tall" would then become a simple, unsupported claim.

The Principle of Fairness

If someone wanted to challenge Anne's argument, he could question her assumption. They might offer each other examples as well as examine Anne's definition of the term *tall*. But the person advancing the argument is not always present. Arguments are often found in books or may be reported secondhand or thirdhand. In these cases, a critical thinker should try to determine what the unstated premises actually are. But there is a danger here. When we assert that a person has made an assumption that has not been explicitly stated, we are liable to attribute to that person the premise that is the easiest to refute. If Dave wants to argue against Anne's conclusion he might assume that her hidden assumption was that *"All basketball players are tall."* This claim would be relatively easy to refute. Dave might simply point to several examples of "short" basketball players at the college and professional levels. Since the premise would turn out to be false, it would provide no support for the conclusion.

But is this being fair to Anne? She might also have assumed a slightly different claim. Perhaps she was reasoning that *"Most basketball players are tall."* In this case the premise is not as easy to refute. If Dave mentions a few short basketball players, Anne can simply retort that anyway most players are tall so Serge *probably* is tall too and that that's all she meant to say.

Now if Anne is not present to defend herself, and Dave has to attribute another premise to the argument, a choice must be made. Which assumption should Dave choose? By choosing the easiest assumption to refute, he is not really being fair to Anne. In those cases where the speaker cannot be questioned directly, the **principle of fairness** suggests that we try as best as possible to attribute the hidden premise *most likely* to be asserted by the speaker if she were thinking critically *and* which is the minimal assumption necessary to link the premises with the conclusion. It is easy to tear down an argument to which we have attributed flawed premises. The principal of fairness states that we should attribute to our opponent the interpretation that makes the best possible case for her conclusion. If Dave had thought about it, he may have decided that Anne would not be likely to make the assertion that *all* basketball players are tall. (Perhaps Dave knows that Anne is a real fan of the game and that she knows there are short players.) How we apply the principle will differ with the situation as well as our familiarity with the context of the argument.

SPOTTING ASSUMPTIONS FOR FUN AND PROFIT

A look at an older piece of reasoning may show why being able to spot logical assumptions can be lucrative as well as helpful in analyzing arguments. Back in the early 1980s a conversation was overheard between two professional gamblers. One had just finished claiming that the stock market would drop tomorrow because the Super Bowl was played today. By now, we should recognize this as an *inductive argument:*

> Premise 1: The Super Bowl was played today.
> Conclusion: The stock market will drop tomorrow.

The conclusion certainly goes beyond anything contained in the premise, first because the premise concerns the Super Bowl and the conclusion mentions the stock market (which is not mentioned in the premise) and second because the premise concerns what happened today and the conclusion concerns what *will* happen tomorrow (a prediction based on the present).

It would be a simple matter to add this presupposition A_1: "If the Super Bowl was played today, then the stock market will drop tomorrow." The addition makes the argument deductive, but does it take us anywhere? That is, what is interesting in this argument is the relationship between the professional football championship and the performance of the stock market; and although adding assumption A_1 transforms that relationship from an argument into a hypothetical statement within the argument, nothing has been explained, justified, or even illustrated. Worse yet, no one is likely to make such an assumption, even though it is logically possible.

But the point is to try to be as fair as possible in attributing hidden assumptions and to avoid the tendency to attribute the premise that presents the easiest target.

Sometimes, however, hidden assumptions are not easy to spot. Consider the following example presented in a format that often is employed in standardized testing:

Statistics indicate that, on the average, women executives' salaries are about 20% lower than those of men in comparable jobs. This is true in spite of job discrimination suits filed by the U.S. government against firms such as AT & T and Bank of America in the early 1970s as well as the passage of laws forbidding job discrimination by gender in many states and localities. In the face of this unrelenting prejudice against women, it is plain that only an amendment to the Constitution can fully remedy the present inequities.

Question Which of the following is assumed by the author of the above argument?

    A. All women executives are at least as well qualified as their male counterparts.

    B. A constitutional amendment is more likely to influence employment practices than separate state laws and court actions.

    C. Legal remedies for discrimination can only be effective when coupled with a sincere desire for reform.

What is more plausible is that these two professionals, familiar with both pro sports and the world of financial investments, observed some sort of correlation between the behavior of each and generalized or made the inductive leap, which may have become the principal working assumption A_2, here:

> Whenever the Super Bowl is played, the stock market drops on the following day

or

> The stock market always drops on the day after the Super Bowl is played.

An assumption such as A_2 still makes the argument deductive, but it also gives focus to subsequent inquiry. If the premises turn out to be true, the conclusion will have to be true too, and it would be a very likely consequence that people who are aware of this fact and who have available capital may try to utilize this information. After all, if it were true, it would be a much surer wager in the market than on the football game. And, interestingly enough, if a sufficient number of people were to capitalize on this new information, what do you suppose might happen to our newfound truth? What does that tell you? And also of interest: What reasons or premises would support the conclusion that has now become premise A_2?

D. Average salaries are misleading indicators of the real status of a particular social group.

E. Discrimination against women is as serious and widespread as discrimination against members of racial and ethnic minorities.

Before attempting to answer this question, we should first identify the conclusion. The conclusion of this argument is indicated by the phrase "it is plain that. . .," which occurs before the last statement in the argument. The other statements are either premises or extraneous statements. Let's examine the possible answers. Answer A may be assumed by many who read the argument, but it is not a necessary part of this argument. If A were a hidden assumption, it would be a useless one because we have not been given any link between equal qualifications and a constitutional amendment. It would also violate the principle of fairness since it is unlikely that most of those in favor of a constitutional amendment would accept such an assumption. Indeed, it is only necessary that fifty percent of women executives be as well qualified as their male counterparts. If *all* of them were, then perhaps their salaries should be commensurately higher! Answer C presents another difficulty. Although it does mention the need for legal remedies, it qualifies this with the claim that "a sincere desire for reform" is also necessary. Such an assumption could even count as evidence *against* the author's conclusion. Without the desire for reform, would the constitutional amendment even be enough? Answer E makes a point that is tangential to the argument. There is no indication of a comparison between ethnic and racial minorities in either the explicit premises or the conclusion. This answer doesn't offer a premise that establishes a connection between it and other premises. It introduces an entirely new claim. Answer E is therefore incorrect. Even if it were correct, it would have no bearing on *this* argument.

Answer B, however, would seem to be an assumption to which the author of the argument must be committed. If a constitutional amendment is seen as necessary for fair employment practices, then there must be a link between the two. Statement B is a hidden assumption of this argument. Answer D provides us with another example of a statement likely to be made by someone who was opposed to the conclusion of the argument. The author of the argument attempts to link a statistical difference in average salaries to the charge of unfairness in the workplace. The attempt to call these indicators "misleading" is an attempt to discredit one of the alleged links with the conclusion of the argument. Hence, it is not an assumption of this line of reasoning.

Unstated Conclusions

The conclusion of an argument may also remain unstated. This may be done because the arguer, having stated his premises, believes that the connection to the conclusion is inevitable for anyone following his line of reasoning. Consider, for example, the following argument:

> *Annual Stockholder Report:* Our company showed a larger gross profit than Acme did last year and theirs was larger than our biggest competitor.

Although not explicitly stated, the author of this argument wants to lead stockholders to the conclusion that their company had a larger gross product than their biggest competitor. The connection between the two premises is easy to spot. So is the line of reasoning: Our company is bigger than Acme and Acme is bigger than our competitor. Just as in the case of unstated premises, the author of the argument did not feel it necessary to state the conclusion. Two points need to be stressed at this juncture:

First, there is a world of difference between the *logical implications* of a statement or set of statements and the *psychological implications* thereof. The latter could be anything the speaker or writer has in mind or anything conjured up in the thought processes of the hearer or reader. For instance, upon turning on the radio and hearing the words, "That is his third strike," one listener may be reminded of the time her grandfather bowled a perfect game, while the announcer psychologically intended her audience to draw the conclusion that the batter was out. Because the psychological implications that grow out of statements and arguments vary from person to person, depending upon context and set of conditions, they are subjective and beyond the purview of logic or critical thinking. On the other hand, the logical implications (the unstated conclusions) that follow from a statement set or an argument set are assessable, capable of being evaluated by an objective set of logical rules, criteria, and operations. Some of the more prominent of those rules and principles will be examined in Part Two.

Second, *logical implications* differ in an important way from *logical assumptions*. Logical assumptions are easier to detect because they are a part of *all* inductive lines of reasoning. While there are an indefinite number of ways of expressing the same statement, the unstated premise or logical assumption always links

ADVERTISING THAT LETS YOU DRAW CONCLUSIONS

Have you ever stopped to ask yourself how many commercials are designed to "let you do your own thinking," meaning that they give you the premises from which you draw the conclusion that they have designed for you. For example, we will paraphrase a few such jingles:

> The larger the chicken, the better the chicken and
> Our stores have the largest chickens anywhere around.

> If you want to buy a car you can trust, then you should buy a Belchfire, and if you are going to buy a Belchfire, then you ought to consider one of your Metro Belchfire dealers. And, if you are going to consider one of your Metro Belchfire dealers, then you should pick the one with the lowest overhead. The Metro Belchfire dealer with the lowest overhead is Acme Belchfire. So. . . .

> "Red Dots is a great candy. . . ."
> "No! It's a great breath-o-lizer."
> "Wait! You're both right."

Generally, they do not make the conclusion too difficult to recognize.

the content of the premises which is not included in the conclusion with the content of the conclusion that is not expressed in the premises. There are no such easy marks to know when conclusions are not being stated.

EXERCISES

A LEVEL

Short Answers

  1. What is an assumption?

2. What is the difference between an explicit assumption and an implicit assumption?

3. What is a hidden assumption? What is an unstated conclusion?

4. What is an implication and how does it differ from a hidden assumption?

5. What is the principle of fairness?

True or False

* **6.** _F_ An assumption is always an unstated part of an argument.
* **7.** _T_ Explicit assumptions are always easier to spot than implicit assumptions.
* **8.** _T_ Unstated conclusions are usually more difficult to spot than unstated premises.
* **9.** _F_ Every argument has at least one unstated premise.
* **10.** _T_ The principle of fairness requires us to listen to an argument with an open mind.

B   LEVEL

List the premises and conclusion for each of the following arguments, then identify any unstated premise or conclusion.

 1. You must be a registered voter because you were asked to serve on the jury.
 2. Obviously you've never been to Manhattan, you'd have seen the Empire State Building.
 3. I'll bet you wrecked the car. Every time you wreck it, you get a stupid look on your face.
 4. Coroner's report: "We still haven't identified the hit-and-run victim, but he's not from around here. His lungs are too clean."
 5. I guess your parents won't let you drive the car anymore. I've seen you walking to school for the past week.
 6. You really should take it easy tonight, you have a big test tomorrow.
 7. Anyone who makes more than $400 in interest income has to report it on a tax return, and last year you made about three times that much.
 8. A karaoke bar is a great place for a person to make a spectacle of herself so Cathy would really enjoy going to one.
 9. John must have been behind the wheel because he was the only person in the car.
 10. Bob just graduated with honors, and you have a better grade-point average than he does.

C   LEVEL

The following questions are of the type found in the analytical reasoning sections of standardized tests. Try to find the best answer for each.

 1. Psychiatrists and laypersons both agree that the best sort of adjustment is founded on an acceptance of reality, rather than an escape from it.

The author of this passage assumes

  I. there are many sorts of adjustment

  II. escaping reality is possible

  III. psychiatrists and laypersons usually disagree

  A. I only

  B. I and II only

  C. II only

 D. I, II, and III

 E. III only

 2. "Sandra must be a soccer player; she's wearing a soccer jersey."

The author of this argument is assuming

 A. All soccer players wear soccer jerseys.

 B. Soccer players are required to wear soccer jerseys.

 C. Soccer players never wear any kind of jersey except a soccer jersey.

 D. Only soccer players wear soccer jerseys.

 E. Sandra is a woman.

3. Contemporary research reveals that 45% of all Americans are displeased with the shape of their nose. Which of the following is assumed or implied by this statement?

 I. Many American adults wish they could have their noses fixed.

 II. Many Americans are dissatisfied with one or more of their facial characteristics.

 III. Most American adults are displeased with one of their physical attributes.

 A. I only

 B. II only

 C. I and II only

 D. II and III only

 E. I, II, and III

 4. Only people with valid licenses can legally drive. Only people who pass the driving test can have valid licenses. Therefore, only those who pass the driving test can legally drive.

Assume that all of the statements in this argument are true. Which of the following must also be true?

 I. If a person does not have a valid license, then he cannot legally drive.

 II. If a person does not have a valid license, then she has not passed the driving test.

 III. Anyone who has not passed the driving test cannot legally drive.

 A. I only

 B. I and II only

 C. I and III only

 D. II and III only

 E. I, II, and III

5. There are no fewer than three but no more than five people in this class who understand the nature of this problem.

If this statement is true, which of the following must also be true?

 I. There are four people in this class who understand the problem.

 II. There are more than two people in this class who understand the problem.

 III. There are more than three people in the class who understand the problem.

 A. I only

 B. II only

 C. III only

 D. II and III only

 E. I, II, and III

6. The greatest chance for the existence of extraterrestrial life is on a planet beyond our solar system. After all, the Milky Way Galaxy alone contains a hundred billion other suns, many of which could be accompanied by planets similar enough to Earth to make them capable of supporting life.

This argument assumes which of the following?

 A. Living creatures on another planet would probably have the same appearances as those on Earth.

 B. Life cannot exist on other planets in our solar system.

 C. If the appropriate physical conditions exist, life is an inevitable consequence.

 D. More than one of the suns in the galaxy is accompanied by an Earth-like planet.

 E. It is likely that life on another planet would require conditions similar to those on Earth.

7. In a taste test, nine out of ten Brits preferred Earl Blue tea to the top-selling Lippy's. Not only that, but Earl Blue is less than half the price of Lippy's. So, get with it America; buy Earl Blue, the Brits favorite, and save, save, save!

This advertisement assumes or concludes that

 A. A cheaper brand of tea must be better.

 B. American tastes in tea are similar to those of the Brits.

 C. Lippy's is a tea of poor quality.

 D. Teas are all alike in quality, so people should buy the cheapest brand.

 E. Earl Blue is the best and cheapest brand of tea available.

8. Scientific testing shows a significant correlation between cardiovascular fitness and exercise.

Therefore, it is essential that everyone run or swim for at least half an hour three times a week.

 A. People must achieve cardiovascular fitness in order to be considered in good health.

 B. People will definitely achieve cardiovascular fitness if they run or swim for at least thirty minutes three times a week.

 C. Only the frequency and the length of exercise sessions will determine their effectiveness.

 D. Running and swimming are the only important forms of exercise for cardiovascular fitness.

 E. It is only by running or swimming for thirty minutes three times a week that people can bring about cardiovascular fitness.

3.2 DIAGRAMMING ARGUMENTS

Having examined the internal components of arguments, it is now time to take a step back and see how they relate to one another. One way of doing this is by assigning numbers to each of the premises, as well as the conclusion, and then drawing a diagram. The diagram should express the connections among all of the argument's statements. The simplest relationship among premises and conclusion is a *linear* one. Consider the following example:

Because your car ran out of gas, it will not run. It obviously ran out of gas because you did not put any in the tank. Now I realize that you couldn't have put any gas in the tank because you were out of money.

This argument contains four statements:

1. Your car ran out of gas.
2. Your car will not run.
3. You did not put any gas in the tank.
4. You were out of money.

The line of reasoning presented in this argument would begin with statement #4, "You were out of money." But the truth of this statement led the speaker to see that statement #3, "You did not put any gas in the tank" followed from the truth of #4. Because #3 is true, so is #1. ("Your car ran out of gas.") Finally, statement #2 ("Your car will not run") follows directly from #1. Since one statement leads directly to the next, we would diagram this argument as follows:

This diagram shows that the premises are connected to one another in such a way that the truth of each supports or establishes the truth of the next. If the first premise turns out to be true, then the second should be true. And if the second is true, then so must the third, etc. Sometimes, however, premises do not lead directly from one to the next. In some cases they are said to "converge" on the conclusion. Such a structure is called a *convergent* one, and it occurs when the truth of the premises are independent of one another, but when taken together lead to the conclusion. This is the case in the following example:

Because your radiator is clogged and your electrical system is also malfunctioning, your car will not run.

There are three statements in this argument:

1. Your radiator is clogged.
2. Your electrical system is malfunctioning.
3. Your car will not run.

In this example, each premise is sufficient in and of itself and *does not depend on the other premises* to support the conclusion. A malfunctioning electrical system will probably cause a car to quit running, and so will a clogged radiator. Since either of the premises leads independently to the conclusion, we indicate this by drawing separate lines from the circles indicating the premises (#1 and #2) to the circle representing the conclusion (#3):

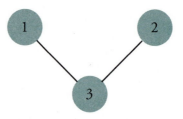

Sometimes one premise will independently support more than one conclusion. To distinguish these cases, we call such lines of reasoning *divergent,* in that more than one conclusion follows from the premise. This is the case with the following example:

Because your car will not run, you are going to be late for work and you are going to incur some expenses you had not expected.

This argument also has three statements:

1. Your car will not run.
2. You are going to be late for work.
3. You are going to incur some unexpected expenses.

This argument would be diagrammed as follows:

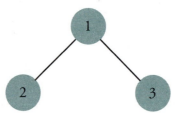

Being late for work and paying to fix the car follow from the premise. In still other arguments, the conclusion does not follow independently from each of the premises. Cases such as this show the conclusion following from the compounding or bringing together of the premises. Arguments such as the following are structured as *compound arguments:*

Since noncarnivorous dinosaurs ate a diet that included pinecones, they eventually became extinct, because eating pinecones caused fatal bone deficiencies.

The component statements of this argument are:

1. The diet of noncarnivorous dinosaurs included pinecones.
2. Noncarnivorous dinosaurs eventually became extinct.
3. Eating pinecones caused fatal bone deficiencies.

The conclusion statement (#2: Noncarnivorous dinosaurs became extinct) is not explained simply by the fact that they ate pinecones (statement #1). But in combination with statement #3 the conclusion naturally follows. Since the premise statements must be compounded in order to produce the conclusion, we represent this in our diagram with a horizontal line first linking the premises:

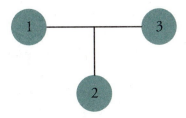

In some arguments the premises are not of equal weight. In such cases it is important to try to establish the relative importance of the various premises. Suppose, for instance, that you are taking a course and you have an excellent opportunity to steal an advance copy of the upcoming test. You mention this to a close friend in the course and he replies:

No! You should not steal the test, first and foremost because it is morally wrong. And besides, what if it's a trick or you get caught?

The statements involved here are:

1. You should not steal the test.
2. Stealing the test is morally wrong.
3. The opportunity to steal may really be a trick.
4. You may be caught stealing the test.

Each of the premises of this argument (statements #2, #3, and #4) gives independent reasons for the conclusion (statement #1). Yet the arguer indicates that some of the reasons are more important than others. The phrase "first and foremost" placed before statement #2 tells us that our friend places more "weight" (i.e., more importance) on this premise than on the others. Statements #3 and #4 are offered as additional disincentives, but their lesser weight or importance is suggested by the term "besides" which precedes them. Even if statements #3 and #4 were deleted from the argument, we would not have affected the main line of reasoning. To diagram an argument where one premise is more important than the others we should use a bold line to connect it to the conclusion:

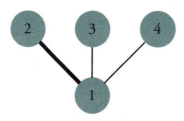

There are doubtless many other combinations of premises that could be rendered into diagram form. What we have learned in this section are some of the basics. But if we can get a basic overview of the relationships among the premises and the conclusion, we at least have an indication of which statements are important to challenge and which are not.

SUMMARY

In this chapter we learned how to analyze the claims that make up an argument. This chapter corresponds with Step 3 of *the Technique: spotting assumptions and implications*. To begin with, we must first distinguish explicit claims (those actually stated) and then implicit claims (those not stated, but assumed by the argument). Implicit assumptions are also known as *hidden assumptions,* logical presuppositions, and *unstated premises*. It is also often the case that conclusions to arguments are not explicitly stated. Spotting unstated claims as well as implications is extremely important in the analysis of an argument since it is often the unstated claims that can make or break an argument.

When trying to determine an implicit assumption or implication, it is important to invoke the principle of fairness. This is a principle designed to prevent us from imputing an assumption to an opponent simply on the basis that it would be an easy one to refute. The fairest way to determine an implicit assumption is to ask the arguer when possible what she had in mind. In those cases where the arguer is unavailable, it is necessary to study the context of the argument and to call on our background knowledge to determine the *minimal* assumption needed to guarantee the truth of the conclusion.

Once we have determined all of the claims involved in an argument, it is helpful to examine their relationships to one another. Some premises imply other premises directly. This type of relationship between premises is linear. In other cases, premises independently offer evidence for the same conclusion. This relationship is known as a *convergent one*. A *divergent argument* occurs when a claim implies two independent conclusions. Finally, in a *compound argument* the premises depend on one another to imply the conclusion. It is also helpful to indicate the relative importance of premises within an argument to produce a conclusion.

EXERCISES

A   LEVEL

Short Answers

1. What is meant by a convergent argument?
2. What is a divergent argument?
3. What is the difference between a divergent argument and a compound argument?
4. Draw a simple diagram illustrating a convergent argument.
5. Draw a simple diagram illustrating a divergent argument.

True or False

* 6. ___F___ A divergent argument is one in which all the disputants agree on the conclusion but not the premises.
* 7. ___F___ All arguments are either convergent or divergent.
* 8. ___T___ A linear argument is one in which each premise leads to the next.
* 9. ___(F)___ Most arguments are linear.
*10. ___T___ In some arguments, some premises are more important than others.

B   LEVEL

Diagram the following arguments according to the methods of this section. Be sure to assign numbers to all of the statements.

1. Since Ben is a member of Congress, he can send all of his official mail for free.
2. Since Ben is a member of Congress, he can send all of his official mail for free. Since he doesn't have to pay postage, he doesn't have to worry about licking stamps.
3. Betty didn't invite Veronica to her party because they had just had a fight. Besides, their husbands often get into heated arguments when they are together.
4. Clinton ought to be able to help the economy. To begin with, he wants to bring down the cost of health care. He also intends to try to reduce the budget deficit.
5. I was late for the examination, so Professor Reed gave me an "F." Now my grade-point average is going to go way down. If that happens, I'll lose my scholarship and my parents will take away my car.
6. Cigarettes cause health problems. They also can cost a lot of money. You should give up smoking because of the health problems. But even if that doesn't convince you to give up smoking, the fact that it is an expensive habit should.

7. The United States ought to try to make peace with Iraq. After all, Iraq is one of the most powerful nations in the region and we should try to be on peaceful terms with all influential nations. Besides, we've lost enough lives already trying to solve our differences through the use of force.

8. The United States ought never make peace with Iraq. Look at the way they tortured American prisoners. Besides, Hussein is power hungry and he'll try to take over all the oil in the region. If he does that, we'll be at his mercy economically.

9. If Senator Gramm runs as the Republican nominee for president in 1996, that will mean that the conservative wing of the party has taken control. If that happens you can be sure that abortion will be a big issue. You can also be sure that gun control will be an issue. If abortion becomes the big issue, the Republicans will lose. If gun control becomes the big issue, the Republicans have a chance. But either way, it doesn't work very good for the Republicans in 1996.

10. If the economy is bad in 1996 and Clinton's popularity starts slipping, the Republicans will recapture the White House. This would mean that five of the last seven presidential elections were won by Republicans. If that doesn't tell you which party is the most popular, nothing will.

C   LEVEL

1. Create an argument in which you have three premises that independently support the conclusion.
2. Create an argument in which you have two premises that depend on one another to support the conclusion.
3. Create an argument in which one of your premises is more important than the others for reaching the conclusion.
4. Try to create a complex argument that includes divergent, convergent, linear, and compound elements.

CASE STUDY

An Application of Step 3 of the Technique

The case study for this chapter consists of an application of Step 3 to a passage by B. F. Skinner. First study the passage, and then see if your understanding of Step 3 would have caused you to offer a similar analysis.

> But the triumph of democracy doesn't mean it's the best form of government. It was merely the better in a contest with a conspicuously bad one [i.e., Nazi Germany in World War II]. It isn't and can't be the best form of government, because it's based on a scientifically invalid conception of man. It fails to take account of the fact that *in the long run* man is determined by the state [that his behavior is totally conditioned]. A *laissez-faire* philosophy which trusts to the inherent goodness and wisdom of the common man is incompatible

with the observed fact that men are made good or bad and wise or foolish by the environment in which they grow.

—from *Walden Two* by B. F. Skinner

Since the premises of this argument mention only alleged "facts" and "observations" about how things are or have been and the conclusion is a normative statement about what may or may not be the best form of government, the conclusion "goes beyond" what is contained in the premises. The argument, therefore, is *inductive*. Notice also that it would not be a contradiction to say that the premises may be true, but the conclusion may be false; this will give us some clues as to what presuppositions underlie the reasoning.

Since there are two distinct lines of argumentation here, both of which are inductive each step of the way, several assumptions may be involved. To determine those presuppositions precisely as well as to analyze the structure of the entire argument, it will be helpful to display the structure of the argument as actually stated. There are six statements, which can be listed by number:

1. The triumph of democracy doesn't mean it's the best form of government.
2. Democracy was merely the better in a contest with a conspicuously bad one [Nazi Germany].
3. Democracy isn't and can't be the best form of government.
4. Democracy is based on a scientifically invalid conception of man.
5. Democracy fails to take account of the fact that in the long run man is determined by the state [viz. that his behavior is totally conditioned].
6. A *laissez-faire* philosophy, which trusts to the inherent goodness and wisdom of the common man, is incompatible with the observed fact that men are made good or bad and wise or foolish by the environment in which they grow.

The structure of the argument comprised by these six statements can be displayed in the following manner:

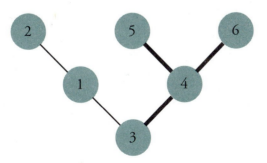

The minor reasoning from #1 to #3 is inductive and is based on the assumption that *"Winning a war does not necessarily mean that the victor has a better form of government."* The major line of reasoning from #4 to #3 is likewise inductive. The "fact" that a government is based on a scientifically invalid conception of human nature does not guarantee that that particular form of government is not the best form. The premise concerns a scientifically invalid psychology, and the conclusion concerns an evaluation of a political organization. The major assumption that connects the two could be expressed in a number of ways. For example, negatively put, it would be that

> *If a form of government is based on a scientifically invalid conception of human nature, then it cannot be the best form of government.*

Or phrased in a positive manner:

> *The best form of government will be based on a scientifically valid conception of human nature.*

Two premises support Skinner's contention—Statement #4—that democracy is based on a scientifically invalid conception of man. Statement #6 presupposes that democracy is in fact based on a *laissez-faire* philosophy and that such a philosophy betokens an invalid conception of human nature. Statement 5 makes use of the logical assumption that any nonbehaviorist theory of human nature is scientifically invalid in order to make the link with Statement #4 that democracy is based on a scientifically invalid concept of man. To the extent that Statements #5 and #6 are somewhat interdependent in supporting Statement 4 it is perfectly permissible to connect those two statements (#5 and #6) with a straight line between them to indicate this.

4

CLARIFYING MEANING

step one
What is the main claim?

▼

step four
What is the meaning of the terms employed?

step two
Is there an argument?

▼

step five
Are there any fallacies?

Only to the white man
was nature a 'wilderness' and
only to him was the land
'infested' with 'wild' animals
and 'savage' people.
To us it was tame.
—*Luther Standing Bear (1909)*

Fixed Asset, n.
A small, neutered donkey.
—*Brother John Economics (1992)*

Happiness is a warm puppy.
—*Charles Monroe Shultz (1962)*

Conservative. A statesman who is
enamored of existing evils,
as distinguished from a Liberal,
who wishes to replace them with others.
—*Ambrose Bierce (1891)*

4.1 Ambiguity and Vagueness
Exercises
4.2 Definitions
Summary
Exercises
Case Study

KEY TERMS

Ambiguity - The confusion that results from the fact that a word or phrase has multiple, definite meanings and in which the intended meaning is not apparent.

Connotation - The set of conditions for a term's use.

Definition - What a word means and the conditions governing how to use it.

Denotation - The set of objects, events, or conditions to which a term is taken to refer.

Equivocation - Occurs when a crucial word or phrase is used in two or more different senses in different contexts in an argument.

Grammatical ambiguity - Confusion resulting from faulty sentence construction that is open to two or more distinct interpretations and the context does not help clarify which one is meant.

Meaning - What a word or phrase signifies, represents, or portends or how it is used in a particular context.

Quantitative vagueness - Occurs when an expression is employed that refers to an indefinite amount of something.

Referential ambiguity - Occurs when a word or phrase can refer to two or more things, and it is not clear which of the two is intended.

Referential vagueness - Results from the use of a term that is not specific enough to indicate the conditions under which the term would apply.

Reportive definition - States how a term is actually used in normal language, or technically, or in the past.

Stipulative definition - Specifies the precise meaning of how a term is going to be used in a specific context.

Term mention - A referral to the actual word or phrase itself—a term is mentioned when we talk about a term itself rather than using it.

Term use - The actual employment of a word or phrase in referring to a situation, event, or object.

Vagueness by stress - The fact that the same set of words may be understood differently depending on how the words are stressed or accentuated.

The fourth step in the Technique asks you to consider the question "What do the terms mean?" The **meaning** of a term is that which a word, phrase, or sentence signifies, represents, or portends and includes the set of conditions under which the language is used correctly. Clarifying the meaning of words, phrases, and sentences allows you to better understand the intended meaning of the speaker. Words, phrases, and sentences sometimes have more than one possible meaning. Confusion and misunderstandings often result from the speaker intending that his words have one particular meaning, while his audience understands the term differently. This will allow a more informed application of *the principle of fairness*. It will also teach you how to construct clearer and less obscure arguments. An understanding of the meaning of a term or phrase will also help in the spotting of hidden assumptions and implications. In Chapter 4 we present a method for the clarification of the meaning of the words, phrases, sentences, and sometimes even the gestures from which the argument is constructed.

Whether we are analyzing the reasoning of others, or are attempting to construct arguments of our own, it is important to understand the meaning of the statements we employ. If someone is speaking a language we don't understand, the examination of their argument would be much more difficult. But sometimes, even when we do understand an arguer's language, the intended meaning is not readily apparent. Words and phrases can often be understood differently by the speaker and her audience. This can lead to a variety of misunderstandings. This chapter is devoted to an analysis of the concept of *meaning* and its function in human reasoning.

Many attempts have been made by philosophers over the years to zero in on the concept of meaning—and there has been much disagreement. In general, though, we can say that when we speak of the meaning of a word or phrase, we are indicating what it signifies, represents, or portends as well as those conditions that govern its usage. Remember that in any conversation (including a dispute between two individuals) both the speaker and his audience believe that the terms used have a certain meaning. Although there is often agreement as to the intended meaning, many times the participants understand the terms differently. When this occurs, verbal disagreements may result and the task of the critical thinker is to try to clarify the meaning of the terms being used.

4.1   AMBIGUITY AND VAGUENESS

One of the most common difficulties associated with the conveying of meaning from one person to another is linguistic ambiguity. **Ambiguity** occurs when there is more than one definite meaning for a word or phrase and the intended meaning is not immediately apparent. Consider the following statement:

> Heidi is a German shepherd.

This statement could mean that Heidi is a particular type of a dog. But it could also mean that Heidi is a person who lives in Germany and works as a shepherd. (You might think that the first possible meaning is the obvious one, but what if the sentence had been found in a story about fifteenth-century Germany?) Sometimes the ambiguity may even be intentional and designed to produce an emotional effect. The famous Abbott and Costello comedy routine, for instance, which begins with the confusion over a first baseman named "Who" and which results in a total misunderstanding of the answer to the question "Who's on first?" is an example of the use of ambiguity for comic effect. Advertisements sometimes use ambiguity to catch the attention of the public. A pizza parlor, for instance, which advertises "We don't cut corners," tells potential customers that the chefs use the finest ingredients. But it could also refer to the fact that the product is, in fact, round. The term *dog* could refer to a pet or to a snack at the ballpark or even to one's foot. Ambiguity becomes problematic in cases where there are verbal disagreements. It can also cause an apparently good line of reasoning to break down because the link from one premise to the next is illusory. Consider the following conversation:

Cathy: Nothing would make me happier than a diamond ring.

George: Great, now I know what to get you: nothing.

Cathy: What do you mean?!

George: Well you said that nothing would make you happier than a diamond ring. Since I know that you really want a diamond ring, and that "nothing" would make you happier, that's what I'll get you. Nothing.

The difficulty in this conversation results from the fact that Cathy is using the term *nothing* as part of a larger phrase "nothing would make me happier." But its inclusion in this phrase changes its meaning from what it might indicate if it appeared alone. "Nothing would make me happier" is generally taken to mean that the thing in question is that which would make her happier than any other possibility. But in this example, George interpreted the statement to mean "Getting her nothing at all would make Cathy happier than anything else. She really doesn't want a gift." This miscommunication resulted from the ambiguous use of the term *nothing*. It has one distinct meaning for Cathy and a different distinct meaning for George.

Regardless of whether the ambiguity is intentional a critical thinker will always be on the lookout for ambiguity. The ambiguous use of expressions can produce faulty communication and sometimes needless disagreement. There are several types of ambiguity.

Equivocation occurs when a critical word or phrase is being used ambiguously with two different meanings in the same context. A defendant in a burglary trial who, for instance, might try to claim that she did not really *rob* the victim's home would be relying on the ambiguous nature of the term *robbery*. A common understanding of this term would lead us to understand that a burglary was just a particular kind of robbery. A legal definition of the term, however, requires that for a crime to be considered a robbery, there must be a direct confrontation between the criminal and the victim and a threat must also have been made. The burglar in this example knew her law, and she recognized an ambiguity in the use of the term *robbery* that would allow her to "truthfully" proclaim her innocence of that crime.

Grammatical ambiguity is the result of sentence construction. It occurs when the structure of the sentence itself results in two or more possible interpretations. It is possible that two disputants agree on the individual meaning of every term in isolation, but disagree on the meaning of the statement when taken as a whole. In the advertisement of Figure 4.1, the "World's Largest Plant Sale," for instance, the sentence structure permits several possible interpretations. One might be that some of the largest plants to be found in the world are on sale. Or, two, it might mean that the most plants ever found in one place are all on sale. Three, it might mean that the largest plant in the world is on sale, or, the word "plant" may refer to a physical building or a business, rather than a piece of vegetation. Notice, though, that it was not a single word

FIGURE 4-1 GRAMMATICAL AMBIGUITY

or phrase that was the culprit, but the way the words were put together and the sentence structure that resulted.

Referential ambiguity occurs when a word or phrase can refer to two or more things, and it is not clear which one is intended. This sort of problem can occur because of the use of words such as *this, that,* and *its.* It is often compounded by poor sentence structure. The following conversation is an example of referential ambiguity:

Peter: You go on and take the other side of the court.

Patti: (not moving at all) Okay, I'm on the other side of the court.

Peter: No you're not, you're right here.

Patti: But if you walk around the net and back to the base line, then I'll be on the other side of the court.

In this example, Peter and Patti have different things in mind when they refer to "the other side of the court."

One particular type of referential ambiguity occurs when it is unclear whether the speaker is using a word to refer to something or is talking about the word itself. An elementary school child may, for instance, offer the following when asked to use the word *inundate* in a sentence:

Inundate is a word with eight letters.

Since the child is referring to the word and not to the situation that the word signifies, he is not really *using* the word. In this case we say he is *mentioning* the word. The **mention of a term** involves a referral to the actual word or phrase itself. The **use of a term** or phrase refers to its actual employment in referring to a situation, event, or object. Had the previous example read

The peaceful village was inundated with lava from the volcano

the term *inundated* would be used in the sentence rather than just mentioned. To be perfectly clear about whether we are merely mentioning a term or actually using it, we will follow the convention in this book of using italics for terms that are being mentioned rather than used. So the correct way of putting the child's sentence would be to have it read

Inundate is a word with eight letters.

By using this device we see one way referential ambiguity can be avoided.

Vagueness

Besides being ambiguous, the intended meaning of a term may suffer from vagueness. This occurs when a speaker uses expressions that are not precise enough, given the context, to convey what the speaker has in mind. Expressions such as "a whole bunch of" and "lots of" do not give very specific information.

Quantitative vagueness occurs when an expression is employed that refers to an indefinite quantity. Terms such as *many, a whole lot, a bunch of, quite a few, only a few, barely any,* etc., are often vague enough to be misleading. If Steve asks Shirley what she talked to their mutual friend Ernest about in a recent phone conversation, the reply that "We talked a while about a bunch of stuff" would not be very helpful.

Referential vagueness results from the use of a term that is not specific enough to indicate the conditions under which the term would apply. If a professor asks you to use "good paper" when you type an assignment, what does she mean? What counts as "good paper"? If she asks you to put that assignment in a "blue notebook," would you know exactly what she meant?

Vagueness by stress is the result of different understandings of a term due to different ways the words involved are stressed or accented. The late President Harry Truman was reported to have said, "You can't spend too much to win an election." When asked to clarify what he meant to a group of reporters, Truman allegedly said that politicians should not be able to purchase an office simply by outspending their opponents. Contemporary politicians have understood Truman's words as meaning that the ends justify the means and that a politician should do whatever it takes to win an election. Similarly the expression "All men are created equal" seems to have different meanings when we stress the term *men* and when we stress the term *created*.

EXERCISES

A   LEVEL

Short Answers

* **1.** What is meant by the term *ambiguity?*
* **2.** What is equivocation?
* **3.** What are some common expressions that convey referential ambiguity?
* **4.** Give some common expressions conveying referential vagueness.
* **5.** Give an example of quantitative vagueness.

True or False

* **6.** _____ Ambiguous terms are terms with more than one possible meaning.
* **7.** _____ In the sentence "The egg is cracked," the term *egg* is mentioned.
* **8.** _____ In the sentence "The word *egg* has three letters," the term *egg* is mentioned.
* **9.** _____ Vagueness by stress occurs when the meaning of a sentence is affected by accenting certain terms.
* **10.** _____ Ambiguity and vagueness are always unintentional.

B   LEVEL

Underline for italics when necessary in the following to distinguish the use of a term from its mention. Note that there may be more than one correct way of punctuating these sentences.

* **1.** You say yes while I say I'll think about it.
  2. Every time you say now it is always then.

  * **3.** Magic Johnson got his name from his mother.

     4. James wrote the name Jim on his notebook.

  * **5.** I know what I mean, but you don't know what you means.

     6. Anyone who can write well can write well.

  * **7.** Nick wrote his name in the margin on the first page.

     8. Stupid is a stupid word to spell.

  * **9.** The sign said The Greatest Show on Earth is playing at the bigtop.

    10. Life is the name of a magazine.

Identify any examples of vagueness or ambiguity in the following and state which type each is.

 ***11.** Last summer I went to a bunch of Braves games.

   12. For your assignment, purchase a large notebook.

 ***13.** All *men* are created equal.

   14. Al: When I get to the third traffic light do I turn left?

       Ellen: Right.

       Al: But you just said to turn left.

 ***15.** *Love* is a four-letter word.

   16. After Maggie insulted Mary, she slapped her.

 ***17.** Cathy didn't have too much to drink *tonight.*

   18. But Mom, I just failed the exam by a few points.

 ***19.** Reformer: I hate hate.

       Skeptic: How can you hate a word?

   20. I prefer only the best wines.

C   **LEVEL**

Try to find several examples of vagueness and ambiguity in news reports in the paper or on television. Discuss the ways such vagueness and ambiguity may be misleading. (Hint: *Consumer Reports* often cites wonderful examples of product advertising.)

4.2 DEFINITIONS

To settle disputes about meaning, disputants often rely on definitions. Definitions tell us what a word means and how to use it. The most common place for you to find a definition is in a dictionary. There are two major types of definitions.

A **reportive definition** is one that states how a term is (*or was*) actually being used. This is the type of definition found in a dictionary. This sort of definition appeals to the common usage of terms within the language.

A **stipulative definition** states the precise meaning of a term in a specific context. Sometimes in such areas as business and the legal profession, it is important to be very specific about the meaning of a particular term. It may also occur in a set of instructions, as in the following example:

Father: Now don't be late.

Daughter: OK. Don't worry, Dad.

Father: And by late I mean after midnight.

Daughter: But DAD!

A term such as *late* is too vague in this context. The Father thought that it was important to specify a time.

Another common type of stipulative definition occurs when a new discovery or invention must be named. The mathematician Edward Kasner, for instance, found it necessary to find a name for the frequently used number 10^{100}. He called it a *googol,* thereby stipulating that the definition of a googol was 10^{100}. (The name was supposedly provided by his young grandson.) Stipulating that the name of the smallest bit of matter should be the *quark* is another example of this type of definition.

Sometimes not only the definition itself is in dispute, but the type of definition that is called for. The abortion controversy in the United States is a good example. The Pro-Lifers generally believe that the definition of human life as beginning at conception is a reportive one. Finding out when life begins is a matter that they believe can be settled by examining evidence and making observations. Many Pro-Choicers believe, on the other hand, that the issue of when to define the beginning of life is a matter of stipulating a definition, rather than reporting one.

Before analyzing the possible types of definition you might offer, it is important to clarify a few terms. The **connotation** of a term is the set of conditions for its use. A word's connotation is usually what the dictionary offers as the definition of the term. But a term also denotes certain objects or events. The **denotation** of a term is the set of objects or events or conditions to which the term is taken to refer. Dictionaries often include examples of the term's denotation. The following definition includes both the denotation and connotation of the term *nation:*

A nation is a centralized political union such as Ghana, China or Germany

The connotation of the term is given by the phrase "a centralized political union," whereas the phrase "Ghana, China, or Germany" provides denotative examples. The use of the terms *connotation* and *denotation* will help in the understanding of the different ways that a definition can be formulated:

1. **Ostensive definitions:** An ostensive definition is perhaps the simplest. It involves simply pointing to an example of the term. A child learning the word *couch* might first understand its meaning when his mother points to the living room sofa.
2. **Citing examples:** A slightly more sophisticated form of definition occurs when we use examples. If you were to define *rock groups* as ". . . groups like R.E.M., the Spin Doctors, and En Vogue. . ." you would be offering a definition by example.
3. **Complete inventory:** Another type of definition cites all of the things to which the term refers. This type of definition applies only when the set of things that the term denotes is relatively small. An example is the definition of a continent as one of seven land masses: North America, South America, Africa, Europe, Asia, Australia, and Antarctica.
4. **Synonym:** A term that is not understood can often be defined by a more familiar term. A criminal can be defined, for instance, as a lawbreaker.

CARTOONS FOR COLOR

When President Clinton began to address the nation concerning his health care and national health insurance proposals, someone had loaded the wrong speech into the teleprompter. In a cartoon in the *Philadelphia Inquirer,* artist Tony Auth depicts with humorous insight what goes through a president's mind under such circumstances:

WHAT GOES THROUGH A PRESIDENT'S MIND WHEN
THE WRONG SPEECH COMES UP ON THE TELEPROMPTER?

While this represents Mr. Auth's interpretation of the different reactions of Clinton, Bush, Reagan, and Nixon, and while there may be a great deal of interpretive disagreement in the way other people might understand those reactions, there is also some very persuasive nonverbal argumentation at play in this cartoon. For example, which presidential responses are depicted favorably and which unfavorably?

5. **Connotation:** This is the best type of definition since it gives instructions as to when a term may be used. A good connotative definition will also include an example or two.

Evaluating Definitions

Once a definition is offered, criteria are available for evaluating that definition. You can question the accuracy, adequacy, clarity, and fairness of a definition.

Accuracy   It is important to know how accurate and precise the definition is. We can evaluate the accuracy of a definition by comparing its connotation with its denotation. If a peacock were to be defined as "a bird often found wandering free in zoos" and we were to accept this definition, we would find it exceedingly inaccurate. There would be many birds wandering around zoos that would not be peacocks, and there would be many peacocks that would not be found wandering around zoos. The definition simply does not zero in on the intended denotation. This definition picks out an *irrelevant feature*.

Adequacy   A definition can be inadequate when the connotation given is too broad or too narrow. A definition is too broad when it does not specify enough. Calling a triangle a "closed geometrical figure" is too broad because this definition would allow us to call things that we know are not triangles (such as circles and squares, which are also closed geometrical figures) by that name. A definition is too narrow, on the other hand, when it specifies too much. To say that to be a triangle the figure must have three equal sides would provide a good example of a definition that is too narrow.

Clarity   Definitions should also be as clear as possible. Since the purpose of any definition is to clarify the meaning of a term, to offer unclear definitions would defeat the purpose. It makes little sense if the language used in a definition is more difficult to understand than the term being defined. John Dewey, for instance, once defined *inquiry* as "the controlled or directed transformation of an indeterminate situation into one that is so determinate in its constituent distinctions and relations as to convert the elements of the original situation into a unified whole" (From *Logic: The Theory of Inquiry*). It is unlikely that anyone unfamiliar with the term *inquiry* would be aided by a definition such as this one.

Note also that sometimes lack of clarity is intentional. This is often the case with figurative or metaphorical language. G. K. Chesterton, for instance, once defined a *yawn* as "a silent shout." While this definition is neither clear nor accurate, it does have a certain poetic effect that could not be conveyed by a more "scientific" definition. Again it is the context in which the definition occurs that determines whether or not it is clear enough.

One form of definition that invites a lack of clarity is a circular definition. Definitions become circular when they simply repeat, in other words, the term being defined. To define *freedom* as "the state of being free" doesn't get us anywhere unless we know the meaning of the term to begin with.

Another major cause of lack of clarity is the tendency to define words in negative terms. To say, for instance, that *love* is "not lust" gives us very little clarification about what love actually is. Such negative definitions should be avoided. Two points need to be mentioned in this connection. First, by "negative" characterizations, we are referring to *descriptively* negative, not *judgmentally* negative characterizations. To define a "car" as "not a truck, or a bus, or a van" is a descriptively negative definition. To define the "Independent Political Party" as "the political group of losers" is judgmentally negative. We will see how to handle judgmentally negative definitions under the topic of *fairness*. The second point of note is that on rare occasions, descriptively negative definitions cannot be completely avoided. So, the rule of thumb is to avoid negative characterizations to the extent possible.

Fairness. One of the most common yet serious problems with definitions is bias. Perhaps every word or phrase has some sort of emotional connotations, positive or negative, associated with it. For this reason it is extraordinarily easy to prejudice one's case when giving a definition. A person who is ideologically conservative is likely to define political disagreements in this way:

> The major difference between political conservatives and liberals today is that conservatives consider the entirety of human nature, while liberals can see only the materialistic side of people.

A person who is ideologically liberal might offer a counter-definition:

> A conservative is a person who fights against nature by trying to stop the ongoing processes of change in order to protect his own economically privileged position. A liberal, on the other hand, knows those processes will occur—the question is whether to direct them intelligently or to fight against them irrationally and futilely.

Both sides may fervently believe in the justness of their cause but the strength of one's belief is not a logical warrant for its correctness. In each of these cases the definer is hardly being fair; each has tried to persuade the audience that the other side is by definition untenable, without giving concrete or descriptive evidence to support the conclusion.

SUMMARY

The fourth step in *the Technique* is concerned with *meaning*. The meaning of a term is that which a word, phrase, or sentence signifies, represents, or portends and it also includes the set of conditions governing the use of that term. Clarifying the meaning of words, phrases, and sentences allows you to better understand the intended meaning of the speaker. In this chapter, we studied the meaning of the term *meaning* and its many aspects, which must be taken into account by a critical thinker. The meaning of a word, phrase, or sentence is that which it signifies, represents, or portends. Clarifying the meaning of words, phrases, and sentences allows you to better understand the meaning of the language being used. It also allows you to construct clearer and less diffuse arguments. An understanding of the meaning of a term or phrase will also help in the spotting of hidden assumptions and unstated conclusions. The meaning of a term can often cause confusion because it is ambiguous. This means that the term has two or more possible, very definite meanings and the intended meaning is not apparent. *Equivocation* occurs when the term in question is used in an ambiguous way that misleads others. It does so by relying on one meaning in one use, and a different meaning in another use, so that a link which is supposed to be made is not in fact present. *Referential ambiguity* results when the connotation of the term is apparent but the denotation of the term is not. Problems in understanding may also result from the confusion of the *use* of a term and its *mention*. *Vagueness* results when the application of the term is not apparent or is unclear. *Quantitative vagueness* results from the use of open-ended quantity terms such as *lots* and *a few*. *Referential vagueness* occurs when it is not clear to what specific objects or events the term is meant to apply. Vagueness by stress results from the intonation or stress given to a particular part of a statement.

We also saw in this chapter that the purpose of definitions was to help clarify the meaning of a term. *Reportive definitions* indicate the way terms are actually used, whereas *stipulative definitions* specify how a particular definition should be used in a specific context. Finally, definitions should be evaluated on the

WILEY DEFINES THE FARMER

Johnny Hart's cartoon "B.C." depicts the character "Wiley" giving his definition of the word *farmer*. The clever answer, however, contains almost no descriptive content at all, except perhaps the word *feed*. Everything else is calculated to raise the ironic feeling that while the farmer is responsible for feeding the world, he cannot make enough of a living at doing so even to feed his own family. What happens is that the connotative content of the definition is geared to raise sympathy for the plight of the farmer. This would be a persuasive definition.

B.C.   **BY JOHNNY HART**

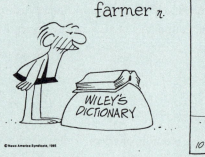

(By permission of Johnny Hart and Creators Syndicate, Inc.)

basis of their accuracy, adequacy, clarity, and fairness. Within these four categories we can distinguish seven criteria for evaluating reportive definitions:

1. Avoid using irrelevant features
2. Avoid characterizations that are too broad or too narrow
3. Avoid circular definitions (repeating the term being defined)
4. Avoid obscure characterizations (definitions that are harder to understand than the word being defined)
5. Avoid language that is vague, ambiguous, metaphorical or figurative
6. Avoid descriptively negative characterizations
7. Avoid persuasive or judgmentally loaded characterizations.

EXERCISES

A LEVEL

Short Answers

* 1. What is a reportive definition?
* 2. What is a stipulative definition?
* 3. What is the difference between connotation and denotation?
* 4. List at least five ways of formulating definitions.
* 5. What is meant by the adequacy of a definition?

True or False

* 6. _____ Definitions found in dictionaries are always stipulative.
* 7. _____ The best sort of definition is an ostensive one.
* 8. _____ A fair definition is one that is unbiased.
* 9. _____ A definition which is too broad does not specify enough information to adequately apply the term.
* 10. _____ A circular definition is one that "goes around" the term but never quite gets to the point.

B LEVEL

State the type of definition in each of the following. Then evaluate it in terms of fairness, adequacy, accuracy, and clarity.

* 1. A human being is a featherless biped.
  2. A triangle is a closed geometric figure.
* 3. The president is the one who presides.
  4. "Love is a rose. . ."
* 5. An upper classman is a sophomore, a junior, or a senior.
  6. By *good car* I mean a car like a Mercedes or an Infiniti.
* 7. (Mother pointing out the window of a car while talking to her young child): "That's a cow."
  8. A pentagon is a closed geometrical figure with five equal sides and five equal angles.
* 9. A liberal is really a communist in disguise.
  10. A U.S. citizen is anyone who was born in the country or who was legally naturalized.
* 11. "Instructor": one who guides or teaches children.
  12. "Faith:" believing in something you know ain't true.
* 13. "Good": not being evil, bad, malicious, or spiteful.
  14. "Denver:" mile high city; home of the Broncos.
* 15. Life's a beach.

16. A "portrait" is an oil painting done on canvas depicting a person.

*17. "Anti-social": not social

18. "Singletree": a whiffletree

*19. Hereinafter in this contract, the term "recreational vehicle" shall be used to mean a self-contained, motorized vehicle.

20. "Sleeping pills": pills that make you go to sleep.

*21. "Check": a negotiable instrument.

22. "Honesty": chronic, habitual absence of the intent to deceive.

*23. Mars is what I mean by a "planet".

24. "Solar planet": the nine major heavenly bodies revolving around our sun and including Mercury, Venus, Earth, Mars, Jupiter, Saturn, Uranus, Neptune, and Pluto.

*25. "SAT": a culturally biased test designed to prevent certain minority students from being accepted for college admission.

 LEVEL

Look for four or five examples of definitions in your college textbooks (including this one) and criticize those definitions on the basis of the criteria presented in this chapter.

CASE STUDY

Countdown to the Election

(Reprinted with permission from *Listening to America,* Transcript #127 Copyright © 1992 PBS Video.)

This case study is excerpted from a Public Affairs Television production hosted by Bill Moyers. It consists of a discussion of television's effect on the presidential campaign of 1992. It provides a good example of how the meaning of statements can be affected by modern campaigning and advertising techniques. As you read through the transcript, pay attention to the ways in which television advertising can convey meanings that are not explicitly stated nor implied by the text.

Bill Moyers   . . . Welcome to this final edition of *Listening to America.* As the presidential election appears to tighten in the last days before the election, we'll look at the battleground state of New Jersey. But first, our resident analyst of campaign rhetoric, Kathleen Hall Jamieson, Dean of the Annenberg School for Communication at the University of Pennsylvania. . .

Kathleen Hall
Jamieson: What we have in the final weeks of the campaign is a test of the credibility of Ross Perot, the candidate who has purchased more total air time in the general election than any can-

didate in the history of television. . . . [W]e have an interesting test of the kinds of claims you saw in the opening of the program because news is a highly credible medium. We trust those unscripted encounters. And now the question about Ross Perot is, is that person we saw in the press conference after the debate . . . the real Ross Perot, or is Ross Perot, the real Ross Perot, the person we see in those half-hour presentations or in the debates? And news is going to win out in that encounter. We trust news at the same time as we say, "Oh , those media people! I don't like any of them."

Moyers: Well, I was going to ask, if news is trustworthy, why does President Bush keep—about all he can say these days is "Attack the media, attack the media."

Jamieson: I'm going to surprise you by defending George Bush. One of the things that we looked at about four or five weeks ago was the tendency of the news media when somebody's been the front-runner for a while to disadvantage the person who's behind in the polls. Now the conservatives charge that that's a conspiracy, that basically the "liberal media," "liberal reporters" are out to get George Bush. It's not a conspiracy at all, but there is a tendency in the structure of news as we know it now to say of the front-runner in news stories, "This person must be doing something right to be the front-runner. Let's now run stories which account for this person's success." The news stories pick decisive moments that show that the person is doing really well. And, of the person who is behind in the polls, the questions change. When George Bush was interviewed by Bryant Gumbel this week, for example, the poor President spent much of his time having to dodge questions which said "How can you possibly win?" in essence. What we basically do is make it harder for the person who's behind to get his message through. We make it easier for the person who is ahead to duck accountability. We spend too much time talking about strategy, who won and lost the debates, instead of what was the substance disclosed.

Moyers: Nonetheless, the President is constantly on the attack against his opponent and against the media and it's getting really tough in these last few days against Bill Clinton.

* * * At this point a Bush campaign commercial is shown * * *

Moyers: Now, those are real people, but those photographers are professionals pretending to be amateurs, home videos. What do you make of that?

Jamieson: This form of advertising, which emerged in the 1976 campaign, deliberately takes the techniques of the news, the hand-held camera, the documentary look, the quick cuts between individuals to suggest to you that in a news-like encounter, here we have typical citizen reactions to a candidate. What we're missing, of course, in these kinds of encounters is a sense of typicality. These aren't actually real citizens. These are people the camera-holder knows are Bush supporters and they're saying things that we would find far more controversial if they were uttered by the candidate, George Bush. People in the street are able to make stronger attacks with more impunity because, after all, they're just expressing their own point of view.

Moyers: These are people we might know down the street, around the corner, in the shops?

Jamieson: They're selected to look like us and they're also selected to sound like us, but occasionally the ads misfire. One of these ads, which has been aired repeatedly by the Bush campaign, shows a woman who, on first exposure, seems genuinely concerned about whether there'll be clothes on her child's back. But what we found in focus groups is that as people see this ad repeatedly—and that's a characteristic of advertising, we see it again and again—people step back from her and say, "I don't like her. I don't trust her. She sounds highly partisan. She sounds unfair." So as we get repeated exposure to any communication, we become more likely to test it.

Moyers: Politicians cannot always get away with saying something ugly about the other guy or the other woman, but if you take the man or woman "on the street" saying the same thing, we're more inclined to believe that.

Jamieson: To accept it, yes.

Moyers: What does that say about politics today, that the professional politician must use amateur techniques in order to get the message across?

Jamieson: I think what it says is that your strongest attacks, historically, have always been carried by surrogates and we now have a surrogate who has emerged as a representative of the American people, actually a pseudo-representative of the American people. Basically, these people on the street are surrogates for the candidate. They're surrogates in the same sense that the people who introduce the candidates are surrogates. They're surrogates in the same way that the anonymous print of the nineteenth century was a surrogate. You notice we don't have on the screen an identification. We don't know who the person is, where the person lives, what the person does. This is supposed to be Everywoman and Everyman.

2

THE EVALUATION OF ARGUMENTS

Two main parts of the critical technique include (1) analyzing arguments and (2) evaluating arguments. During the analytical phase the primary focus concerns breaking down arguments into their component statements (claims), identifying premises and conclusions, distinguishing deductive from inductive reasoning, spotting assumptions and implications, portraying the structure of the reasoning involved, and clarifying meaning as necessary. All of this part of phase one has been covered in the first four chapters and is preliminary to a fair, adequate, and accurate assessment of the argument.

Now we are ready to begin the second major phase of the critical technique: evaluating arguments. Two principal ways of assessing the worth of a line of thinking explore alternately the *content* or the *form* of the reasoning. In Chapter 5, we begin to evaluate the content of arguments by noting when the evidence presented may be irrelevant, insufficient, unfair or inaccurate. Traditionally, this area of study has been called that of *informal fallacies.* In Chapters 6 and 7, the form of the argument becomes the central focal point when we turn our attention to syllogisms or classical categorical logic. A prime reason for still studying such argument structures is their continued appearance on standardized testing.

In Chapters 8 through 11 the form of the argument remains on center stage, but we shift perspective to the propositional forms both simple and complex statements can assume in creating the actual structure of any particular argument. We will also look at truth tables, proofs, and derivations within this format. One reason for emphasizing understanding the form of arguments in this section is that in the normal course of daily living we are more familiar with criticizing arguments on the basis of their content. By developing our awareness of the structure of arguments as well we become better listeners and can assess reasoning from an internal, rather than external perspective.

5

FALLACIES

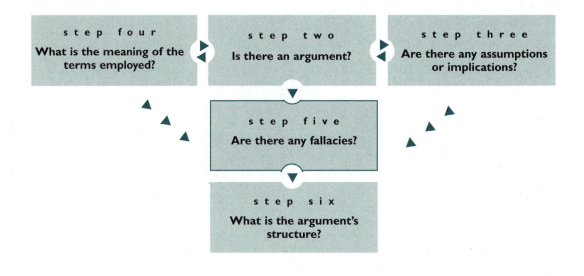

step four
What is the meaning of the terms employed?

step two
Is there an argument?

step three
Are there any assumptions or implications?

step five
Are there any fallacies?

step six
What is the argument's structure?

If you engage people's pride, love, pity, ambition (or whatever is their prevailing passion), on your side, you need not fear what their reason can do against you.

—Lord Chesterfield (1759)

Somewhere out in this audience may even be someone who will one day follow in my footsteps and preside over the White House as the President's spouse. I wish him well.

—Barbara Bush (1990)

CHAPTER OUTLINE

KEY TERMS

Fallacy - A mistake in the alleged connection between the premises and conclusion of an argument or within a premise.

Fallacy of inadequate premise - One in which the premise is relevant to the conclusion but actually provides insufficient support for that conclusion, or not as much as it claims to provide.

Fallacy of irrelevant premise - One in which the premise seems to support a conclusion but is in fact irrelevant to that conclusion.

Fallacy of unfair premise - A fallacy which unfairly stresses a fact or misconstrues an opponent's claim or argument.

With this chapter, we begin the second major division of the Technique: The *evaluation* of arguments. Step 5 will teach you how to identify any fallacies that are being employed. Fallacies are forms of bad reasoning that are often accepted by *uncritical* thinkers as good evidence for the conclusion. In this chapter arguments will be evaluated by asking the following questions:

1. Are the premises relevant to the conclusion? To what degree?
2. Are the premises true? If you disagree with them, is the disagreement factual, evaluative, interpretive, or verbal?
3. Are the premises fair? Or are they slanted or biased? How so?
4. Are the premises adequate? Is there a need for more evidence? Are important objections to the argument considered or are they ignored?

One common mistake people make is to confuse a fallacious argument with a *false* claim. If someone were to say, for instance, "It is a fallacy to think that we are now in a depression," she is using the term incorrectly. She should have said instead something like "The belief that we are now in a depression is false." A **fallacy** is not a false statement; instead, it is a faulty connection between statements. It is important not to confuse these terms because the discovery of a fallacy within an argument does not mean that the conclusion to the argument is necessarily false, it only means that the conclusion does not follow from *this* particular set of premises.

Fallacies may or may not be intentional. In some cases, fallacies are used intentionally to dupe or trick an audience; in others, however, fallacies are used unintentionally. Their unintentional use usually results from poor habits of reasoning. But whether or not they are intentional, it is important to detect fallacies and to show why they can be misleading.

Remember also that fallacies are context dependent. This means that a fallacy can be cited as one only because of its role in the reasoning process. A joke made to sidetrack an opponent in a debate can be considered a fallacy. But a humorous political cartoon would not normally be considered fallacious. In this chapter we try to set some guidelines to determine when the context of an argument shows that a fallacy has occurred.

One of the reasons fallacies are so seductive is that they sometimes tend to parallel good forms of reasoning. This is another reason to be aware of the context in which an alleged fallacy is thought to occur. By examining the context, we may also determine whether or not a fallacy has indeed occurred. As we examine the individual fallacies, we will also try to show the viable forms of reasoning which they resemble.

Finally, the number of actual fallacies that can occur is indefinite. It is doubtful that there could ever be an exhaustive list of all the mistaken forms of reasoning. This is partially because people are continually coming up with new ways of supporting their beliefs. From Aristotle's earliest attempt to identify and catalog fallacies to the present day there has been no agreement as to the number or even the types of fallacies. What we have done in this text is to come up with a workable number of the most frequently occurring fallacies. They fall into two general categories:

1. Fallacies caused by problems with the evidence or premises, as a result of which three general types of problems can occur:

a. The premises are irrelevant to the conclusion (either psychologically or grammatically misleading).
b. The premises are inadequate support for the conclusion.
c. The premises are unfair or biased in relation to the conclusion.

2. Fallacies caused by problems with the alleged link between premises and conclusion.

In the explanation of fallacies that follows, we have tried to keep the technical terms to a minimum. Although you should learn the names of these fallacies, the more important thing is to recognize the error in each and why it prevents the particular argument from establishing the truth of its conclusion.

5.1 FALLACIES OF IRRELEVANT PREMISES

An argument can be considered fallacious when its premises, whether they are true or not, are logically irrelevant to establishing the truth of the conclusion. Although this may be accomplished in a variety of ways, the common error is that the evidence presented seems convincing when in fact it does not contribute any real support for the conclusion. The emotions evoked by the use of certain terms may make an unsupported conclusion psychologically more acceptable.

Psychologically Irrelevant Premises

Premises are psychologically irrelevant when they attempt to manipulate psychological states to cloud the issue being discussed or to divert one from that issue entirely. The following are some of the common fallacies that occur in this category.

Personal Attack The Personal Attack fallacy is traditionally referred to as an *ad hominem* argument. It is an attack directed at the person making the argument, rather than at the argument itself. It works by drawing attention away from the subject matter of the argument and directing it toward the character or behavior of the arguer. Often the fallacy is effective because it shifts the focus from what the person is saying to who is saying it. When the attack is directly leveled at the person, the fallacy is called *abusive*. A recurring *Saturday Night Live* parody of news discussion shows featured Dan Akroyd's character beginning his argument with Jane Curtain with the phrase "Jane, you ignorant slut," to which she would retort "Dan, you pompous windbag." (Reprinted with permission from *Saturday Night Live*.) Name-calling among children is a very basic form of this fallacy. (Unfortunately, many retain the habit into their adulthood.)

Some varieties of the Personal Attack are called circumstantial. A circumstantial personal attack occurs when the person under attack is being abused because of some special feature or characteristic that is supposed to render her unworthy of belief. For instance, if someone reasons that we cannot take Jamal's conclusion about the basketball game seriously because he is short, that person's premise is completely irrelevant to the line of questioning we should be considering.

Another form of the personal attack works by degrading the source or genesis of a particular argument. Known as the *genetic fallacy,* this reasoning error may take several forms. One, for instance, would be to argue that we should not consider a female sports reporter's comments on the Super Bowl with seriousness because she is, after all, a woman. Or, conversely, that an argument by a white male should be completely discounted because he couldn't possibly understand an issue involving Native American women.

A second type of genetic fallacy occurs in what might be called the blanket "Praise-by-Association" or "Blame-By-Association". For example, if someone were to argue that we should oppose a policy of paid vacations for employees because Adolph Hitler used to favor the idea, this would be a form of blame-by-association. Remember, the argument stands or falls on its own merits, not because of who said it.

A person commits the fallacy of *Poisoning the Well* when she attempts to forestall a dispute by making it embarrassing to disagree with the speaker or writer. Phrases like "any intelligent person would know that . . ." or "only a complete idiot would believe that. . ." or "no true patriot would be opposed to . . ." are examples of this form of personal attack.

The final form of personal attack we consider is known as the *you too* fallacy. This fallacy is sometimes referred to by its Latin name *tu quoque.* This fallacy may rely on the belief that two wrongs make a right. Instead of addressing the charges made or the conclusions drawn by someone else, the speaker tries to turn the line of inquiry to the person making the charges. A candidate for political office, for instance, might respond to a charge of political favoritism made by his opponent by accusing her of being unethical herself. Children are often eager to justify their actions by claiming that their friends "did the same thing."

Each of the varieties of personal attack can be psychologically persuasive because they seem to address a real issue. The problem from a critical thinking perspective is that it shifts attention from the issue at hand. Remember, however, that like all other fallacies, the personal attack fallacy is context dependent. A defense lawyer in a criminal trial may legitimately attempt to destroy the credibility of a witness for the prosecu-

WHAT IF?

Fallacies that are closely related to each other often occur in the same piece of reasoning. Suppose a national scandal magazine ran a story about a feud between two television stars, Celebrity A and Celebrity B, detailing the dispute chronologically. At one point, Celebrity A's reasoning is featured:

> Celebrity A is outraged. He told his friend: "I'd always heard stories about what a lowlife jerk Celebrity B is. This note on my wife's car and everything else reinforces that. Only someone with the IQ of pond scum would do that."

The epithet "lowlife jerk" in this context is a Personal Attack of the abusive kind. The continuation, "Only someone with the IQ of pond scum," is a blanket Poisoning the Well fallacy. It is not that name-calling is always fallacious *per se,* but when that name-calling cannot be backed up with descriptive phraseology and evidence, then one may suspect that it is empty of true content and occurs for the sake of swaying opinion in the place of real proof.

tion by questioning his character and reliability. But in the case of a trial the integrity of the witnesses *is* a legitimate issue.

Red Herring   The user of this fallacy attempts to draw one's attention away from the issue in question and sidetrack it to a different set of concerns. It gets its name from the fish used by British fox hunters to weed out the inexperienced hunting dogs by creating a false trail. (The well-trained hounds would stay on the fox's trail.) This fallacy is a very general one. You might have noticed already that all the varieties of the personal attack fallacy can be put into this category. Some of the fallacies that follow in this chapter can also be placed in this category. We will reserve the use of the Red Herring fallacy to cover those general cases not included in the more specific uses. The political candidate attacked by his opponent, for instance, might respond by offering a red herring of his own: "Tricks of this nature have been typical of this whole election, where people have tried to slander me and my family, but it won't work." The candidate is trying here to draw our attention away from the charges made against him by substituting the issue of his opponent's tactics.

Appeal to Fear   This fallacy involves the use of threats or an appeal to force to appeal to a special kind of self-interest. It is an attempt to change people's minds or behavior by replacing rational reflection with an emotional response. Parents are often guilty of this fallacy. A father, for instance, might try to justify a curfew to his daughter by threatening to take away her allowance. In such a case, an appeal to fear would fail to address the reasons that the father might offer to try to persuade his daughter rationally that the curfew should be obeyed. Similarly, a religious figure might try to argue that a person should observe the rules of morality "because sinners go to hell."

Like the other fallacies, this too is context dependent. The question the critical thinker should ask in this case is this: Is the appeal to fear being offered rationally as a reason for the arguer's conclusion? Is an attempt being made to override thoughtful deliberation and replace it with the emotion of fear? If the answer to these questions is yes, then the fallacy has been committed. But if rational consideration is given to the possible consequences, the appeal might be legitimate. A political candidate might legitimately use an opponent's record to warn of the possible consequences of voting for her opponent. If the issue is rationally addressed and the opponent offered a chance for rebuttal, the appeal may be legitimate.

Appeal to Pity   This fallacy redirects the thought processes from a rational consideration of the issues to the emotional reactions inspired by our tendency to sympathize with a person's misfortunes. An applicant for a job might, for instance, attempt to advance his cause by telling the interviewer that his wife just lost her job, his children have fallen ill and need medicine, his home just burned to the ground, and his dog was hit by a car. Although these are surely sad circumstances, they are irrelevant to the question of job qualifications. Remember, even this fallacy is context-dependent.

Misuse of Humor   Like pity, humor is an emotion that can be used to seduce an audience into a feeling of sympathy or closeness to the arguer. This fallacy occurs when humor, jokes, or comical "put downs" are used to divert attention away from an argument. When asked whether he thought Nancy Reagan had too much influence on her husband's policies as president, Senator Bob Dole chuckled and replied that "Well, sometimes we're all a bit *too* married." He was attempting to draw attention away from the issue.

Humor, however, can be legitimately useful in some contexts. Editorial cartoons, for instance, often attempt to take a humorous approach to political issues. In such cases, the humor is not an attempt to divert the discussion, but to provide another perspective. To try to *use* a political cartoon to establish the conclusion of an argument would, on the other hand, be a misuse of humor.

Appeal to Tradition When a person begins to question why something is done in a particular way, the answer is sometimes "Because we have always done it this way." This type of response is an example of an appeal to tradition. Like any other practice, traditions may be questioned. To respond to a question about a tradition by merely stating that it *is* a tradition avoids the issue entirely. For example, remember that at one time slavery and burning heretics at the stake were considered traditional. If a tradition is a valid one, it ought to be capable of standing up to the scrutiny of critical thinking. The same holds true for novelty: just because something is "new and improved" does not necessarily make it a better product for you.

Popular Appeals This fallacy involves the use of carefully chosen emotive language to sway a person's opinions. While he was running for president, then-governor Jimmy Carter was addressing an audience in Cleveland on the issue of school busing for the purpose of integration. As he explained his support for this method, he sensed an uneasiness in the audience. At this point, he decided to talk about the need for preserving the "ethnic purity" of neighborhoods in an attempt to win back the support of his audience.

Popular appeals are the stock-in-trade of much modern advertising. The cologne or perfume that is offered as assuring one of success with the opposite sex is one example. Popular appeals may be directed toward any sort of emotional need—snobbery, envy, loyalty, security, and greed, for example.

Bandwagon Fallacy Sometimes cited as a particular example of a popular appeal, the Bandwagon Fallacy occurs so frequently that it deserves special recognition. This is the attempt to prove that a conclusion is true by citing the fact that a majority of people believe that it is true. Many religious leaders, for instance, have argued that since most of the people in the world believe that God exists, God must therefore be a reality. (If this type of argument appeals to you, you might want to consider that for hundreds of thousands of years most of the people in the world believed that the earth was flat.) Neither the number of people who hold a belief nor the fervency with which that belief is held provides reasonable grounds for believing it to be true.

Emotional Appeals These fallacies result from the use of emotion to cloud or to bypass issues. Like the Red Herring fallacy, emotional appeals encompass a number of specific fallacies we have already studied. The Fallacies of Popular Appeals, Appeals to Fear, Pity, Humor, and Tradition as well as the Bandwagon Fallacy have their effects through the evocation of emotional responses. In themselves, there is nothing wrong with emotional appeals. They become fallacious when they are used to draw attention away from the issues being considered. This should not be taken to imply that one's emotions should play no role whatsoever in the formulation of a person's position. To deny the role of the emotions in thought processes of human beings would be patently unfair. A fear of burglary in a crime-ridden neighborhood would be both legitimate and reasonable. However, an exaggerated fear of crime caused by a television commercial for a home security system would be an abuse of the emotion. When emotions are used to distract from serious consideration of the issues, they become detriments to clear-headed reasoning.

WHY DO WE DO IT THAT WAY?

The Appeal to Tradition is not always wrong or fallacious; rather, we often lose sight of the original reason why something was a good idea in the first place, but why that reason is no longer pertinent now. For example, a woman once asked her husband why he cooked a particular roast by cutting off the ends. He replied that was the way his mother had cooked the roast for over thirty years and it tasted better and made nice brown gravy. So, the woman decided to call her husband's mother and ask why she cooked the roast that way. The mother replied, because *her* mother had cooked the roast that way for more than thirty years and it tasted better and made great brown gravy. The woman resolved to try one last time, and called her mother-in-law's mother, asking her why she had cut the ends off of this kind of roast when she cooked it. The elderly woman responded, "To make it fit in the pan."

According to the Critical Technique, if the roast pan we now have is too small for the roast we just bought, then this may still be a viable line of reasoning (for the same type of roast, of course.) But, if the roast fits just fine in the pan we have, then the original reason is absent and it may be even better if we do not cut the ends off the meat and possibly cause it to dry out more than it should.

It is also possible that emotions are inflamed by erroneous lines of reasoning. In such cases as hypochondria, for instance, a critical assessment of the reasons for one's beliefs might eliminate the fear of illness. So although emotions do play a legitimate role in our lives and even in our reasoning, they should also be subject to the same critical scrutiny as the other elements of our thought processes.

Emotional appeals often use the connotative aspects of language to evoke an appropriate response. The definition of abortion can be stated as "the murder of a defenseless human being." But it can also be formulated as "a woman's fundamental right to choose what to do with her body." Both definitions attempt to evoke an emotional appeal: the first a negative abhorrence of murder, the second a positive commitment to human rights.

Descriptions too can be deeply colored by emotionally charged language. The same person's housekeeping techniques may be alternately described as "neat and tidy" or "compulsively neurotic."

Misuse of Authority This fallacy occurs when a person makes a claim based on an authority or expert who is unqualified to render a judgment on the issue under consideration. A person may be unqualified for several reasons. The question at issue may be outside of her field of specialization. It may be an issue for which she is no more qualified to make a judgment than most other people (for instance, a nationally known doctor being asked his opinion on the benefits of a new social security program). It could also be the case that the authority appealed to is an outdated one whose ideas have been clearly superseded (citing Issac Newton, for instance, to try to refute Einstein's theory of relativity). Sometimes the authority is not even identified specifically but alluded to in general terms such as "an inside source" or "expert witness." Finally, the authority may be one who is not recognized by others in the field.

Grammatically Irrelevant Premises

Each of the fallacies studied in the first section has the common feature of being psychologically persuasive because the evidence distracts the audience from considering the material that would be pertinent to the conclusion. Now we will look at fallacies in which the evidence presented is irrelevant to the conclusion because of grammatical mistakes.

Equivocation This fallacy relies on the ambiguous use of a word, phrase, or sentence in order to effect an apparent link between premises and the conclusion when in fact the link does not exist. The following argument is based on equivocation:

> The chapter on writing is at the conclusion of this book because it is concerned with the correct formulation and support of the conclusions of arguments, and conclusions of books come at the end.

The use of the term *conclusion* is equivocal in this case because in the premise it refers to the "points made by an argument," whereas in the conclusion it means the "end" or "termination" of this book. (Remember, the conclusion of an argument is often stated *first* in an argument.)

Amphiboly This is the traditional name for the kind of fallacy that involves mistaken inferences of grammatical or syntactic ambiguity. It's not that the term itself has more than one meaning, but that the arrangement of the words or punctuation leaves one unsure of the meaning of the entire sentence. The wording on a leaflet such as the following is a good example:

> Hurry on down to your Big Orange Grocers tomorrow!!! We will give to our first fifty customers and to those who spend more than $100 a Thanksgiving Turkey *absolutely free*. So hurry on down to Big Orange tomorrow.

It is not clear from this ad whether or not you would need to spend $100 *and* be one of the first fifty customers in order to get your free turkey. The way the ad reads, it seems possible that doing only one *or* the other would be sufficient. Whenever one is led to infer a conclusion due to a grammatical ambiguity in the premises or evidence one is a victim of the fallacy of amphiboly. A good deal of bait-and-switch advertising relies on this technique.

Composition A composition mistake occurs when we assume that because some specific parts or pieces of a larger whole have a particular trait or characteristic, the organized whole must possess that particular trait or quality. Suppose, for instance, that several good friends have gotten together and decided to build their own vacation home. Having purchased the land and the best construction materials available, they proceed to build their house. But having purchased the best possible materials does not imply that they will build the best possible house. The friends' abilities to construct things as well as the architectural plans will also affect the quality of the house.

This fallacy may also manifest itself in the assumption that what is true of individuals *distributively* must also be true of them *collectively.* One might conclude, for instance, that because the average Italian drinks more red wine than the average American, Italy consumes more red wine than the United States.

Division This is the converse of the fallacy of composition. It leads one to believe that the qualities or characteristics of an organized whole must be possessed by the individual members. An example of this fallacy would be to conclude that because a university enjoys a reputation for excellence, it's Philosophy Department must also be first-rate. Another example is the assertion that because the Dallas Cowboys possess the best team in the NFL, they also must possess the best quarterback.

The fallacies of composition and division both rely on equivocation between the collective and individual senses of a term. In this sense they are both classified as grammatical rather than psychological fallacies of irrelevant premises.

EXERCISES

 LEVEL

Short Answers

* **1.** All of the variations of the Personal Attack fallacy can be considered as specific instances of which more general fallacy?
* **2.** What is the difference between the Bandwagon Fallacy and the Popular Appeals Fallacy?
* **3.** What is the difference between a fallacy of Psychologically Irrelevant Premises and one of Grammatically Irrelevant Premises?

True or False

F * **4.** _____ The Appeal to Tradition Fallacy means that it is a mistake to continue to do things the same way that they were always done in the past.

F * **5.** _____ Popular Appeals, Appeals to Fear, and the Fallacies of Composition and Division are all examples of emotional appeals.

T * **6.** _____ When one is aware of the persuasive and connotative aspects of language, one is less likely to fall victim to emotional appeals.

F * **7.** _____ The Red Herring Fallacy gets its name from the fact that red herrings are the cheapest and least tasteful forms of the fish.

F * **8.** _____ Whenever a person attacks the character of another person presenting an argument or tries to damage the opponent's reputation, she is committing the Poisoning the Well Fallacy.

T * **9.** _____ It is usually a Misuse of Authority to fail to identify the source of expert testimony except as an "inside source."

F * **10.** _____ It is never fallacious to point out that your opponent is guilty of the same type of behavior that he is charging you with committing.

B   LEVEL

Identify the fallacies involved in the following. Be sure to state in your own words the errors in reasoning involved.

Popular Appeal (Emotional) **1.** You folks should elect me to the Senate because I can promise you that every one of you will have a voice in government. My door will be open to all. There will be no forgotten citizens and no special favors for special interests at the expense of my constituents.

Emotional Fear **2.** I know how much you like this job here in the mailroom, so I am sure you will reconsider sending that letter to the editor. You have a family to feed and it is extremely difficult to find work during this recession.

Personal attack *** 3.** Dr. Martin Luther King's views about racial equality can be dismissed as myths, because he learned them from his father who just wanted his very bright son to grow up without becoming conceited.

Red Herring, You too **4.** Sam Porkbarrel, candidate for the 5th District congressional seat responded to charges that he faces criminal indictment by charging his opponent Mary X Torter with not being entirely honest about her own arrest record.

Bandwagon *** 5.** Muhammed Ali has to be the greatest heavyweight boxing champ of all time. More people are in agreement about this point than have ever been with respect to any other boxer.

Poisoning the well **6.** During the 1990s we are going to have to elect public officials who are sensitive to the environment. Any person with half a brain can see that it is economic suicide for us not to pursue an aggressive energy policy, including alternative energy sources, conservation measures, and vigorous recycling programs.

Emotional *** 7.** And, while we are on the topic, we are simply going to have to discontinue strip-mining. It is degrading, disgusting, and produces nothing but eyesores.

Tradition **8.** Ever since critical thinking became part of the college curriculum students have had to work exercises on fallacies. So you students are going to have to work them too.

Misuse of Authority *** 9.** Cigarette smoking cannot be that bad for you. Take it from Bronco Kazonka, this year's Super Bowl Most Valuable Player.

Pity, Red Herring **10.** Yes, Ms. Walters, I know what the *Times* is saying about me and my candidacy and those alleged affairs. But don't you realize that this is just one more attempt to discredit me. They tried to threaten me and my family, have the IRS investigate me, sabotage my home and car, and now this. But it's not going to work.

Composition ***11.** The Wolverines have five of the top eight recruits in the country today, not to mention the best coach. They are bound to be the best team in the nation this year.

Amphiboly **12.** This new foreign hotel may have some questionable activities going on inside, Lieutenant. Here, look at this brochure, which says, "You are invited to take advantage of the chambermaid."

Emotional Pity ***13.** Professor Meany, I really think you ought to reconsider raising my grade to an "A." If I don't maintain my 3.5 grade-point average, I will lose my scholarship money. And, my mom was really counting on me to become the first college graduate in my family.

"You too" **14.** George Bush has no business criticizing Bill Clinton's policies; just remember all the policy failures Bush had when he was president!

*15. The ACME 9890 is the newest computer on the market, totally state of the art. So, it has to be the best one for you! Hurry now, supplies are limited!!

16. You just bought that Toyota and it is brand-spanking new. Therefore, the battery must be new too.

*17. Wait, I don't think that hospital will take our daughter: She's Buddhist and the sign says "Christian Children's Hospital."

18. Jenny, you'd better reconsider going out on a date with Professor Ewing; Fred saw him standing right next to a gay bar not too long ago.

*19. National health insurance is the most important political topic of the 1990s; even marginally informed voters know that.

20. Well, you have seen how one of your classmates, Mr. Smarty, analyzes this argument and you have seen the way that I, your Professor, analyze it. You'll have to conclude that my way is better; after all, you could flunk this course if you see it as Mr. Smarty does.

*21. Jell-o brand instant pudding has to be the most nutritious and tasty treat you can buy for kids today; Bill Cosby says so.

22. Yes, I think you can find her hanging out by those people getting ready to raft down the river because I just heard someone saying that she was telling jokes that had everyone hanging by the rafters.

*23. You might think of trying to outgrow that naive view of human nature as mechanistic, robot-like, and deterministic in favor of the much more informed and sophisticated view of people as autonomous, free, and responsible for their own behavior.

24. Interest rates have become stable and dependable, there is growth in the new home industry, even suicides are down. Therefore, the economy must be doing well.

*25. I don't care what Professor Dullard says about how trashy Grisham's new novel is—everyone I know is reading it. It must be great!

26. You really care about her? Then buy her a champagne no one else has ever bought for her—Dom Perignon!

*27. Senator Snort, accused by his Republican opponent of misappropriating funds, responded to charges today by saying, "Let him who is without sin cast the first stone."

C **LEVEL**

Find examples of the fallacies discussed in this section in newspapers, magazines, and television advertisements. Be sure to identify which fallacies occur, and why the particular fallacy is a case of bad reasoning. Also state how the article or advertisement in question could have been written without invoking the fallacy.

5.2 FALLACIES OF INADEQUATE PREMISES

Some premises, though relevant to their conclusions, are far from sufficient to warrant accepting the conclusion on their basis alone. The problem here is not that these premises have no worth as evidence, but that they cannot do the job by themselves of supporting the conclusion. The following are some of the more common examples of **fallacies of inadequate premises.**

Hasty Generalization This mistake in reasoning involves jumping to a conclusion prematurely. Most often this occurs because one has not examined enough cases to support the conclusion adequately. If a person were to conclude that since the weather in the Virgin Islands has been beautiful for three days in February the weather there must be always beautiful at that time of year, the conclusion is not adequately supported even if it turns out to be true subsequently.

A Hasty Generalization does not always involve reasoning from specific instances to some general conclusion. Sometimes one jumps directly to another specific conclusion. Having spent an enjoyable evening at a motel that was part of a national chain, a traveler might be led to conclude that the next night ought to be spent at another motel in the same chain. But the fact that one motel in the chain was comfortable is not sufficient to conclude that another would provide similar accommodations.

Accident The reasoning error referred to as Accident is that of taking something that is true *as a general rule* and misapplying it to some particular case that has some accidental circumstances making the rule inapplicable. Normally, for instance, we would say that exercise is beneficial. To conclude that therefore Sonya should exercise may be a fallacy: Perhaps she is recovering from an illness and is refraining from exercising on a doctor's orders.

In just about every case in which a generalization is held to be correct, there can be some circumstances in which the rule is not meant to apply. The sixty-five mile per hour speed limit may be a law on many interstates, but is a breakable rule for emergency vehicles responding to a call. A rule posted by means of a sign saying "Keep Off the Grass" would not likely be enforced if it were broken to save a child from a burning house.

A particularly dangerous form of the fallacy of accident is known as stereotyping. *Stereotyping* occurs when an individual member of a group is attributed to have characteristics that are thought to be typical of that group. Stereotyping often leads to racial, ethnic, religious, gender, and other forms of prejudice. It has the further drawback that stereotypes are all too often based not on the general characteristics that the group has been shown to possess, but on myths and tales with no basis of support.

Argument from Ignorance This argument boils down to the fact that a conclusion is taken to be true because it has never been proven false. Alternately, it occurs when a conclusion is taken to be false because it has never been proven true. If someone were to argue, for instance, that the stories depicted in the Bible must be true because they had never been proven false, she would be guilty of this fallacy. The assumption in the American legal system that a defendant is "innocent until proven guilty" is an attempt to force the criminal justice system to avoid this fallacy.

Begging the Question The fallacy of Begging the Question occurs when the conclusion of the argument is surreptitiously introduced as one of the premises. The basic form of question begging is "A is true because A is true." Of course real arguments may not be stated so simply. A sportswriter, for instance, might reason that the Braves are the best baseball team this year because they have gotten together the best pitching staff, and that they have the best pitching staff because the owner believes that they deserve to win the

World Series this year. Finally, he might assert that they deserve to win the World Series because the Braves are the best baseball team. This is called circular reasoning.

Question begging may also employ terms whose definitions already contain (either denotatively or connotatively) the conclusion the arguer wishes to prove. If someone were to argue, for instance, that ACME Industries is the country's most prosperous first-rate business concern, an opponent might retort that "ACME Industries is not what I would call a first-rate business." The opponent would be guilty of begging the question. By defining ACME Industries as *not* a first-rate business concern, she has begged the question with her definition.

Assuming the Cause   Sometimes called *False Cause* or *Post Hoc, Propter Hoc* (after this, therefore on account of this), this fallacy assumes that since A precedes B in time, A must therefore be the *cause* of B. Someone who decided not to take up jogging because a friend took up jogging and had a heart attack would be guilty of this fallacy. Similarly, a person who came down with a case of measles and then stated that the rash (which accompanies the disease) caused the disease would be making an illegitimate assumption. To establish the

BEWARE THE HEADLINES

Because a number of sources have been reluctant to grant permission to use some of their "real-life" examples, we have come up with several that may inadvertently parallel the original sources:

Headline in a grocery-store checkout-line magazine:
"BABY BORN PURPLE AFTER MOM EATS TOO MUCH EGGPLANT!"

Astrologist's warning to a person about to go on a job interview:
"You should come up with an excuse to miss your appointment because the stars are all out of line for any chances of success for you."

A friend who teaches logic once told us the story that in his class he tells his students the only stupid question is an unasked one. Soon after, a young student took him at his word and asked him why so many Civil War battles were fought in national parks.

Each of these cases in its own way typifies "Post Hoc" or Assuming the Cause reasoning:

The first, because it reasons that Event B happened (the baby was born purple) AFTER Event A happened (the mother ate too much eggplant), and that therefore (and on no other basis) Event A was the cause of Event B.

The second, because it reasons that Result B (the predicted disastrous interview) will occur because of some occult and unexaminable Cause A (the "stars being out of line").

The third, because it mistakenly reverses the cause and the effect. Which do you suppose came first, the battles or the parks?

cause of a given effect requires a variety of observations and experiments. This requirement is not satisfied by the simple assertion that one event preceded the other in time and so must be its cause.

Assuming Existence   It is fallacious to assume that because a phrase or word exists to describe a thing or situation that that thing or situation must actually exist. Children are particularly susceptible to this fallacy, but it sometimes comes to haunt adults as well. UFOs, ghosts, and other "paranormal" phenomena are often taken to exist for the simple reason that if they didn't there wouldn't be terms describing them. Philosophers like Decsartes even argued that God must exist because that's the only way the term *God* could have originated. (This argument is a bit more complicated, but boils down to this assumption.)

Fakey Precision   This fallacy is caused by the use of unnecessarily precise data when the situation does not warrant such precision. The intended effect here is the production of timidity or confusion in one's opponent. Fakey Precision has the effect also of diverting a line of reasoning into a dispute about the precision of a particular claim. If a representative of the National Rifle Association were to argue that a proponent of a gun control law was off by a few hundredths of a percentage point in the citation of a statistic, he could be guilty of this fallacy. Fakey Precision thus also has the psychological component of making an inadequate set of premises seem adequate. An uncritical thinker can often be fooled into thinking that a precisely stated statistic can establish support for a conclusion. But the question that can always be asked in such a case is "How does this precisely stated fact or statistic provide support for your conclusion?" A critical

BLAME IT ON ANYBODY

Making the rounds on business and office fax machines are many clever little stories whose authors often do not get the credit (or sometimes the blame) they richly deserve. Here is one such story:

> This is a story about four people named Everybody, Somebody, Anybody, and Nobody. There was an important job to be done and Everybody was sure that Somebody would do it. Anybody could have done it, but Nobody did it. Somebody got angry about that, because it was Everybody's job. Everybody thought Anybody could do it, but Nobody realized that Everybody wouldn't do it. It ended up that Everybody blamed Somebody when Nobody did what Anybody could have done.

By reifying the indefinite pronouns "Everybody," "Somebody," "Anybody," and "Nobody" (that is, treating them as if they were concrete, tangible, individual entities), this little story seems to be guilty of the Fallacy of Assuming Existence. A closer inspection reveals that because those indefinite pronouns are being used equivocally (that is, they have more than one distinct meaning here) that something else is also happening. Is there a nonverbally argued point to this story?

thinker need not be intimidated by the presentation of even well-researched evidence. Even a precisely stated set of claims must answer to the question of relevance and fairness as well as adequacy. Notice, for example, in televised political debates that each side can bring up startlingly well-researched facts and figures to back up their case. But usually neither side can address the other side's statistics.

Faulty Analogy Probably one of the most unreflectively used modes of day-to-day reasoning is the employment of analogies. An analogy is the comparison of one thing or event to another. Analogies play an important and useful part in our reasoning processes. But they are often misused. Whether or not an analogy is a viable one depends on several factors. First, it depends on whether there are many crucial similarities between the things being compared, particularly in the area of comparison. Second, the validity of an analogy depends on the dissimilarities between the two. The question should be asked whether the differences are strong enough to prohibit a valid comparison. The comparison of a strong American president like Franklin Roosevelt to a dictator like Joseph Stalin might establish some points of similarity, but the strong differences between the two would preclude any meaningful comparison except in the most incidental ways. Faulty analogies are often criticized because the analogy is said to be "like comparing apples and oranges."

EXERCISES

 LEVEL

Short Answers

* 1. What is the difference between the fallacies of Hasty Generalization and Composition?
* 2. When does one commit the fallacy of Begging the Question?
* 3. What happens when one commits the fallacy of Accident?

True or False

* 4. _____ It is always a fallacy to support a conclusion by offering only the evidence that it has never been proven true.
* 5. _____ It would not be a fallacy of Assuming the Cause if one used reasoning in which the presumed cause turned out on further investigation to be the real cause.
* 6. _____ Whenever a conclusion is supported solely by an argument that uses an analogy, then the fallacy of Faulty Analogy has been committed.
* 7. _____ Whenever a term is used in an argument and that word or phrase stands for something that may not actually exist, then the fallacy of Assuming Existence has been committed.
* 8. _____ It would always be a fallacy to use information or data that is unnecessarily precise in the course of an argument.
* 9. _____ The fallacy of Accident involves the accidental or unintentional use of a word or phrase that has more than one meaning.
*10. _____ Arguments by analogy are relatively infrequent.

B   LEVEL

Identify the fallacies involved in the following. Be sure to state in your own words the errors in reasoning involved.

Begging the Question

* **1.** Capital punishment for repeatedly convicted drug dealers is absolutely justifiable because people who are found guilty of selling drugs again and again should be given the death penalty.

Hasty General

2. I really don't think that you should buy that Volvo. I had one once and spent a fortune replacing every part of the car. In fact, every part of it made a noise except for the horn.

Assuming cause

* **3.** The economy started to improve right after President Clinton was elected. I am certain that he must be the reason why we have turned the corner on this depressed economy.

Bad Analogy

4. When you are boiling mad, don't hold it in. If the tea kettle couldn't blow off steam it would explode. So if you don't let your anger out when you are mad, you'll blow up too.

Faulty Analogy

* **5.** In most civilized nations today, freedom of reference is an accepted way of life. Doctors may consult books, x-rays, test results, and other doctors. Lawyers may refer to case studies, precedents, briefs, and other materials. Therefore, students should be allowed to use their books and notes when they are taking tests or examinations.

Argument from ignorance

6. Well, the files on the new transfer student are virtually empty. Still, I think that we can conclude that she must be a fine student since there's nothing in the records to say that she's not.

Assuming existence

* **7.** You really ought to accept that job opportunity. You were absolutely born for it. It's your fate. And remember, you are a Pisces.

Begging the question A→B ←B

8. You can be sure that everything written in the Holy Book is true because it is the word of God. The way that we know that the Holy Book is the word of God is that the great prophets tell us that it is. And the word of the prophets must be trusted, since it says we must do so in the Holy Book.

Assuming the cause

* **9.** ACME Industries has tripled in size since Mr. Iasmoka became CEO. Give credit where credit is due. He must be an incredible financial wizard.

Faky Precision

10. I disagree with your assessment of the Kennedy assassination. Your argument is based on the premise that it takes 2.3 seconds to operate the bolt on the type of rifle used by Oswald. Our experts have determined that including the time that it takes to reaim the rifle, it actually takes 2.313 seconds for a very competent marksman to operate the bolt on that rifle.

Hasty Generalization

* **11.** I don't think the clerks at ACME Department Stores are capable of filling an order correctly. They certainly messed up two of mine during the holiday season.

Accident

12. U.S.-made cars do not seem to hold their value as well as foreign-made cars do, at least during the 1980s and 1990s. Therefore, this Saturn won't hold its value as well as this Yugo will.

Argument from ignorance

* **13.** It seems to me that some kinds of extrasensory perception have to exist. In all these years no one has ever proven conclusively that the reports of its occurrence are unfounded.

Begging Question

14. When you think about it, democracy is one of the most desirable forms of government because it fosters both freedom and equality, which are essential to any democratic form of government.

Assuming cause

* **15.** We need to get Hillary out of Washington, D.C.: We haven't had a decent day's weather since she and her husband moved to the White House.

Faky precision.

16. I don't know where you Republicans come up with the figures you do. You claim that 128,356 more people are out of work under the Clinton administration than under the Bush administration. But we have proof from independent government researchers that the unemployment rate has fallen by 2.613% under the Clinton administration. So, you must be wrong.

*17. Wait a minute, Your Honor. This country is allegedly a democratic one, is it not? One of its founding principles is that all persons who live here are free, equal, and cannot be deprived of our rights and liberties. Therefore, you cannot lock me up, because you would be depriving me of any rights and liberties.

18. An invisible hand guides all capitalistic economies toward their ultimate destiny. For this reason, we should be able to devise some sort of empirical test to detect this phenomenon.

*19. There is absolutely no way that Ronald Reagan was involved in the Iran-Contra scandal. If he had been, surely someone would have been able to prove it by now.

20. There seem to be more and more students from Eastern Runovya coming to this university. I have met three of them this semester. I will bet they all have those shifty little eyes, dark curly hair, and funny, bent noses!

*21. I am telling you there are no great prima ballerinas who are under five feet three inches tall. So, if you're telling me that Dame Margot von Furstenburg is only five feet two, then I am telling you that she cannot be a great prima ballerina.

22. Have you ever noticed that the most successful junior executives wear expensive, tailor-made Italian suits and drive terribly expensive foreign cars? Therefore, I think one of the best ways you can become a successful junior executive is to go out and buy some expensive, tailor-made Italian suits and a nifty foreign car like an Infiniti, or a BMW, or perhaps a Lexus.

*23. Doing a great job around here is like wetting your pants in a dark suit: you get a nice warm feeling temporarily but nobody really seems to notice. Then, all of a sudden you're just sort of feeling all wet. Therefore, in answer to your question, do I think you should go out of your way to do a bang up job on this project, I say, "No way!"

C   LEVEL

Find examples of the fallacies discussed in this section in newspapers, magazines, and television advertisements. Be sure to identify which fallacies occur, and why the particular fallacy is a case of bad reasoning. Also state how the article or advertisement in question could have been written without invoking the fallacy.

5.3 FALLACIES INVOLVING UNFAIR PREMISES

Besides being inadequate or irrelevant, premises may also be slanted or biased. Sometimes the premises are stated in such a way as to limit the range of options or alternatives available for consideration. In other cases the premises are stated in such a way as to offer only undesirable alternatives—and in still other cases only the positive ones. The range of choices may be restricted in order to present one option in its best light. And by quoting things out of context, positions may be misrepresented. The remaining fallacies represent kinds of bias that can be present in arguments.

Misrepresentative Generalization This fallacy occurs when a generalization is made on the basis of data that are not typical or fairly representative of the population in question. This fallacy differs from that of Hasty Generalization in that it is possible to commit this fallacy with a sufficient number of instances. The problem with a Misrepresentative Generalization is not the number of particulars, but with the way in which the particulars are chosen. In the presidential election of 1948, for instance, polls taken before the election predicted that New York Governor Thomas Dewey would be the winner. The population samples were more than adequate statistically, so this was not a case of Hasty Generalization. President Truman, in fact, won reelection. The problem turned out to be the way in which the data were gathered. Random phone calls were made and a majority of respondents declared their support for Dewey. But it turned out that at the time only about half of the U.S. population had telephones in their homes. Those that did tended to be wealthier than those who didn't, and those who were rich tended to vote Republican—Dewey's party. The result was a Misrepresentative Generalization and a mistaken prediction.

Leading Question This fallacy is also known as that of Complex Question. It occurs when a question includes a background assumption that may or may not be true. If a person were asked the question "When did you stop drinking?," the assumption of the questioner would be that the respondent was at one time a drinker. If the respondent were not a drinker, it would be extremely difficult to answer this question since any answer at all seems to confirm that he was indeed a drinker.

The problem with a Leading Question is that it is essentially two questions disguised as one. The fair way of asking the question would be to turn it into two separate questions and to allow the respondent the opportunity to answer both independently: "Were you ever a drinker?" would be the first question. Depending on the answer to this, the second question, "When did you stop?" might follow.

Limited Options Sometimes known as a *False Dilemma,* this fallacy unfairly offers fewer options than may actually be present. Slogans like "America, love it or leave it" and "You're either for me or against me" are examples of this fallacy. Similarly, a student who asks a teacher for a special dispensation from a test because "either I will fail or I will have to find some way to cheat" is not stating all the possible options. The answer to this fallacy is to offer some other desirable alternative as being viable in the situation.

Straw Man This occurs when an arguer offers an unfair and easily criticized summary of her opponent's argument. It may be the case that the opponent's position is made out to be stronger than he intended. If a person argues that most criminals return to prison after their release, he might be misrepresented as arguing that *all* criminals return to prison. The Straw Man fallacy is unfair because it attributes a position to an opponent that she would not likely take herself.

Fallacious Extension Closely related to the Straw Man fallacy, Fallacious Extension involves the exaggeration of the consequences of an opponent's position. If someone were to argue, for instance, that there should be a waiting period before the purchase of handguns, an opponent would commit Fallacious Extension by claiming that his opponent was in favor of letting only criminals possess weapons. Fallacious Extension involves the misrepresentation of the consequences of a person's position when those consequences do not necessarily follow from that position.

Slippery Slope This is a special form of Fallacious Extension. It involves the erroneous claim that adopting a particular position or taking a particular action will result in inevitable and undesirable consequences. During the Vietnam War, for instance, it was often argued that "If we don't stop the Communists in Vietnam, they'll take over all Southeast Asia and we'll wind up fighting them in Australia."

The following argument against the practice of artificial insemination is an example of the Slippery Slope:

> If we start allowing surrogate mothers to carry to term the fetuses of other women, we can soon expect to find population increases out of hand, artificial insemination and test tube babies the norm, and the end of motherhood as we know it. And with the end of motherhood comes the end of the family.

One interesting aspect of the Slippery Slope is that it is often thought to be a valid form of reasoning. The phrase "Once we do that, we start down that slippery slope. . ." is often used to begin arguments. But despite its popularity, this form of reasoning is fallacious and unfairly projects a string of consequences for which little or no evidence has been offered.

Misuse of Hypothesis This is a fallacy that employs an "if. . .then" statement as the basis for a conclusion even though there is little or no evidence to support it. After the presidential election of 1992, for instance, former President Bush was criticized by his supporters for not campaigning more vigorously. It was thought that "If he had campaigned harder, Bush would have won the election." There is no way to prove such an assertion true. The election happened and Bush lost. It is easy enough after the fact to offer "if. . .then" statements that might suggest a different outcome had things gone differently. But it is difficult to prove that things would happen in a certain way on the basis of things that in fact had not happened.

Stress The fallacy of Stress or Accent involves the use of emphasis to manipulate the meaning of a statement. The preamble to the Constitution of the United States can be alternately read as stating that "*all* men are created equal" or "all *men* are created equal." In each case the Constitution is read in distinctively different ways.

Another way of committing this fallacy is to quote out of context. This is often accomplished in writing by inserting three dots (or ellipses points) to indicate that part of the quote is not being mentioned. A movie reviewer, for instance, might say that "Only if you have an IQ of less than 40 would I suggest that you see the movie *The Killer Monsters From Outer Space*.." The company that produced the movie could easily run an ad saying that that same movie critic said ". . .I suggest that you see the movie *The Killer Monsters From Outer Space*."

SUMMARY

Step 5—the identification of fallacies—begins the second major division of the Technique. The evaluation of arguments commences with the identification of fallacies. Fallacies are forms of bad reasoning that are often accepted by *uncritical* thinkers as good evidence for the conclusion. *Fallacies* are mistakes made in the

WHAT IF?

Reasoning from counterfactuals is not necessarily fallacious. For example, we are often asked to change one or more variables in a situation and then hypothesize what might happen. This is perfectly legitimate. The trick is to be sure not to overstate the case beyond the degree to which it can be justified. Here is a case from William Kienzle's *Chameleon*:

> . . . Jackson turned. "Larry, if this game were yours to call . . . if you didn't have to answer to anyone else, what would you do? Would you really close all these parishes?"

> "In a minute."

> They fell silent. But Jackson knew that this hypothetical question to his boss involved a condition contrary to fact.

How often have you been asked what you would do if such and such were the case, when that qualification means that it is unlikely or impossible for the conditions to really be that way? Is there any way for you to *know* that you would respond in the way you *think* (let alone say) you would?

(William X. Kienzle, Chameleon, *Ballentine Books: New York, 1991, page 36. Ballentine is a Division of Random House, Inc. of New York. For further information write to Andrews and McMeel, A Universal Press Syndicate Company, 4900 Main Street, Kansas City, MO 64112.)*

connection of premises and the conclusion of an argument. They may also occur within the premises themselves. Although they are not always intentional, fallacies seem to support a conclusion when in fact that support is irrelevant, inadequate, or unfair. Those fallacies that consist of irrelevant premises may be further subdivided into those that are *psychologically* or *grammatically* misleading. Psychologically irrelevant premises are misleading because they divert attention away from the line of reasoning through an appeal to various psychological or emotional states such as fear, anger, humor, or other emotions. Those that are grammatically irrelevant rely on the confusions caused by language—terms may have more than one meaning and the intended meaning is unclear, or the sentence structure itself may provide room for more than one interpretation.

Fallacies may also be relevant to the conclusion, but inadequate to support that conclusion. In these cases the problem is one of "jumping to conclusions." These premises are misleading in that the support given for the conclusion is based on evidence which *seems* adequate, but upon closer inspection reveals itself to be insufficient and illusory.

Finally, premises may be unfair. This occurs when the evidence is presented in such a way as to falsely limit the available options beyond what is called for or to offer only undesirable alternatives when a positive one is available. These fallacies violate the principle of fairness, which demands that the restatement of an opponent's argument be done in such a way as to present that argument in a way that is not misleading and is true to the intentions of the arguer.

An unlimited number of possible fallacies may be involved in the reasoning process. In this chapter, the most common of these fallacies have been examined. The point, though, is not so much to be able to place the fallacious reasoning in a certain category, but to be able to recognize and explain the mistakes that have been made.

EXERCISES

 A   LEVEL

True or False

* 1. _____ Fallacies are always intentional.
* 2. _____ Fallacies are always context dependent.
* 3. _____ A fallacy of Irrelevant Premise is one in which the premise may in fact be true, but is irrelevant to the conclusion.
* 4. _____ The fallacy of Personal Attack involves the use of violence or force to try to win an argument.
* 5. _____ The use of an editorial cartoon to make a point about a political dispute is usually an example of the fallacy of Appeal to Humor.
* 6. _____ A Faulty Analogy could not be an example of a fallacy of Unfair Premises.
* 7. _____ It would not be an example of Fallacious Extension to apply a rule or principle to another case which is similar to a precedent that has already been set.
* 8. _____ It would not be a case of the Slippery Slope fallacy to argue that a teacher cannot curve grades by one percent because the next test will have to be curved by two percent, the following exam by four percent, etc.
* 9. _____ The Straw Man fallacy involves the intentional misrepresentation of an opponent's argument.
*10. _____ If one were to quote an opponent out of context, he would be guilty of the fallacy of Stress or Accent.

B   LEVEL

Identify the fallacies involved in the following. Be sure to state in your own words the errors in reasoning involved.

* 1. You may be right about the Yankees now, but if Billy Martin were still alive and managing the team, they would be in first place today.

2. I really don't think we should be lowering our interest rates by a quarter of a percent right now. People will expect us to drop it another quarter of a percent next month, and another quarter the month after that. Before you know it, the interest rate will be less than five percent.

* 3. Opponents of tuition increases argue the since our state benefits from well-educated university graduates, the state should pay more for higher education through taxes. They'll probably have to pay all the costs of everyone's food, housing, and health care since it could be argued that the state also benefits from a well-fed, well-housed, healthy population.

4. Most people in town are against the All-Nude Night Club. Letters in the paper are four to one in opposition to it and the local neighborhoods are incensed about it.

* 5. Why is higher education such a waste of time?

6. Mr. President, we only have two options: back down or fight!

* 7. I definitely think you should purchase that extra ten million dollars of advertising time. After all, Harry Truman said that you can't spend too much to win an election.

8. I know that you think that the West is not keeping pace with Eastern nations when it comes to training in math. But you're wrong. Not every Eastern person is better. Just look at Simone. She placed third in the international math competitions for her age group and she's a Westerner.

* 9. If we are going to buy a car we have to buy either a good one or a cheap one. We can't afford a good one and we don't want a cheap one. So we'll just have to do without a car.

10. Americans are simply tired of dishonesty from their politicians. This conclusion is borne out by a recent comprehensive survey of more than 100,000 college students.

*11. Prosecutor to defendant on the witness stand: "It seems pretty clear that the accident was your fault. Did you see the traffic light turn red before or after you ran it?"

12. No, I disagree with your conclusion about the Bulls. If Jordan hadn't retired, they would definitely have won the NBA title again this year.

*13. Now I realize that you were in surgery when I gave the examination. But I cannot let you take a make-up exam. If I do that, then people who were absent due to car accidents or illnesses in the family or just plain "had the flu" would demand make-up exams, too. Then, pretty soon anyone who was scared of taking one of my tests or had something better to do that day would be asking for make-up exams.

14. The way I see it, we might study hard for this test and still fail it. On the other hand, we might not study at all and get lucky and have the test curved in our favor. So, we might as well have fun and take our chances!

*15. I guess he's not a *real* doctor yet. You said he was just a *practicing* physician, didn't you?

16. Fellow committeepersons, I think that we should deny this request for relief funds for the homeless. I do realize that it is twenty degrees below zero outside right now, but what are we going to do when food prices skyrocket and the AFDC people want relief for their folks? What if gas prices go up exorbitantly and all the commuting little junior executives want some kind of support. What about earthquake and fire victims?

*17. What an interesting conclusion: I always thought lawyers were a very conservative political group. But here, according to one survey, they are, contrary to public opinion, a very moderate to liberal group. In a nationwide poll of law students, 57% voted for Clinton; 21% for Bush; and 21% for Perot.

18. Noted astronomer and scientist Carl Sagan has remarked that human beings now have the capability to send people to the moon and to Mars. However, I think he has overstated his case: There is no way that we can send any number of people anywhere in space any time we want, and certainly not right now.

*19. It sure seems like a Hobson's choice to me: Either we look like the big, bad aggressor nation sending troops into a tiny country as if we were the pope of moral opinion, or we do nothing, which makes us look like a bunch of scared little wimps who won't even stand up for basic human rights.

20. The market strategy I was using should have worked. Too bad we had that unexpected setback at the summit meeting this morning; if that hadn't occurred, the stock market absolutely would have gone through the roof.

*21. The problem, as I see it, is if we give the okay for this play, there won't be any effective way for us to censor future plays that have more nudity, violence, or offensive language. In effect, we will have given a license to pornography. We might as well legalize drugs, prostitution, and organized crime while we're at it.

22. My opponent claims that he cannot tell you unequivocally that he will not have to raise taxes. Now how can you vote for someone who has just told you to your face that he is going to double or triple your taxes?

*23. Look, Mom, I know my grades have fallen tremendously this semester, but there's a method to my madness. If you read this school catalog carefully, it says that you have to have a 2.0 average in order to graduate. With two or more semesters worth of grades as low as mine are this quarter, I should be able to bring my GPA down to 2.0 by graduation time.

The following passages contain a variety of argument types. The fallacies in these exercises may come from any one of the sections in this chapter. Some of the passages may contain no fallacies at all and others contain two or more. For each fallacy you find, explain why it constitutes a mistake in reasoning.

24. ACME Parcel Service is an aggressive young company. So, Sam, the parcel package delivery woman, must be an aggressive young driver.

*25. Congratulations!! I see you are expecting to be a mother soon. Too bad you'll have to give up your medical career.

26. I started getting all these headaches right after I changed from tap water to bottled water. So, I am sure that the bottled water must be the cause of my headaches.

*27. There is absolutely no reason for us to consider this guy's arguments concerning reproductive rights: Not only is he a male, but he's gay and doesn't even have children of his own.

28. I'll tell you why we can't tolerate abortions in the case of incest and rape. First of all, the Pro-Choice people are in favor of this and we should oppose anything these idiots favor. Secondly, if we let them get their feet in the door on these issues, then we will have to grant certain first-trimester abortions. Once we do that, anyone who wants to terminate their pregnancy can do so at any time they want.

*29. Premarital sex is definitely immoral. Not only did my father and my priest tell me so, but everybody knows that sex before marriage is wrong.

30. The hamburgers at that place on the other side of town must be pretty good for you. For one thing, they have sold an awful lot of them. For another, if there was something non-nutritional about them, somebody would have proven it by now.

*31. Employee to supervisor: "I definitely deserve a bonus and a raise. I'm behind on my house payments and my wife just lost her job. Not only that, but Junior needs braces and tutoring. Things are tough all over. Also, you might remember that I could take what I know to our competitors and they could bury you tomorrow."

32. To be a feminist these days is to be a Nazi and a Fascist. I know this is so because I hear Rush Limbaugh refer to them as *feminazis* and no one has called in so far to refute the correctness of that name.

*33. What do you mean, "Why do we play the national anthem before the ballgame?" What a stupid question! We've always done it that way.

34. Your Honor, I think you're being a little unfair to my client. Two weeks ago in a case exactly similar to this one you found the defendant guilty but made him serve twenty hours of community service. Therefore, you should reconsider your decision to imprison my client.

*35. Our home was burglarized after they decreased the penalty for burglary. Quite frankly, we fully expect to be robbed again until the old law is reinstated.

36. You want to be the talk of the neighborhood? Every woman will look for an excuse to go for a ride with you and every man will be jealous. You're guaranteed to turn heads wherever you go. Buy a Belchfire and watch your life change!

*37. "President Bush has accused my economic recovery plan as being one of 'smoke and mirrors.' Well, if anyone should know, he would be the one." (Candidate Bill Clinton, on the campaign trail)

38. "How can you trust the Governor of a small, failed state?" (Candidate George Bush)

 C   L E V E L

Listen to a political debate on a news show such as the *MacNeil-Lehrer News Hour* or on C-Span. Try to identify any fallacies that occur. Also note the way in which particular fallacies are answered by the opponent. (It might help to look at these programs on videotape.)

C A S E   S T U D Y

The case study for this chapter is an often-quoted, old, yet timeless, essay written by Max Shulman, entitled "Love is a Fallacy." It is included for several reasons. One, it should warn all of us about the perils of taking this chapter and fallacies too seriously. This is not to say that fallacies are not serious, but is merely meant as a reminder not to be too trigger-happy about showing off our skills at spotting them. Second, notice that some of the fallacies mentioned by Shulman have different names than those designated in this chapter. See if you can determine which ones these are.

Love Is A Fallacy

by Max Shulman

(Copyright © 1951, © renewed 1979 by Max Shulman. Reprinted by permission of Harold Matson Company, Inc.)

Cool was I and logical. Keen, calculating, perspicacious, acute and astute—I was all of these. My brain was as powerful as a dynamo, as precise as a chemist's scales, as penetrating as a scalpel. And—think of it!—I was only eighteen.

It is not often that one so young has such a giant intellect. Take, for example, Petey Bellows, my roommate at the university. Same age, same background, but dumb as an ox. A nice enough fellow, you understand, but nothing upstairs. Emotional type. Unstable. Impressionable. Worst of all, a faddist. Fads, I submit, are the very negation of reason. To be swept up in every new craze that comes along, to surrender yourself to idiocy just because everyone else is doing it—this to me is the acme of mindlessness. Not, however, to Petey.

One afternoon I found Petey lying on his bed with an expression of such distress on his face that I immediately diagnosed appendicitis. "Don't move," I said. "Don't take a laxative. I'll get a doctor."

"Raccoon," he mumbled thickly.

"Raccoon?" I said, pausing in my flight.

"I want a raccoon coat," he wailed.

I perceived that his trouble was not physical, but mental. "Why do you want a raccoon coat?"

"I should have known it," he cried, pounding his temples. "I should have known they'd come back when the Charleston came back. Like a fool I spent all my money for textbooks, and now I can't get a raccoon coat."

"Can you mean," I said incredulously, "that people are actually wearing raccoon coats again?"

"All the Big Men on Campus are wearing them. Where've you been?"

"In the library," I said, naming a place not frequented by Big Men on Campus.

He leaped from the bed and paced the room. "I've got to have a raccoon coat," he said passionately. "I've got to!"

"Petey, why? Look at it rationally. Raccoon coats are unsanitary. They shed. They smell bad. They weigh too much. They're unsightly. They—"

"You don't understand," he interrupted impatiently. "It's the thing to do. Don't you want to be in the swim?"

"No," I said truthfully.

"Well, I do," he declared. "I'd give anything for a raccoon coat. Anything!"

My brain, that precision instrument, slipped into high gear. "Anything?" I asked, looking at him narrowly.

"Anything," he affirmed in ringing tones.

I stroked my chin thoughtfully. It so happened that I knew where to get my hands on a raccoon coat. My father had one in his undergraduate days; it lay now in a trunk in the attic back home. It also happened that Petey had something I wanted. He didn't HAVE it exactly, but at least he had first rights to it. I refer to his girl, Polly Espy.

I had long coveted Polly Espy. Let me emphasize that my desire for this young woman was not emotional in nature. She was, to be sure, a girl who excited the emotions, but I was not one to let my heart rule my head. I wanted Polly for a shrewdly, calculated, entirely cerebral reason.

I was a freshman in law school. In a few years I would be out in practice. I was well aware of the importance of the right kind of wife in furthering a lawyer's career. The successful lawyers I had observed were almost without exception, married to beautiful, gracious, intelligent women. With one omission, Polly fitted these specifications perfectly.

Beautiful she was. She was not yet of pin-up proportions, but I felt sure time would supply the lack. She already had the makings.

Gracious she was. By gracious I mean full of graces. She had an erectness of carriage, an ease of bearing, a poise that clearly indicated the best of breeding. At table her manners were exquisite. I had seen her at the Kozy Kampus Korner eating the specialty of the house—a sandwich that contained scraps of pot roast, gravy, chopped nuts, and a dipper of sauerkraut—without even getting her fingers moist.

Intelligent she was not. In fact, she veered in the opposite direction. But I believed that under my guidance she would smarten up. At any rate, it was worth a try. It is, after all, easier to make a beautiful dumb girl smart than to make an ugly smart girl beautiful.

"Petey," I said, "are you in love with Polly Espy?"

"I think she's a keen kid," he replied, "but I don't know if you'd call it love. Why?"

"Do you," I asked, "have any kind of formal arrangement with her? I mean are you going steady or anything like that?"

"No. We see each other quite a bit, but we both have other dates. Why?"

"Is there," I asked, "any other man for whom she has a particular fondness?"

"Not that I know of. Why?"

I nodded with satisfaction. "In other words, if you were out of the picture, the field would be open. Is that right?"

"I guess so. What are you getting at?"

"Nothing, nothing," I said innocently, and took my suitcase out of the closet.

"Where you going?" asked Petey.

"Home for the weekend." I threw a few things in the bag.

"Listen," he said, clutching my arm eagerly, "while you're home, you couldn't get some money from your old man, could you, and lend it to me so I can buy a raccoon coat?"

"I may do better than that," I said with a mysterious wink and closed my bag and left.

"Look," I said to Petey when I got back Monday morning. I threw open the suitcase and revealed the huge, hairy, gamy object that my father had worn in his Stutz Bearcat in 1925.

"Holy Toledo!" said Petey reverently. He plunged his hands into the raccoon coat and then his face. "Holy Toledo!" he repeated fifteen or twenty times.

"Would you like it?" I asked.

"Oh yes!" he cried, clutching the greasy pelt to him. Then a canny look came into his eyes. "What do you want for it?"

"Your girl," I said, mincing no words.

"Polly?" he said in a horrified whisper. "You want Polly?"

"That's right."

He flung the coat from him. "Never," he said stoutly.

I shrugged. "Okay. If you don't want to be in the swim, I guess it's your business."

I sat down in a chair and pretended to read a book, but out of the corner of my eye I kept watching Petey. He was a torn man. First he looked at the coat with the expression of a waif at a bakery window. Then he turned away and set his jaw resolutely. Then he looked back at the coat, with even more longing in his face. Then he turned away, but with not so much resolution this time. Back and forth his head swiveled, desire waxing, resolution waning. Finally he didn't turn away at all; he just stood and stared with mad lust at the coat.

"It isn't as though I was in love with Polly," he said thickly. "Or going steady or anything like that."

"That's right," I murmured.

"What's Polly to me, or me to Polly?"

"Not a thing," said I.

"It's just been a casual kick—just a few laughs, that's all."

"Try on the coat," I said.

He complied. The coat bunched high over his ears and dropped all the way down to his shoe tops. He looked like a mound of dead raccoons. "Fits fine," he said happily.

I rose from my chair. "Is it a deal?" I asked, extending my hand.

He swallowed. "It's a deal," he said and shook my hand.

I had my first date with Polly the following evening. This was in the nature of a survey; I wanted to find out just how much work I had to do to get her up to the standard I required. I took her first to dinner. "Gee, that was a delish dinner," she said as we left the restaurant. Then I took her to a movie. "Gee, that was a marvy movie," she said as we left the theater. And then I took her home. "Gee, I had a sensaysh time," she said as she bade me good night.

I went back to my room with a heavy heart. I had gravely underestimated the size of my task. This girl's lack of information was terrifying. Nor would it be enough merely to supply her with information. First she had to be taught to THINK. This loomed as a project of no small dimensions, and at first I was tempted to give her back to Petey. But then I got to thinking about her abundant physical charms and about the way she entered a room and the way she handled a knife and fork, and I decided to make an effort.

I went about it, as in all things, systematically. I gave her a course in logic. It happened that I, as a law student, was taking a course in logic myself, so I had all the facts at my finger tips. "Polly," I said to her when I picked her up on our next date, "tonight we are going over to the Knoll and talk."

"Oo, terrif," she replied. One thing I will say for this girl: you would go far to find another quite so agreeable.

We went to the Knoll, the campus trysting place, and we sat down under an old oak, and she looked at me expectantly. "What are we going to talk about?" she asked.

"Logic."

She thought this over a minute and decided she liked it. "Magnif," she said.

"Logic," I said, clearing my throat, "is the science of thinking. Before we can think correctly, we must first learn to recognize the common fallacies of logic. These we will take up tonight."

"Wow-dow!" she cried, clapping her hands delightedly.

I winced, but went bravely on. "First let us examine the fallacy called Dicto Simpliciter."

"By all means," she urged, batting her lashes eagerly.

"Dicto Simpliciter means an argument based on an unqualified generalization. For example: Exercise is good. Therefore everybody should exercise."

"I agree," said Polly earnestly. "I mean exercise is wonderful. I mean it builds up the body and everything."

"Polly," I said gently, "the argument is a fallacy. EXERCISE IS GOOD is an unqualified generalization. For instance, if you have a heart disease, exercise is bad, not good. Many people are ordered by their doctors NOT to exercise. You must QUALIFY the generalization. You must say that exercise is USUALLY good, or exercise is good FOR MOST PEOPLE. Otherwise you have committed Dicto Simpliciter. Do you see?"

"No," she confessed. "But this is marvy. Do more! Do more!"

"It will be better if you stop tugging at my sleeve," I told her, and when she desisted, I continued. "Next we take up a fallacy called Hasty Generalization. Listen carefully: You can't speak French. I can't speak French. Petey Bellows can't speak French. I must therefore conclude that nobody at the University of Minnesota can speak French."

"Really?" said Polly, amazed. "Nobody?"

I hid my exasperation. "Polly, it's a fallacy. The generalization is reached too hastily. There are too few instances to support such a conclusion."

"Know any more fallacies?" she asked breathlessly. "This is more fun than dancing even."

I fought off a wave of despair. I was getting nowhere with this girl, absolutely nowhere. Still, I am nothing if not persistent. I continued. "Next comes Post Hoc. Listen to this: Let's not take Bill on our picnic. Every time we take him out with us, it rains."

"I know somebody just like that," she exclaimed. "A girl back home—Eula Becker, her name is. It never fails. Every single time we take her on a picnic—"

"Polly," I said sharply, "it's a fallacy. Eula Becker doesn't CAUSE the rain. She has no connection with the rain. You are guilty of Post Hoc if you blame Eula Becker."

"I'll never do it again," she promised contritely. "Are you mad at me?"

I sighed. "No, Polly, I'm not mad."

"Then tell me some more fallacies."

"All right. Let's try Contradictory Premises."

"Yes, let's," she chirped, blinking her eyes happily.

I frowned, but plunged ahead. "Here's an example of Contradictory Premises: If God can do anything, can He make a stone so heavy that He won't be able to lift it?"

"Of course," she replied promptly.

"But if He can do anything, He can lift the stone," I pointed out.

"Yeah," she said thoughtfully. "Well then I guess He can't make the stone."

"But He can do anything," I reminded her.

She scratched her pretty, empty head. "I'm all confused," she admitted.

"Of course you are. Because when the premises of an argument contradict each other, there can be no argument. If there is an irresistible force, there can be no immovable object. If there is an immovable object, there can be no irresistible force. Get it?"

"Tell me some more of this keen stuff," she said eagerly.

I consulted my watch. "I think we'd better call it a night. I'll take you home now, and you go over all the things you've learned. "We'll have another session tomorrow night."

I deposited her at the girls' dormitory, where she assured me that she had had a perfectly terif evening, and I went glumly home to my room. Petey lay snoring in his bed, the raccoon huddled like a great hairy beast at his feet. For a moment I considered waking him and telling him that he could have his girl back. It seemed clear that my project was doomed to failure. The girl simply had a logic-proof head.

But then I reconsidered. I had wasted one evening; I might as well waste another. Who knew? Maybe somewhere in the extinct crater of her mind a few embers still smoldered. Maybe somehow I could fan them into flame. Admittedly it was not a prospect fraught with hope, but I decided to give it one more try.

Seated under the oak the next evening I said, "Our first fallacy tonight is called Ad Misericordiam."

She quivered with delight.

"Listen closely," I said. "A man applies for a job. When the boss asks him what his qualifications are, he replies that he has a wife and six children at home, the wife is a helpless cripple, the children have nothing to eat, no clothes to wear, no shoes on their feet, there are no beds in the house, no coal in the cellar, and winter is coming."

A tear rolled down each of Polly's pink cheeks. "Oh, this is awful, awful," she sobbed.

"Yes, it's awful," I agreed, "but it's no argument. The man never answered the boss's question about his qualifications. Instead he appealed to the boss's sympathy. He committed the fallacy of Ad Misericordiam. Do you understand?"

"Have you a handkerchief?" she blubbered.

I handed her a handkerchief and tried to keep from screaming while she wiped her eyes. "Next, I said in a carefully controlled tone, "we will discuss False Analogy. Here's an example: Students should be allowed to look at their textbooks during examinations. After all, surgeons have X rays to guide them during an operation, lawyers have briefs to guide them during a trial, carpenters have blueprints to guide them when they are building a house. Why then shouldn't students be allowed to look at their textbooks during an examination?"

"There now," she said enthusiastically, "is the most marvy idea I've heard in years."

"Polly," I said testily, "the argument is all wrong. Doctors, lawyers, and carpenters aren't taking a test to see how much they have learned, but students are. The situations are altogether different, and you can't make an analogy between them."

"I still think it's a good idea," said Polly.

"Nuts," I muttered. Doggedly I pressed on. "Next we'll try Hypothesis Contrary to Fact."

"Sounds yummy," was Polly's reaction.

"Listen: If Madame Curie had not happened to leave a photographic plate in a drawer with a chunk of pitchblend, the world would not know about radium."

"True, true," said Polly, nodding her head. "Did you see the movie? Oh, it just knocked me out. That Walter Pidgeon is so dreamy. I mean he fractures me."

"If you can forget Mr. Pidgeon for a moment," I said coldly, "I would like to point out that the statement is a fallacy. Maybe Madame Curie would have discovered radium at some later date. Maybe somebody else would have discovered it. Maybe any number of things would have happened. You can't start with a hypothesis that isn't true and then draw any supportable conclusions from it."

"They ought to put Walter Pidgeon in more movies," said Polly. "I hardly ever see him any more."

One more chance, I decided. But just one more. There is a limit to what flesh and blood can bear. "The next fallacy is called Poisoning the Well."

"How cute!" she gurgled.

"Two men are having a debate, The first one gets up and says, 'My opponent is a notorious liar. You can't believe a word that he is going to say.' . . . Now, Polly, think. Think hard. What's wrong?"

I watched her closely as she knit her creamy brow in concentration. Suddenly a glimmer of intelligence—the first I had seen—came into her eyes. "It's not fair," she said with indignation. "It's not a bit fair. What chance has the second man got if the first man calls him a liar before he even begins talking?"

"Right!" I cried exultantly. "One hundred percent right. It's not fair. The first man has POISONED THE WELL before anybody could drink from it. He has hamstrung his opponent before he could even start. . . . Polly, I'm proud of you."

"Pshaw," she murmured, blushing with pleasure.

"You see, my dear, these things aren't so hard. All you have to do is concentrate. Think—examine—evaluate. Come now, let's review everything we have learned."

"Fire away," she said with an airy wave of her hand.

Heartened by the knowledge that Polly was not altogether a cretin, I began a long, patient review of all I had told her. Over and over and over again I cited instances, pointed out flaws, kept hammering away without letup. It was like digging a tunnel. At first everything was work, sweat, and darkness. I had no idea when I would reach the light, or even IF I would. But I persisted. I pounded and clawed and scraped, and finally I was rewarded. I saw a chink of light. And then the chink got bigger and the sun came pouring in and all was bright.

Five grueling nights this took, but it was worth it. I had made a logician out of Polly; I had taught her to think. My job was done. She was worthy of me at last. She was a fit wife for me, a proper hostess for my many mansions, a suitable mother for my well-heeled children.

It must not be thought that I was without love for this girl. Quite the contrary. Just as Pygmalion loved the perfect woman he had fashioned, so I loved mine. I decided to acquaint her with my feelings at our very next meeting. The time had come to change our relationship from academic to romantic.

"Polly," I said when next we sat beneath our oak, "tonight we will not discuss fallacies."

"Aw, gee," she said, disappointed.

"My dear," I said, favoring her with a smile, "we have now spent five evenings together. We have gotten along splendidly. It is clear that we are well matched."

"Hasty Generalization," said Polly brightly.

"I beg your pardon?" said I.

"Hasty Generalization," she repeated. "How can you say that we are well matched on the basis of only five dates?"

I chuckled with amusement. The dear child had learned her lessons well. "My dear," I said, patting her hand in a tolerant manner, "five dates is plenty. After all, you don't have to eat a whole cake to know that it's good."

"False Analogy," said Polly promptly. "I'm not a cake. I'm a girl."

I chuckled with somewhat less amusement. The dear child had learned her lessons perhaps too well. I decided to change tactics. Obviously the best approach was a simple, strong, direct declaration of love. I paused for a moment while my massive brain chose the proper words. Then I began:

"Polly, I love you. You are the whole world to me, and the moon and the stars and the constellations of outer space. Please, my darling, say that you will go steady with me, for if you will not, life will be meaningless. I will languish. I will refuse my meals. I will wander the face of the earth, a shambling, hollow-eyed hulk."

There, I thought, folding my arms, that ought to do it.

"Ad Misericordiam," said Polly.

I ground my teeth. I was not Pygmalion; I was Frankenstein, and my monster had me by the throat. Frantically I fought back the tide of panic surging through me. At all costs I had to keep cool.

"Well, Polly," I said, forcing a smile, "you certainly have learned your fallacies."

"You're darned right," she said with a vigorous nod.

"And who taught them to you, Polly?"

"You did."

"That's right. So you do owe me something, don't you, my dear? If I hadn't come along you never would have learned about fallacies."

"Hypothesis Contrary to Fact," she said instantly.

I dashed perspiration from my brow. "Polly," I croaked, "You mustn't take all these things so literally. I mean this is just classroom stuff. You know the things you learn in school don't have anything to do with life."

"Dicto Simpliciter," she said, wagging her finger at me playfully.

That did it. I leaped to my feet, bellowing like a bull. "Will you or will you not go steady with me?"

"I will not," she replied.

"Why not?" I demanded.

"Because this afternoon I promised Petey Bellows that I would go steady with him."

I reeled back, overcome with the infamy of it. After he promised, after he made a deal, after he shook my hand! "The rat!" I shrieked, kicking up great chunks of turf. "You can't go with him, Polly. He's a liar. He's a cheat. He's a rat."

"Poisoning the Well," said Polly, "and stop shouting. I think shouting must be a fallacy too."

With an immense effort of will, I modulated my voice. "All right," I said. "You're a logician. Let's look at this logically. How could you choose Petey Bellows over me? Look at me—a brilliant student, a tremendous intellectual, a man with an assured future. Look at Petey—a knothead, a jitterbug, a guy who'll never know where his next meal is coming from. Can you give me one logical reason why you should go steady with Petey Bellows?"

"I certainly can," declared Polly. "He's got a raccoon coat."

6

THE CATEGORICAL SYLLOGISM

step five
Are there any fallacies?

▼

step six
What is the argument's structure?

▼

step seven
What other conclusions can be drawn?

No race has a monopoly on vice or virtue, and the worth of an individual is not related to the color of his skin.
—*Whitney Moore Young, Jr. (1969)*

In proportion as the antagonism between classes within the nation vanishes, the hostility of one nation against another will come to an end.
—*Karl Marx and Frederich Engels (1848)*

C H A P T E R   O U T L I N E

6.1 Categorical Syllogism
Exercises
6.2 The Rule Method for Testing Categorical Syllogisms
Exercises
6.3 The Venn Diagram Method for Evaluating Syllogisms
Summary
Exercises
Case Study

KEY TERMS

Categorical logic - The study of arguments from the standpoint of the relationships between classes of entities or events.

Categorical statement - A premise or conclusion in a categorical argument and in which members of one class are said to be included in or excluded from another class.

Categorical syllogism - A two premise, one conclusion deductive argument in which all three of the statements are categorical in form.

Distribution - That property of a class or term referring to the members of that class individually. A term is said to be distributed when reference applies to each and every member of that class. A term is said to be undistributed when reference does not necessarily apply to each and every member, but only to some.

Existential fallacy - The violation of Rule 4 of the Rule Method for testing the validity of categorical syllogisms and which holds that whenever both premises are universal statements (A- or E-Form) and the conclusion is a particular statement (I- or O-Form), all three of the terms or classes of the syllogism must be known to have at least one member for the syllogism to be valid.

Fallacy of faulty exclusions - The violation of Rule 2 of the Rule Method for testing the validity of categorical syllogisms and which holds that a valid categorical syllogism has either (A) no negative (that is, E- or O-Form) statements or (B) one negative statement in the conclusion and one negative statement in the premises.

Fallacy of illicit distribution - The violation of that part of Rule 3 of the Rule Method for testing the validity of categorical syllogisms and which holds that any term which is distributed in the conclusion must also be distributed in the premises.

Fallacy of the undistributed middle term - The violation of that part of Rule 3 of the Rule Method for testing the validity of categorical syllogisms and which holds that the Middle Term must be distributed at least once.

Formal reasoning - The assessment of arguments on the basis of their structure and without regard to the actual truth or falsity of the premises.

Four terms fallacy - The violation of Rule 1 of the Rule Method for testing the validity of categorical syllogisms and which holds that a valid categorical syllogism has exactly three class terms each used twice and in precisely the same sense in each of the statements in which it occurs.

Invalid syllogism - A categorical syllogism in which the truth of the premises does not guarantee the truth of the conclusion.

Major premise - The premise of a categorical syllogism containing the predicate class from the conclusion.

Major term - The predicate class in the conclusion of a categorical syllogism.

Middle term - The class or term in a syllogism connecting the major and minor terms, and which occurs only in the premises of the argument.

Minor premise - The premise of a categorical syllogism containing the subject class from the conclusion.

Minor term - The subject class in the conclusion of a categorical syllogism.

Particular term - A term indicating one or more members of a class. It is represented by the quantifier some and can actually refer to any part of that whole, up to and including every member.

Predicate - The second class in a categorical statement and from which some portion of the subject class is being excluded or included.

Quantifier - A term which indicates which part of a class from none to some to all is being included in or excluded from another class. The three standard quantifiers are All, No, and Some.

Singular term - An individual thing or event that can serve as an entire class term, even though there is only one member. It is usually quantified by the terms all or no.

Subject - The class or category which is being included in or excluded from some relationship with a second class in a categorical statement.

Universal term - A term indicating every member of the class, usually represented by the quantifier all or no.

Valid syllogism - A categorical syllogism in which the truth of the premises guarantees the truth of the conclusion.

With Chapter Six we begin the study of the formal relationships that exist within arguments. This corresponds to Step Six of the Technique. The previous chapter concentrated on the assessment and analysis of arguments in terms of the fallacies that may be included in them. Chapters 6 through 11 concern the formal relationships which obtain within an argument. Formal reasoning examines the structure of the argument. This can be done without even considering the meaning and the possible truth of the statements involved. With formal reasoning, we focus on certain key terms that occur in the arguments and how they are related among the premises and the conclusion. In this and the following chapter, we will consider primarily the terms all, some, and no. These terms are indicative of a type of formal reasoning known as categorical logic, which is based on the relationships among classes or categories of things or events. In later chapters we will examine the use of terms such as if . . . then, and, or, and not.

6.1 CATEGORICAL SYLLOGISM

A categorical syllogism is a special kind of argument with two premises and one conclusion. A categorical syllogism (or "syllogism" for short—although there are other kinds of syllogisms) is composed of categorical statements. These categorical statements assert that one class, set, or category is related to a second class, set, or category by way of being included in it or excluded from it. A *categorical statement* is determined by a quantifier. A quantifier is a term that indicates which part of the class (if any) is being included in or excluded from another class. The terms used as quantifiers in syllogisms are all (as in "All birds reproduce by laying eggs"), some (as in the "Some birds can fly"), and no (as in "No birds are elephants").

A correctly formed syllogism expresses the relationship between three classes. It does this by employing two categorical premises and a categorical conclusion. In a categorical statement, one of the terms or classes functions as the subject and the other as the predicate. A subject term is the class or thing that is being included in or excluded from the second or other class term in the statement. The predicate term is the class in which or from which the subject term is being included or excluded. In the statement

"No elephants are pink"

the subject term is "elephants" and the predicate term is "pink things". Note that "pink" does not express a class at all, while "pink things" does. The quantifier in this instance is "no" and the word "are" expresses the relationship. What happens when an individual happens to be the subject or the predicate of a statement? Take for instance the statement:

"Bill Clinton is President of the United States."

The subject term, "Bill Clinton," is an individual. When we use an individual as a subject term we are talking about a singular term. We will treat a singular term as a class term which has only one entity or member. This would mean that in a statement such as "Bill and Nick walked to the store," the subject class is "Bill and Nick" and the quantifier is "all" because it is all of them that walked to the store, not just their feet or legs. So, a categorical statement has four ingredients:

1. *A quantifier:* All, Some, or No
2. *A subject term:* expressed as a class term
3. *A relationship:* is included or is not included in . . .
4. *A predicate:* again, always expressed as a class term.

We must become acquainted with a few other terms before we continue. In each syllogism, as we have said, there are three classes or "terms" involved. Each of these plays a role in syllogistic reasoning. The major term is the term that is the predicate of the conclusion. The minor term is the subject of the conclusion. A third term links or connects the major and the minor term and is known as the middle term. The middle term does not appear in the conclusion at all, but only in the premises.

Each syllogism also contains a major and a minor premise. The major premise is the premise that includes the predicate term of the conclusion (the major term of the syllogism). The minor premise is the one that includes the minor term or subject class of the conclusion. Consider the following argument:

All beagles are dogs.
All dogs are mammals.
_____
Therefore: All beagles are mammals.

In this example the predicate of the conclusion is mammals, so it is the major term of the syllogism. Since "mammals" appears in the second premise, that premise is the major premise in this particular example. The term "beagles" is the minor term of this syllogism since it is the subject class of the conclusion. The first premise contains the minor term "beagles" and so it is the minor premise. The term "dogs", the only term which does not appear in the conclusion at all, is the middle term.

The final element in understanding the structure of a syllogism is to be able to differentiate the four possible forms that the categorical statements can take within a syllogism. These four forms of categorical statements are designated by the letters.

1. A-Form: All A's are B's. (e.g. "All of the sandwiches are in the basket").
2. E-Form: No A's are B's. (e.g. "None of the sandwiches are in the basket").
3. I-Form: Some A's are B's. (e.g. "Some of the sandwiches are in the basket").
4. O-Form: Some A's are not B's. ("Some of the sandwiches are not in the basket").

Notice that the A- and the I-Forms are positive or affirmative. They assert that one thing or class is included in another class. These terms originated in the letters for the Latin phrase "I affirm" *AffIrmo*. The E- and O-Forms deny that a thing or class is included in another class. These letters originate in the Latin n*EgO* or "I deny."

A Special Note About Particular Statements

Before we examine the rules for differentiating good from bad syllogisms, it should be noted that the I- and O-Forms of categorical statements do not involve an assumption that is often present in the ordinary language uses of the term "some". In the example cited above for the I-Form, for instance, a person hearing the claim "Some of the sandwiches are in the basket" might assume that if some of the sandwiches are in the basket, then some of the sandwiches are not in the basket. We will not make such an assumption. The I-Form and the O-Form do not imply one another.

Some Points About Putting Ordinary Language Into Standard Form

Some categorical statements do not appear in any of these standard forms (A, E, I or O) but they can nevertheless be recast into one of the four standard forms. For instance, the old saying

"Every dog has his day."

can be recast as an A Statement:

A-Form: All [dogs] are [things which have their day]

In this case we needed to determine that the statement was a universal (requiring the term "all") and that it included one class within another. The term "dogs" is the subject term and "things which have their day" is the predicate term. ("Have their day" does not express a class or set of things at all.) Since the statement is both universal and affirmative, it must be an A-Form statement. Although recasting a categorical state-

> ## WAS HE OR WASN'T HE (A GENTLEMAN)?
>
> "Don't be silly" she protested. "He's not a gentleman. He's from Epidaurus; there are no gentlemen in Epdaurus ."
>
> This dialogue, from Robert Ludlum 's spy thriller, *The Parsifal Mosaic,* shows that people do occasionally reason syllogistically without even recognizing that they are doing so. Is our Grecian courtesan's reasoning valid or not? What makes you think so?
>
> *Reprinted with permission from* Robert Ludlum, The Parsifal Mosaic, p. 28, New York: Grenada Publishing Limited (1982).

ment into standard form sometimes tends to butcher language, it is extremely helpful in analyzing the worth of the syllogism.

Statements with singular terms can be recast easily into standard form categorical statements:

"Jan and Emily saw the movie last week"

is put into standard form beginning with the subject term, "Jan and Emily." The predicate of the sentence, "saw the move last week," has to be made into a class term: "people who saw the movie last week," or "beings who saw the movie last week". The relationship is one of inclusion—Jan and Emily are included in the larger group of people who saw the movie last week—so, the relationship is "are." The quantifier in this instance is "all" because we are talking about all of Jan and all of Emily, not just their eyes or their brains, i.e., not just some of them, went to see the movie. Hence, it is an A-Form statement:

A-Form: All [Jan and Emily] are [people who saw the movie last week]

A final point to mention at this juncture concerns a structure that seems as if it were in standard form, when in fact it is not. Take the statement:

All A is not B.

The quantifier, "All," is a perfectly legitimate quantifier. The class terms, "A" and "B," are not problematic either. And, the relationship, "is not", is a viable one for O-Form statements. The problem is that this statement does not fit neatly into one of the patterns for the four Standard Forms for categorical statements, and moreover, it is ambiguous as it stands. Does it mean (1) that none of the A's are B's (an E-Statement) or (2) that some of the A's are not B's (an O-Statement)? The way to handle such statements is to ascertain from the context which of the two meanings is intended. Consider the statement:

Glenn is not a gambler.

In standard form the statement is NOT "All Glenn is not a gambler," but rather

E-Form: No [Glenn] is [a gambler]

On the other hand, take the statement:

Not all people were unhappy about the decision.

Here, we are saying that it is not the case that everybody was unhappy about the decision, or, in standard form:

O-Form: Some [people] are not [people who were unhappy about the decision]

Translating statements into standard form definitely takes some practice. As you do so, ask yourself, is this statement universal or particular; is it affirmative or negative?

EXERCISES

 **A**   LEVEL

Short Answers
1. What is a universal term ?
2. What is a particular term ?
3. Which of the categorical statement forms are positive?
4. Which of the categorical statement forms are negative?
5. What is the quantifier in an E-Statement?
6. What is the quantifier is an A-Statement?
7. Which is the only statement form that employs the term "not" as part of the relationship?
8. How many things or events does the quantifier "some" indicate?
9. What is the major term in a categorical syllogism?
10. What is the middle term in a categorical syllogism?

B   LEVEL

Translate each of the following statements into standard categorical form (A, E, I, or O), and then tell which of the four forms it is, and identify the subject class, the predicate class, the relationship, and the quantifier precisely.
1. All low-flying, high-speed aircraft are planes which will have to use the city's alternative airport.

2. Some extremely low-budget Hollywood movies are films of distinctive quality and taste.

3. No person who has filed a tax extension is eligible for a refund at this time.

4. Some overpaid ball players are not fit to play on the second string of the better professional teams.

5. Many of the recipe cards that she uses came from her grandmother's side of the family.

6. There are not any medical procedures which are completely risk-free.

7. Every street light in town is lit tonight.

8. A great many of the excellent skiers from countries around the world are not Olympic gold medal hopefuls this year.

9. A number of students who were thought to be too uninterested showed up for the rally that was held in the quad last night.

10. No one who has not actually played a Rachmaninov Piano Concerto should criticize the way Andre played in the performance tonight.

11. Anyone who ever had a heart that was not made of cast-iron would be sorry for behaving that way.

12. There are some possible courses of action which have not been overlooked.

13. These shoes are way too tight.

14. No parking is allowed here.

15. ACME Industries does not make the strongest widgets in the business.

16. "Sausage and Peppers" is a wonderful Italian dish.

17. In fact, there's some sausage and peppers ready right now.

18. Some of the most intelligent and sensitive physicians are not board-certified.

19. Just about everyone I know attended the opening-day ceremonies at the stadium.

20. Dogs with long hair stay warmer in winter than people with long hair.

21. Almost no one walks ten miles to school uphill in the snow anymore.

22. A number of these examples have been exaggerated for heuristic purposes.

C   LEVEL

Find examples of statements in television commercials or magazine advertisements and try to restate them in standard categorical form. Be sure to be faithful to the original, intended meanings.

6.2 THE RULE METHOD FOR TESTING CATEGORICAL SYLLOGISMS

As deductive forms of reasoning, categorical syllogisms are either valid or they are invalid. A valid categorical syllogism is one in which if the premises are both true, then the conclusion must be true. An invalid categorical syllogism is one in which even the truth of the premises does not guarantee the truth of the conclusion. There are several methods for determining the validity of such syllogisms: we will consider two: a Rule Method and a Diagramming Method. The Rule Method presented here centers around three things to watch for and which correspond to the three parts of Standard Form Categorical Statements—(1) the classes, (2) the relationship, and (3) quantifier.

Rule One: The Classes

The first rule of evaluating the validity of categorical syllogisms has to do with the classes involved in the reasoning and the meanings of the terms that are used to refer to those classes.

> *RULE ONE*: A valid categorical syllogism has exactly three class terms, each used in the same sense in both of the statements in which it occurs.

This rule is sometimes known as the Three Term Rule. There are at least three distinctive ways that this rule may be broken. First, a syllogism may actually involve four instead of three terms because two of the classes in the reasoning overlap, but are not identical. For instance, take a look at the argument:

> All outstanding financial advisors are extremely well-paid professionals.
> Sandy is a financial advisor with a great deal of education.
> ———————————————————————————————
> So, Sandy must be an extremely well-paid professional.

What has happened here is that the reasoning has four terms: (1) outstanding financial advisors, (2) extremely well-paid professionals, (3) Sandy, and (4) financial advisors with a great deal of education. What looks like it should be the Middle Term, the one occurring in the premises only and not in the conclusion is actually not one term, but two overlappping classes: (1) outstanding financial advisors and (4) financial advisors with a great deal of education. Of course there are probably people who fit into both of these categories, that is, who are both outstanding financial advisors and who are financial advisors with a great deal of education. Still, it is highly possible that there are some outstanding financial advisors who do not have a great deal of education. And, there may likewise be some financial advisors with a great deal of education but who are not particularly outstanding. It would require a leap of reasoning to assume that because Sandy is a member of one of these classes that she must be a member of the other class as well.

A second way that Rule One is often violated occurs when the meaning of a term shifts between a class and a larger class in which it is included as a member. Consider the following line of reasoning:

> All happy, well-adjusted children love the Amusement Park.
> Laura is a child.
> ———————————————————————————————
> Thus: Laura loves the Amusement Park.

Again, in this example it is the middle term which shifts its meaning from premise one to premise two. "Happy, well-adjusted children" is the subject class of the first premise. But "children", the predicate class of premise two is a much more inclusive class containing as part of itself "children of the happy, well-adjusted sort". So in reality, there are actually four terms in this syllogism. What is interesting in many cases which are similar to this second example is to notice what happens if the classes are reversed in their order. If the syllogism were

All children love the Amusement Park.
Laura is a happy, well-adjusted child.
_____

So: Laura loves the Amusement Park.

This syllogism would be valid, although the full line of reasoning would require two syllogisms: Laura is a happy, well-adjusted child and (we add) happy, well-adjusted children are children, so Laura is a child. This conclusion (Laura is a child) is now combined with the premise "All children love the Amusement Park" to generate the necessary conclusion: "Laura loves the Amusement Park."

The third way Rule One may be broken is actually a form of the *Fallacy of Equivocation:* in other words, one of the class terms is used in such a way as to shift or change meaning between the two occurrences. Consider a line of reasoning which seems fairly airtight:

B weighs more than C
A weighs more than B
_____

So: A weighs more than C

If this line of reasoning were tested by computer, the result is going to be "Valid Argument". Suppose we put in deliberately tricky content:

Nothing weighs more than lead.
You weigh more than nothing.
_____

Therefore: You weigh more than lead!

What is wrong here?!? The computer is going to say this is a valid line of reasoning. The problem is that unless the computer is so programmed, it will not recognize that the word "nothing" is used in two different senses in this argument to generate the apparently wacky conclusion. There are two ways of handling this kind of situation: one, call this another instance of the Four Terms Fallacy because there are really four different classes in the argument. Or, two, you can say that this is a content problem and since the question of validity is a question of form, the argument is in fact a valid one with the content problem of the *Fallacy of Equivocation.*

Rule Two: The Relationship

The second rule has to do with the relationship element of categorical statements insofar as the relationships may be either one of inclusion or one of exclusion; that is, they may be affirmative or negative.

> *RULE TWO:* A valid categorical syllogism has either (A) *no* negative statements at all, or (B) one negative statement in the premise and one in the conclusion.

If there is more than one negative statement in the premises the conclusion cannot necessarily follow. It might be true, but it does not *have* to be true. This is because negative statements function by exclusion. Take a look at this argument:

> No current NBA players are current NFL players.
> Larry Johnson is not currently playing in the NFL.
>
> Therefore: Larry Johnson is not a current NBA player.

The classes of current NBA players and current NFL players are excluded from one another in the major premise. This means that the two classes are entirely separate and distinct. The minor premise established the fact that Larry Johnson is excluded from the class of current NFL payers. So, both Larry Johnson and all of the current NBA players are excluded from the class of current NFL players. But this does not and cannot establish whether or not Larry Johnson is excluded from the class of current NBA players. According to the information established in the premises, the truth of the conclusion does not necessarily follow from the premises. This syllogism is therefore invalid. When Rule Two is broken or violated, the fallacy is known as Faulty Exclusions.

Rule Three: The Quantifier

Before explaining the third rule, we need to recognize a distinction in the way we talk about a class of things. We may refer to a class distributively or collectively. When referring to a class distributively, we mean to refer to each and every member of the class. Collective reference to a class, however, is not intended to apply to every member of the class, but to the class of things taken as a whole. For instance, in the statement, "The Americans were first to put a man on the moon", the term "Americans" is being used collectively. It was not each and every American who put a man on the moon, literally, but the collective entity which accomplished this feat. On the other hand, the statement "Americans tend to be very proud of their individualism and self-reliance", employs the term "Americans" distributively. When a term is used distributively to refer to each and every member of the class that term is said to be distributed. (Think back also to the connection that this concept of "distribution" may have with the fallacies of Composition and Division.)

A-Form statements have distributed subjects but undistributed predicates. In the statement "All cats are mammals" the subject term "cats" is distributed because the reference is to each and every member of the class of cats. But the statement does not refer to each and every member of the class of mammals (but only to some of them—namely, the cats). Since this is the case, the predicate "mammals" is undistributed.

E-Form statements have distributed predicates as well as distributed subjects. The statement "No hemophiliacs are blood-donors" refers to the entire class of hemophiliacs (there is not a one of them who is a blood-donor) and to the entire class of blood donors (none of them are hemophiliacs). Any one entity in either class is excluded from the entirety of the other class.

I-Form statements contain undistributed subjects and undistributed predicates. The statement "Some surfers are Republicans" refers to neither the entire class of surfers nor the entire class of Republicans. In fact, all it says is that there is at least one surfer who is also a Republican, or conversely, that there is at least one Republican who is also a surfer.

O-Form statements have subjects that are undistributed, but predicates which are distributed. A variation on the last example will show how this is so. Consider the statement "Some surfers are not Republicans." In this case the term "surfers" is undistributed because each and every surfer is not what is meant; we need find only one surfer who is not a Republican to ascertain that this statement is true. However, the term "Republicans" *is* distributed because we know something about the entire class of Republicans: namely, that the surfers mentioned in the subject class are not part of that class. The statement says of each and every Republican that he or she is not a member of that group of "some surfers", or, put another way, that the entire class of Republicans is excluded from at least some of the class of surfers.

Figure 6.1 summarizes distribution for the four standard forms.

FIGURE 6-1
DISTRIBUTION IN STANDARD CATEGORICAL STATEMENTS

	Subject Term	Predicate Term
A-FORM	Distributed	Undistributed
E-FORM	Distributed	Distributed
I-FORM	Undistributed	Undistributed
O-FORM	Undistributed	Distributed

With this discussion of the concept of distribution, we are in a position to understand the third rule, which has two parts to it:

> *RULE THREE:* In a valid categorical syllogism, (A) the Middle Term must be distributed at least once, and (B) any term that is distributed in the conclusion must also be distributed in the premises.

Taking the (B) part of this rule first, if a term is distributed in the conclusion and not in the premises, in effect you have a kind of Hasty Generalization Fallacy, because the undistributed class in the premise refers only to some of its members while the distributed class in the conclusion refers to all of its members. There is no guarantee that what is true of some parts of a whole must be true of all of those component parts. With respect to the (A) part of Rule Three, if a middle term is not distributed at least once, it may turn out not to apply to either the major or the minor term. A vital link, then, that is supposed to be made between the subject term and the predicate term may be an illusion. (Remember, if it is not distributed, it does not apply to each and every member.) Consider the following example:

All seniors are students.
All freshmen are students.
_____

Therefore: All seniors are freshmen.

This syllogism is invalid because it violates Rule 3(A). Let's put it in standard form, letting "D" stand for "distributed" and "U", for "undistributed", so we can see why this is the case:

                 D   U

A-Form All [seniors] are [students]

                 D   U

A-Form All [freshmen] are [students]
_____

                 D   U

A-Form All [seniors] are [freshmen]

Students is the middle term of this argument. It occurs in both of the premises, and not in the conclusion at all. In this particular argument, it is undistributed both times. Because the middle term is supposed to link the subject class with the predicate class, there must be some overlap. But, in this case, freshmen constitute one part of the class of students and seniors constitute a completely different part of that class. There is no overlap at all. When the middle term is undistributed, this is known as the Fallacy of the Undistributed Middle Term.

Let us take a look at another example:

> All atomic explosions are things that produce radiation.
> Some things that produce radiation are beneficial to human beings.
> _____
> So: All atomic explosions are beneficial to human beings.

The term "things which produce radiation" is undistributed in each of the premises. Even if the conclusion had been weaker—"Some atomic explosions are beneficial to human beings"—the argument would still be invalid because there is no guarantee of a vital connection between subject and predicate classes when the middle term is not distributed at all.

Now, consider an example where a term is distributed in the conclusion but not in the premises, thus violating the second part of Rule Three:

> Most truly famous authors did not achieve fame during their own lifetime.
> Leo Tolstoy did become famous during his lifetime.
> _____
> Leo Tolstoy must not have been a truly famous author.

Let's set this one up using "D" = Distributed, "U" = Undistributed and "TFA" = Truly Famous Authors "PWAFDTL" = People Who Achieved Fame During Their Lifetime "LT" = Leo Tolstoy

                         U   D

O-Form: Some   TFA   are not   PWAFDTL

TECHNICAL BACK TO ORDINARY LANGUAGE

Part of the reason for the Technique was to be able to evaluate lines of reasoning in order to apply them to real-life situations. Sometimes, as we get into analyzing deductive arguments we seem to be getting further and further from that objective. Let's look at a line of reasoning that occurred recently, especially since it parallels a number of arguments that share a common flaw.

Overheard in the midst of an evaluative and interpretive disagreement:

> Just about every socialist and leftist I have ever heard of believes in national health care and insurance, and you'll have to agree, Hillary certainly believes in national health care and insurance. See! I told you she had to be a socialist and leftist.

From the standpoint of the Technique as it applies to this type of reasoning, there is little that needs to be done to recast it in standard categorical form:

I—Some [Socialists^U and Leftists] are [Proponents of Nat'l H.C.^{U} & I]

A—All [Hillary^D] is [Proponent of Nat'l Health Care^U & Insurance]

A—All [Hillary^D] is [a Socialist and Leftist^U]

And, according to our Technique, this breaks Rule 3 because it has an Undistributed Middle Term, *Proponents of National Health Care and Insurance*. But, to explain it in this way to someone unfamiliar with logical terminology might be an exercise in futility. One may consider beginning with the point that according to this reasoning, there could be other groups as well who also favored national health care and insurance and that possibly Hillary could be aligned with one or more of them *without* necessarily being aligned with socialists or leftists. It might be even more graphic, however, to use an argument by analogy to make the point: "Gee! By your own line of reasoning here, since ducks are animals, and since rabbits are animals, therefore ducks have to be rabbits!"

A-Form:	All	LT^D	is	PWAFDTL^U

E-Form:	No	LT^D	is	TFA^D

The term "truly famous author" is distributed in the predicate of the conclusion, since the conclusion is an E-Form Statement. But this same term, "TFA", is undistributed in the first premise, where it is the subject of an O-Form Statement. Thus, a term which is distributed in the conclusion is not distributed in the premises and the syllogism is invalid. This mistake is known as the Fallacy of Illicit Distribution, and in this instance, the term that is illicitly distributed is "truly famous authors". Notice the difference, by the way, if we were to be talking about all of the truly famous authors and had cast premise number one as an E-Statement:

> No truly famous authors became famous during their lifetime.
> Leo Tolstoy did become famous during his lifetime.
>
> Leo Tolstoy must not have been a truly famous author.

In this case, all of the rules for correctly forming a syllogism have been met, including the provisions for distribution. This reconstituted version of the syllogism would be valid. (An interesting sideline to note here is that even though the syllogism is valid, it has a conclusion which happens to be false. This can be the case because the first premise turns out to be false also.)

A Corollary to Rule One: A Special Feature of the Quantifier "Some"

The final rule for determining the validity of categorical syllogisms involves the concept of existential import. When a Universal Statement (A- or E-Form) is made, it is understood that the subject term includes all members of the class *if* there are any members. But, it does not necessarily imply that there are any members. For instance, the statement, "All leprechauns are Irish", really states that all leprechauns (if indeed there are any) would be Irish. But one cannot conclude from this statement that there are any leprechauns. On the other hand, particular statements (I- and O-Form) do imply that some (or at least one) member of the subject and the predicate class actually exists. The statement, "Some Americans are of Irish descent" implies that at least one American exists and that he or she is a member of the class of people who are of Irish descent. It is directly from this feature of "some" statements that the fourth rule derives. We can call it the Corollary to Rule One because it too pertains to the classes involved in the syllogism:

> *COROLLARY TO RULE ONE:* In a valid categorical syllogism, whenever both premises are universal statements (A- or E-Form) and the conclusion is a particular statement (an I- or O-Form), all three classes in the syllogism must be known to have at least one member.

The consequences of the violation of the corollary can be seen in the following syllogism:

> All illegally parked cars are towed to ACME garage.
> All cars towed to ACME garage cost $100 service charge.
>
> Some illegally parked cars cost $100 service charge.

Because the conclusion is an I-Statement, it implies that there actually is an illegally parked car and that it cost $100 service charge for that illegally parked car. But, the premises are both A-Statements which are universals. Neither one of them actually implies that there is an illegally parked car or that one was towed to ACME garage. Look at it this way: the sign, "No parking allowed here", is put there in the hopes of keeping the classes empty. That is, they do not want any cars parked here. When this particular rule is violated, the mistake is called the Existential Fallacy. Figure 6.2 shows a step by step application of the Rule Method for evaluating categorical syllogisms. It is followed immediately by Figure 6.3, which shows how Figure 6.2 may be applied to a concrete example.

FIGURE 6.2
USE OF THE RULE METHOD TO EVALUATE CATEGORICAL SYLLOGISMS

STEP 1:   Identify premises and conclusion. Write them down and make a "mistake box." Is anything omitted (e.g., an unstated premise or conclusion)? If so, specify exactly what is implicit. If not, proceed on to the next step.

STEP 2:   Put both the premises and the conclusion in *standard form.* That is, for each of the three statements
        A. Determine the two classes *precisely.*
        B. Specify the quantifier (all, no, or some).
        C. Specify the relationship between the two classes. (Is the subject class supposed to be included in the predicate class or excluded from it?)
        D. Identify the statement form (A, E, I, or O).
        E. Determine the distribution of each class or term.
Now that the argument is in standard form, go to the next step.

STEP 3:   Evaluate the resulting form of the argument using the rules.
  A. Check Rule 1: Are there exactly three classes or terms, each one occurring twice with precisely the same meaning both times? If yes, put a check by this block and proceed to the next step; if not, figure out what is wrong and put an "X" by this rule, stating "Four-Terms fallacy" and what each of the terms is. Then, go to the next step.
  B. Check Rule 2: How many E or O statements occur? If there are none put a check by this block and go to the next step. If there are one or three "exclusions," then go to the mistake box, put an "X" by this rule and write "Faulty Exclusions," stating how many E- or O-statements there are and where they occur (i.e., in the premises or conclusion). Then proceed to the next step. If there are two E- or O-statements , does one of them occur in the conclusion? If yes, put a check by the rule and go on to the next step. If no, put an "X" by the rule and write "Faulty Exclusions—two exclusions in the premises," then go to the next step.
  C. Check Rule 3(A): What is the middle term (the one occurring in both the premises and not in the conclusion)? Is that middle term distributed at least once? If yes, put a check by this rule and go to the next step. If not, go to the mistake box and write "Undistributed Middle Term" and state what that term is. Then go to the next step.
  D. Check Rule 3(B): Is either term in the conclusion distributed? If not, put a check by this rule and go to the next step. If yes, look back up in the premises to determine whether that term is

also distributed. If it is, put a check by the rule and go on to the next step. If not, go to the mistake box, put an "X" by the rule, and write "Illicit Distribution," stating which term is illicitly distributed. Then go to the next step.

E. Check the Corollary: Are both of the premises universal (A or E) statements? If not, put a check by this rule and go to the next step. If yes, is the conclusion a universal statement too? If yes, put a check by this rule and go to the next step. If no, look at each one of the three classes: Are they known to have at least one member? If yes, put a check by this rule and go to the next step. If no, go the the mistake box and write "Existential Fallacy," specifying which classes are empty or at least may not have any members. Then go to the next step.

STEP 4:   Wrapping it up. Check the mistake box: Is anything written in it? If not, and if there are all checks by the rules, then congratulations, the argument is a valid one. Indicate this by writing "Valid" next to the argument. If yes, write "Invalid" and fill in the mistakes that have been committed, *UNLESS* the only mistakes that occur are *both* the Four-Terms fallacy and the Faulty Exclusions fallacy. In this event, go back to each one of the statements and see if an immediate inference (explained in Chapter 7) can reduce the number of classes to three, exactly. If not, then the argument is still invalid. If it can be reduced to three terms, does that process also change the number and position of negative statements in the argument? If not, the argument remains invalid. If so, is the argument valid now?

FIGURE 6.3

AN EXAMPLE OF THE RULE METHOD TO EVALUATE A CATEGORICAL SYLLOGISM

Suppose we are given the following argument "It looks like birds must live in this neighborhood after all, because robins live in this neighborhood and they are birds." Is this a valid argument? Does the conclusion HAVE TO follow from the premises? This is, if the premises are true, would the conclusion have to be true too? How does the argument sound to common sense? Well, let's check it out using the step by step technique in Figure 6.2.

Step 1: Identify premises and conclusions and write them down.

Answer:	Robins live in this neighborhood	p1
	Robins are birds	p2
	Birds live in this neighborhood	c

Mistake Box
Rule 1
Rule 2
Rule 3A
Rule 3B
Cor.

Step 2: Put the premises and conclusion in standard form.

A. What are the classes, precisely?

Answer: In the first premise, the subject class is "robins". The predicate class cannot be "live in this neighborhood" because that grouping of words does not express a class term. It could be "things (or creatures or beings, etc.) that live in this neighborhood". In the second premise, the subject class is "robins", the predicate class is "birds". In the conclusion, the subject class is "birds" and the predicate class would be the same one we expressed as the predicate of the first premise: "things that live in this nieghborhood ".

B. What are the quantifiers?

Answer: In the first premise, common sense tells us that not every robin in the universe lives right here, so the answer is "some". For the second premise, "robins are birds", the quantifier intended is probably "all". And, in the conclusion, since we don't mean to say all the birds in the world live here, the quantifier is "some".

C. What is the relationship between the classes?

Answer: In each one of the statements, the relationship is "are" because in each case the subject class is alleged to be included in the predicate class.

D. What are the statement forms (A, E, I, or O)?

Answer: The first premise is an I-Statement; the second, an A-Statement; and the conclusion, an I-Statement

E. What is the distribution of each class or term?

Answer: In the first premise, "robins" is undistributed (we are only talking about some of them); "things that live in this neighborhood" is also undistributed (again, we are only talking about some of them). In the second premise, "robins" is distributed (here, we are talking about *all* of them); and "birds" is undistributed (we are not talking about all of them—just the robins). In the conclusion, "birds" and "things that live in this neighborhood" are both undistributed.

Now that the argument is in standard form it looks something like this—

			U		U
P₁	I	Some	Robins	are	things that live in this neighborhood

			D		U
P₂	A	All	Robins	are	birds

			U		U
c	I	Some	Birds	are	things that live in this neighborhood

Now that the argument is in standard form, we can move to the evaluation phase.

Step 3:   Evaluate the resulting form by the rule method.

A.   Check Rule 1: Are there three classes or terms each occurring twice with the same meaning both times?

Answer: Yes; "robins" is class 1, and it occurs in both the premises. "Things that live in this neigh-borhood" is class 2, and it occurs as the predicate class of the first premise and the predicate class of the conclusion. "Birds" is class 3, and it occurs as the predicate class of the second premise and the subject class of the conclusion. None of the terms is used equivocally, so we can put a check by Rule 1 of the Mistake Box and move to the next step.

B. Check Rule 2: How many E or O Statements are there?

Answer: None, they are all A or I Statements. So, we can put a check in the Mistake Box by Rule 2 and proceed to the next step.

C. Check Rule 3A: What is the Middle Term? Is it distributed at least once?

Answer: The Middle Term (the one in both the premises and not in the conclusion) is "Robins". It is distributed in the second premise, so we can put a check in the Mistake Box by Rule 3A and continue on to the next step.

D. Check Rule 3B: Is any term in the conclusion distributed?

Answer: No, so we can put a check by 3B in the Mistake Box and proceed to the next step.

E. Check the Corollary: Are both of the premises universal statements (A or E forms)?

Answer: No, so again, check the Mistake Box and we can proceed to wrap things up.

Step Four: The "Wrap Up" Phase. Since there are all checks and no "X"s in the Mistake Box, this turns out to be a valid argument, and we can indicate this by writing "Valid" in the Mistake Box. In final form the argument looks something like this—

		U		U		
I	Some	[Robins]	(T-I) are	[Things that live in this neighborhood]	(T-2)	P

		D		U		
A	All	[Robins]	(T-1) are	[Birds]	(T-3)	P

		U		U		
I	Some	[Birds]	(T-3) are	[Things that live in this neighborhood]	(T-2)	C

```
              Mistake Box
     Rule 1:     ok     √
     Rule 2:     ok     √
     Rule 3A:    ok     √
     Rule 3B:    ok     √
     Corollary:  ok     √

         VALID ARGUMENT!!
```

EXERCISES

A LEVEL

Short Answers

1. What is meant by a valid categorical syllogism?
2. What are two ways of showing categorical syllogisms to be invalid?
3. Does the categorical statement, "All Quarks have Charm," necessarily mean that there have to be quarks, i.e., that quarks necessarily exist? Why or why not?
4. What is meant by an empty class?
5. What is meant by a term's being distributed? What does it mean to say that a term is undistributed?
6. Which Statement Forms have distributed predicate terms? Which ones have distributed subject terms?
7. What is meant by the Fallacy of Faulty Exclusions?
8. What is meant by the Four Terms Fallacy?
9. Explain the Fallacy of Illicit Distribution and which Rule does it break?
10. What is the Fallacy of the Undistributed Middle Term? Which Rule does it violate?
11. What is the Existential Fallacy? Explain how it is committed and what Rule it violates.
12. How are we to treat proper names and singular terms in categorical syllogisms?

B LEVEL

Test each of the following arguments for validity as a categorical syllogism, using the Rule Method. Make sure to put each statement into Standard Categorical Form. Use the Flow Chart in Figure 6.2 as an aid in determining the steps to take, if you need.

1. Since every economic theory is a theory about human beings in society and a lot of philosophical theories are theories about human beings in society, it follows that a lot of philosophical theories must be economic theories.
2. We know that some people in the political spotlight cannot tell the truth. And, all people who cannot tell the truth are liars. Therefore, some liars must be people in the political spotlight.
3. No traffic cops are one-armed people. Some Vice-Presidential candidates are not one-armed people. So, some Vice-Presidential candidates are not traffic cops.
4. Any person who can run a three minute mile is a potential Olympic Gold Medal winner. Any potential Olympic Gold Metal winner is a person who will make a fortune in advertising endorsements. Therefore, some people who will make a fortune in advertising endorsements are people who can run a three minute mile.
5. Multigrain cereals are an important source of fiber. Some kinds of fruit are not important sources of fiber. Thus, any multigrain cereal is a kind of fruit.
6. Some automobile drivers are not licensed drivers. Some licensed drivers are people who have never had an accident. Consequently, some automobile drivers are not people who have never had an accident.

7. Some automobile drivers are licensed drivers and some licensed drivers are not people who have never had an accident. Thus, some automobile drivers are not people who have never had an accident.

8. Some cigarettes are not particularly good for your health. Since all cigarettes are tobacco products, it must be the case that some tobacco products are not particularly good for your health.

9. Nothing that tastes good is good for you. And nothing that is good for you is something that you like. Therefore, nothing that tastes good is something that you like.

10. Evidently, some cars are not vehicles that have to be inspected because no vehicles that have to be inspected are pre-1985 vehicles and some cars are not pre-1985 vehicles.

11. Not every philosophy course is a skills course, so logic must not be a skills course, since it is a philosophy course.

12. No irresponsible people should be camp directors. Most Republicans are irresponsible. Therefore, most Republicans should not be camp directors.

13. No true Scotsman would ever make fun of the bagpipes. Michael is a Scotsman all right. Consequently, he would never make fun of the bagpipes.

14. Artistic people have a very special way of seeing things, so they must be autistic, since autistic people have a very special way of seeing things.

15. Everyone who puts her own interests before others is an egoist. And people who put the interests of others before their own are altruists. Therefore, some egoists must be altruists too.

16. Anything worth doing is worth doing well. Some useless tasks are obviously not worth doing. So, some useless tasks are not worth doing well.

17. No invalid syllogisms are sound arguments. But then, no true act of reasoning is an invalid syllogism. So, no true act of reasoning is a sound argument.

18. All people born in the States are free. Anything that is free is cheap. Therefore any person born in the States is cheap.

19. Anything that is logical makes sense to me. But, your explanation doesn't make sense to me. Therefore, your explanation is not logical.

20. Anyone who is a taxpayer is eligible for this position. Solomon is a U.S. citizen, so he is thereby eligible for this position.

21. Any course in critical thinking is a basic skills course, so some critical thinking courses are not worthless, because no basic skills courses are worthless.

22. There simply aren't any didlips which are eables. But, there have been known to be eables which are foints. This has to mean that some of the foints are didlips.

C   LEVEL

Select a passage containing arguments and pick out a deductive one (or turn an inductive argument into a deductive one). Try to recast that argument in categorical form. Then, evaluate the resulting syllogism on the basis of the Rule Method presented in this chapter.

6.3 THE VENN DIAGRAM METHOD FOR EVALUATING SYLLOGISMS

Categorical statements can be symbolized through the use of Venn diagrams. These are circles representing the terms of the syllogism. We begin our discussion by looking at the method for diagramming two terms, and then show how a third term can be added. When the three terms of a syllogism are correctly diagrammed, the validity or invalidity of the syllogistic argument can be determined.

The two classes to be diagrammed are represented by overlapping circles. For instance, the statement "Some students write excellent essays" includes two terms, *students* and *those who write excellent essays.* The circle on the left represents the first class while that on the right represents the second.

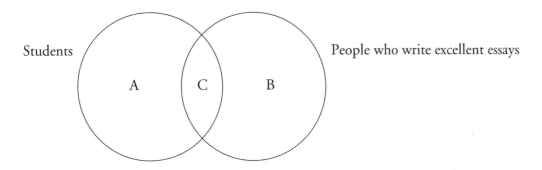

The parts of the circle indicated by the letters "A" and "C" represent the class of students. The circles represented by the letters "B" and "C" indicate the class of people who write excellent essays. The overlapping portion "C" represents those people who are both students and who write excellent essays. The statement "some students write excellent essays" can be diagrammed by placing an "X" in area "C." This means that there are some (at least one) person who is both a student and who writes excellent essays.

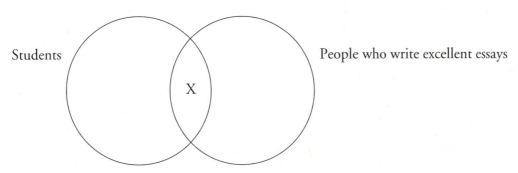

Some students write excellent essays

Similarly, we can indicate the fact that "Some students did not write excellent essays" by putting an "X" in region "A," which is in the class of those people who are students but outside of the class of people who write excellent essays.

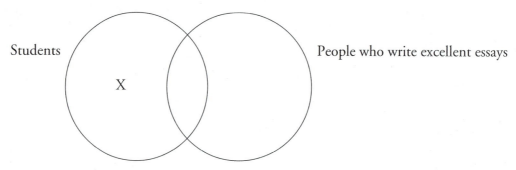

Some students do not write excellent essays

The rule for diagramming particular statements is therefore to place an "X" in the region of the diagram in which the members of that class are asserted to exist. By placing an "X" in this region, existential import is established for the class of students: At least one member of the class actually exists.

Universal statements do not establish existential import. The Venn diagram, therefore, does not represent these statements as having existential import. To diagram the statement "All freshmen are students" we therefore shade in area "A" to show that there are no freshmen who are not students:

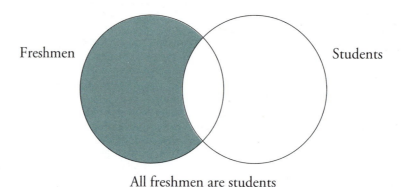

All freshmen are students

This diagram indicates that freshmen (if any exist) would all be included in the class of students. Negative universals are diagrammed by placing the shading in section "C," which indicates that there is no overlap between the classes. The statement "No freshmen are upperclassmen" is diagrammed as follows:

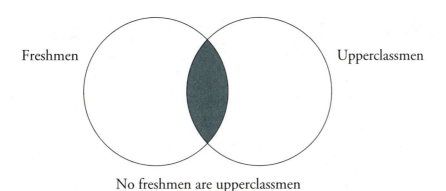

No freshmen are upperclassmen

This diagram shows that there is nothing in the section that represents freshmen who are upperclassmen. This says, in effect, that the subclass represented by the shaded portion is empty.

Three-Term Venn Diagrams

Having learned to express a categorical statement with two terms, it is a simple step to diagram three terms. In this case three overlapping circles must be drawn. This results in eight possible areas within the diagram (if you count the region outside all of the circles). Employing the letters "S", "P", and "M" to represent the three classes, the three-term diagram would look like this:

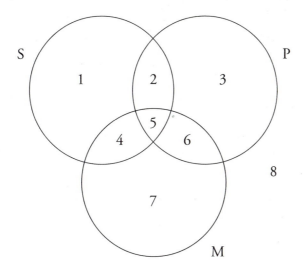

Diagram showing the eight possible regions of a three-term Venn diagram

This diagram represents the eight possibilities as follows:

A NOVEL REPLAY?

The following dialogue occurs in John Grisham 's *A Time to Kill*. In this instance a lawyer is trying to decide who to strike from a prospective jury.

> "Joe Kitt Shepherd."
> "Sounds like a redneck," said Lucien.
> "Why do you say that?" asked Harry Rex.
> "The double first name," Lucien explained. "Most rednecks have double first names. Like Billy Ray, Johnny Ray, Bobby Lee, Harry Lee, Jesse Earl, Billy Wayne, Jerry Wayne, Eddie Mack. Even their women have double first names. Bobbie Sue, Betty Pearl, Mary Belle, Thelma Lou, Sally Faye ."
> "What about Harry Rex?" asked Harry Rex.
> "Never heard of a woman named Harry Rex."
> "I mean for a male redneck."
> "I guess it'll do."
> Jake interrupted. "Dell Perry said he used to own a bait shop down by the lake. I take it no one knows him."
> "No, but I bet he's a redneck," said Lucien . "Because of his name. I'd scratch him."

Grisham has beautifully captured the way in which many people reason when they are thinking prejudicially. It is also a wonderful example of the fallacy of the Undistributed Middle Term. Note that the syllogism would read something like this:

> Most rednecks are people with two first names.
> (All) Joe Kitt is a person with two first names.
> So, (All) Joe Kitt is a redneck.

28, New York: Grenada Publishing Limited, (1982).

The problem in reasoning here is that it is very possible that Joe Kitt comes from a different part of the class of "people with two first names" than the class of "rednecks " occupies.

(Reprinted with permission from John Grishman, A Time to Kill, *p. 331, New York: Doubleday, Division of Bantam, Doubleday, Dell Publishing Group, Inc., 1989.)*

Region   Classes Included

1.   Things that are in the class of S, but not in the classes P or M.
2.   Things that are both S and P, but not M.
3.   Things that are P, but not S or M.
4.   Things that are S and M, but not P.

5. Things that are S, M, and P.
6. Things that are P and M, but not S.
7. Things that are M, but not S or P.
8. Things that are not included in any of the three classes. (Things which are not S, nor M, nor P.)

To draw a Venn diagram representing the entire syllogism, diagram each of the two premises, considering only the two circles representing the two classes or terms contained in that premise. It is important to remember that in evaluating these diagrams, *we do not diagram the conclusion*. The validity of the syllogism is tested by determining whether or not the conclusion is *already contained* in the diagram representing the premises. If the conclusion can be seen in the diagram of the premises, the syllogism is valid. If the conclusion is not represented in the diagram of the premises, the syllogism is invalid. Consider the following syllogism:

All Nigerians are African.
Some residents of Lagos are not African.

Therefore: Some residents of Lagos are not Nigerian.

For our diagram, we will let the letter "N" stand for the class of Nigerians, "L" will represent the class of citizens of Lagos, and "A" will represent Africans. To diagram the first statement we will consider only the circles N and A and diagram them without reference to the class L:

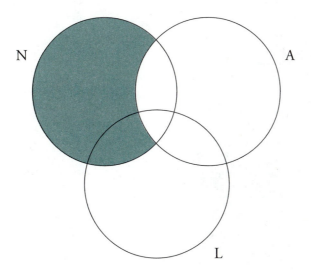

All Nigerians are African

This diagram shows that the first premise of the syllogism is a universal statement showing that there is no one who is a Nigerian but not an African. Regions 1 and 4 are thus represented as empty classes. We now diagram the second premise by putting an X in region 7:

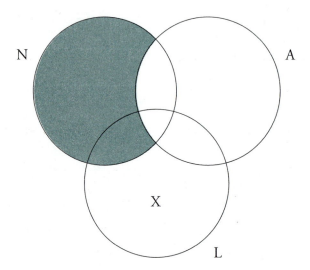

This is the resulting diagram of two premises. Since the conclusion is " Some residents of Lagos are not Nigerian," the argument is valid. This can be seen because there already is an "X" in region 7 representing people who are residents of Lagos, but not Nigerian.

It is important to remember that the universal premise must be diagrammed first. This will allow us to more easily place the "X" for the particular statement in the proper region. (It would not be clear whether the "X" would be placed in region 4 or region 7.) The next example shows how an invalid syllogism can be read from the premises:

> All Nigerians are African.
> Some Africans speak French.
> ───────────────────────
> Therefore: Some Nigerians speak French.

Using the letters "N," "A," and "F," we diagram the first premise in the same way as the last example:

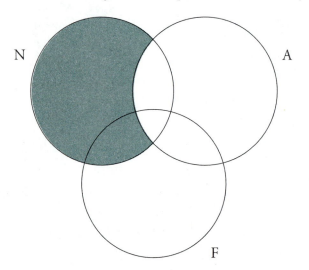

We go on to symbolize the second premise. But there's a problem here. We need to place an "X" in the area where the A class and the F class overlap. But there are two regions of the diagram—regions 5 and 6—that may be intended. The statement offers us no clue as to which one it is. So in order to show that the "X" falls into either one region or the other, we place it on the border between the two regions:

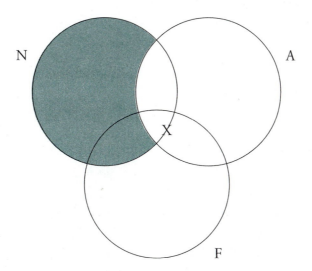

The conclusion of this argument is that "Some Nigerians speak French." But since the "X" is not necessarily in the area indicating French-speaking Nigerians, the conclusion does not necessarily follow. And a valid syllogism requires that the conclusion does necessarily follow from the premises. Thus this diagram shows that the syllogism is invalid.

Figure 6.4 summarizes the use of Venn diagrams to evaluate categorical syllogisms, with a step by step technique of application.

SUMMARY

Step 6 of the Technique is concerned with the analysis of the structure of arguments. This chapter focuses on a particular type of structure known as the *categorical syllogism*. The syllogism is composed of two statements and a conclusion, all of which are categorical statements. A categorical statement is one in which an individual, set of individuals, or a class is said to be included or excluded from another class. Categorical statements are indicated by the quantifiers *all, some,* or *no.* The subject of a categorical statement is the class or individual or group of individuals said to be included or excluded from another class. The predicate term is the class in which the subject is said to be included, or from which the subject term is said to be excluded. A syllogism requires exactly three class terms. The major term of the syllogism is the predicate of the conclusion. The major premise of the syllogism is the premise containing the major term. The minor term of a syllogism is the subject term of the conclusion. The minor premise of a syllogism is the one in which

FIGURE 6-4

USE OF VENN DIAGRAMS TO EVALUATE CATEGORICAL SYLLOGISMS

Step 1:   Identify premises and conclusion, making sure everything is stated.

Step 2:   Put each of the three statements into *standard form* (i.e., tell whether it is an A-, E-, I-, or O-form).

Step 3:   Draw the diagram and test the inference.

     A. Begin by drawing the three overlapping circles representing each of the three classes, and label each one to show which class it symbolizes.

     B. Apply the rules of thumb previously discussed:

        1. Diagram any universal (A- or E-form) statements that occur in the premises.

        2. Now diagram any particular I- and O-Form premises. If there are two or more possible locations where the "X" could be placed, draw both or all of them and connect them with a dotted or squiggly line to remind you that later all but one of them can be erased or deleted, or draw an "x" or the border line between the two regions in the question.

Step 4:   Look at the completed diagram of the premises. Compare the actual conclusion of the syllogism (that is, what the conclusion would look like if it were diagrammed by itself) with the diagram of the premises: Is the former (the conclusion as diagrammed) *necessarily* contained in the latter (the premises as diagrammed)? If the conclusion is not represented at all, or if it might be true or false, then the argument form is invalid (in the same way that we might respond ordinarily or informally by saying, "not necessarily"). If the conclusion cannot possibly be true if the premises are true, we still call the argument form invalid (but this time in a way we would ordinarily express, "necessarily not . . ."). Only if the conclusion is an inescapable consequence of the premises do we call the argument form a valid one.

the minor term is mentioned. The middle term of a syllogism serves to link the major and minor terms, and is included in the premises, but not in the conclusion.

A syllogism is said to be valid when it establishes that the truth of its conclusion necessarily follows from the truth of its premises. There are three rules for evaluating categorical syllogisms and one corollary to the first rule. Rule 1 is that a valid categorical syllogism has exactly three class terms, each one occurring twice with precisely the same meaning in both of the statements in which it occurs. Violation of this rule constitutes the Four Terms Fallacy. Rule 2 is that a valid categorical syllogism has the same number of negative (E- or O-Form) statements in the premises as it has in the conclusion. In other words, a valid categorical syllogism has either no negative statements at all, or it has one negative statement in the conclusion and one in the premises. When Rule 2 is violated, the Faulty Exclusions Fallacy is committed. Rule 3 maintains

FIGURE 6-5

RECAP OF THE RULES FOR DETERMINING VALIDITY OF CATEGORICAL SYLLOGISMS

RULE 1: A valid categorical syllogism has exactly three class terms each used in the same sense in both of the categorical statements in which it occurs.

   COROLLARY: In a categorical syllogism whenever both premises are universal statements (A- or E-form) and the conclusion is a particular statement (I- or O-form), all three classes in the syllogism must be known to have at least one member.

RULE 2: A valid categorical syllogism has either (a) no negative statements (E- or O-form) at all or (b) one negative statement in the premises and one negative statement in the conclusion.

RULE 3: In a valid categorical syllogism, (a) the middle term must be distributed at least once and (b) any term that is distributed in the conclusion must also be distributed in the premises.

that in a valid categorical syllogism, (A) the middle term must be distributed at least once, and (B) any term that is distributed in the conclusion must be distributed in the premises too. If a term is undistributed in the conclusion, it does not matter whether that term is distributed or undistributed in the premises. Violation of Rule 3A constituted the Fallacy of the Undistributed Middle Term. When Rule 3B is broken, the Fallacy of Illicit Distribution occurs. The Corollary to Rule 1 is that in a valid categorical syllogism, whenever both of the premises are universal statements (A- or E-Form) and the conclusion is a particular statement (I- or O-Form), all three of the classes of the syllogism must be known to have at least one member. If any one (or more) of the classes is empty, the Existential Fallacy is committed.

Venn diagrams may also be used to test syllogisms for validity. In a Venn diagram, two or three classes can be represented. To test for the validity of a categorical syllogism properly, the Venn diagram must contain three classes. The premises of the argument are diagrammed, but the conclusion is not. If the syllogism is valid, it should be possible to read the conclusion in the diagram of the premises, because the truth of the conclusion will be necessarily contained in the premises. Figure 6.5 summarizes the rules for determining the validity of categorical syllogisms.

EXERCISES

 A   LEVEL

Short Answers
 1. What is represented by a circle in a Venn diagram?
 2. Venn diagrams can be used to indicate the relationship between how many terms?
 3. What is indicated by the shaded portion of a Venn diagram?

4. What is indicated by the placement of an "X" in an area of a Venn diagram?

5. How many areas are represented in a two-term Venn diagram?

6. How many areas are represented in a three-term Venn diagram?

True or False

7. _F_ When testing a syllogism with a Venn diagram, the conclusion should be diagrammed before the premises.

8. _T_ The area outside all of the circles in a Venn diagram indicates those things that do not fall into any of the three classes named in the syllogism.

9. _F_ An "X" placed on the border line between two areas of a Venn diagram indicates that there is at least one thing that exists in *both* of the bordering classes.

10. _T_ Some syllogisms that contain only two terms can be tested by the Venn Diagram method.

B   LEVEL

Using Venn Diagrams, test for validity the arguments you tested at the end of section 6.2, where you used the Rule Method. Use the Flow Chart in Figure 6.4 as an aid in determining the steps to take, if you need. Those syllogisms are reprinted here for your convenience.

1. Since every economic theory is a theory about human beings in society and a lot of philosophical theories are theories about human beings in society, it follows that a lot of philosophical theories must be economic theories.

2. We know that some people in the political spotlight cannot tell the truth. And, all people who cannot tell the truth are liars. Therefore, some liars must be people in the political spotlight.

3. No traffic cops are one-armed people. Some Vice Presidential candidates are not one-armed people. So, some Vice-Presidential candidates are not traffic cops.

4. Any person who can run a three minute mile is a potential Olympic Gold Medal winner. Any potential Olympic Gold Medal winner is a person who will make a fortune in advertising endorsements. Therefore, some people who will make a fortune in advertising endorsements are people who can run a three minute mile.

5. Multigrain cereals are an important source of fiber. Some kinds of fruit are not important sources of fiber. Thus, any multigrain cereal is a kind of fruit.

6. Some automobile drivers are not licensed drivers. Some licensed drivers are people who have never had an accident. Consequently, some automobile drivers are not people who have never had an accident.

7. Some automobile drivers are licensed drivers and some licensed drivers are not people who have never had an accident. Thus, some automobile drivers are not people who have never had an accident.

8. Some cigarettes are not particularly good for your health. Since all cigarettes are tobacco products, it must be the case that some tobacco products are not particularly good for your health.

9. Nothing that tastes good is good for you. And nothing that is good for you is something that you like. Therefore, nothing that tastes good is something that you like.

10. Evidently, some cars are not vehicles that have to be inspected because no vehicles that have to be inspected are pre-1985 vehicles and some cars are not pre-1985 vehicles.

11. Not every philosophy course is a skills course, so logic must not be a skills course, since it is a philosophy course.

12. No irresponsible people should be camp directors. Most Republicans are irresponsible. Therefore, most Republicans should not be camp directors.

13. No true Scotsman would ever make fun of the bagpipes. Michael is a Scotsman all right. Consequently, he would never make fun of the bagpipes.

14. Artistic people have a very special way of seeing things, so they must be autistic, since autistic people have a very special way of seeing things.

15. Everyone who puts her own interests before others is an egoist. And people who put the interests of others before their own are altruists. Therefore, some egoists must be altruists too.

16. Anything worth doing is worth doing well. Some useless tasks are obviously not worth doing. So, some useless tasks are not worth doing well.

17. No invalid syllogisms are sound arguments. But then, no true act of reasoning is an invalid syllogism. So, no true act of reasoning is a sound argument.

18. All people born in the States are free. Anything that is free is cheap. Therefore any person born in the States is cheap.

19. Anything that is logical makes sense to me. But, your explanation doesn't make sense to me. Therefore, your explanation is not logical.

20. Anyone who is a taxpayer is eligible for this position. Solomon is a U.S. citizen, so he is thereby eligible for this position.

21. Any course in critical thinking is a basic skills course, so some critical thinking courses are not worthless, because no basic skills courses are worthless.

22. There simply aren't any didlips which are eables. But, there have been known to be eables which are foints. This has to mean that some of the foints are didlips.

C   LEVEL

1. Select a passage containing arguments and pick out a deductive one (or turn an inductive argument into a deductive one). Try to recast that argument in categorical form. Now, evaluate the resulting syllogism on the basis of the Rule Method presented in this chapter. Then, evaluate it again on the basis of the Venn Diagram Method. Do you find the results to be the same or different?

2. Use the Venn Diagram Method to show an invalid instance (you can use letters to represent classes) of each one of the Rules for testing the validity of Categorical Syllogisms. In other words show what a diagram would look like if Rule One were broken, and so forth through the Rules. If you are having a hard time doing this with the Four Terms Fallacy, can you explain why?

CASE STUDY

Diagramming techniques for testing the validity or invalidity of categorical syllogisms are extremely helpful shortcuts and in many cases are easier to remember than the Rule Method. They are becoming more plentiful and ingenious each year. One particularly interesting one, devised by Professors Armstrong and Howe and reprinted courtesy of *Teaching Philosophy*, is presented here.

A Euler Test for Syllogisms

excerpted from Robert Armstrong and Lawrence Howe. (*Teaching Philosophy*, vol. 13, March 1990. Used with the permission of the Philosophy Documentation Center, publisher of *Teaching Philosophy*.)

. . . Our method [of testing syllogisms] employs the circle diagrams used by the Swiss mathematician Leonhard Euler in 1761. We have devised a *reductio ad absurdum* version of Euler's circle diagram method. It teaches the students to take a critical, challenging attitude toward the evaluation of arguments presented for analysis. The student tries to prove the argument invalid by showing that a false conclusion can be derived from the purportedly true premises of the argument. This is done by contradicting the conclusion of the argument and showing that it is consistent with the truth of the premises. If it is possible to represent the premises as true and the conclusion as false in a single Euler circle diagram, then the argument is proved to be invalid. If the argument is actually valid then the attempt to draw such a diagram will be impossible.

. . .(T)he student must first grasp two important concepts—contradiction and invalidity. Students learn contradiction by mastering the square of opposition. [The important feature is that an A-Statement and an O-Statement are contradictory, and an E-Statement and an I-Statement are contradictory.] They are then taught the concept of invalidity, namely, that an argument form is invalid if even one case with true premises and a false conclusion can be presented. Thus the student is trained to recognize counter-examples to supposedly valid arguments. . . .(W)e usually teach the counter-example method of proving invalidity by contructing a substitution instance of the argument which has obviously true premises and a false conclusion. This method proves invalidity but not validity. Thus a proof of validity is needed to be used in conjunction with the effective but incomplete counter-example method.

Also, prior to the introduction of the test, the student is shown how Euler Circles can be used to diagram (not prove) valid argument forms. This has the advantage of teaching . . . the most primitive uses of the circles, that is, to represent statements in the form of diagrams. For example, take the . . . [A A A] syllogism:

     All M are P
     All S are M
     ——————
     All S are P

This argument form can be diagrammed using three circles in the following way:

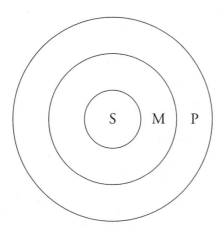

By merely looking at the diagrammatic representation of the argument, one can see that the conclusion "All S are P" follows from the circles representing the first two premises. The conclusion is "contained" in the premises. This exercise is helpful since the students get used to representing statements by drawing circles which enable them to "picture" the truth of the conclusion given the correct diagrammatic representation of the premises.

With this background information in mind, the student is ready to apply the circle test to categorical syllogisms. The student learns that a deductive argument is shown to be invalid by producing an instance of the argument form where the conclusion is false when the premises are assumed to be true. We begin by presupposing that all arguments presented for evaluation are valid and teach our students to take a critical stance. That is, they are to try to prove that the argument is invalid. To prove it invalid they must produce a counter-example in the form of a diagram with three circles which show the premises to be true while the conclusion is false.

The steps of the proof are as follows:

1. Diagram the major premise as true. This diagram will fix the position of two of the three terms [or classes] of the argument. [Either premise will do, but it is easier to pick a premise which is a universal (A or E) statement.]
2. Contradict [that is, substitute an O-Statement for an A-Statement, an I-Statement for an E-statement, and so forth] the conclusion and consider the possibilities of fixing the position of the third term. Sometimes there are as many as three possible positions for it.
3. Inspect the minor premise [or the remaining, undiagrammed premise] to see which drawing of the third term permits it.

If such a diagram can be drawn then the argument is shown to be invalid. The completed diagram would have three circles, one for each term, showing the premises as true and the conclusion as false (since the contradictory of the conclusion rather than the original conclusion is diagrammed).

Let us apply the method to the valid . . . [A A A] syllogism. We would outline it as follows.

All M are P
All S are M
_____
All S are P—contradict → Some S are not P

Step 1: Diagram the major premise as follows:

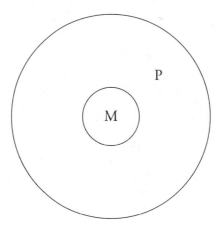

Step 2: Take the contradicted conclusion and "plug" it into the diagram of the first premise. Thus we add the circle for the "S" term which means that some members of "S" are not members of "P." The diagram looks like this:

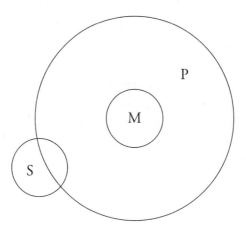

Alternative diagrams are possible for representing "Some S are not P." Thus,

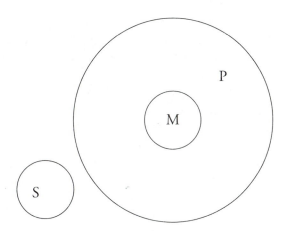

also represents "Some S are not P," but the natural or intuitive preference for "Some are" and "Some are not" is the intersecting diagram

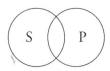

Having diagrammed the contradicted conclusion, we must now direct our attention to the second premise. Does it, or does it not, permit the contradicted conclusion? In the present case, neither possible drawing of "Some S are not P" is permitted by the second premise, "All S are M." Thus, we indicate this impossibility by drawing an "X" through our drawing of the third term to present the contradicted conclusion. Therefore, our assumption that the argument is invalid is reduced to an "impossibility." That is, it turned out to be impossible to represent the truth of the premises and the falsity of the conclusion in the same diagram.

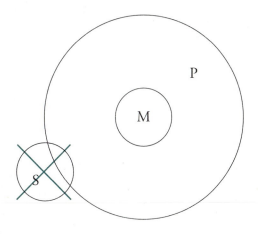

Our final diagram looks like this:

All valid syllogisms yield a diagram with an "X"ed out term indicating the impossibility of representing the truth of the premises and the falsity of the conclusion. Since this absurd or impossible diagram results from our assumption that the initial argument was invalid, that assumption is reduced to absurdity. Therefore, the only other logical possibility is that the original argument form is valid. Its validity is thus proven.

Let us now apply the test to an invalid argument:

All P are M
All S are M
—————————————
All S are P—contradict ➝ Some S are not P

After contradicting the conclusion, we now draw circles for the major premise, then for the contradicted

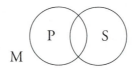

conclusion, and finally, for the remaining premise. This yields the following:

The minor premise permits the drawing of the contradicted conclusion. We find that it is possible to draw circles so that all statements are represented without inconsistency or the impossibility of drawing a circle. Thus, our assumption, that the argument form is invalid, succeeds. This diagram constitutes a substitution instance with true premises and a false conclusion. Thus the argument form is proven to be invalid.

7

THE SYLLOGISM REFINED

step five
Are there any fallacies?

step six
What is the argument's structure?

step seven
What other conclusions can be drawn?

No man who worships education has got the best out of education . . . Without a gentle contempt for education no man's education is complete."
—G. K. Chesterton (1911)

All men are mortal,
Socrates is a man:
Therefore, all men are Socrates.
—Woody Allen (ca. 1964)

KEY TERMS

Contradictions: - Two statements with the same subject and predicate, one of which must be true and the other false. Categorical contradictions are either A-Form versus O-Form or E-Form versus I-Form.

Contraries: - Two statements with similar subjects and predicates, one A-Form and the other E-Form, both of which cannot be true at the same time but which may both be false.

Conversion: - Switching subject and predicate terms.

Enthymeme: - A syllogistic argument with a missing premise or a missing conclusion.

Immediate inference: - A conclusion drawn from a single statement.

Mediate inference: - A conclusion (such as that of a syllogism) reached through the connection of two terms by a "mediate" or third term that bridges the gap between the other two terms.

Obversion: - Changing affirmative or positive statements to negative ones and negatives to positive or affirmative ones.

Sorites: - An argument composed of a string of categorical syllogisms, the conclusion of one becoming a premise for the next. Because sorites usually do not state the implied conclusions, they are examples of enthymemes.

Square of opposition: - A diagram showing the truth-relationships between different forms of categorical statements.

Subalterns: - Two statements with the same subject and predicate, one of which is a universal statement (A-Form or E-Form), the other of which is a particular statement (I-Form or O-Form). If the universal statement is true and the class is known to contain at least one member, then the particular statement must also be true.

Subcontraries: - Two statements with the same subject and predicate, one I-Form and the other O-Form, which cannot both be false but may both be true.

Step 6 of the Technique is concerned with the assessment of argument structures. In the previous chapter you learned some of the methods for evaluating the forms taken by categorical arguments. In this chapter we continue our discussion of categorical syllogisms.

The conclusion from the two premises of a categorical syllogism is sometimes known as a **mediate inference** because the middle term bridges the gap or *mediates* between the subject term in the minor premise and the predicate term in the major premise. But categorical statements also lend themselves to unmediated or immediate inferences. **Immediate inferences** are conclusions that can be drawn from a single statement. For instance, a spokesperson for an industry that is largely responsible for pollution might make the statement

POSSIBLE VERSUS NECESSARY IMMEDIATE REFERENCES

Perhaps part of what it means to be a human being is to draw inferences from a single piece of information, i.e., to draw further conclusions from a single, sometimes unsupported premise. This being the case, we need a part of the Technique to help us determine when the inferences are legitimate or warranted and when they are not. Consider for a minute the little tidbit of information that pops up somewhere almost every day: "Seventy-five percent of all automobile accidents occur within 25 miles of home." Are we supposed to file this ostensibly isolated datum in the deep RAM of our brains, or are we supposed to *do something* with it? Some of the possible ramifications of this piece of information are explored in slightly tongue-in-cheek manner by John Hickey in an article in the *Journal of Irreproducible Results*. With apologies, we will take a few liberties with them.

Let us suppose that it is true that 75% of all automobile accidents occur within 25 miles of home. What conclusions are different people likely to draw from this?

1. The "Normal Chuck" reaction: Wow! That is a lot of accidents, SO I had better drive just as carefully near home as I do out on the highway.
2. The "Deb L" Response: That IS a lot of accidents, and since I am almost always within 25 miles of SOMEBODY's home, I had better drive carefully all the time.
3. The "Kelly A" Reaction: Well then, I had better drive like a bat-out-of-you-know-where to get outside of the danger area near my house and into the surrounding "safe" zone.
4. The "Dr. Dave Statistician" Response: Well, since only 75% of the accidents occur where I do 95% of my driving, the 25-mile zone surrounding my home is a "safe zone" where I can let down my guard a little and relax while I am driving.

No city in the United states has a dangerous level of pollution.

Now if a reporter were to question this spokesperson about her statement, he might ask "Well then, does the city of Detroit have a dangerous level of pollution?"

The spokesperson could easily respond by saying "Didn't I just tell you that?"

While the spokesperson did not actually say that Detroit was not dangerously polluted, she did in fact imply that with her statement. Detroit is a city in the United States. Because no U.S. cities were said to have a dangerous level of pollution, and Detroit is a city in the United States, the conclusion that Detroit does not possess a dangerous level of pollution is an immediate inference from the original statement. This can be shown with a Venn diagram of the two terms involved:

> 5. The Actuarial Savant Response: Okay; I am going to register my car at a "home" at least a thousand miles away from where I actually live and I will never go anywhere near there.
>
> 6. The Logic Professor's Corollary: Not a bad idea, but why not go on and register your car at a location at which (a) you will never have any chance of ever going near and which (b) has an automobile collision rate of exactly 0%. The South Pole immediately comes to mind.
>
> Now all of these conclusions are *inductively* drawn. None of them is remotely guaranteed by the premise itself. In fact, the conclusions that necessarily and deductively follow from this premise include:
>
> I—Some automobile accidents are things that occur within 25 miles of home
>
> or
>
> I—Some things that occur within 25 miles of home are automobile accidents
>
> or
>
> O—Some automobile accidents are not things that do not occur within 25 miles of home.
>
> To be sure, this is an extension of the Technique we began developing back in Chapter 2 and 3 when covering the concepts of inference and logical implications.
>
> *(Reprinted with permission from John Hickey,* "The Journal of Irreproducible Results, 2nd printing, 1981, p. 175.

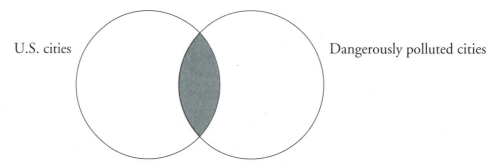

No U.S. cities possess a dangerous level of pollution

The diagram of this E statement shows that there is nothing in the overlapping class of *dangerously polluted U.S. cities.* Since we know that there are cities in the United States and Detroit is one of those cities, it must fall in the region of the diagram in which there is no shading.

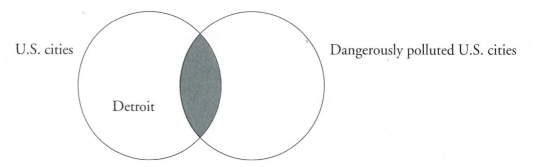

No U.S. cities possess a dangerous level of pollution

This diagram demonstrates one of the more general forms of immediate inference: If an E-form statement is true and the subject class contains at least one member, then the O-form statement about a member of that class must also be true.

Other relationships between statement forms can be characterized with what has come to be known as the square of opposition. The **square of opposition** is a diagram showing the truth-relationships between different forms of categorical statements (Figure 7.1).

The square of opposition is designed to show the relationships between the various categorical statement forms (A, E, I, O). The square shows that A-form statements and E-form statements are **contraries.** Two statements are contrary to one another if they cannot both be true, but can both be false. It cannot be true at the same time, for instance, to say that "All college instructors have Ph.D.'s" and "No college instructors have Ph.D.'s." If we know that one of the statements is true, we can immediately infer that the other is false. On the other hand, it is possible for them both to be false. If some college instructors have Ph.D.'s while others do not (which is in fact the case), then both statements turn out to be false. Thus if you should determine that an A statement is true, you can conclude that the corresponding E statement is false and

FIGURE 7-1

THE SQUARE OF OPPOSITION.

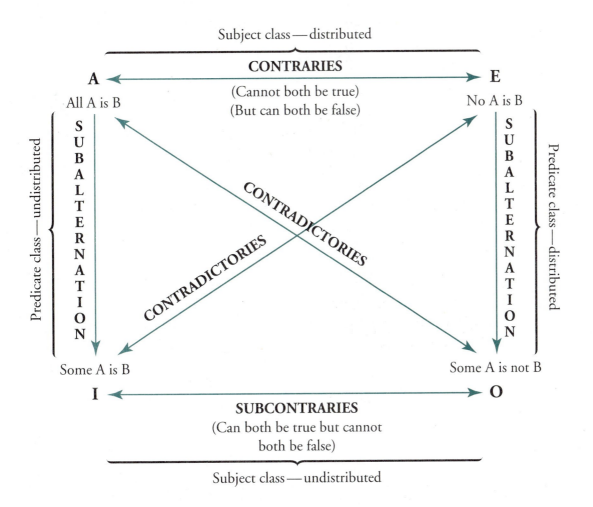

Subject class — distributed

CONTRARIES

A (Cannot both be true) (But can both be false) E

All A is B   No A is B

Predicate class — undistributed

SUBALTERNATION

CONTRADICTORIES

CONTRADICTORIES

Predicate class — distributed

SUBALTERNATION

Some A is B   Some A is not B

I

SUBCONTRARIES

(Can both be true but cannot both be false)

O

Subject class — undistributed

vice versa. If, however, you know that the E-Statement is false, you cannot be sure that the A-Form is either true of false.

I-form and O-form statements are subcontraries. **Subcontraries** are statements that cannot both be false, but can both be true. For instance, the statements "Some architects are Australian" and "some architects are not Australian" cannot be mutually false. (Either some architects are Australian or some are not.) Since I- and O-form statements cannot both be false, knowing that one or the other is in fact false will lead us to legitimately conclude that the other is true. If it were to turn out that the statement "Some architects are not Australian" were a false statement, the corresponding I-form statement, "Some architects are Australian," must in fact be true.

When two statements **contradict** one another, exactly one of the statements must be true and the other false. Another way of putting this is to say that contradictory statements cannot both be true and cannot both be false. A-form statements contradict O-form statements and E-form statements contradict I-form statements. If it is true, for instance, that "All architects have college degrees," then it must also be false that "Some architects do not have college degrees." Similarly, the false statement "No architects have college degrees" will lead us to the inference that the statement "Some architects have college degrees" is a true statement.

Another relationship expressed in the square of opposition is that of subalternation. **Subalternation** expresses the relationship between universal statements and particular statements. I-form statements are subalternates to A-form statements and O-form statements are subalternates to E-form statements. In each case the particular statement form is true as long as the corresponding universal statement is true and as long as the classes in the universal statement contain at least one member. If it is true that "All apples are fruits" that it is true that "Some apples are fruits." This relationship holds only in one direction—from the universal to the particular. It does not hold in the other direction. For instance, one should *not* infer from the statement "Some apples are red" the universal statement that "All apples are red." That would be a *Hasty Generalization* fallacy.

7.1 IMMEDIATE INFERENCES

Three kinds of immediate inference may be supported by the information contained in the square of opposition:

1. Inferences from the known or supposed truth of a statement
2. Inferences from reversed subject and predicate terms (called **conversion**)
3. Inferences from changing affirmative to negative statements or vice-versa (called **obversion**).

Knowledge of the rules for each of these three types of immediate inference will permit us to immediately infer true statements from other statements we know to be true without the intervention of a categorical syllogism.

Inferences from the Known or Supposed Truth of a Statement

If a categorical statement is known to be true, the truth or falsity of at least one other categorical statement can be immediately inferred. For instance, since A-form and O-form statements are contradictory, and since one of those statements must be true and the other false we can determine the truth or falsity of one if we know that of the other. If it is false that "All apples are red" then it must be true that "Some apples are not red." Since it is true that "No human is immortal" it must also be false that "Some humans are immortal."

Contraries cannot both be true but can both be false. If we know that one of a pair of contraries is true (for instance, "All apples are fruits") then the contrary statement must be false ("No apples are fruits"). On the other hand, since contraries can *both* be false, knowing that one of a pair of contraries is false tells us nothing about the other member of the pair. "All bananas are blue" is a false statement. But knowing this does not ensure that its contrary "No bananas are blue" is also false.

> ## ▶ REAL-LIFE CONTRADICTIONS? ◀
>
> Note that most boxes of powder laundry detergent contain a special, fairly prominent sign: CONTAINS NO PHOSPHORUS. Surprisingly, on the same box of detergent there appears another statement: "This product contains less than 0.5% phosphorus." What is going on here!?!?
>
> In other words we have an outright contradiction between an E-statement and an I-statement in one and the same place. The first is the E-statement:
>
> > "No phosphorus is an ingredient in this box."
>
> The second is the I-statement:
>
> > "Some phosphorus is an ingredient in this box."
>
> How could both of them be true at the same time? The answer is that they cannot be. This could be another example of your tax dollars hard at work. In other words, it may be a compromise that legislators have devised to appease environmental groups who insist that the amount of ecologically hazardous material be displayed on the box for environmentally conscious consumers, while at the same time appeasing those manufacturing interests who have persuaded government officials to believe that 0.5% phosphorus or less is "not environmentally hazardous."

Subcontraries can both be true, but cannot both be false. So the fact that one of a pair of subcontraries is false (e.g., "Some bananas are blue") will lead us to the immediate inference that the other member of the pair is true ("Some bananas are not blue"). However, since they can both be true, knowledge that one member of the pair is true will not ensure that we can immediately infer that the other member of the pair is false (or that it is true).

Finally, we can immediately infer that, if a universal statement is true and the class terms contain at least one member, then the particular form of the statement is also true.

Table 7.1 shows the more complete set of immediate inferences from known truth conditions.

Conversion: Reversing Subject and Predicate Terms

One common form of immediate inference is the conversion of the subject and predicate terms of a categorical statement. A categorical statement is converted when the subject and predicates are switched with one another. While some statement forms can be converted directly, others require changing a universal statement to a particular statement. A-form statements, for instance, can be converted only when they are transformed into particular statements. Consider a class in which all of the students failed their first examination. Following the second examination the teacher announces:

TABLE 7-1

IMMEDIATE INFERENCES FROM KNOWN TRUTH CONDITIONS

		Resulting Truth Value for These Statement Forms			
		A	**E**	**I**	**O**
Given truth values	A = T	T	F	T*	F
	E = T	F	T	F	T*
	I = T	?	F	T	?
	O = T	F	?	?	T
Given that these	A = F	F	?	?	T
forms are known	E = F	?	F	T	?
to be false	I = F	F	T	F	T
	O = F	T	F	T	F

*Note: T= true; F=false; ?=cannot be determined; *=true by limitation (provided classes are not empty).*

All those who passed this second examination are those who failed the first.

If you were a student could you thereby infer that you must have passed the second examination because you failed the first? Such a conclusion would not be legitimate. We can illustrate this with a Venn diagram. The original statement would be diagrammed as follows:

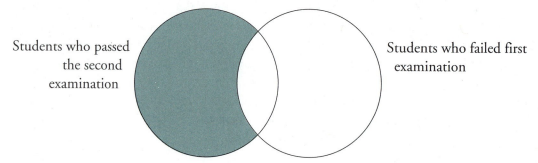

All those who passed the second examination failed the first.

This diagram clearly shows that the converted statement "All whose who failed the first examination passed the second" is not implied by the original statement. Assuming that the classes each contain at least one member, the most we can infer from the original statement by conversion is that "*Some* students who failed the first examination passed the second." The region of the diagram representing those students who failed the first examination is clearly not empty. So the rule for the conversion of A-form statements is

A-form statements can be converted into I-form statements as long as there is at least one member of each class.

Both E-form and I-form statements present less of a problem. This is because these types of statements can be directly converted into statements of the same form. Note that the distribution of subject and predicate terms is the same in both the case of E-statements (where they are both distributed) and I-statements (where they are both undistributed.) The statement "No automobiles can fly" can be directly converted into the statements "No flying things are automobiles." E-form statements such as this present us with two mutually exclusive classes. If "No A are B" then it must be equally true that "No B are A." When we use a Venn diagram to illustrate an E-form statement, we can see that it can be read either way:

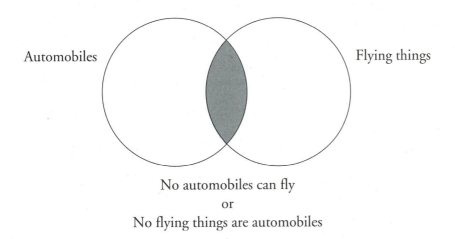

No automobiles can fly
or
No flying things are automobiles

Looking at the Venn Diagram, we see that the two statements are equivalent. The same is true for I-form statements. If it is true that "Some automobiles have air bags," it must also be true that "Some things with air bags are automobiles":

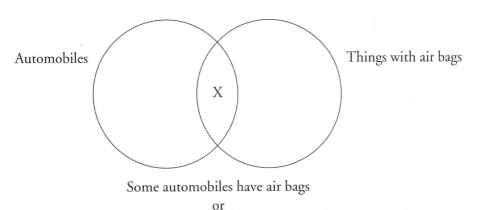

Some automobiles have air bags
or
Some things with air bags are automobiles

Again, by examining the Venn Diagram, the two statements turn out to be equivalent. So the rules for the conversion of E-form and I-form statements are

E-form statements can be directly converted into E-form statements

and

I-form statements can be directly converted into I-form statements.

Finally, it is the case that O-form statements cannot be converted at all. If we know that "Some citizens are not taxpayers" we *cannot* legitimately conclude that "Some taxpayers are not citizens." The first statement tells us nothing about the taxpaying habits of noncitizens, but only that some citizens do not pay taxes:

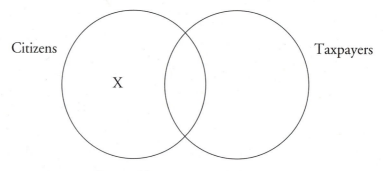

Some citizens are not taxpayers

There is just no way of knowing, from the original statement whether or not any or all taxpayers are or are not citizens. The final rule of conversion is therefore:

O-form statements cannot be validly converted.

Table 7.2 presents a summary of the findings about converting subjects and predicates for categorical statements.

TABLE 7-2

CONVERSION TABLE FOR CATEGORICAL STATEMENTS

A-statments (All A is B)	convert to	I-statemnents (Some B is A)*
E-statements (No A is B)	convert as	E-statements (No B is A)
I-statements (Some A is B)	convert as	I-statements (Some B is A)
O-statements (Some A is not B)	*cannot be validly converted*	

* In this case, both classes must be examinined to ensure that they are not empty.

ILLEGITIMATE CONVERSIONS?

Suppose you are thinking of joining the crew team and you see a sign advertising for people to join, and it says

ONLY PEOPLE IN EXCELLENT SHAPE WILL MAKE THE TEAM.

If you were to reason that "since only people in excellent shape will make the team and I am in excellent shape, therefore I will make the team," you would be guilty of fallacious reasoning. The argument is not valid, but it is likely that you misconstrued the first premise to mean "*All* people in excellent shape will make the team." By its content, you know that cannot be correct, for if it were true, then everyone in the universe who was in excellent shape would make the team, and hence the team would have to be very, very big. But, even from its form, what has happened is that you illegitimately converted the A-Statement, "Everyone who makes the team is a person who is in excellent shape" into an A-Statement, "Everyone who is in excellent shape is a person who makes the team," instead of into an I-statement, "Some people in excellent shape are people who will make the swim team."

Obversion: Changing Affirmatives to Negatives or Negatives to Affirmatives

Another common form of immediate inference is obversion. Obversion occurs when a positive statement is changed to a negative statement or a negative statement is changed to a positive one. Although such a change often leads to some language construction that would not be ordinarily found in everyday speech, it can show us which statements can be immediately inferred from a categorical statement. A-form statements, for instance, can be obverted into E-form statements. From the statement "All beagles are dogs" we can immediately infer that "No beagle is a non-dog." While the second statement is grammatically cumbersome, it correctly captures the relationship expressed by the first statement. A Venn diagram helps us to understand this:

Beagles   Dogs

All beagles are dogs
or
No beagle is a non-dog

Similarly E-form statements can be directly obverted into A-form statements. If it is true that "No cats are dogs" it must be equally true that "All cats are non-dogs." The E-form statement expresses the fact that the classes of cats and dogs are mutually exclusive. The obverted A-form statement yields the same result:

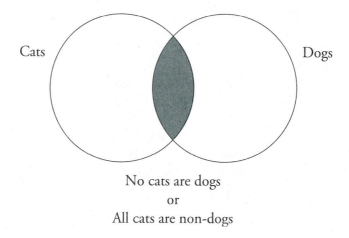

No cats are dogs
or
All cats are non-dogs

The Venn diagram shows us that both readings of the relationship between the classes of cats and dogs are correct. The obversion rules for A-form and E-form statements are therefore:

A-form statements can be obverted into E-form statements

and

E-form statements can be obverted into A-form statements.

This is done by (1) changing the quantifier (All to No or No to All), which (2) changes the relationship (from inclusion or exclusion to inclusion) and (3) changing the predicate class to its complementary class. *Nothing* is done to the subject class.

I-form and O-form statements present more of a problem. While it may be true, for instance, that "Some automobiles are Fords" we cannot therefore conclude that "Some automobiles are not Fords" since it may in fact be the case that Ford makes all of the automobiles that are produced. Similarly, the statement "Some automobiles are not Edsels" cannot be legitimately obverted into the statement "Some automobiles are Edsels" since we do not know whether or not there are any Edsels at all.

Notice that in the attempt to obvert I-form and O-form statements, we still can *not* negate the subject class. This is because a direct negation of the subject class would make the negated subject class everything else in the universe besides the subject class. The class of nonautomobiles, for instance, includes everything that is not an automobile. This is a pretty large class to consider. In effect, it includes so much that it would be impossible to say anything significant about it. Nevertheless, both I- and O-form statements may be obverted legitimately. Table 7.3 presents a quick recap of the obversion forms for each of the four categorical statement types.

TABLE 7-3

OBVERSION TABLE FOR CATEGORICAL STATEMENTS

A-form (All A is B)	becomes	E-form (No A is non-B)
E-form (No A is B)	becomes	A-form (All A is non-B)
I-form (Some A is B)	becomes	O-form (Some A is not non-B)
O-form (Some A is not B)	becomes	I-form (Some A is non-B)

EXERCISES

 **LEVEL**

Short Answers

1. What is an *immediate inference?*
2. Under what conditions would the statement "All P is Q" *not* imply the statement "Some P is Q"?
3. If it is known that the E-form of a statement is false, what do we know about the A-form of that statement?
4. If it is known that the O-form of a statement is true, what do we know about the A-form of that statement?
5. What is meant by *conversion?*
6. Which statement forms can be legitimately converted into the same statement form?
7. What is meant by *obversion?*
8. Which statement forms can be obverted? Which cannot?
9. How would the statement "All wizards know magic" be obverted?
10. How would the statement "No wizards know magic" be converted?

B   LEVEL

State the form of the following statements (A, E, I, or O). Assuming the original statement to be true, state whether the other three forms of the statements are true, false, or unknown.

1. All persons in attendance were carrying wallets.
2. No cookies were made with chocolate chips.
3. Some rap singers are true artists.
4. Some accountants are not punctual.
5. All salespersons meet their quotas.
6. No sailboats are over 300 feet long.

7. Some knowledge is a dangerous thing.

8. Some children are not over 5 feet tall.

9. All wizards are magicians.

10. Some people are not popular.

Convert the following statements:

11. No sculptors are skydivers.

12. Some trees are coniferous.

13. All kittens are lovable.

14. Some cans are not recyclable.

15. Some people who love classical ballet are not people who love modern dance.

16. No Model-T cars had automatic transmissions.

17. Some people who came late to the theater were not admitted.

18. Every day that I don't have to work is a day that I am extremely productive.

19. Just about every hand tool is good for a number of purposes.

20. Every TV commercial seeks to influence the viewer.

Obvert the following statements:

21. All doughnuts are tasty treats.

22. No pterodactyls are lazy beasts.

23. Some articles of clothing are useless.

24. Some bananas are not ripe.

25. Every scientific experiment is repeatable.

26. No polluted cities are desirable habitats.

27. Some children were curious.

28. Some automobiles are not electrically powered.

29. No one who heard the lecture remained unmoved.

30. First-place blue ribbons were not achieved by everyone.

C   LEVEL

The following syllogisms require some type of immediate inference to test them for validity. Figure out which immediate inferences must be made in order to evaluate the syllogisms and then evaluate them by the Rule Method of Chapter 6.

1. All mortals are imperfect beings and no humans are immortal, so it follows that all perfect beings are nonhumans.

2. Since no nonresidents are citizens and all citizens are nonvoters, it must be the case that all voters are residents.

3. Joe must have flunked the 401 class after all. Only those who passed 401 are in the 402 class and he is not in it.

4. It is simply false that all architects are good engineers. But it is true that they all know something about construction. This leads us to the conclusion that some people who know something about

construction are not good engineers.

5. Things that are inflammable are unsafe. So, things that are safe must be nonexplosive, since all explosives are flammable. (*Warning:* Be careful of definitions in this one.)

6. This painting can't possibly be by the master Steen because it is in watercolor and Steen only painted in oils.

7.2   ENTHYMEMES AND SORITES

An **enthymeme** is a syllogism with either a premise or a conclusion omitted. The omitted statement is implied. Usually, the omission occurs because the speaker assumes that the listener understands that the missing statement is part of the argument. For instance, consider the following argument:

> Pendleton must be an outstanding ballplayer. Anyone who was named MVP two years in a row would have to be.

This argument never explicitly mentions the fact that Pendleton won the MVP two years in a row. But this statement must clearly be assumed for the argument to make any sense. Put in categorical form the argument would read

> Anyone who was named MVP two years in a row would have to be an outstanding ballplayer.
> (Pendleton was named MVP two years in a row.)   Missing Premise
> _____
> Therefore: Pendleton must be an outstanding ballplayer.

The second or minor premise in this case is put in parentheses because it is assumed but not explicitly stated. Many times the missing premise or conclusion is obvious. But if we are aware of the fact that a statement is missing, we can employ the Rule Method of Chapter 6 to help us determine what might have been meant. (We are assuming here that the arguer is presenting her argument correctly.) We could apply this method to determine the missing premise as follows. The argument can be schematized as follows:

> All Class 1 (Players named MVP two years in a row) are Class 2 (Outstanding ballplayers)
> (Missing Premise)
> _____
> Therefore: All Class 3 (Pendleton—he's the only one in his "class") are Class 2

According to Rule 1, we need to have three classes or terms, each of which occurs twice. Class 2 shows up twice, but Classes 1 and 3 appear only once. So the missing premise should include Classes 1 and 3. But what should the relationship be between these classes? We have two options. We can either say "All Class 1 are Class 3" or "All Class 3 are Class 1." But if we state it as the first, "All players named MVP two years in a row are named Pendleton," we could be violating Rule 3(B) which states that any term distributed in the conclusion must be distributed also in the premises. Class 3 (Pendleton) would, in this case, be distributed in the conclusion but not in the premises. That leaves us with the second option "All Class 3 are Class 1" or "All Pendleton is a person who won the MVP two years in a row" or more simply "Pendleton won the MVP two years in a row." This being the case, the last statement adheres to all of the rules. We would therefore assume that it is the missing premise.

Sorites are simply chains of arguments that include enthymemes. When sorites are evaluated, they can be recast into individual syllogisms, the conclusion of one becoming the premise of the next. Consider the following argument from Lewis Carroll:

> Babies are illogical.
> No one who is despised can manage a crocodile.
> Illogical people are people who are despised.
> ──────────────────────────────
> Therefore: Babies cannot manage crocodiles.

To evaluate this line of reasoning we can recast it into several syllogisms. To form the first syllogism, we take the two premises that contain similar terms. In this case the first and the third. We form the premises of the first syllogism as follows:

> All babies are illogical.
> All illogical people are people who are despised.

By the Rule Method we can determine that the missing conclusion would have to be

> All babies are despised

since the alternative "All despised people are babies" would violate Rule 3(B), which states that anything distributed in the conclusion must also be distributed in the premises.

Combining this with the second premise, we can now formulate the second syllogism by using the conclusion of the first as a premise in the second:

> All babies are despised.
> No one who is despised can manage a crocodile.
> ──────────────────────────────
> Therefore: Babies cannot manage crocodiles.

By evaluating the two syllogisms we can determine that the conclusion of the original sorites must be legitimate.

SUMMARY

Step 6 of the Technique requires us to evaluate the forms or structures of arguments and to assess their validity. Categorical statements can be the subject of immediate inferences. An immediate inference is a

AN ENTHYMEME IN THE MARKET

Several years ago, a major fast food restaurant chain began a series of advertisements by urging people to *think* for themselves and to taste the difference between their hamburgers and those of their competitors, and *not* to be swayed by fancy advertising. Whereupon they closed the ad with the slogan: "The bigger the burger, the better the burger; the burgers are bigger at Burger King." Here is a perfectly valid enthymeme with a unstated conclusion. By "thinking for yourself" as they told you to do, you can come up with the conclusion all by yourself: "Ergo, the burgers are better at Burger King." They didn't even have to tell you; you figured it out all by yourself.

(Slogan reprinted courtesy of Burger King.)

truth that can be extracted from a categorical statement without the use of a syllogism. The square of opposition provides a diagram by which the truth or falsity of a statement can be determined given the truth or falsity of another statement with the same subject and predicate terms. Contraries are the A- and E-forms of categorical statements. Contraries cannot be true but may both be false. Subcontraries are the I- and O-forms of categorical statements. Subcontraries cannot both be false, but may both be true. Contradictions are opposed forms of categorical statements (A-form and O-form or E-form and I-form). Exactly one of the contradictory statements must be true and the other false. The subaltern of a universal statement is a particular statement. If the universal statement is true and the classes it represents contain at least one member, then the particular statement must also be true.

Conversion is the switching of the subject and predicate terms of a categorical statement. Obversion is the changing of affirmative statements to negative statements and negative statements to positive ones.

Enthymemes are categorical arguments with unstated premises or an unstated conclusion. A sorites is an argument composed of a string of categorical syllogisms, the conclusion of one becoming a premise for the next. Since sorites usually do not state the implied conclusions, they are examples of enthymemes.

EXERCISES

A   Level

True or False

* 1. ___F___ Enthymemes contain unstated premises, but the conclusion of an enthymeme is always explicitly stated.

* 2. ___T___ The unstated parts of an enthymeme are sometimes obvious.

* 3. ___T___ The unstated parts of an enthymeme can sometimes be determined by the Rule Method.
* 4. ___T___ Sorites are chains of reasoning based on categorical statements.
* 5. ___T___ Sorites include enthymemes.
* 6. ___T___ Sorites can be recast as a series of categorical syllogisms.
* 7. ___T___ "All good actors win an Oscar at least once and Sally Starr never once won an Oscar" is an example of an enthymeme.
* 8. ___T___ "All people are created equal. Sam is a citizen of Wisconsin and so is Sally. All citizens of Wisconsin are persons, so Sam and Sally must have been created equal." This argument is an example of a sorites.
* 9. ___F___ "Some Coloradans are Democrats and Gerry is a Coloradan, so Gerry is a Democrat" is an example of an enthymeme.
*10. ___F___ The argument in Exercise 9 is an example of a sorite.

B   LEVEL

The following arguments are all enthymemes that can be represented in syllogistic form. Put each of them into standard form and supply the missing conclusion or premise. Then determine whether or not each is a good argument by the Rule Method.

1. Andy's a politician, so he's looking out for himself.
2. This stuff must be good for us, it's natural food.
3. You just passed that state trooper at 90 mph. You're going to get a ticket.
4. I know these aren't rose bushes, they don't have any thorns.
5. Dr. K. can't be a reputable teacher because he's not listed in the *Encyclopedia of Reputable Professors*.
6. Vegetarians don't eat Bigga Burgers, and this is a Bigga Burger.
7. The *Journal* is an awful paper. But that is not the *Journal*.
8. Interest rates must be down: A lot more houses are for sale. (This one is difficult. Think in terms of time.)
9. It will rain today. I know because I just washed my car.
10. I know I'll get a bad grade in that class. After all, it is a Geology class.

Recast each of the following sorites as a series of categorical syllogisms. Then determine whether or not each is a good or bad argument.

11. Ronnie is a lawyer. She makes a lot of money. All lawyers argue well. So, anyone who argues well makes a good deal of money.
12. All good actors can play any role. Role-players are people who live well. Nancy is a good actor, so she must also be a good liar.
13. Whenever it rains the streets get wet, and whenever the streets get wet, there are many more accidents. On days that there are more accidents, the police department has much more work. So, on rainy days police departments have much more work to do.

14. I'm taking a Geology class. Classes in Geology require much memorization, and I'm really bad at memorizing things. When I can't memorize class material, I always get a bad grade in that class. So I guess I'll get a bad grade in Geology.

*15. Watching the television tends to deaden our imaginative powers. Peter's imaginative powers are almost nonexistent. Peter watches television whenever he gets the chance. So it must be the case that Peter's imagination was diminished by watching too much television.

C   LEVEL

1. Construct three examples of enthymemes and two sorites based on your own beliefs or experience. Then analyze each of them according to the Rules Method. If you determine that any of your examples are bad arguments, change them so that they turn out to be good arguments.

2. Construct Venn diagrams for each of the categorical syllogisms in Exercises 11 through 15 of Level B. Determine whether or not your evaluation of the Venn diagrams agrees with the answers you got according to the Rule Method.

CASE STUDY

A Brown Bag Lecture

Reasoning occurs at different levels of sophistication. Surely, most of us have attended a lecture, listened to a speech, or read a book where we sincerely wondered if the author were even using the same language. Individually, the words may each have made sense. But, put together as they were, they seemed intelligible beyond our comprehension. Let us look at how to apply the Critical Technique back to reasoning of this convoluted sort to show how it can be put into a standard form so that we can not only understand it, but are able to assess its worth.

While you are attending a "brown bag" lecture, the speaker says at one point:

> *I have definitely come to the conclusion that it is simply untrue that college-educated persons always make better voters and citizens than their nongraduate counterparts. It may be true that there is no way for a non-college-educated person to be exposed to the wealth of perspectives on current events that college-educated persons are. But, just because they are exposed to such a wealth of perspectives does not mean that necessarily all persons so exposed are inevitably better voters and citizens. . . .*

Applying the Technique to such a jumbled piece of reasoning, we first need to determine the major claim being advanced. Here, it is not totally clear whether the speaker intends the first sentence or the last one to be the major point. (We would have to listen to the rest of the speech to extract from the context which point seemed to be the main one.) If the indicator words are at all reliable, however, the first sentence, prefaced by the words "I have definitely come to the conclusion that. . .," is the stated conclusion based on the next two statements. If this analysis is correct then we can set forth this part of her argument as follows:

> *P–1: (It may be true that) There is no way that a noncollege-educated person is exposed to the wealth of perspectives on current events that college educated persons are.*
> *P–2: (But, just because they are exposed to such a wealth of perspectives does not mean that necessarily) all persons exposed to such a wealth of perspectives are better voters and citizens.*
>
> ───
>
> *C: (I have definitely come the conclusion that it is simply untrue that) College-educated persons always make better voters and citizens than their nongraduate counterparts.*

Schematically, the argument would be diagrammed according to the Technique as developed in Part 1:

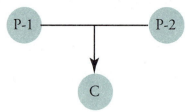

But, because the line connecting P–1 and P–2 shows that the two reasons are integrally connected in support of the conclusion, we can use the more sophisticated techniques developed in Part 2 to demonstrate and explore the relationship between the evidence presented and the claim itself. Now, according to the Technique, we need to determine whether the argument as explicitly stated is inductive or deductive. What we find is that all of the information contained in the conclusion is also contained in the premises. Our first indication, then, is that the argument is deductive in form. And, the premises *seem* to be put forth as if their truth guaranteed the truth of the conclusion. The question at this point is whether it would be a contradiction to agree that the premises are true (whether they in fact are or not) but to maintain that the conclusion could still be false. To make that determination, we need to take each of the statements individually and put them into a standard form that simplifies, yet preserves, their meaning.

> *P–1 says in effect that "No noncollege-educated person is a person who is exposed to the wealth of perspectives on current events that a college educated person is." We can abbreviate this: P–1: No [non CEP] is [PWIETTWOPOCE].*

P–2 says in effect that "It is not the case that all persons exposed to the wealth of perspectives on current events are better voters and citizens than their nongraduate counterparts." This can be abbreviated:

> *P–2: It is false that All [PWIETTWOPOCE] are [BVACTTNCEC].*

The conclusion, C, says the same thing as "It is not the case that college-educated persons are better voters and citizens than their nongraduate counterparts." This would be abbreviated:

C: It is false that All [CEP] are [BVACTTNCEC]

Now, putting the argument in standard form for syllogistic reasoning we have:

P–1: E No [non CEP] is [PWIETTWOPOCE].
P–2: O Some [PWIETTWOPOCE] is not [BVACTTNCEC] (from immediate inference that the A-form is false).

C: O Some [CEP] is not [BVACTTNCEC] (from immediate inference that the A-form is false).

Now, we can proceed to test the form of the argument to see what it really means and entails before we have to examine whether the content is true, relevant, fair, and adequate. Using our Rule Method, we can see from the foregoing that Rules 1 and 2 are broken to begin with, before we have even taken a look at the distribution for each term. Rule 1 is broken because we have four classes or terms: (1) non-CEP, (2) PWIETTWOPOCE, (3) BVACTTNCEC, and (4) CEP. Class 1 and class 4, however, are complementary classes, so we may be able to use obversion to reduce the number to three. Rule 2 is also broken insofar as there are three negative (E or O) statements in the argument. To that extent we could try obverting the first premise in order to have an argument of the form A O O, which is valid in a number of cases, depending on the placement of the middle term. But, before we obvert P–1, we will have to convert it first, since the term *non-CEP* is in the subject position and we cannot change it to the complementary class until it is in the predicate. That being the case, the argument would look something like this:

$$P–1: E \ no \ [non\text{-}CEP] \ is \ [PWIETTWOPOCE] \overset{convert}{\longrightarrow} E \ No \ [PWIETTWOPOCE] \ is \ [non\text{-}CEP] \overset{obvert}{\longrightarrow}$$

$$\overset{D}{} \quad \overset{U}{}$$
$$A \ All \ [PWIETTWOPOCE]_1 \ is \ [CEP]_2$$
$$\overset{U}{} \quad \overset{D}{}$$
$$O \ Some \ [PWIETTWOPOCE]_1 \ is \ not \ [BVACTTNCEC]_3$$

$$\overset{U}{} \quad \overset{D}{}$$
$$O \ Some \ [CEP]_2 \ is \ not \ [BVACTTNCEC]_3$$

According to the Rules Method, this form of argument is actually valid, because it has three classes or terms: (1) PWIETTWOPOCE, (2) CEP, and (3) BVACTTNCEC; because it has one O-statement in the premises and one O-statement in the conclusion: because the middle term, PWIETTWOPOCE, is distributed in at least one premise (here, it is the first premise); and because there is a term in the conclusion that is distributed (in this case it is the predicate term, BVACTTNCEC) and it is also distributed to the second premise. The corollary has not been violated either since one of the premises is a particular statement. (In this case, it is P–2, which is an O-statement.)

Now, putting this argument back in ordinary language, the initial convoluted argument says essentially the same thing as the following:

> Any person who is exposed to the wealth of perspectives on current events is a college-educated person and since persons who are so exposed to the wealth of perspectives on current events are not necessarily better voters and citizens, therefore some college-educated persons are not necessarily better voters and citizens than their nongraduate counterparts."

From here it is easier to critique the reasoning. Even though the reasoning is valid—if the premises are true, then the conclusion has to be true too—there may be some trouble with the truth and accuracy of the premises themselves. Surely, there are good grounds for believing that the first premise is false. One need only find a single example of a person who has been exposed to a wealth of perspectives on current events, but who is not a college-educated person, and that would destroy the truth of the first premise. Even so, P–1 is much more open to scrutiny because it is much more understandable in its reconstructed form than in the form it took originally: "there is no way that a non-college-educated person is." As we proceed, we will find that there are even easier techniques for portraying different structures of arguments that will make them that much easier to critically assess. This was one of the purposes of the critique: to increase our ability to process and understand information and reasoning and to increase thereby our power to deal more effectively with a wider variety of situations.

8

SYMBOLIZING STATEMENTS

step five
Are there any fallacies?

▼

step six
What is the argument's structure?

▼

step seven
What other conclusions can be drawn?

If triangles had a god,

he would have three sides.

—*Baron de Montesquieu (1791)*

When I search for man

in the technique and the

style of Europe, I see only

a succession of negations of man . . . .

—*Frantz Fanon (1961)*

KEY TERMS

Antecedent - The "if" part of a conditional statement. Symbolized, it is always placed to the left of the arrow.

Biconditional - Represented by a "⇔", a biconditional asserts that one component is true if and only if the other is true.

Conditional - Represented by a "⇒", a conditional or hypothetical statement asserts that if the first component (or antecedent) is true, then the second component (or consequent) is also true.

Conjunction - Represented by the symbol "&," a conjunction asserts that the two conjoined statements are both true.

Consequent - The "then" part of a conditional statement. Symbolized, it is always placed to the right of the arrow.

Disjunction - Represented by the symbol "▼," a disjunction asserts that one of the two component statements is true. If it is possible that both statements are true, the disjunction is said to be *inclusive*. If only one of the statements may be true, the disjunction is said to be *exclusive*.

Logical Connective - A term that connects statements together into a complex statement or that changes the truth value of a statement.

Necessary condition - A condition that must be present for another to occur. It is symbolized as the consequent of a conditional.

Negation - Represented by a "~", a negation asserts that the following statement is *false*.

Propositional logic - The study of relationships among specific assertions and denials and the assessment of the validity or invalidity of resulting argument forms.

Sufficient condition - A condition the presence of which is sufficient to conclude that another condition is also present. It is symbolized as the antecedent of a conditional.

Symbolic logic - The use of symbols to designate the logical connections between statements in order to assess the validity of arguments.

Truth value - Whether a statement is true or false.

Not all deductive arguments can be easily stated in categorical form. Many arguments consist of claims that can best be analyzed and assessed through the use of **propositional logic.** Propositional logic examines the relationships among the claims and conclusions of arguments. The premises of a propositional argument usually include premises composed of two or more claims connected by the terms *if . . . then, and, either . . . or* and *if and only if,* or modified by the term *not.* Each of these would be a complex statement. For instance, the statement

> It is raining and the streets are wet

is composed of two claims ("It is raining" and "The streets are wet") connected by the term *and.* Similarly, the statement

> If you pass the final exam, then you will pass the course

is composed of two claims: "You pass the final exam" and "You will pass the course" joined by the connective *If . . . then.*

It is important to learn to symbolize propositional arguments, since it is the argument's symbolic form that will determine whether or not the argument is a valid one. The form of a deductive argument determines that argument's *validity.* A valid deductive argument is one that is structured in such a way that if and only if all of the premises turn out to be true, *necessarily* the conclusion must be true. In an *invalid* deductive argument, the conclusion need not be true, even if all of the supporting premises are true. Valid deductive arguments give us a way of "extracting" information from information we already possess. For instance, if I know that "Whenever it rains, the streets get wet" and I also know that "The streets are not wet," I can validly "extract" from these two premises the information or conclusion that "It is not raining."

Because validity is determined by the patterns formed by the component statements of the argument, it is easier to represent an argument symbolically. By symbolizing the component statements and their connectives, the argument pattern can be more easily recognized. This is referred to as **symbolic logic.** Differentiating valid from invalid arguments can be of great practical benefit. Many of the decisions we make are the conclusions of arguments we offer ourselves or accept from others. Sound decisions cannot be made on the basis of fallacious reasoning.

Symbolization

In propositional logic, simple statements are symbolized with capital letters. Although these letters can be any of the 26, it is usually helpful to pick the first letter of an important word in the statement. So the statement "The Mississippi River is the longest in the United States" is best symbolized by a capital M, although any other letter will do equally well. But consistency is important. If M means that "The Mississippi River is the longest in the United States," we should not assign any other meaning to M and we should not let any other letter stand for the same statement. In this text, we will underline the word whose first letter is to symbolize the statement in which it is included. For instance, if we make the claim just stated, the word Mississippi will be underlined: "The <u>Mississippi</u> is the longest river in the United States." This tells us that we should symbolize the statement with the letter *M*.

Another important element of propositional logic is the logical connective. A **logical connective** is a term that connects statements to one another. The connectives we will study are *and, or, if . . . then, not,* and *if and only if.* These connectives determine the logical form of the resulting argument, and will help us to assess the validity or invalidity of the conclusion. The term *and* as well as its synonyms form statements that are known as **conjunctions. Disjunctions** result from the use of the connective *or. If . . . then* statements are known as **conditionals,** while the use of the term *not* turns the statement into a **negation.** (Strictly speaking, negations do not connect statements, they simply deny that the statement is true). Finally, *if and only if* is a connective that forms a **biconditional** from the component statements. The truth value of complex statements is determined not only by the truth value of its components, but by the rules applicable to that particular logical connective. The statement "Albany is the capital of New York *and* Albany is the capital of Georgia" is a complex statement that turns out to be false. On the other hand, "Albany is the capital of New York *or* Albany is the capital of Georgia" is a complex statement that is true. In the following sections we examine the basic rules for determining the truth value of complex statements.

Truth Values

When we talk about the **truth value** of a statement, we are talking about whether that statement is *true* or *false.* In Western logic we always assume that every statement is either one or the other, and is never both. (Logicians have studied and developed "multivalued logics" in which more than two truth values are recognized. This is an interesting topic in itself, but beyond the scope of this book.) This does not mean that we always know what this truth value is in a particular case, but only that it must be one or the other. And, remember, even false statements can be symbolized.

In the case of simple statements, the truth value can be determined by observation , or perhaps by "looking it up" or asking someone who knows. Sometimes we cannot determine the truth value of a statement, but hope that perhaps it might be determined in the future. (For instance "There is life on the planet Mars.") When we look at a *complex* statement, however, we need to know how its truth depends on the truth values of its component statements. Consider two statements, "Sacramento is the capital of California" and "Los Angeles is the capital of California." The former statement is true, but the latter is false. If we were to connect these statements with the term *and,* the resulting conjunction would be false. It is *false* to say that "Sacramento is the capital of California *and* so is Los Angeles, If, on the other hand, we were to form a disjunction by connecting these statements with the term *or,* the resulting statement would be true: *Either* Sacramento *or* Los Angeles is the state capital. In this chapter we also study the rules for determining the truth value of complex statements.

8.1 SYMBOLIZING CONJUNCTIONS AND DISJUNCTIONS

Conjunctions

The most easily understandable logical connective is the *conjunction.* It is usually represented in the English language by the word *and.* Its logical symbol is an ampersand (&). An ampersand has the function of connecting into a single statement two independent statements. For instance, if W means that "Washington D.C. is the capital of the United States" and M symbolizes "Moscow is the capital of Russia," we can

THE TECHNIQUE GOES HORIZONTAL

We have seen in Part 1 and up until now how the Technique uses *vertical* diagrams to display argument structures.

P
|
C

Now we can refine the Technique further to reflect the difference between simple and complex statements. This we can display *horizontally*. For example, note that statement A can be shown on its own line:

A

But, a complex statement, (A and B) or (A or B) or (If A, then B) can also be shown on the same line now (whereas heretofore we just gave the whole statement a letter or number):

(A & B)   (A ▼ B)   (A ⇒ B)   (~A)

This will allow us to capture the relationship between simple and complex statements or even that between two different complex statements in a way we could not do up until now. The reason for this will be seen as we get into the importance of being able to determine the deductive relationship between statements. Heretofore, we did not need to distinguish between good and

combine these two statements into the single statement W & M. The two statements do not need to refer to one another, nor do they even need to be on the same topic. We can combine such disparate statements as "Jupiter is the largest planet in our solar system" with a statement like "Alison expects to get a B in history" into a complex statement reading J & A. In a conjunction the *order* of the two letters does not really matter. Our last example could have as easily been rendered A & J.

The term *and* is not the only English term symbolized by an ampersand. There are several others. For instance, the term *but* is also symbolized by an ampersand. So are the terms *while, even though, even if, however, although, nevertheless, yet, still, moreover, in addition* and *whereas*. This should not be taken to mean that all of these terms have exactly the same function or meaning in the spoken language, but merely that they are *logically* equivalent. The difference can be made clear by considering the differences in the following two statements:

Lisa attended the meeting and so did Joey.
Lisa attended the meeting even though Joey also attended.

bad *forms* of argumentation (since we had not reached the level of "evaluating arguments" at that point). Now, it will be crucial for us to make these distinctions in order to be able to assess the value of any line of reasoning *from the standpoint of its structure*. For example, take two arguments, (A) and (B):

Given our initial way of representing arguments, both argument (A) and argument (B) would be represented identically:

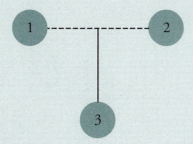

Note, however, that we would fail to recognize a very important difference between the structure of the two arguments, and we will need a slightly more sophisticated technique to show this.

Both of these statements are logically symbolized L & J, and they are logically equivalent. They both tell us that Lisa attended and that Joey attended as well. Thus the statement represented by L is true and the statement represented by J is also true.

But of course there is *some* difference in the meaning of the two sentences. The second implies that for some reason we might not have expected Lisa to attend given Joey's presence. This is not conveyed by our first sentence. The second sentence in effect gives us more information than the first. However, the logical structure of the two remains identical. The information that we "lose" when we formalize the second sentence is not important to its formal structure. (It may, however, be important to an argument's content. Remember Step 3 of the Technique where we consider what is being presupposed or assumed by the premises and Step 4, where we consider meaning.)

When symbolizing a statement as a conjunction, remember that a conjunction implies that *both* of the component statements are true and that their truth is independent of one another. The truth value of a conjunction depends on the truth values of its two components. A conjunction is true when, and only when, both of its conjuncts are true. A conjunction is false when either or both of its conjuncts are false.

The truth value of a conjunction is determined by the truth value of its component statements according to the following rule: A conjunction is true when and only when both of its component statements are true. Otherwise it is false. For example:

Albany is the capital of New York State while Atlanta is the capital of Georgia

is a *true* statement because both conjuncts are true. But

New York City is the capital of New York State while Atlanta is the capital of Georgia

is *false* because the first statement happens to be false. It would still be false if the second statement were also false. Symbolically, we can represent the truth values for the conjunction by letting a "T" stand for the fact that a statement is true and an "F" represent that a statement is false:

$$
\begin{array}{cccc}
T & \& & T & = T \\
T & \& & F & = F \\
F & \& & T & = F \\
F & \& & F & = F \\
\end{array}
$$

This shows that the only case in which a conjunction is true is when both of its conjuncts are true. Otherwise it is false.

Disjunctions

Another common connective is that represented by the phrase *either . . . or*. These are called *disjunctions* and are represented by a "▼" or "wedge." Either . . . or statements, or disjunctions, are not simply the combination of two previously known statements, as was the case with the conjunction. Instead they represent a more subtle relationship between the two statements joined by the wedge. A wedge tells us that we know that one or the other (or *perhaps* both) of the connected statements is true, but it does not indicate which one. (Remember that, in a conjunction, both statements are held to be true.)

Suppose, for example, that you remember that either Senator Moynihan or Senator Kennedy represents the state of New York, but you're not quite sure which. You can symbolize the statement "Either Senator Moynihan or Senator Kennedy represents the State of New York" as

M ▼ K

thus indicating that you believe that either M or K is a true statement, but that they are not *necessarily* both true.

When we connect statements with a disjunction, we are stating that *at least* one or the other statement is true. But what about the situation where *both* statements are true? For instance, the statement "Either Washington is the capital of the United States or Moscow is the capital of Russia" is a statement with two true disjuncts. Whether or not we count a disjunction with two true disjuncts as true depends on the type of disjunction we have in mind. An *exclusive* disjunction is one in which the possibility that both disjuncts are true is counted false. For instance, the statement "Either the National League team or the American League team will win the next World Series" is *not* meant to convey the possibility that both teams win, but that only one or the other—but not both—will win. The truth value of an exclusive disjunction is that it is true when either disjunct is true, but is false whenever both disjuncts turn out to be true or both turn out to be false.

An *inclusive disjunction,* on the other hand, takes into account the possibility that both disjuncts may be true. It essentially says "either this or that is true, or possibly both." The statement "Either Rome or Athens is a city in Georgia" is a true statement if meant as an inclusive disjunction. The truth value of an inclusive disjunction is that the inclusive disjunction is true whenever either or both of its disjuncts are true. It is false only when both of its disjuncts are false.

Disjunctions are true when *either* disjunct is true, and also when *both* disjuncts are true. (Remember, our characterization of *either . . .or* implies *either . . . or, or both.*) The only condition under which a disjunction is false is when both elements are false.

Thus,

> Either Albany or Atlanta is the capital of Georgia

is a true statement, and so is

> Either Albany is the capital of New York or Atlanta is the capital of Georgia

But the statement

> Either Albany or Macon is the capital of Georgia

is a false statement. Again using "T" to represent true statements and "F" to represent false statements, the truth calculations for disjunctions are as follows:

$$T \ \blacktriangledown \ T \ = T$$
$$T \ \blacktriangledown \ F \ = T$$
$$F \ \blacktriangledown \ T \ = T$$
$$F \ \blacktriangledown \ F \ = F$$

This shows that the only case in which a disjunction is false is when both disjuncts are false, otherwise it is true.

But there is a further complication here. We have already noted that disjunctions may be either *inclusive* or *exclusive.* The above truth calculations represent an inclusive disjunction. This means that either one or the other or perhaps even both of the disjuncts ae true. Sometimes, however, a disjunction is meant in the *exclusive* sense. An *exclusive* disjunction states that one or the other of the disjuncts is true *but not both.* The statement "Either Bush or Clinton won the presidential election of 1992" is *not* meant to imply that "perhaps both won." To show the difference, we will symbolize an exclusive disjunction by adding the symbolization for "but not both." So if we want to say "Either Bush or Clinton won the election of 1992" and we mean it to be an *exclusive* disjunction, we would *not* write

B ▼ C

since this would imply that perhaps both won. Rather, we would use parentheses to group these statements and add the proviso that "they did not both win" or ~(B & C). These two complex statements, moreover, would be connected with an ampersand resulting in the following symbolization :

(B ▼ C) & ~(B & C)

When symbolizing disjunctions it is therefore important to determine whether it was meant to be read inclusively or exclusively.

EXERCISES

   LEVEL

Short Answers

1. What is a conjunction?
2. What is a disjunction?
3. Describe the difference between an inclusive and an exclusive disjunction.
4. What is meant by the *truth value* of a statement?
5. For a conjunction to be true, what must be the truth values of the two conjuncts?
6. For a disjunction to be false, what must be the truth values of the two disjuncts?

True or False

* 7. ___F___ Disjunctions are false when either one of the disjuncts is false.
* 8. ___T___ Conjunctions are false when either one of the conjuncts is false.
* 9. ___T___ A conjunction is a complex statement which implies that both of its elements or conjuncts are true.
*10. ___T___ An exclusive disjunction is one in which either one or the other of the components or disjuncts is true, but not both.
*11. ___F___ An inclusive disjunction asserts that either both disjuncts are true or neither is true.
*12. ___F___ The symbol for a conjunction is the letter "v."
*13. ___F___ A disjunction may have only one disjunct.
*14. ___T___ The term *but* is usually an indication that the connected statements together form a conjunction.

*15. 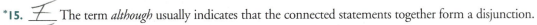 The term *although* usually indicates that the connected statements together form a disjunction.

*16. _____ The only way a conjunction can be true is if both its conjuncts are true.

B | **LEVEL**

Symbolize the following statements:

1. Stop or I'll shoot. (Let T = "I'll shoot")

2. It's raining and the streets are wet.

3. Blue and yellow are Sara's favorite colors.

4. Either green or orange is Marty's favorite color.

5. Nero fiddled while Rome burned.

Given the truth values of the following statements, give the resulting truth value of the complex statements that follow.

"Tom went to the concert" is a true statement.

"Jane went to the concert" is a false statement.

6. Jane went to the concert, while Tom did not.

7. Either Tom or Jane went to the concert .

8. Either Tom or Jane went to the concert, and Tom went to the concert while Jane did not.

"Red is Sara's favorite color" is a false statement.

"Orange is Sara's favorite color" is a true statement.

9. Either red or orange is Sara's favorite color.

10. Both red and orange are Sara's favorite colors.

C | **LEVEL**

Find a one-page passage from a textbook used for another course. List all of the conjunctions and disjunctions found on that page. For the disjunctions, be sure to state whether they are meant to be inclusive or exclusive disjunctions.

8.2 SYMBOLIZING NEGATIONS AND CONDITIONALS

The simplest type of complex statement is the negation. In fact, the tilde symbol (~) doesn't really "connect" two simpler statements, it "negates" the meaning of a statement for which we have already assigned a symbol. For instance, if we have already let the symbol P stand for the statement "Peter is chairperson of the advisory committee," we can symbolize the statement "Peter is *not* chairperson of the advisory committee" by placing a *tilde* before the statement's symbol: ~P. This is useful in that it shows the negative relationship between P and ~P that would not be apparent if we chose another letter (say, Q) to represent the negation of P. While the latter is allowable, strictly speaking, it would have the unwanted effect of concealing the relationship between the two closely related statements. Many of the rules discussed in the next chapter depend on the use of this symbol.

Strictly speaking, the tilde translates as the phrase "it is false that. . . ." But as long as the negated sentence means the same, it is allowable to insert the term *not* in the apppropriate place in the sentence. Be careful though. If J for instance means "Jill intends to make the trip to Minneapolis," ~J should be translated as "It is false that Jill intends to make the trip to Minneapolis." Otherwise it would not be clear which of the following statements would negate the original:

(1)   Jill does *not* intend to make the trip to Minneapolis,

or

(2)   Jill intends to *not* make the trip to Minneapolis.

Statement 1 tells us that Jill does not have any intention of making the trip (but might, perhaps, be talked into it). Statement 2, on the other hand, tells us that Jill has a specific intention, namely, to *not* make the trip. Since the context does not tell us which of these meanings is intended, it is simpler to render the negated statement:

(3)   It is false that Jill intends to make the trip to Minneapolis.

It should also be clear that if the statement represented by J turns out to be true, that represented by ~J must turn out to be false, and vice versa.

Negations have the opposite truth value of the statements they negate. So putting a tilde at the beginning of a statement changes its truth value. Thus the statement

Hillary Clinton is the president of the United States

is a false statement. But its negation

It is false Hillary Clinton is president of the United States

is a true statement. Symbolically, we can say that the negation of a true statement is false, while the negation of a false statement is true:

$$\sim T \ = \ F$$
$$\sim F \ = \ T$$

Double Negations

Perhaps when you were younger you were warned by your parents or a teacher that something you said was a *double negative*. While they may not have told you why this was wrong, it should be obvious at this point that the problem is a result of the fact that by negating a negation, an affirmative statement results. Consider the doubly negated statement:

It is *false* that Lagos is *not* the capital of Nigeria.

If we were to symbolize "Lagos is the capital of Nigeria as L, then the two negations would be symbolized as two tildes. As a result the preceeding statement would be symbolized as

~~L

But this is clearly equivalent to the statement L. We can indicate this truth value calculation by showing that two tildes cancel one another:

~~T = T
~~F = F

In those rare cases where there are more than two tildes, the rule is that every two cancel each other. As a result, an odd number of tildes leaves you with a negation, while an even number leaves you with an affirmative statement. [But, remember, do not cross the grouping parentheses: ~(~A ▼ B) contains *no* double negations.]

Conditionals

A conditional statement is a complex statement that expresses a hypothetical relationship between the truth values of its two component statements. The most common ordinary language phrase that is symbolized as a conditional is *if . . . then*. For instance, if I make the statement "If I wash my car, I'm sure it's going to start raining," I have expressed a conditional or hypothetical relationship between the statements "I wash my car" and "It will start raining." An arrow is used to express this relationship. The statement "If I <u>wash</u> my car, I'm sure it will start to <u>rain</u>" is symbolized

W ⇒ R

Unlike the conjunction and the disjunction, the order of the two components of a conditional statement is extremely important. It would be *wrong* in this case to symbolize this statement as

R ⇒ W

This would mean "If it starts raining, then I wash my car." In general, the statement that comes immediately after the word *if* goes to the left of the arrow. It is known as the **antecedent.** The statement that follows the term *then* goes to the right of the arrow (the arrow *always* points to the right) and is known as the **consequent.**

Ordinary language uses several terms and phrases other than *if . . . then* to express a conditional relationship. The following statements all express conditional relationships; each is a different way of saying "If someone wears a <u>hearing aid</u> then they have a hearing <u>problem</u>":

> <u>Whenever</u> someone wears a hearing aid, they have a hearing problem.
> <u>If</u> someone wears a hearing aid, they have a hearing problem.
> <u>Anyone</u> who wears a hearing aid has a hearing problem.
> <u>Should</u> someone wear a hearing aid, they have a hearing problem.
> Only people with hearing problems wear hearing aids.
> Someone has a hearing problem <u>if</u> they wear a hearing aid.

Notice that the order of the two statements in the actual sentence does not matter. Our only concern is to determine which statement follows the term *if* or its equivalent. The term *when* can also indicate a conditional, but only when it is used in the sense of *whenever.* For instance, the statement "When Nancy learned she had a hearing problem, she purchased a hearing aid" is *not* a conditional statement because the term *when* refers to a particular time and does not mean *whenever.*

While the conditional may *seem* to express a "causal" relationship between the antecedent and the consequent, this is not necessarily the case. What a conditional states is simply that *if* the antecedent is true, then so is the consequent. It *does not* mean that the antecedent somehow causes the consequent. It might be the case, for instance, that I only wash my car on cloudy days because my owner's manual tells me it's better for the car's finish not to wash it on sunny days. So on the days I choose to wash my car, there happens to be a better chance of rain. But it would be wrong to conclude that somehow my washing my car causes it to rain. That would constitute a Fallacy of Assuming the Cause. To cite another example, I might correctly believe the statement that "If a woman is wearing a hearing aid, she has a hearing problem." But we would not want therefore to conclude that wearing the hearing aid is the cause of her problem.

Conditionals are useful in that they allow us to connect the information conveyed by the component statements to make predictions about the consequences of our actions. When a conditional is a true reflection of reality, it helps us to respond appropriately to problematic situations. Anyone who happened to be ignorant of the conditional "If it runs out of gas, my car will stop running" probably would not pay attention to their gasoline gauge and find themselves bemoaning the fact that their automobile turned out to be such a "lemon."

The truth values of conditionals are not as intuitively obvious as those of other connectives. They can be easily determined, however, by using the following example. Suppose that you just purchased a new automobile. The auto dealer gives you the following guarantee (which we'll simplify for purposes of this example):

> If the car <u>breaks</u> down, the dealer will <u>fix</u> it for free.

This can be symbolized

$$B \Rightarrow F$$

The truth values can be determined by looking at the possibilities of B and F being true, and in each case determining whether the auto dealer has kept his bargain. For instance, assume that the car breaks down, and the dealer fixes it for free. B is true, and F is true. The dealer kept the bargain, and so the truth value of the conditional as a whole is true.

Now suppose that the car breaks, but the dealer doesn't fix it. B is true but F is false. In this case the dealer is clearly not fulfilling the guarantee, so the resulting conditional is false. In fact, this will turn out to be the only case where a conditional is false: when its antecedent is true and its consequent false.

It is also sometimes the case that a car is recalled by the dealer to correct possible problems that may not yet have manifested themselves. In this example, the car did not break (so B is false) but the dealer "fixed" it anyway (making F true). Again, since the dealer did not break any promises, the resulting conditional is true.

If B and F are both false, this would indicate that the car did *not* break down, and the dealer did *not* fix it. But the dealer has not done anything wrong in this case. This leads to the curious result that *when both the antecedent and the consequent of a conditional are false, the resulting conditional is true.* This is known in logic as a *counterfactual* and is the subject of much debate among logicians. In everyday discussions it is most often used to indicate the falsehood of an antecedent. For instance, someone might say: "If she's a good cook, then I'm a monkey's uncle." Since a person making such a statement clearly cannot be a monkey's uncle, the statement is taken to indicate (by *modus tollens*) that the person in question is *not* very good in the kitchen.

So the only time a conditional is false is when the antecedent is true and the consequent is false. In all other cases, the conditional is considered true. We can summarize the truth values of the conditional as follows.

$$T \Rightarrow T = T$$
$$T \Rightarrow F = F$$
$$F \Rightarrow T = T$$
$$F \Rightarrow F = T$$

If this seems a bit strange, try to remember that in a conditional, we are not saying that either element *is* true, but merely that the truth of one is dependent on the other.

Necessary and Sufficient Conditions

Some conditionals are not as easily symbolized as those we just examined. In these cases the term *if* or its equivalent may not even occur in the sentence we are trying to symbolize. Often the component statements of these sentences can be symbolized by determining whether they are necessary or sufficient conditions for one another. Consider the following conditional statement:

> In order to be <u>president</u> of the United States, it is necessary for a person to be at least <u>thirty-five</u> years old.

This true conditional states that a person *must* be at least thirty-five years old in order to be president. The question is, how should we symbolize this conditional in order to "capture" this fact. Consider the two alternatives:

(1)   T $\Rightarrow$ P
(2)   P $\Rightarrow$ T

Now remember that even though the phrase *if . . . then* does not appear in the original statement, we should be able to place it in the statement correctly when we translate it back into ordinary language. If we do this, statement 1 becomes

(1)   If a person is at least thirty-five years old, then he or she is president of the United States.

But this is clearly not what was intended by the original statement. If we were to symbolize our original statement T $\Rightarrow$ P we would be making the clearly absurd statement that anyone who was at least thirty-five years of age was president of the United States.

Statement 2, however, would be translated as

(2)   If a person is president of the United States, then he or she is at least thirty-five years old.

This second statement captures the meaning we intended with our original statement. The statement T, which means that a person is at least thirty-five years old, is a *necessary* condition for being president. This leads to our first rule concerning necessary and sufficient conditions.

A necessary condition is always a consequent and is placed to the right of the arrow.

In the following examples, the underlined statements are the necessary conditions for the nonunderlined statements:

You have to break an egg in order to make an omelet.
Before a team can play in the World Series, it must win its league championship series.
High fevers always accompany cases of the measles.
A student can graduate only if she has attained at least 120 credits.

Notice that the last sentence contains the phrase *only if* and that this phrase introduces a **necessary condition**, which is thus symbolized and placed to the *right* of the arrow. This is an important exception to the rule stated earlier: that what follows the term *if* is always placed to the *left* of the arrow. We must therefore modify that rule to read as follows:

The phrase *only if* introduces a *necessary condition* and the statement that follows it becomes the consequent and is placed to the *right* of the arrow. But if the term *if* is not preceded by the term *only,* the statement that follows remains the antecedent.

So if I know that a person is president, I know that he is at least thirty-five, because being thirty-five is a necessary condition for being president. But this also means that the knowledge that one is president is a

sufficient condition for concluding that he is at least thirty-five. Being president is *not* a necessary condition for being thirty-five (if that were so, the president would be the only person to attain that age), but it is a sufficient condition. So our second rule is:

> A sufficient condition is always an antecedent and is placed to the left of the arrow.

A sufficient condition is one that justifies our belief in the truth of the consequent. In the following statements, the sufficient conditions are underlined:

> <u>An apple a day</u> keeps the doctor away.
> <u>Should Socrates drink the goblet of hemlock,</u> he will die.
> <u>If she has the measles,</u> then she is running a high fever.

Notice that the last statement is simply a restatement of one of the examples of necessary conditions given earlier. This is because necessary and sufficient conditions complement one another. In fact, in any conditional statement, regardless of the phrases used to introduce the component statements, the antecedent can always be seen as the sufficient condition, while the consequent can similarly be viewed as the necessary condition. This can be summarized by the following schema:

> Sufficient condition $\Rightarrow$ Necessary condition

or

> If Y is a necessary condition for X,
> then X is a sufficient condition for Y.

and

> If X is a sufficient condition for Y,
> then Y is a necessary condition for X.

Other Problems.

Some terms are difficult to symbolize and cannot be easily analyzed in terms of necessary and sufficient conditions. For instance, consider the terms *unless* and *without*. Assuming that P means that Phil goes on the picnic and J means that Jane goes, the following statement

> Jane won't go on the picnic unless Phil goes too

or

> Jane won't go to the picnic without Phil

WOULD IT HOLD UP IN COURT?

Often in ordinary language we use the phrase *only if* to mean *if and only if,* when technically it does not. The latter indicates both necessary and sufficient conditions, but the former indicates only a necessary condition.

"YOU CAN HAVE DINNER ONLY IF YOU CLEAN UP YOUR ROOM!"

If little "Howie" here takes his parent to mean that he can't have dinner unless he cleans his room *AND* that he can have dinner when he finishes cleaning his room, then he may be in for a rude awakening. The first half of what he understands is correct: He cannot have his dinner if he does not clean his room (assuming the parent is willing to back up the threat). But the second half is not warranted by what the parent actually says. In other words, the parent would not be lying if Howie were to clean up his room and still not get to eat dinner.

While this may not be an earth-shattering consequence in the contrived scenario of Howie and his parent, it may behoove us to check out the contracts we sign a little more closely, now that we are aware of this feature of the words, *only* and *only if.*

should be read

> If Phil doesn't go on the picnic, Jane won't go

and should be symbolized

> $\sim P \Rightarrow \sim J$

In general, the terms *unless* and *without* should be translated as *if not.*

EXERCISES

A   LEVEL

Short Answers

1. What is a negation?
2. What is a conditional?
3. Describe the relationship between the antecedent and the consequent of a conditional statement.
4. Under what conditions is a conditional false?

True or False

* 5. ___T___ A counterfactual is a conditional with a truth value of true but whose antecedent and consequent are both false.
* 6. ___F___ "If the moon were made of green cheese, then Washington, D.C., is the capital of the United States" is an example of a counterfactual.
* 7. ___F___ A necessary condition always becomes the antecedent of a conditional.
* 8. ___F___ A sufficient condition may or may not become the consequent of a conditional.
* 9. ___F___ Statements connected by the phrase *only if* are symbolized in the same way as statements connected by the term *if.*
*10. ___F___ A tilde is a symbol connecting two or more statements.
*11. ___T___ A conditional statement asserts that if the antecedent is true then the consequent must also be true.
*12. ___F___ "Jim decided to accept the new job whether or not it paid the same as his current job" is an example of a conditional statement.

B   LEVEL

Symbolize the following statements:

1. If <u>Clinton</u> is reelected, then <u>Gore</u> will still be vice president in 1998.
2. If you can't do the <u>time</u>, then don't do the <u>crime</u>.
3. The insurance company will give you lower <u>rates</u>, but only if you stop <u>smoking</u>.
4. If you are out of <u>sugar</u>, you may substitute <u>honey</u> in this recipe.
5. Whenever I watch a <u>movie</u> by Ingmar Bergman, I begin to question the meaning of my <u>life</u>.
6. Anyone who watches too much <u>television</u> does not get a chance to use his or her <u>imagination</u>.
7. <u>Exercising</u> regularly is a necessary condition for remaining <u>healthy</u>.
8. Not being <u>color-blind</u> is a sufficient condition for enjoying the <u>works</u> of Dali .
9. Should you misplace your <u>passport</u>, you should <u>report</u> it as lost.
10. Sign up for the <u>course</u> only if you are prepared to <u>work</u>.

Given the truth values of the following statements, give the resulting truth value of the complex statements that follow.

"Tom went to the concert" is a true statement.

"Jane went to the concert" is a false statement.

11. If Tom went to the concert, then so did Jane.

12. Tom went to the concert, if Jane did.

13. Tom and Jane did not both go to the concert.

14. If Jane did not go to the concert, then neither did Tom.

15. Jane went to the concert only if Tom did not.

C   LEVEL

Construct four or five complex statements using both true and false statements. Determine the truth value of each. Then determine how changes in the truth conditions of the component statements will affect the truth conditions of the complex statements. (You may use a truth table to help you determine the various truth conditions and their effects.)

8.3 SYMBOLIZING BICONDITIONALS

One particular type of conditional must be considered separately. It is called a *biconditional* because, in effect, each of the statements is both a necessary and sufficient condition for the other. Let's consider two simple conditionals and see how they can be combined into a biconditional .

(1)   If Sam goes to the party, then so will Phyllis.

(2)   Phyllis will go to the party only if Sam goes.

The first sentence states that Sam's going to the party is a sufficient condition for Phyllis's going. But it does *not* say that it is a necessary condition. If we take sentence 1 by itself we can conclude that if Sam is there, then so is Phyllis. But Sam does not need to be there in order for Phyllis to come. Even if he's not there, Phyllis might come anyway (since his coming is not a necessary condition).

Sentence 2, however, says that Sam's coming to the party is a necessary condition for Phyllis's coming. As far as Phyllis is concerned (according to sentence 2), Sam needs to be there in order for her to show up. To put it another way, Phyllis won't come unless Sam does too. Now if we put these two sentences together (and change the wording just a bit) we have a combined sentence which reads.:

(3)   Phyllis will go the party *if and only if* Sam goes.

According to this third, combined sentence, Phyllis's going is both a necessary and sufficient condition for Sam's going. But this also means that Sam's going is both a necessary and sufficient condition for Phyllis's going. We would symbolize sentence 3 with a double arrow:

$$P \Leftrightarrow S$$

This shows that P and S are both necessary and sufficient conditions for one another. This being the case, the order of the letters does not really matter. It should be noted that

$$P \Leftrightarrow S$$

is logically equivalent to

$$(P \Rightarrow S) \ \& \ (S \Rightarrow P)$$

Translated back into English, this last statement would read

> If Phyllis goes to the party then Sam will go, and
> if Sam goes then Phyllis will go.

In other words, a biconditional is really just a *conjunction* of two conditionals with the same statement on opposite sides of the arrow.

The phrase *if and only if* is not the only one that is symbolized by a biconditional. The following statements are also symbolized as biconditionals.

> A team wins the World Series *just in case* it wins four games.
> Having 120 credits and a C average is a *necessary and sufficient* condition for graduating.
> Phyllis won't go *unless* Sam goes and Sam won't go *unless* Phyllis does.

In a biconditional, one element is true *if and only if* the other element is true. As a result, either element is false *if and only if* the other element is false. The truth values of biconditionals are easy to remember. A biconditional is true when its two truth values are the same, and false when its truth values are different.

To understand the truth conditions for the biconditional, it is helpful to consider the example of a mother promising her young son that "You can <u>watch</u> TV tonight if and only if you do your <u>homework</u>." We'll symbolize this as "W ⇔ H." As in our example for the conditional, we'll assume that the conditional is true if the mother keeps her promise, and false if she doesn't.

The first case to consider is when the child does his homework and is allowed to stay up late to watch TV. Both W and H are true in this instance, and the mother has kept her promise. Similarly, if the child does not do his homework, we would expect his mother *not* to allow him to watch television. Both W and H are false in this instance, but the biconditional is true because the child's mother again did not break her promise.

But if the child does not do his homework, yet his mother allows him to watch television anyway, we would say that she has gone back on her word. W is true and yet H is false. So the biconditional in this case turns out to be false. It also turns out to be false when W is false but H is true: The child did his homework but his mother does not allow him to watch television. In this case we might want to say that the mother broke her promise to her son. So again the biconditonal turns out to be false. We can summarize the truth conditions for the biconditional as follows:

$$T \Leftrightarrow T = T$$
$$T \Leftrightarrow F = F$$
$$F \Leftrightarrow T = F$$
$$F \Leftrightarrow F = T$$

Statements with More Than One Connective

Sometimes a complex sentence will have more than one logical connective and more than two statements. When this happens it is important to "group" the appropriate statements together using *groupers*. Groups are essentially parentheses "( )" but can also be brackets "[ ]". For example, consider the sentence:

If <u>Anne</u> and <u>Jill</u> attend the party, then so will <u>Peter</u>.

First of all, we should notice that the sentence, taken in its entirety, is a *conditional*. It does not say that Anne, Jill, or even Peter will attend the party. What it *does* say is that *if* Anne and Jill do, *then* so will Peter. "Anne attends and Jill attends" thus becomes the antecedent of the conditional, and "Peter attends" becomes the consequent. Since the antecedent is itself a conjunction, it should be symbolized as such. The resulting conditional looks like this:

$$(A \ \& \ J) \Rightarrow P$$

It would be wrong, however, to symbolize this conditional as

$$A \ \& \ (J \Rightarrow P)$$

This second symbolization says in effect that Anne *will* attend, and that Peter's attending depends on Jill also showing up. But this is not what the original statement intended. In trying to symbolize these complex statements, you should remember three things:

1. Look at the sentence as a whole, and try to determine what type of sentence it is (conditional, conjunction, etc.).
2. No more than two letters and one symbol (tildes excluded) should appear within any two parentheses.
3. The sentence as a whole should be considered as "grouped," but the outermost parentheses may be dropped unless there is a tilde that applies to the whole sentence.

This last point needs some explanation. Sometimes we may want to negate statements within the sentence and other times we may want to negate the entire sentence. Consider the following two statements:

(1)   If <u>Peter</u> doesn't go to the party, <u>Jane</u> will.

(2)   It is false to say that if <u>Peter</u> doesn't go to the party, <u>Jane</u> will.

The resulting symbolizations would be:

(1)   ~P ⇒ J

(2)   ~(~P ⇒ J)

Sentences that require a tilde outside of the outermost parentheses (or other groupers) usually begin with the phrase "It is false that . . ." or "It is untrue that . . ."

SUMMARY

In this chapter we studied the ways in which simple statements could be joined with other simple statements to form complex statements. This is an important component of Step 6 of the Technique, since it allows us to determine the validity or invalidity of argument forms composed of the resulting statements. Simple statements are symbolized by a capital letter. The symbols that "hold" the complex statements together are known as *connectives* and correspond to the ordinary language words *and, either...or, not, if...then,* and *if and only if.* Complex statements connected by the word *and* are known as *conjunctions* and the simple statements that are connected are called *conjuncts.* They are symbolized by an ampersand or "&." Disjunctions are simple statements connected by the phrase *either . . . or* and their component statements are called *disjuncts. Disjunctions* are symbolized by a wedge or "▼." *Negations* are simple statements to which the equivalent expression *it is false that* or *not* is added. The tilde or "~" symbolizes negations. Unlike the other connectives, the tilde goes *before* the simple statement it modifies.

If . . . then statements are called *conditionals.* They are symbolized by arrows that always point to the right: "⇒." In a conditional the antecedent or statement to the left of the arrow is the sufficient condition of the consequent, which is always placed to the right of the arrow. The consequent is said to be a necessary condition for the antecedent. A biconditional is a special form of the conditional in which each simple statement is both the necessary and sufficient condition of the other. Biconditionals are symbolized by double arrows. "⇔."

In this chapter we also studied the truth value conditions for complex statements. Conjunctions are true only when both conjuncts are true, and are false in every other case. Disjunctions are false only when both disjuncts are false, and are true in every other case. Negations have truth values opposite in truth value to the negated statement without the tilde. Conditionals are false only when the antecedent is true and the consequent is false. They are true in all other cases. Finally, the biconditional is true when both elements are true. It is also true when both elements are false. A biconditional is false when its two components have opposite truth values.

EXERCISES

A   LEVEL

Short Answers

  *1. What is a biconditional?

  *2. Define a necessary condition.

  3. What is a sufficient condition?

  4. How does a conditional differ from a biconditional?

True or False

  *5. __T__ In a biconditional, each component statement is a necessary condition of the other.

  *6. __F__ A biconditional differs from a conditional in that a biconditional must have two component statements while a conditional requires only one.

  *7. __F__ The phrase 'only if' when used in a complex statement is a sure indication that we are dealing with a biconditional.

  *8. __F__ The statement "If <u>Vinny</u> and <u>Natasha</u> go to the party then so will <u>Louis</u>" can be correctly symbolized as V & (N ⇒ L).

B   LEVEL

Symbolize the following conditional statements and negations using the first letters of the underlined words to symbolize the appropriate statement.

  *1. If you give me the <u>directions,</u> I can find the <u>house.</u>

  2. <u>Cindy</u> can come, provided that we also invite <u>Jack.</u>

  3. If you want to make a <u>cake mix,</u> you have to add <u>eggs.</u>

  4. Whenever <u>Pete</u> shows up at a party, <u>Lisa</u> usually shows up to.

  5. If <u>Jill</u> doesn't come to school today, I can't <u>repay</u> her the money I owe her.

  6. I will <u>repay</u> her the money I owe her, provided <u>Jill</u> does come to school today.

  *7. I can't get a <u>job</u> without <u>experience.</u>

  8. Unless you get 120 <u>credits,</u> you can't <u>graduate.</u>

  *9. Only <u>dog owners</u> know how much of a <u>mess</u> a dog can make when left alone.

  10. The manufacturer guarantees that if the product should fail to <u>operate</u> it will be <u>repaired</u> free of charge.

*11. The statement that neither <u>Olivia</u> nor <u>Gerry</u> will attend the party is false.

12. It is untrue that either <u>Kennedy</u> or <u>Eisenhower</u> is currently president.

*13. We can visit <u>Paris</u> or <u>Rome,</u> but not both.

14. Either we both go, or no one goes. (Let Y = "you go" and I = "I go.")

*15. It is not true that only <u>Republicans</u> are <u>conservatives.</u>

16. The party will be a <u>success</u> if and only if you don't invite both <u>Lisa</u> and <u>Jill.</u>

*17. A society can only be called a <u>Utopia</u> if it can boast of no <u>crime</u> or <u>poverty.</u>

Symbolize the following statements:

18. Either I'm <u>mistaken</u> or it's not <u>raining.</u>

*19. It's not <u>raining</u> and the streets are not <u>wet.</u>

20. It's not <u>raining,</u> but the streets are <u>wet</u> anyway.

*21. Either <u>green</u> or <u>orange</u> is Marty's favorite color, while <u>purple</u> is Barbara's favorite.

22. Neither <u>wealth</u> nor <u>fame</u> can ensure happiness, and neither can a life of <u>pleasure.</u>

*23. I'd like to be either <u>wealthy</u> or <u>famous,</u> and I'd also like to have as much <u>fun</u> as I can.

24. We can visit either <u>Paris</u> and <u>Rome</u> or <u>Timbuktu</u> and <u>Lagos.</u>

*25. We can visit either <u>Paris</u> or <u>Rome</u> and either <u>Timbuktu</u> or <u>Lagos.</u>

26. If the <u>Spurs</u> win their division championship, they will be league <u>champions</u> only if they can defeat the <u>Pistons.</u>

*27. Winning <u>four</u> games is a necessary condition for a team's winning the <u>World</u> Series.

28. While the <u>Spurs</u> will probably win their division championship, they will be league <u>champions</u> only if they can defeat the <u>Pistons.</u>

*29. Although the Democrats control <u>Congress,</u> if the Republicans control the <u>presidency</u> then they control the <u>Supreme</u> Court as well.

30. A team wins the <u>World Series</u> if and only if they win <u>four</u> of its games.

*31. If anyone who is <u>liberal</u> is a <u>Democrat,</u> then anyone who is <u>conservative</u> is a <u>Republican.</u>

32. Only <u>Democrats</u> are <u>liberal.</u>

*33. <u>Phil</u> is planning to attend and so is <u>Rebecca,</u> provided of course that <u>Denise</u> isn't invited.

34. If I buy the <u>Ford</u> no one will be <u>impressed,</u> but if I purchase the <u>Mercedes</u> all my yuppie friends will be <u>jealous.</u>

*35. <u>C</u> is a sufficient condition for <u>D,</u> provided that <u>B</u> is a necessary condition for <u>A.</u>

36. According to <u>Gautama,</u> if you can stop having <u>desires</u> you can stop <u>suffering.</u>

*37. In order to be <u>president</u> a person must be at least <u>thirty-five</u> years old.

38. Winning the <u>seventh</u> game is a sufficient condition for winning the <u>World</u> Series.

*39. A person is eligible to serve on a <u>jury</u> only if he or she is registered to <u>vote.</u>

40. Only the people who enjoyed the play <u>Hamlet</u> would appreciate <u>King Lear.</u>

Translate the following symbolized statements into meaningful English sentences:

Y = Yellow is Lisa's favorite color.

G = Blue is Lisa's favorite color.

41. Y ▼ G

42. Y ▼ ~G

43. G ⇒ ~Y

44. G & ~Y

45. G ⇔ ~Y

46. G & (G ⇒ ~Y)

R = It is raining.
W = I wash my car.

47. W ⇒ R

48. R ⇒ W

49. W & R

50. ~W ▼ R

51. R ⇔ W

52. ~R ⇔ ~W

C   LEVEL

Find an argument in a magazine article and try to symbolize the premises and the conclusion using the symbols learned in this chapter.

CASE STUDY

Aiding Upper Slobovia

We can continue to refine our Technique to handle arguments in greater complexity. The steps of the Technique discussed and developed in Part 1 were designed principally to display the "vertical" structure of arguments. That is, we were concerned with showing which claims followed from which pieces of evidence and the "arrows down" portrayed which "becauses" led to which "therefores." But as we increase the complexity of the argument forms we need to be able to show that complexity "horizontally " as well. For instance, a single, simple statement is displayed by a single, simple symbol on a line by itself. Now, we need to be able to display the complex statement forms discussed in Chapter 8 on the same line. Let us then look at an argument that has been compressed from several pages into the following rather terse prose.

If the United States sends aid to Upper Slobovia, then U.S. resources at home will be diminished. And, if the United States sends aid to Upper Slobovia and domestic resources are diminished, then either the United States will experience its own domestic shortage or troubles will emerge somewhere else in the U.S. economy. If either of these troubles emerges somewhere else in the U.S.

economy or the United States experiences its own shortage, then economic conditions in the Unit-ed States will worsen. If economic conditions in the United States worsen, then either the reces-sion will sharpen or the workforce will experience rising unemployment. If troubles emerge else-where in the U.S. economy, the recession will sharpen. If either the recession in the United States sharpens or the workforce experiences rising unemployment, then the U.S. stock markets will decline severely. Public confidence in the new administration will be eroded, unless the U.S. stock markets do not decline seriously. Also, if the recession in the United States sharpens, then the poor, the homeless, and the elderly will be hurt tremendously. If the United States sends aid to Upper Slobovia, then it will not experience its own domestic shortage. Thus, if the United States sends aid to Upper Slobovia, then its poor, its homeless, and elderly citizens will be hurt and also the public confidence in the new administration will be eroded. And so, if the United States does not want to hurt its poor, homeless, and elderly, and it does not want to erode public confidence in the new administration, then it will not send aid to Upper Slobovia.

Now, we could diagram this argument using earlier techniques from Part 1, but much of the interrelated-ness of the premises would be lost if we were to miss the deductive relationships obtained between the given statements. Accordingly, we will let a letter of the alphabet, beginning with the letter "A," stand for each simple statement in the argument. We could have used the same form of symbolization used earlier in the chapter, underlining the key word or phrase and using the first letter as the symbol, but the "alphabetical" method will work just as well if not better for a longer or protracted argument.

A = The U.S. sends aid to Upper Slobovia.
B = U.S. resources at home (domestic resources) will be diminished.
C = The U.S. will experience its own domestic shortage.
D = Troubles will emerge elsewhere in the U.S. economy.
E = Economic conditions in the U.S. will worsen.
F = The recession in the U.S. will sharpen.
G = The workforce will experience rising unemployment.
H = U.S. stockmarkets will decline severely.
I = Public confidence in the new administration will be eroded.
J = The poor, the homeless, and elderly U.S. citizens will be hurt tremendously.

At this point we have a symbol for each of the individual, simple statements in the argument. We now have to read back through the argument and take each statement, one at a time, and display it on its own line, whether simple or complex. The result for this particular argument is shown thusly:

1. A⇒B   Given
2. (A & B) ⇒(C ▼ D)   Given
3. (C ▼ D)⇒E   Given
4. E⇒(F ▼ G)   Given
5. D⇒F   Given
6. (F ▼ G)⇒H   Given

7. ~(~H)⇒I   Given
8. F⇒J   Given
9. A⇒~C   Given

Thus, 10. A ⇒ (I & J)

As we proceed, we shall try to show the benefits of being able to portray the structure of arguments in this fashion. One immediate and tangible practical use, for example, is the facility it affords in working the seemingly intractable pieces of reasoning one may find on standardized tests. A second benefit is the simplification that results in being able to digest long, complex reasoning in any field and make it manageable, easier to understand, and easier to evaluate.

9

ARGUMENT FORMS

step five
Are there any fallacies?

▼

step six
What is the argument's structure?

▼

step seven
What other conclusions can be drawn?

"She would of been a good woman,"
the Misfit said, "if it had been
somebody there to shoot her
every minute of her life."
—*Flannery O'Connor (1955)*

"If I can go in there
and clean them toilets,
why can't I use them?"
—*Annie Adams (1958)*

KEY TERMS

Affirming the consequent - An invalid argument of the form A $\Rightarrow$ B, B therefore A.

Affirming a disjunct - An invalid argument of the form A ▼ B, A therefore ~B.

Broken chain - An invalid argument form in which the consequent of neither conditional premise is identical to the antecedent of the other. For instance, A $\Rightarrow$ B, C $\Rightarrow$ D therefore A $\Rightarrow$ D.

Chain argument - A valid argument of the form A $\Rightarrow$ B, B $\Rightarrow$ C therefore A $\Rightarrow$ C.

Complex dilemma - A valid argument of the form A ▼ B, A $\Rightarrow$ C, B $\Rightarrow$ D, therefore C ▼ D.

Conjunctive argument -A valid argument of the form ~(A & B),A therefore ~B.

Denying a conjunct - An invalid argument of the form ~(A & B), ~A therefore B.

Denying the antecedent - An invalid argument of the form A $\Rightarrow$ B, ~A therefore ~B.

Disjunctive argument - A valid argument of the form A ▼ B, ~A therefore B.

Invalid arguments - Deductive arguments in which the conclusion is not necessarily true even if all the premises should turn out to be true.

Modus ponens - A valid argument of the form A $\Rightarrow$ B, A therefore B.

Modus tollens - A valid argument of the form A $\Rightarrow$ B, ~B therefore ~A.

Simple dilemma - A valid argument of the form A ▼ B, A $\Rightarrow$ C, B $\Rightarrow$ C therefore C.

Sound argument - A valid argument in which all of the premises are in fact true. The conclusion of a sound argument *must* be true.

Valid arguments - Deductive arguments in which if and only if all the premise all turn out to be true, does the conclusion *have* to be true.

Having learned to symbolize statements, you are now at the point where you can use your symbolization skills to determine the *propositional form* of an argument. The propositional form of an argument (from now on we'll simply refer to it as the *form* of the argument) allows us to see patterns that are created. The form of an argument is determined by the placement of the simple statements or claims within the argument and the manner in which they are joined or modified by the connectives. By symbolizing the claims made in the following argument, for instance,

> If you fly into <u>Atlanta,</u> you will land at <u>Hartsfield</u> International Airport.
> You are flying into Atlanta
> _____
> Therefore: You will land at Hartsfield International Airport.

we can show the resulting form:

Argument 1:
A ⇒ H
<u>A</u>
H

In this argument one of the premises is a conditional statement. The other premise *affirms* that the antecedent of that conditional is true. The conclusion affirms that the consequent of that conditional is true. We can schematize this argument as follows:

> Antecedent ⇒ Consequent
> The antecedent of the above conditional is true.
> _____
> Therefore: The consequent of the above conditional is also true.

But if we were to switch the secondary premise with the conclusion, we'd have an entirely different argument form:

Argument 2:
A ⇒ H
<u>H</u>
A

In this argument, the second premise affirms that the *consequent* of the conditional is true, while the conclusion affirms that the antecedent is true. The form of an argument therefore depends on whether or not a claim is made as a premise, or whether it is advanced as a conclusion.

Steps 6, 7, and 8 of the Technique question whether a deductive argument is valid or invalid. Discovering the form of an argument can be useful if not essential in assessing the validity of arguments. Arguments that exhibit certain forms are valid, while argument forms that take other structures are invalid.

Argument 1, for instance, represents a valid argument form. It is valid because if and only if all of its premises turn out to be true, its conclusion must also be true. Argument 2, on the other hand, represents an invalid argument form. Even if it turns out that both premises are true, in Argument 2, it still does *not necessarily* follow that the conclusion must be true as well.

In deductively valid arguments it is *impossible* for the conclusion to be false if all of the premises are true. This is because the conclusion does not really introduce any new information. It asserts information already contained in the premises. But if this is the case, one might ask, why bother with an argument? Why not simply state the information? The answer to these questions rests on the fact that the information is "implicit" in the premises, and not readily apparent. **Valid arguments** extract information that is actually present in the premises. **Invalid arguments,** on the other hand, offer conclusions that are not contained in the premises but only appear to be.

The concept of *validity* is comparable to the rules one follows when playing a game. For instance, it is a rule in the game of chess that a bishop moves diagonally and can land on any square that is not blocked by an intervening piece, and it can capture any opposing piece on a square to which it may legally move. Because of this rule, a bishop cannot move from a light square to a dark square (since this would cause it to move off of its diagonal). Now suppose you were playing a game of chess and you moved your bishop in such a way as to take one of your opponent's knights. Assuming you obeyed all of the relevant rules, your move would be "valid." But if you inadvertently (or even maliciously) moved your bishop from a light to a dark square your move would be "invalid." It is quite possible that your opponent might not have noticed the invalid move, but if your opponent or the referee had noticed the invalid move, your taking of the knight simply would not count.

The case is similar in the presentation of arguments. If an argument is valid the conclusion *must* be true if the premises are in fact true. When this is the case, i.e. all of the premises are true and the form is a valid one, we say that the argument is **sound.** A sound argument is a valid argument in which all of the premises are true. The conclusion of a sound argument is necessarily true. It would be impossible for the conclusion to be false if the premises were true. Another way of putting this is to say that in a sound argument, the truth of the premises guarantees the truth of the conclusion.

Invalid arguments, however, present a more difficult case. Assuming that the premises are all true, the conclusion of an invalid argument is *not necessarily* true. This means that the conclusion of such an argument may or may not turn out to be true. The conclusion of an invalid argument asserts information that is not actually contained in the premises, but which may appear to be. Consider the following *invalid* argument:

> Whenever it rains, my basement floods (because of a crack in the foundation of my house).
> I find that my basement is flooded.
> _____
> Conclusion: It must be raining.

While it is quite *possible* that it is in fact raining and that the rain is responsible for the flooding, given my premises, it need *not necessarily* be the case. It is possible that a broken water pipe or an overflowing sink is causing the problem. This is one major way arguments can be invalid: If we accept their conclusions, we eliminate possibilities that might in fact turn out to be true. Based on this conclusion, the simple solution to the problem (turning off the faucet) may be ignored.

Now we will consider a *valid* form of this argument by reversing the conclusion with one of the premises. Suppose Premise 1 is still true and I look out my window and see that it has begun to rain. At this point I can validly conclude that my basement will begin to flood (if it has not already) and I should take action to perhaps protect any valuables stored there, which might be damaged by the water. A *valid* version of this argument would look like this:

> Whenever it rains my basement floods.
> It is raining.
> _____
> Conclusion: My basement will flood.

Unlike that of the previous argument, the conclusion of this one *must necessarily* follow. Assuming the premises are true, the conclusion is inescapable. At this point you may be wondering why necessary conclusions are so important. After all, very little in life is certain. By asking for necessary conclusions in logical thinking are we not demanding too much?

We can answer this question by first of all thinking of statements as conveying information. Complex statements convey more than the information contained in their component statements; information is also conveyed in the way these statements are connected. In the first premise of the last argument, we're not only speaking of rainy days and flooded basements, but are asserting a relationship between the two events. And when we combine this complex statement with the second premise, we're stating a further piece of information; namely, that both of these statements happen to be true. But since they are both true, we now can "extract" a further piece of information that is not explicitly stated, but is contained within the two premises. The conclusion of the argument is just that information which was revealed by bringing all of these premises together. It is much like a chemist mixing otherwise inert chemicals to produce an explosion. By themselves these chemicals are nothing, but put together in the right way they produce an explosion. Put your premises together in the right way and you produce a conclusion.

Just as a good chemist should know her formulas, so should we thinkers know our argument forms. When an argument is valid its conclusion *must* follow, but when an argument is invalid, its conclusion need not. It 's important to remember this when we're either trying to solve problems for ourselves (and thus constructing our own arguments) or listening to others trying to influence the way we think. For instance, a politician may tell us a a series of things (premises) that we all know to be true. He then attempts to get his audience to agree with his conclusion. Someone not paying attention to the *form* of the politician's argument might be misled into accepting its conclusions simply because the premises happen to be true. But not all true sets of premises lead to true conclusions. We examine the differences between *valid* arguments, which lead to necessarily true conclusions if their premises are true, and *invalid* arguments, which do not guarantee the truth of their conclusions.

9.1 CONDITIONAL ARGUMENT FORMS

We are now ready to consider argument forms that are associated with particular types of connectives. We begin with a consideration of conditional argument forms. They are called *conditional* forms because the complex statement associated with all of them is a hypothetical or conditional one. The most common argument forms make use of conditional statements. Remember that in a conditional statement we are not asserting that anything *is* in fact the case, but only that *if* it were the case, we could be sure that something else would also be true. In the argument forms that contain conditionals, another statement is added which says that either the antecedent or the consequent is, in fact, either true or false. The conclusion of these arguments is a result of the combination of the conditional and the assertion or denial of one of its elements.

AFFIRMATIVE FORMS

There are basically two affirmative types of conditional argument forms. The first is named **modus ponens**, which is a Latin term meaning "the way of affirmation." In a *modus ponens* argument, there are two statements, one of which is conditional, the other being the *affirmation of the antecedent*. Consider, for instance, the conditional statement

> (1)   Whenever it rains, the streets get wet.

This is a *conditional* statement. It does *not* assert that it is raining, nor does it assert that the streets really are wet. But if we add another piece of information, namely,

> (2)   It is raining.

(Assuming it to be true) we can arrive at the *conclusion* that

> (3)   The streets are wet.

Notice that statement (3) *must* be true if statements (1) and (2) are true. To put it in other words, there is no way that statement 3 can be false if 1 and 2 are true. So we have our first *valid* argument form:

Modus Ponens (Valid):
$$A \Rightarrow B$$
$$\underline{\quad A \quad}$$
$$B$$

where A and B stand for any statements at all which fit into this format. What is important here is that the second statement A (or ~A) be identical to the antecedent of the conditional. A variation of this form occurs when either the antecedent or consequent is a *negation*. In these cases the second premise or the conclusion must also be negated accordingly. Take, for instance, the following argument:

> Whenever it *doesn't* rain, Diane goes for a morning walk.
> It is not raining.
> _____
> Therefore: Diane will go (has gone) for a morning walk.

We would symbolize this argument

$$\sim R \Rightarrow W$$
$$\underline{\sim R}$$
$$W$$

Notice again that the second statement is identical to the antecedent of the conditional, while the conclusion *exactly* matches the consequent. Similarly, when the consequent of the conditional is a negation, so must be the conclusion of the argument. This results in the four possible forms that a *modus ponens* argument can take:

$A \Rightarrow B$	$A \Rightarrow \sim B$	$\sim A \Rightarrow B$	$\sim A \Rightarrow \sim B$
A	A	$\sim A$	$\sim A$
B	$\sim B$	B	$\sim B$

Closely related to *modus ponens* is an invalid argument form that looks almost like it. It is called **affirming the consequent.** It occurs in an argument with a conditional statement. But unlike *modus ponens,* in this case it is the *consequent* that is affirmed in the second premise. Consider the example we used for *modus ponens,* but with a slight change:

Whenever it rains the street gets wet.
The streets are wet.
_____
Therefore: It is raining.

The problem with this argument form is that the consequent is merely a *necessary* condition for the antecedent. It is not a sufficient condition. This means that even though the consequent of the conditional turns out to be true, the antecedent need not be so. When an argument is in this form, the information specified in the conclusion *is not* contained in the premises. In this case the supposed fact that the streets are wet together with the conditional *does not* guarantee that it is raining. The streets being wet is not a sufficient condition for the assertion that it is raining because there are other possible reasons for thinking that the streets may be wet. It may have rained earlier, or a water main might have broken, or the city may have washed down the streets. There may be any number of other sufficient conditions that would make the second premise true. So while it *may* be true that it was the rain that caused the streets to be wet, this information was *not* included in the premises. The conclusion is illegitimate. Thus we have an invalid argument form, which like *modus ponens* has four possible schemas.

$A \Rightarrow B$	$A \Rightarrow \sim B$	$\sim A \Rightarrow B$	$\sim A \Rightarrow \sim B$
B	$\sim B$	B	$\sim B$
A	A	$\sim A$	$\sim A$

Notice that in all cases the second premise is identical to the consequent of the conditional, while the conclusion matches the antecedent. Thus in the second example even though the consequent is a negation (~B), it looks exactly like the consequent of the first premise, so it is still considered an affirmation.

Another form of argument involving the conditional includes two conditionals as premises, with the consequent of one forming the antecedent of the other. This is known as a **chain argument.** Embellishing our previous argument we can form a "chain" as follows:

> Whenever it rains, the streets get wet.
> If the streets get wet, they get slippery.
> _____
> Therefore: Whenever it rains the streets get slippery.

We can formalize this argument:

$$R \Rightarrow W$$
$$\underline{W \Rightarrow S}$$
$$R \Rightarrow S$$

The W that forms the consequent of the first conditional is the antecedent of the second. They must match exactly for this argument to be valid; otherwise the chain would be "broken." The following argument is an example of a **broken chain** argument:

> Whenever it rains, the streets get wet.
> If the streets become slippery they become dangerous.
> _____
> Therefore: Whenever it rains the streets become dangerous.

This broken chain can be symbolized

$$R \Rightarrow W$$
$$S \Rightarrow D$$
$$R \Rightarrow D$$

In a broken chain, the consequent of one of the premises does *not* match the antecedent of the other. There is thus no guaranteed connection between the premises and the conclusion. Broken chain arguments are therefore invalid.

Negative Forms

There are essentially two negative forms of conditional arguments, one valid and one invalid. In these cases the second premise is *opposite in sign* to either the antecedent or the consequent.

The valid form occurs when the consequent of the conditional is negated by the second premise. It is known as **modus tollens** or "the way of denial." That this argument form is valid should be obvious when we consider the fact that the consequent names the necessary condition. If B is a necessary condition for

VALID, BUT FALLACIOUS REASONING?

During the rather controversial Senate Judiciary Committee hearings for Supreme Court Nominee Clarence Thomas, one distinguished senator offered the following rather astounding piece of reasoning which aired before the American public on national network television:

> For a person to say what Professor Anita Hill claims Judge Clarence Thomas said, he would have to be seriously emotionally disturbed. But obviously Judge Thomas is not emotionally disturbed. Therefore, Judge Thomas did not say what Professor Hill claims that he said.

As far as the form of this argument is concerned, it appears to be valid (taking the form "If A, then B; but not B. Therefore, not A"—which is Denying the Consequent). If each of the statements in this argument is offered as a serious claim, however, there may be a problem in terms of content. The first statement—phrased hypothetically as "If Thomas said what Hill claims he said, then he would have to be emotionally disturbed,"—is put forth as if it were an empirical claim, capable of being tested as either true or false, when it is almost assuredly a definitional and analytical claim, which cannot be assailed at all. Therefore, this is a fairly good real-life example of the fallacy of Begging the Question by Definitional Dodgeball (see Chapter 5). So, even though an argument can have a perfectly valid form, it may still be a fallacious piece of reasoning due to a defect in the content.

A, and B happens to be false, then it should be clear that A would be false as well. Let's go back to our example from the last section, again rearranging it just a bit:

> Whenever it rains, the streets get wet.
> The streets are *not* wet.
> _____
> Therefore: It is not raining.

This argument may be symbolized

$$R \Rightarrow W$$
$$\frac{\sim W}{\sim R}$$

By asserting that the consequent of the conditional is false, we are ensuring that the antecedent is also false. The statement W must be true in order for R to be true. But the second premise asserts that W is *not* true. Lacking a condition necessary for its truth, the antecedent cannot be true. The information in the conclusion is thus contained in the premises. The following are examples of forms that *modus tollens* may take:

Modus Tollens (Valid)

$A \Rightarrow B$	$A \Rightarrow \sim B$	$\sim A \Rightarrow B$	$\sim A \Rightarrow \sim B$
$\sim B$	B	$\sim B$	B
—	—	—	—
$\sim A$	$\sim A$	A	A

In each of these cases, both the second premise as well as the conclusion are opposite in sign from the two elements of the conditional. Notice also that it is the *consequent* and not the antecedent which serves as the negated second premise.

Another negated form of argument employing the conditional is known as **denying the antecedent.** In this form, the antecedent of the conditional is said to be *false,* and the argument erroneously concludes that the consequent is also false. The problem with this argument is much like the problem we ran into when we discussed the fallacy of "Affirming the Consequent." Just because one sufficient condition happens to be false does not mean that another sufficient condition for the consequent is not true. Again modifying our example we might want to argue:

> Whenever it rains, the streets get wet.
> It is not raining.
> _____
> Therefore: The streets are *not* wet.

As we saw earlier, the fact that it's raining is not a necessary condition for the streets being wet. It may therefore be true that the streets are wet even though it is not raining. The invalid forms therefore look like this:

Denying the Antecedent (Invalid)

$A \Rightarrow B$	$A \Rightarrow \sim B$	$\sim A \Rightarrow B$	$\sim A \Rightarrow \sim B$
$\sim A$	$\sim A$	A	A
—	—	—	—
$\sim B$	B	$\sim B$	B

EXERCISES

A LEVEL

Short Answers

1. Define the difference between a valid and an invalid argument.
2. If the premises of a *modus ponens* argument are all true, must the conclusion also be true? Why or why not?

3. If the premises of an argument in the form of Denying the Antecedent are all true, must the conclusion also be true? Why or why not?

True or False

* 4. ___F___ The conclusion of a valid argument must always be true.

* 5. ___F___ The conclusion of an invalid argument must always be false.

* 6. ___T___ In a *modus tollens* argument, the consequent of the conditional premise is negated in the second premise.

* 7. ___T___ *Modus ponens* is a valid argument in which the antecedent of the conditional is affirmed in the second premise.

* 8. ___T___ Chain arguments have conditionals for their conclusions.

* 9. ___F___ If the premises of an argument in the form of Denying the Antecedent are all false, then the conclusion must also be false.

*10. ___T___ Another way of describing the argument *modus ponens* is to say that it is a case of affirming the antecedent.

B   LEVEL

Symbolize each of the following arguments, then state which type of conditional argument form it exemplifies:

1. Whenever the movie *It's a Wonderful Life* starts appearing on television, you know it's Christmas. So far I've seen it about three times this month. So I'm sure it's Christmastime.

2. Whenever it snows, Lisa goes skiing. Lisa is skiing. So it must be snowing.

3. If Santa Claus didn't exist, we'd have to invent him. But I know that he does exist because I've seen him several times in many different places. Thus we don't have to invent him.

4. Winning four games is a sufficient condition for a team's winning the World Series. The Giants did not win four games of last year's series. Thus the Giants did not win the series.

5. According to the Constitution of the United States an individual is not qualified to be president unless he or she is at least thirty-five years old. If a person is too young to vote then he or she is not yet thirty-five years old. So, anyone who is too young to vote is not qualified to be president.

6. A person can be president only if he or she is at least thirty-five years old. Madonna is not yet thirty-five years old. Therefore, Madonna is ineligible to be president.

7. A student can't graduate unless he or she has 120 credits. Tony does not yet have 120 credits. Therefore she cannot yet graduate.

8. If Jill doesn't go to the concert, then neither will Lisa. Lisa can't go because she has the flu. So I guess Jill's not going.

9. A person is not eligible to become president unless he or she is at least thirty-five years old. Dan Quayle is at least thirty-five. He is therefore eligible to become president.

10. If that car behind us were a police car, it wouldn't have one of its headlights out. But, as you can see, one of its headlights is not working. So don't worry, I don't need to slow down because it's not a police car.

11. You can't get this job without experience. But you don't have the experience, so you don't get the job.

12. You can't get experience without having a job. You don't have the experience, so you don't get the job.

13. If we let the communists win in Vietnam they'll take over Laos and Cambodia. If they get Laos and Cambodia then the Philippines and Indonesia will be next. If we lose them then Australia won't be far behind. So we have to stop them in Vietnam.

14. Either Einstein's theory of relativity is not false or Aristotle's theory of natural place is true. Einstein's theory has proven true. Thus Aristotle's theory is false.

15. If Elvis were alive, somebody would eventually spot him. Every time I read the newspapers they sell in the grocery store I read where people are seeing him all of the time. This proves Elvis is still alive.

16. Man afraid of flying explaining why he is against it: "If God had wanted human beings to fly, He would have given us wings. And it's obvious that we don't have wings."

C   LEVEL

Try to find real-life examples of the conditional argument forms discussed in this section. In each case note also (when you can) whether the premises and conclusion are true or false. Be on the lookout for unstated premises and conclusions when doing this exercise.

9.2 CONJUNCTIVE AND DISJUNCTIVE ARGUMENT FORMS

Just as conditional argument forms contain a conditional as at least one of their complex statements, conjunctive and disjunctive argument forms rely on conjunctions and disjunctions as elements of their premises respectively.

Two argument forms are associated with the conjunction, one of which is valid and the other a fallacy. Both forms contain the negation of a conjunction.

Conjunctive Argument

A **conjunctive argument** begins with a statement of the form *not both* and asserts that two statements cannot both be true at the same time. This means that either one or the other may be true, or they may both be false. Consider the possibility that John and Allison know one another and they don't really get along. Consider also a party that they're both thinking about attending. Assuming that they are aware of each other's intentions, we can also assume that

John and Allison won't both go to the party

which can be symbolized

~(J & A)

Now, before we proceed, it is worthwhile to consider the possibilities. John might decide to go to the party, in which case Allison will not. Or possibly Allison will attend, which would cause John to stay home. Or they both might decide not to go. All three of these possibilities are included in the last statement. In fact, the only thing that *cannot* happen if ~(J & A) is true is that they *both* show up. This gives us a good basis for analyzing the conjunctive argument.

Suppose that I know that John and Allison will not both show up for the party. Suppose also that I know that one of them (say, John) is intent on going. This will allow me to conclude correctly that Allison will not show up:

> John and Allison will not both attend the party.
> John is attending.
> _____
> Therefore: Allison will *not* attend.

TWO FOR THE PRICE OF ONE: INVALID AND STUPID

How often have you encountered a snippet of reasoning such as the following piece taken from a private letter, but which could have occurred anywhere?

> "If you weren't so stupid, you'd understand that she had nothing but good intentions . . . ."

As it stands, this is a statement, not an argument. Indeed, some might call it an "unsupported claim," which is cast in the form of a hypothetical or conditional statement. Nevertheless, implied along with it is one of two unspoken statements: (A-1) "But you are so stupid." Let us consider this scenario first. Just in terms of the parts of the Critical Technique we have covered so far, there are at least three things wrong with this piece of reasoning. First, solely in terms of its form, it is fallacious by Denying the Antecedent:

> If ~S (You were Not so Stupid), then U (You would Understand. . . .)
> ~(~S) (You are so Stupid)
> _____
> (Implied C) ~U (You do not Understand. . . .)

Second, even if we had not discussed form alone, there are other things wrong with this reasoning purely in terms of content. One, for instance, is that it involves a Misuse of Hypothesis Contrary to Fact. Third, again in terms of content, there is either a Poisoning the Well fallacy or a Personal Attack or both occurring when a person's intelligence level is addressed without ever referring to the core of the reasoning issue.

Symbolized it looks like this:

Conjunctive Argument (Valid):

1. ~(J & A)
2. J

Therefore: ~A

By affirming that John will attend in the second premise, and combining it with the first, we can conclude that Allison will not show up.

Denying the Conjunct

Beware, however, of an argument that looks very much like a conjunctive argument but is *invalid*. It occurs when the second premise **denies one of the conjuncts** of the first conjunction. Assume, for instance, that we know that John will *not* attend the party for one reason or another. This would not allow us to conclude that therefore Allison will attend. Remember that one of the possibilities we discussed earlier is that they might both decide *not* to attend. To conclude that Allison will definitely attend because John has decided not to does not follow from these premises. So the following argument is *invalid*.

John and Allison will not both attend the party.
John will not attend.

Therefore: Allison will attend. (Invalid)

Symbolically:

Denying a Conjunct (Invalid):

1. ~(J & A)
2. ~J

Therefore: A (Invalid)

Remember that the first premise lends itself to the possibility that neither of them will show up.

Disjunctive Argument Forms

In the previous chapter we discussed the statement form known as a *disjunction*. Remember that it is symbolized by a ▼ or "wedge," which means that either one or the other, or possibly both, of the statements on either side of the wedge is true (although one *may* turn out to be false).

Disjunctive Argument A **disjunctive argument** consists of two premises. One of these premises is a disjunction and the other is a denial of one of the disjuncts. Since one of the disjuncts must be true, that leaves the remaining one as necessarily true. The following argument, for instance, is valid:

Either Paris or Rome is the capital of Italy.
Paris is *not* the capital of Italy.

Therefore: Rome is the Italian capital.

This argument would be symbolized:

Disjunctive Argument:

1 P ▼ R
2. ~P

Therefore: R

The second premise in this argument was a denial or negation. It essentially eliminated one of the two possibilities stated in the first premise. The conclusion stated that the other possibility must therefore be true.

Affirming a Disjunct   An invalid argument that might look like a disjunctive argument is known as **affirming a disjunct**. It occurs when we begin with a disjunction (as in the previous case) but then the second premise is an *affirmation* rather than a denial. Since both of the disjuncts may turn out to be true, the affirmation of one does *not* necessarily imply the denial of the other. Consider the following argument:

Either The Hague or Amsterdam is the capital of The Netherlands.
The Hague is the capital of The Netherlands.

Therefore: Amsterdam is not the capital of the Netherlands.   (Invalid)

This argument is not only invalid; its conclusion is actually false. As it turns out, The Netherlands is one of several countries that in fact has two capitals. The argument would be symbolized:

Affirming a Disjunct:

1. H ▼ A
2.   H

Therefore: ~A (Invalid)

Again, remember that in a disjunction, both of the disjunctions may turn out to be true.

Dilemma The final form of disjunctive argument we consider is known as a *dilemma*. It is composed of a disjunction and two conditionals. The two conditionals have as their antecedents the two disjuncts, and they have a common consequent. Consider the following argument:

> It is either going to rain or snow today.
> If it snows today, the streets will become wet.
> If it rains today, the streets will become wet.
> _____
> Therefore: The streets will become wet.

This argument, which is a **simple dilemma,** is symbolized as follows:

Simple Dilemma:

1. R ▼ S
2. R ⇒ W
3. S ⇒ W
_____
Therefore: W

Since either R or S (or both) must be true, and since both of them imply that W must be true, we can conclude that W must in fact be true. There is a more complicated instance of the dilemma where the consequents of the conditionals are different from one another. In these cases, the conclusion will turn out to be a disjunction of the two consequents. The following argument is an example of a **complex dilemma:**

> It will either rain or snow today.
> If it rains today, the streets will be wet.
> If it snows today the streets will become icy.
> _____
> Therefore: The streets will be either wet or icy.

Symbolized, the complex dilemma looks like this:

Complex Dilemma:

1. R ▼ S
2. R ⇒ W
3. S ⇒ I
_____
Therefore: W ▼ I

Since either R or S is true, and one implies W while the other implies I, either W or I must also be true.

SUMMARY

An important element in the evaluation of arguments—Step 6 of the Technique—is the determination of the argument's logical form. The logical form of an argument is determined by the types of statements that form the premises and the conclusion, and their relationships within the argument. In this chapter we examined valid argument forms as well as their associated fallacies. Conditional statements generated the valid argument forms *modus ponens, modus tollens*, and the chain argument. Invalid forms or fallacies employing the conditional are known as *affirming the consequent, denying the antecedent* and *broken chain*. When the conjunction is employed, it is usually in the form of a negated conjunction or a *not both* statement, which supplies the first premise of an argument. The valid form associated with a conjunction is known as a *conjunctive argument* and the fallacy is called *denying a conjunct*. The disjunction yields several forms of argument. One valid form is known as a *disjunctive argument*. The other valid forms are the simple dilemma and the complex dilemma. The disjunction also generates a fallacy known as *affirming a disjunct*. If all of the premises of a valid argument are true, then the conclusion must necessarily be true. But the truth of the premises *does not* guarantee the truth of the conclusion of an invalid argument form or fallacy.

Table 9.1 summarizes the argument forms discussed in this chapter.

EXERCISES

 A LEVEL

Short Answers

 1. What is a disjunctive argument? Provide an example.
 2. What is a conjunctive argument? Provide an example.
 3. Explain the differences between disjunctive arguments and those of the form of Affirming a Disjunct.
 4. Explain the differences between conjunctive arguments and those of the form of Denying a Conjunct.
 5. What is the difference between a simple and a complex dilemma? Provide an example of each.

True or False

 *6. ___F___ In a conjunctive argument, one premise is always composed of the denial of a conjunction.
 *7. ___T___ A disjunctive argument always contains the denial of a disjunct as one of the premises.
 *8. ___F___ A disjunctive argument differs from a dilemma in that only the disjunctive argument contains a disjunction.
 *9. ___T___ If the premises of a simple dilemma are all true, then the conclusion must also be true.
 *10. ___F___ If the premises of an argument of the form of Denying a Conjunct are all false, then the conclusion must also be false.

TABLE 9-1
ARGUMENT FORMS

Valid Forms	Fallacies

Modus Ponens

$A \Rightarrow B$

$\underline{A}$

B

Modus Tollens

$A \Rightarrow B$

$\underline{\sim B}$

$\sim A$

Conjunctive Argument

$\sim(A \And B)$

$\underline{A}$

$\sim B$

Disjunctive Argument

$(A \blacktriangledown B)$

$\underline{\sim A}$

B

Chain Argument

$A \Rightarrow B$

$\underline{B \Rightarrow C}$

$A \Rightarrow C$

Dilemma

Simple	Complex
$A \blacktriangledown B$	$A \blacktriangledown B$
$A \Rightarrow C$	$A \Rightarrow C$
$\underline{B \Rightarrow C}$	$\underline{B \Rightarrow D}$
C	$C \blacktriangledown D$

Affirming the Consequent

$A \Rightarrow B$

$\underline{B}$

A

Denying the Antecedent

$A \Rightarrow B$

$\underline{\sim A}$

$\sim B$

Denying a Conjunct

$\sim(A \And B)$

$\underline{\sim A}$

B

Affirming a Disjunct

$A \blacktriangledown B$

$\underline{A}$

$\sim B$

Broken Chain

$A \Rightarrow B$

$\underline{C \Rightarrow D}$

$A \Rightarrow D$

B LEVEL

Decide which type of conjunctive argument form is expressed by each of the following:

1. You can't take both calculus and statistics in the same semester. Since you've already signed up for calculus, you'll have to forget about taking statistics.

2. The New York Giants and the Buffalo Bills don't both play their home games in New York State. The Giants play their home games in New Jersey. So the Bills must play their home games in New York State.

3. Raleigh and Charlotte are not both the capital of North Carolina. Charlotte is not the capital. Therefore, Raleigh must be.

4. It is impossible for a person to both not work and still get paid. Dan Quayle gets paid a pretty good salary. Therefore, he must do some kind of work.

5. The recipe says not to use both sugar and honey. I haven't used any honey. So that must mean that I need to add sugar.

After symbolizing each of the following, state which type of disjunctive argument form is employed:

6. We're suppose to read either *Macbeth* or *King Lear* for English Literature class. Since I really hate all the bloodshed in *Macbeth* I guess I'll read *King Lear*.

7. I have to read either *King Lear* or *Macbeth* for literature class. *King Lear* will depress me and so will *Macbeth*. So either way it looks like this assignment will depress me.

8. Either Brown or White will be elected mayor. But Brown says he doesn't want the job. So White will become mayor.

9. Flight attendant to passenger: "You can't have a cup of coffee because I asked you before if you wanted coffee or tea and I already gave you a cup of tea."

10. Either The Hague or Amsterdam is the capital of The Netherlands. The Hague is the capital. So Amsterdam is obviously not.

11. We're supposed to read either *Macbeth* or *King Lear* for English Literature class. Since I really like *King Lear,* I want to read it. So I guess I won't read *Macbeth*.

C LEVEL

Symbolize each of the following arguments, then state the argument form involved. Be sure to note and supply any unstated premise or conclusion.

1. "Always assume that students will cheat. If you have designed your course in such a way that cheating can occur, you can be sure that it will."
—Memo to teachers from Academic Integrity Board
(Reprinted courtesy of Theodore S. Arrington.)
Professor Spacey reads the newspapers while his students take examinations. Therefore, cheating goes on during his examinations.

2. "Always assume that students will cheat. If you have designed your course in such a way that cheating can occur, you can be sure that it will."

—Memo to teachers from Academic Integrity Board *(Reprinted courtesy* of *Theodore S. Arrington.)* Professor Gilroy found two students cheating on one of her examinations. Thus she must have designed her course in such a way as to allow cheating to occur.

3. In *The Jaguar Smile,* Salman Rushdie concluded that Nicaragua was not a "Marxist-style government" by making the following claim:

". . . if Nicaragua was a Soviet-style state, I was a monkey's uncle." (*Hint:* Be sure to note the unstated premise.)

—From *The Jaguar Smile* by Salman Rushdie. Copyright © 1987 by Salman Rushdie. Used by permission of Viking Penguin, a division of Penguin books USA Inc.)

4. "Death is one of two things. Either it is annihilation, and the dead have no consciousness of anything, or, as we are told, it is really a change—a migration of the soul from this place to another.. Now if there is no consciousness but only a dreamless sleep, death must be a marvelous gain . . . because the whole of time, if you look at it in this way, can be regarded as no more than one single night. If on the other hand death is a removal from here to some other place, and if what we are told is true, that all the dead are there, what greater blessing could there be than this, gentlemen? . . . What would one not give, gentlemen, to be able to question the leader of that great host against Troy, or Odysseus, or Sisyphus, or the thousands of other men and women whom one could mention, to talk and mix and argue with whom would be unimaginable happiness?"

— Socrates' argument that death should not be feared in *The Apology*

(Reprinted courtesy of Princeton University Press.)

5. "That which you fear, you are fighting, and fighting always weakens you. Fear makes you impotent and makes higher levels inaccessible."

—From Dr. Wayne Dyer's self-help book *Real Magic*

(Reprinted courtesy of HarperCollins Publishers.)

6. "If both apelike and manlike wildmen do exist, it seems that the strongest evidence comes from recent or near-recent sightings and descriptions." (These sightings and descriptions were described earlier in the book.)

—Myra Shackly in *Still Living: Yeti, Sasquatch and the Neanderthal Enigma*

(Copyright © 1983 Thames and Hudson Ltd. Reprinted by permission of the publisher.)

7. "There should be no question of what to do about (a city official's) DWI arrest. He must be fired. Public officials should set a good example for all. Let us hope the mayor and city council members have enough good sense to do the right thing."

—Letter to *The Charlotte Observer*

(Reprinted with the permission of *The Charlotte Observer*.)

8. The linguist-philosopher Noam Chomsky offered the following argument to demonstrate that walking was genetically determined:

"If a child is raised by a bird, does he end up flying? No. Or if a dog is raised by a person, does it end up walking on its hind legs? No. That we are designed to walk is uncontroversial. That we are taught to walk is highly implausible."

—Quoted by Russ Meyer in the *New Yorker* article "A Silent Childhood"

(Selected excerpt from *Genie* by Russ Rymer, which originally appeared in *The New Yorker*. Copyright © 1993 by Russ Rymer. Reprinted by permission of HarperCollins Publishers, Inc.)

9. The following was offered as evidence that the skeletons of Adam and Eve had been discovered on a mountainside south of Denver, Colorado:

"Even more compelling, the male skeleton is missing a rib that we found grafted to the female's spine. If you have read the story of creation that appears in the Book of Genesis, you'll recall that God created Adam from clay and then made Eve from one of Adam's ribs. As far as I'm concerned, the couple we found at our dig match that description to the letter."

—*Weekly World News*

(Reprinted courtesy of *Weekly World News*.)

10. "If I discuss the singer (a person named "Orion"), who has since disappeared, it might look as though I'm involved in a scam. . . . If I don't bring up the singer Orion, then it is assumed that I'm covering up something. Either way I can be made to look devious.

—Gail Brewer-Giorgio commenting in the book *Is Elvis Alive?*

(Reprinted courtesy of Tudor Publishing Company.)

11. "Every time I put a line in the water I said a Hail Mary, and every time I said a Hail Mary I caught a fish."

—the character "Fredo" in the movie *The Godfather Part 2* confiding to his nephew the secret of his success as a fisherman.

12. The philosopher Lance K. Stell of Davidson College stated the following in a letter to *The Charlotte Observer* in disagreement with President Bush's desire to define legally protectable life as beginning at the moment of conception:

"If we were to adopt the view that protectable life begins at conception, we would have to support a policy requiring official examination of every woman's menstrual flow for dead human beings. If any were discovered, the medical examiner would have to determine the cause of death . . . recommend legal proceedings if he determined that death resulted from a wrongful act, sign the death certificate and release the "body" for appropriate burial. Such consequences are so outrageous and so costly that it strains credibility to think the president means what he says."

(Reprinted with the permission of *The Charlotte Observer*.)

13. "We are bogged down in abortion politics . . . . A lot of people feel they've paid their dues by being pro-choice, so they don't want to be bothered with this other stuff."

—Linda Tarr Whelan as quoted by Catherine S. Mangold in the *New York Times*.

(Copyright © 1992 by the New York Times Company. Reprinted by permission.)

14. "Why should working mothers pay taxes on day care when without day care they wouldn't be working at all."

—Television advertisement for a U.S. Senate candidate.

15. "I have never understood the animosity, distaste and superiority expressed by the Christian church, especially Baptists, in regard to homosexuals . . . . If there is a heaven and hell—which there isn't—and one must answer for the sins of his forebears, the entire Christian organization is in for a roasting."

—Letter to *The Charlotte Observer*

(Reprinted with the permission of *The Charlotte Observer*.)

16. "Ron Fielder arrived next . . .. Today, he was in an uncharacteristic bad mood, because the previous night a transit cop had issued him a summons for playing his radio too loud on the subway. Hanging up his coat, he told Rose Mary the story, and said 'It couldn't have been too loud. I was sleeping while it was playing.'"

—related by Susan Orlean in *The New Yorker*

(Reprinted by permission; © 1992 Susan Orlean. Originally in *The New Yorker*.)

CASE STUDY

Aiding Upper Slobovia Revisited

We can continue to refine our Technique to handle arguments in greater complexity, using the same argument from the case study in Chapter 8 with a couple of minor modifications. Let us add one more premise to the argument: say "The United States sent aid to upper Slobovia." (This was the statement symbolized by the letter A.) Then, we will see whether the conclusions "Public confidence in the new administration will be eroded (I)," and "The poor, the homeless, and the elderly will be hurt tremendously (J)" necessarily follow from this line of reasoning. Thus, we are checking out the internal consistency and the necessary implications and the "structure" or "form" of the argument before we have to check out the truth, relevance, fairness, and adequacy of the premises. The argument reads:

> If the United States sends aid to Upper Slobovia, then the United States resources at home will be diminished. And if the United States sends aid to Upper Slobovia and domestic resources are diminished, then either the United States will experience its own domestic shortage or troubles will emerge somewhere else in the U.S. economy. If either these troubles emerge somewhere else in the U. S. economy or the United States experiences its own shortage, then economic conditions in the United States will worsen. If economic conditions in the United States worsen, then either the recession will sharpen or the workforce will experience rising unemployment. If troubles emerge elsewhere in the U.S. economy, the recession will sharpen. If either the recession in the United States sharpens or the workforce experiences rising unemployment, then the U.S. stock markets will decline severely. Public confidence in the new administration will be eroded, unless the U.S. stock markets do not decline seriously. Also, if the recession in the United States sharpens, then the poor, the homeless, and the elderly will be hurt tremendously. If the United States sends aid to Upper Slobovia, then it will not experience its own domestic shortage. The United States has now sent aid to Upper Slobovia. Thus, the poor, the homeless, and the elderly United States citizens will be hurt and also the public confidence in the new administration will be eroded.

The symbols for each of the statements in the argument remain the same as they did in the previous case study, because there are no new additional simple statements.

A = The U.S. sends aid to Upper Slobovia.
B = U.S. resources at home (domestic resources) will be diminished.
C = The U.S. will experience its own domestic shortage.
D = Troubles will emerge elsewhere in the U.S. economy.
E = Economic conditions in the U.S. will worsen.
F = The recession in the U.S. will sharpen.
G = The workforce will experience rising unemployment.
H = U.S. stock markets will decline severely.
I = Public confidence in the new administration will be eroded.
J = The poor, the homeless, and elderly U.S. citizens will be hurt tremendously.

The resulting symbolic representation for the argument as presently modified is then displayed in this mode:

1.	$A \Rightarrow B$	Given
2.	$(A \,\&\, B) \Rightarrow (C \blacktriangledown D)$	Given
3.	$(C \blacktriangledown D) \Rightarrow E$	Given
4.	$E \Rightarrow (F \blacktriangledown G)$	Given
5.	$D \Rightarrow F$	Given
6.	$(F \blacktriangledown G) \Rightarrow H$	Given
7.	$\sim(\sim H) \Rightarrow I$	Given
8.	$F \Rightarrow J$	Given
9.	$A \Rightarrow \sim C$	Given
10.	A	Given

Thus, 11. $(I \,\&\, J)$ Conclusion to be proven

Now we are in a position to see what relationships obtain between these several statements and what further conclusions are entailed. We can begin at any number of places, so we must mingle creativity with some insight and also remember what it is that we are trying to prove. Let us start then by noting that if we take Line 1 together with Line 10, we can derive the conclusion B by using our rule *modus ponens* (or affirming the antecedent). This would be displayed:

12. B   Lines 1 and 10   *Modus ponens*

Next, we could conjoin Lines 1 and 12, because we can add together any two lines of the proof, each one either being given to begin with or derived from something initially given. In other words, if A is true and B is true, then A and B are true. This is shown:

13. A & B   Lines 1 and 12   Conjunction

To continue, we may derive the conclusion (C ▼ D) from the complex statement in Line 13, which is identical to the antecedent of the complex conditional statement expressed in Line 2. This is a permissible inference as long as the antecedent that is being affirmed is exactly the same as that expressed in the conditional, or the consequent is precisely the same as the statement that is being denied. Thus, we have:

   14. C ▼ D   Lines 2 and 13   *Modus ponens*

The complex statement, (C ▼ D), is also identical to the antecedent of the conditional statement expressed on Line 3. Thus, we have sort of a chain in the reasoning process:

   15. E   Lines 3 and 14   *Modus ponens*

Continuing with that chain, the simple statement E implies the complex statement (F ▼ G), according to Line 4:

   16. F ▼ G   Lines 4 and 15   *Modus ponens*

That same strain of implication is carried further in Line 6 with (F ▼ G) as the antecedent and H as the consequent:

   17. H   Lines 6 and 16   *Modus ponens*

The antecedent of the conditional statement on Line 7 is the negation of a negative statement; that is, "it is not true that H is not true." Logically, this is equivalent to saying that "H is true." So, the conditional should read, "If H is true, then I is true." With this intermediary step, the next line of proof should read:

   18. I   Lines 7 and 17   *Modus ponens*

We now have half of the conclusion we were seeking. To determine whether the other half, statement J, also follows, we will have to look in a different direction in the case of this particular argument. One way to continue would be to note that Line 9 and Line10 taken together lead to the conclusion that C is false:

   19. ~C   Lines 9 and 10   *Modus ponens*

Since we saw from Line 14 that either C is true or D is true, and since Line 19 tells us that C is not true, D must therefore be true by our rule for Denying one of the Disjuncts. Thus, the next step of the proof should be:

   20. D   Lines 14 and 19   Denying a disjunct or Disjunctive Argument

It can be seen from Line 5 that if D is true, then F must be true, so the argument continues:

21. F   Lines 5 and 20   *Modus ponens*

And, if F is true, according to Statement 8, then J must be true. So, the argument is nearly completed:

22. J   Lines 8 and 21   *Modus ponens*

Line 18 gave us half of the conclusion we sought to prove and Line 22 gives us the other half. We saw earlier that we could conjoin any two lines of the proof that were already given or that were derived from given statements. That gives us:

23. I & J   Lines 18 and 22   Conjunction

The upshot of this phase of the Critical Technique is that we have learned that the argument in question was in fact a *valid* one. This means that if the premises are true, then the conclusion must be true too. It does *not* mean that the conclusion has to be true *no matter what*. For instance, if one or more of the premises turns out to be false, then the conclusion could still be false. So, the next phase of inquiry should be to determine the truth and accuracy of the premises. We must also look at the fairness and relevance of the premises. For example, in order to be fair to the argument, we need to look at the positive consequences of giving aid to Upper Slobovia, as well as the negative consequences. Then, and just as importantly, we need to consider the consequences, both positive and negative, of *not* giving aid to Upper Slobovia, before we begin to be fair to the argument. If all of this checks out, then we may be warranted in claiming that we have a *sound* or *good* argument, which means both that it has a valid form plus true premises.

Now, to recap the formal proof, from a purely structural standpoint the argument is represented:

1. A ⇒ B		Given
2. (A & B) ⇒ (C ▼ D)		Given
3. (C ▼ D) ⇒ E		Given
4. E ⇒ (F ▼ G)		Given
5. D ⇒ F		Given
6. (F ▼ G) ⇒ H		Given
7. ~(~H) ⇒ I		Given
8. F ⇒ J		Given
9. A ⇒ ~C		Given
10. A		Given

Thus, 11. (I & J)   Conclusion to be proven

	Inference	*From*	*Rule*
12.	B	Lines 1 and 10	*Modus ponens*
13.	A & B	Lines 1 and 12	Conjunction
14.	C ▼ D	Lines 2 and 13	*Modus ponens*
15.	E	Lines 3 and 14	*Modus ponens*

16.	F ▼ G	Lines 4 and 15	*Modus ponens*
17.	H	Lines 6 and 16	*Modus ponens*
18.	I	Lines 7 and 17	*Modus ponens*
19.	~C	Lines 9 and 10	*Modus ponens*
20.	D	Lines 14 and 19	Denying a disjunct or Disjunctive Argument
21.	F	Lines 5 and 20	*Modus ponens*
22.	J	Lines 8 and 21	*Modus ponens*
23.	I & J	Lines 18 and 22	Conjunction

10

TRUTH TABLES, EQUIVALENCE, AND VALIDITY

step five
Are there any fallacies?

▼

step six
What is the argument's structure?

▼

step seven
What other conclusions can be drawn?

▼

step eight
Do you agree or disagree with the conclusion?

Consistency is the last
refuge of the
unimaginative.
—Oscar Wilde (1891)

Consistency is contrary to nature,
contrary to life.
The only completely
consistent people are dead.
—Aldous Huxley (1946)

KEY TERMS

Addition - The rule of combining a disjunct to a statement already known to be true.

Combination - The joining of two statements into a single conjunction.

Derivation - This is the extraction of the conclusion from the premises according to the rules of logic.

Formal equivalence - Statements are formally equivalent when they have the same truth values. This is also known as *logical equivalence.*

Simplification - The assertion of one of a pair of conjuncts.

Truth table - A method for determining the truth value of complex statements. They can be used to establish whether or not two complex statements are logically equivalent. They can also be used to determine whether or not an argument is valid.

Valid deductive argument - One that guarantees the truth of its conclusions. Another way of stating this is that if the premises of an argument are true, its conclusion *must* also be true.

Another important element in Steps 6, 7, and 8 of the Technique is to be able to determine whether or not statements are logically equivalent to one another, and also to determine whether longer arguments comprised of several argument forms are valid or invalid. This chapter introduces the idea of truth tables and shows how they may be employed to establish the logical equivalence of statements. Truth tables will also be used to determine the validity or invalidity of arguments. This chapter also introduces you to a method of logical derivations, another means of establishing the validity of an argument.

In our discussion of the formal symbolization of statements, it might have occurred to you that the same statement can sometimes be made using different words. Often the words we choose will determine the logical connective to be used in the statement's symbolization. For instance, a prison guard pursuing an escaping inmate might yell "Stop, or I'll shoot" or he might say "If you don't stop, I'll shoot." Relying on the terms *or* and *if,* the first statement would be symbolized as a disjunction, while the second would be rendered as a conditional. But these two statements convey the same message. They are **formally equivalent.** This means that the circumstances which would lead one to conclude that the first statement were true (or false) are the same circumstances that would make the other statement true (or false). (In both cases, for instance, if the prisoner failed to stop but was *not* shot at, we would conclude that the warning was "false.") In this chapter, we explore ways to determine when statements are logically equivalent to one another, and when they are not.

To determine whether or not statements are logically equivalent we will make use of a truth table. A **truth table** is merely a device for setting up, in tabular form, the truth values learned in Chapter 8. Or, put another way, a truth table is a chart that relates the truth value (true or false) of a complex statement or group of statements to the truth value (true or false) of its component simple statements in all possible cases. We can construct a truth table which shows at a glance how to determine the truth value of complex statements. Instead of using the equal sign (=) though, we will begin to put truth values in tabular form. The following is a truth table that summarizes the truth conditions for five connectives:

A B	A & B	A ▼ B	-A	A ⇒ B	A ⇔ B
T T	T	T	F	T	T
T F	F	T	F	F	F
F T	F	T	T	T	F
F F	F	F	T	T	T

The two left-hand columns are *index columns* and give us the possible truth values of A and B. The other columns tell us the truth values of the resulting complex statements or what they "equal." The reason the truth table contains four lines is that there are two *variables,* A and B. Since each may be either true or false, there are four possible combinations. If there were three variables, we would need eight lines. In general, the rule for determining the number of lines required for a truth table is given by the formula: The number of lines = 2^n where n = the number of variables (or letters) to be considered. As you can see, these truth tables can become very long very quickly: five letters would require 32 lines and seven variables would increase the length of the table to 128 lines.

10.1 TESTING FOR LOGICAL EQUIVALENCE

We are now in a position to address the problem of logical equivalence. The truth table we constructed in the preceding section gives us the ability to do so. Specifically, it will be the case that two statements are logically equivalent when their truth tables are exactly the same. Take, for instance, the statements we mentioned at the beginning of this chapter. The prison guard might say "Stop, or I'll shoot" (which would be symbolized as "S ▼ T" with S meaning "Stop" and T meaning "I'll shoot") or might alternately put it "If you don't stop, I'll shoot" (symbolized as ~S ⇒ T). To test whether or not these statements are equivalent, we must first construct an index column with the two variables S and T and all the possible combinations of truth values. We then look at the truth values of each of the two statements. The truth table would be constructed like this:

S	T	S ▼ T	~S ⇒ T
T	T		
T	F		
F	T		
F	F		

Construction of the values under S ▼ T is relatively easy. We know that the only time a disjunction is false is when both disjuncts are false, otherwise it is true. This leaves us with only the last line under S ▼ T as false:

S	T	S ▼ T	~S ⇒ T
T	T	T	
T	F	T	
F	T	T	
F	F	F	

Since there is a tilde before the S in the expression ~S ⇒ T, however, this one is a bit more complicated. First, we determine the values under the ~S and the T. We get those under ~S by simply reversing those under S in the index column (since ~S has the opposite truth value from S). Since the T has no tilde before it, we simply copy the T column:

S	T	S ▼ T	~S	⇒	T
T	T	T	F		T
T	F	T	F		F
F	T	T	T		T
F	F	F	T		F

To get the truth value of the conditional, we simply combine those of the antecedent and consequent, using the rule we learned earlier: The conditional is false only when the antecedent is true and the consequent is false. We put these final values under the arrow to show that they are the values for the entire statement. At the same time, we cross out the values under ~S and under the T in the conditional to show that we are "through" with them and so that we don't confuse them with the value of the conditional itself. It is also helpful to circle the final truth value under the statement.

S	T	S ▼ T	~S ⇒ T
T	T	T	F T T
T	F	T	F T F
F	T	T	T T T
F	F	F	T F F

Last, to help us pick out the final column under ~S ⇒ T, we "circle" or otherwise highlight the column under the arrow. This is because the arrow is the *main connective* of the expression. We do the same thing under the "▼" column for S ▼ T. (If there had been brackets around the entire expression and a "~" outside those brackets, *it* would constitute the major connective and its column would be circled.)

In this truth table, we see that the truth value on every line under the major connective is exactly the same for both expressions. They are both true on lines 1–3 and false on line 4. Thus the two expressions *are* indeed logically equivalent.

Equivalence Rules for Complex Statements

At this point, we must recall that for any complex expression there are at least three places in which a ~ or negation sign may be placed. It may be placed before either of the two letters, or it may be placed before the statement as a whole outside of the brackets. (If there are no parentheses or brackets around the entire expression, they can be drawn.) In the following example, all three places are held by tildes:

~(~A & ~B)

Going from one symbol to another simply requires knowing which tildes to change as the connectives change. To help in this section we'll designate the three possible positions for tildes as 1, 2, and 3. Position 1 is before the entire expression, 2 before the first letter, and 3 before the second. When we go from one connective to the other we have to be careful not only to change the connective, but also to write the letters down in the same order in which they appeared in the first expression.

Disjunctions and Conditionals. We can state any disjunction as a conditional, and vice versa, as was the case with the warning shouted by the prison guard. When doing so, however, we must change some of the affirmative statements into denials. In the case of the prison example "Stop" became "If you *don't* stop." This gives us the rule by which we can go from a conditional to a disjunction, or a disjunction to the conditional while preserving the logical equivalence. If we symbolize these two logically equivalent statements we get:

~S ⇒ T

HOW MANY TRUTH VALUES ARE THERE?

and

S ▼ T

In this case there was no tilde outside of the brackets in either case (thus we do not need to draw the outer brackets). So position 1 remains the same in both expressions. Similarly the T has no tilde in either case, so position 3 remains the same. But position 2 has changed. While there was a ~ in position 2 in the conditional, there was none in the disjunction. So the first rule is this:

> When changing an expression from a disjunction to a conditional, or vice versa, change only position 2 (i.e., if there is already a tilde, take it out, if there's not, put one in). Leave positions 1 and 3 alone.

The following are logically equivalent:

~A   ▼   ~B is equivalent to   A ⇒ ~B
 A   ▼   ~B   ~A ⇒ ~B
~(A ▼   B)   ~(~A ⇒ B)

Both statements may be uttered as threats, but it turns out that they mean the same thing. In fact, that is why it is sometimes useful to symbolize statements differently. What may be obvious on one rendering, may not be obvious on the other.

Conjunctions and Disjunctions. Conjunctions may be resymbolized as disjunctions. This rule is known as DeMorgan's law, after the logician who conceived it. In this case, however, it is in all positions 1, 2, and 3 that the tilde must be changed. To show this, consider the following statement:

Tom and Jane won't both attend the picnic.

or symbolically:

~(T & J)

Now if we tried to symbolize this as T ▼ J we would realize that it has to be wrong since T ▼ J means that either Tom or Jane or both plan to attend the picnic. But this obviously is not what the ~(T & J) means since the idea behind this expression is explicitly that they will not both come. But when we say that they won't both come, we mean that either one or the other will not show up, and that perhaps even neither of them will show up. But this meaning is captured in the expression:

~T ▼ ~J

which states that either Tom will not show up, or Jane will not, or that neither of them will come. We find that this is the case when we test them with truth tables:

T J	~(T & J)	~T ▼ ~J
T T	F T T	F F F
T F	T T F	F T T
F T	T F T	T T F
F F	T F F	T T T

The only thing that would make either statement false is if Tom and Jane both did attend the picnic. This rule would make the following expressions equivalent:

A ▼ B	~(~A & ~B)
~A ▼ B	~(A & ~B)
~(A ▼ ~B)	~A & B

Conjunctions and Conditionals. When changing from a conjunction to a conditional, or vice versa, positions 1 and 3 must be changed, while position 2 is left alone. In this case, let's consider this conditional:

Whenever it <u>rains</u>, the streets get <u>wet</u>.

or

R ⇒ W

In trying to turn this into a conjunction, we should realize that what is being asserted here is that if one thing is true, another will follow. But the ampersand does not express this type of relationship directly. It can do so, however, if we use the expression *not both*. In this case the conditional expresses the fact that

It will not both be the case that it is raining and the streets are not wet

or

$\sim(R \& \sim W)$

This is in fact what the original conditional statement was asserting—that it wasn't possible for it to be raining and the streets not wet. We can check this out by using a truth table:

R W	R $\Rightarrow$ W	$\sim(R \& \sim W)$
T T	T	T T F
T F	F	F T T
F T	T	T F F
F F	T	T F T

Thus the following expressions are all equivalent:

$R \Rightarrow \sim W$ is equivalent to $\sim(R \& \quad W)$
$\sim(R \Rightarrow W)$ to $R \& \sim W$
$\sim R \Rightarrow W$ to $\sim(\sim R \& \sim W)$

Putting these all together we can chart how one symbol may be translated into another with the *conversion pyramid* (Figure 10.1).

FIGURE 10 - 1

CONVERSION PYRAMID

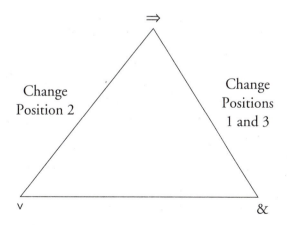

Change all 3 Positions (DeMorgan's law)

When transforming a statement with one connective to an equivalent statement with another connective, change (or negate) the tildes in the three positions as indicated in the chart.

EXERCISES

 A   LEVEL

True or False

* 1. ___T___ Two statements are logically equivalent when all of their truth values match on a truth table

* 2. ___T___ DeMorgan's law is a rule for converting conjunctions into logically equivalent disjunctions and vice versa.

* 3. ___T___ When converting a disjunction into a logically equivalent conditional, only the first disjunct is negated.

* 4. ___F___ Although a disjunction can be converted into a logically equivalent conditional, a conditional cannot be converted into a logically equivalent disjunction.

* 5. ___F___ The truth table for the conditional A ⇒ B is logically equivalent to the conjunction ~(~A & ~B).

* 6. ___F___ "It's raining and the streets are wet" is logically equivalent to "Either it is not raining or the streets are not wet."

* 7. ___F___ "It's raining and the streets are wet" is logically equivalent to "Whenever it rains, the streets are wet."

* 8. ___F___ Two statements are logically equivalent only if the lines marked "true" on the truth table all match.

* 9. ___F___ "Either Perot or Bush lost the election of 1992" is logically equivalent to "It is not the case that both Perot and Bush lost the election."

*10. ___T___ DeMorgan's law requires that all three positions which may contain a negation must be changed when constructing a logically equivalent statement.

B   LEVEL

Using truth tables, determine whether the following formulas are logically equivalent:

* 1. ~A & B and A ⇒ B
2. P ▼ ~Q and P ⇒ ~Q
* 3. R ⇒ ~S and ~R ▼ ~S
4. ~(T ▼ ~V) and T ⇒ V
* 5. ~(M ⇒ N) and M & N

Determine whether the following sets of statements are logically equivalent. To do this, you'll need to symbolize the statements first and then compare them on a truth table.

6. (a) Neither Lois nor Jake will attend the lecture.

   (b) Lois and Jake will not both attend the lecture.

7. (a) If it breaks, we'll fix it.

   (b) If it wasn't broke, we didn't fix it.

8. (a) If pigs had wings, they could fly.

   (b) Either pigs don't have wings, or they can fly.

9. (a) Unless you lower the rent, I won't take the apartment.

   (b) If you lower the rent, I'll take the apartment.

10. (a) Lois will attend the lecture if and only if Jake does.

    (b) Lois will not attend the lecture if and only if Jake doesn't.

11. (a) If Jake doesn't rent the apartment, Lisa will.

    (b) If Lisa doesn't rent the apartment, Jake will.

12. (a) If God had wanted humans to fly, he would have given us wings.

    (b) Either God did not want humans to fly, or he would have given us wings.

13. (a) Albany and Atlanta are not both the capital of Georgia.

    (b) Either Albany is not the capital of Georgia or Atlanta is.

14. (a) If Sacramento is the capital of California, then San Francisco is not.

    (b) Sacramento and San Francisco are not both the capital of California.

Transform the following disjunctions into conditionals:

15. A ▼ B

16. ~A ▼ ~B

17. ~(~A ▼ B)

18. A ▼ ~B

Transform the following statements from disjunctions into conditionals. Use the transformation rules from this chapter. (It might help to symbolize the sentences before applying the rules.)

19. Stop, or I'll shoot.

20. America: Love it or leave it.

21. Either Lisa will go the concert, or Jill will not.

22. Either Lisa or Jill won't go to the concert.

23. You need to take either calculus or logic in order to fulfill the requirement.

Transform the following formulas from conditions into disjunctions:

24. P ⇒ ~Q

25. ~P ⇒ ~Q

26. ~(P ⇒ Q)

27. ~(~P ⇒ ~Q)

Transform the following complex statements from conditionals into disjunctions:

28. Unless you stop smoking, you'll damage your health.

29. If it breaks, we will fix it.

30. If red is not Sara's favorite color, then it's orange.

31. Unless orange is Sara's favorite color, it's red.

32. If it doesn't break, we won't fix it.

C   LEVEL

Find five real-life examples of complex statements. Change these statements into statement forms using the other two connectives. Show the correctness of your changes by constructing truth tables.

10.2 TESTING FOR VALIDITY

A valid deductive argument guarantees the truth of its conclusions. Another way of stating this is that if the premises of a deductive argument are true, its conclusion *must* also be true. There are two methods for demonstrating an argument's validity. One employs truth tables; the other utilizes the argument forms of Chapters 6 through 9 as well as other rules to construct logical derivations.

Testing Validity with Truth Tables

We have already seen that the truth conditions of complex statements depend on the logical structure of those statements as well as the truth values of their components. That this is also the case with arguments employing complex statements should therefore not come as a surprise.

To test the validity of arguments, we will construct a truth table. For example, we can use the disjunctive argument discussed earlier. We will assume it comes in the form:

$$A \blacktriangledown B$$
$$\underline{\sim A}$$
$$B$$

The index columns will list those letter variables which appear in the argument along with the possible combinations of truth values. Since the variable letters in this case are A and B, the index columns are constructed as follows:

A	B
T	T
T	F
F	T
F	F

Across the top of our truth table we next list the premises of the argument. They will each be tested in a separate column:

A B	A ▼ B	~A
T T		
T F		
F T		
F F		

Finally, we list the conclusion of the argument in the last column:

A B	A ▼ B	~A B
T T		
T F		
F T		
F F		

We now test for the truth values of each column according to the rules for each connective. When we have done so, the table will look like this:

	A B	A ▼ B	~A	B
1	T T	T	F	T
2	T F	T	F	F
3	F T	T	T	T
4	F F	F	T	F

The argument turns out to be valid because there are no lines in our truth table where the premises are all true while the conclusion is false. On Line 3, both of the premises do turn out to be true, but so does the conclusion. On Lines 2 and 4, the conclusion is false, but it is not the case that all of the premises are true. So we now can give a specific meaning to our claim that in a deductive argument the truth of the premises guarantees the truth of the conclusion: If we construct a truth table for a valid argument, there will be no lines on which the premises are all true while the conclusion is false. This argument fits into that category, and is therefore valid.

Now let's consider the invalid argument of affirming the consequent:

$$R \Rightarrow P$$
$$P$$
$$\overline{}$$
$$R$$

We construct a new truth table using the two variables R and P for the index column, and then list the premises and conclusion along the top row as we did in the last example:

	R P	R ⇒ P	P R
1	T T		
2	T F		
3	F T		
4	F F		

Now we solve for the truth values under each column:

	R P	R ⇒ P	P R
1	T T	T	T T
2	T F	F	F T
3	F T	T	T F
4	F F	T	F F

In this case, we do in fact find a line on which all of the premises turn out to be true while the conclusion is false. This is Line 3, on which both premises yield a value of T, while the conclusion yields a value of F. This truth table demonstrates that Affirming the Consequent is not a valid argument form since the truth of the premises does not guarantee the truth of the conclusion.

Now we consider an argument with three variables:

$$P \Rightarrow Q$$
$$Q \Rightarrow R$$
$$\sim P$$
$$\overline{}$$
$$\sim R$$

To evaluate this argument, we need three index columns and eight rows:

	P	Q	R	P ⇒ Q	Q ⇒ R	~P	~R
1	T	T	T				
2	T	T	F				
3	T	F	T				
4	T	F	F				
5	F	T	T				
6	F	T	F				
7	F	F	T				
8	F	F	F				

Next, we will solve for the truth values of the premises as well as the conclusion:

	P	Q	R	P $\Rightarrow$ Q	Q $\Rightarrow$ R	~P	~R
1	T	T	T	T	T	F	F
2	T	T	F	T	F	F	T
3	T	F	T	F	T	F	F
4	T	F	F	F	T	F	T
5	F	T	T	T	T	T	F
6	F	T	F	T	F	T	T
7	F	F	T	T	T	T	F
8	F	F	F	T	T	T	T

This argument turns out to be invalid because at least one line yields all true premises and a false conclusion. In fact in this case both Lines 5 and 7 show that the argument is invalid.

The truth table method of showing validity or invalidity will work for any argument of any length. The problem with using it, however, is that for every extra variable, the number of lines must double. If there are four variables, the table requires 16 lines, and with five variables, we would need 32. An easier way of handling these complex arguments is to use the rules learned in Chapter 9 to attempt to "derive" the conclusion directly. This is the subject of our next section.

Derivations

At times arguments can be extremely complex and may involve five or more variables. This would make the construction of a truth table difficult in a manageable amount of space. By combining different premises according to the rules of logic, we can validly derive other statements. The argument forms learned in the preceding chapter are all specific instances of these rules. Once you know these rules, you can begin to derive statements with the express goal of trying to derive the argument's conclusion. If the conclusion of the argument can be derived according to these rules, you will have proven that the conclusion is validly drawn (that is, it is the conclusion of a valid argument).

To understand logical proofs or **derivations**, it is helpful to think of them as games. Consider a game like solitaire. In this game we use a deck of cards and a set of rules to try to reach a certain goal. Although there are a good many variations, the game we are considering here is the one in which seven rows of cards are placed in descending order. The goal is to get down to the aces and then begin piling the cards by suits in ascending order. The game is won if all of the cards in the deck can be placed in these four piles. Sometimes a win is impossible, given the way that the cards are laid out. Other times the game can be won only with innovative strategy.

A logical proof is in many ways similar to a game of solitaire. Instead of cards, one begins with a set of statements. Just as there are rules for stacking the cards, there are rules for putting statements together, or taking them apart, to produce *new* statements. But these new statements do not simply appear "magically". They are the result of the logical combinations of the statements we already possess. The information contained in these new or *derived* statements was already present in the statements we were given at the start of the process. When we reason, we are not simply remembering and stating information we have come to believe. By analyzing this information and combining it with other information we are able to discover information that was not initially apparent.

SUSIE SWEEPSTAKES: A PUZZLE

Suppose Suzie Sweepstakes drops by your residence saying you have a shot at winning one million dollars cash. You and two other persons chosen at random are the potential lucky winners. She explains that she has two $100 bills and three $1 bills in a hat, which she then shows to all three of you. There are five bills all together and while you are not looking, she pins one of them on each of the three of you (let's say, to the back of your shirt where you cannot possibly see it). Each of you three may walk around and look at the bill on the other two people's backs, but you cannot see your own or you are disqualified. If you can tell what denomination the bill is that is pinned to your back, you win the million dollar sweepstakes (*provided* that you can explain how you know). If you guess wrong or cannot explain how you know, then your wages will be garnished for the rest of your life (in other words, there is a rather stiff penalty for guessing). We will also assume that all three of you are of average or above average intelligence, and that each one of you can hear what the other persons have to say.

Contestant #1: "I cannot tell what denomination bill I have."
Contestant #2: "I cannot tell either."
You say: ?

1. What is your answer?
2. How do you know?

(*Hint:* One way of explaining your answer is to use a modified truth table; Try it first before looking at the following solution.)

In the last chapter we compared this to a chemist putting chemicals together to produce an explosive. We then looked at the rules for putting them together correctly. Here we study those arguments in which the conclusion is not as intuitively obvious. This is because the conclusion is not reached in one simple step, but rather several steps. The logical "game" thus becomes one of trying to determine whether the conclusion is *validly* connected to the premises. We can do this by drawing conclusions from our premises, and then recombining the information in those newly drawn statements we have derived with our initial premises to produce even more information. If we can go from our premises to our conclusion validly, step by step, then we are rationally compelled to accept its conclusion if we also accept its premises.

Consider the following four statements:

1. Either Roger Maris or Babe Ruth hit 61 home runs in a single season.
2. If Henry Aaron did not hit 61 home runs in a single season, then neither did Babe Ruth.
3. Henry Aaron never hit 61 home runs in a single season.

Therefore, Roger Maris hit 61 home runs in a single season.

Answer: You must have a $1 bill pinned to your back and here is one way of explaining your answer: There are seven possible combinations of how those five bills may be distributed among three people.

Possibility #	1	2	3	4	5	6	7
Contestant #1	$1	$1	$1	$1	$100	$100	$100
Contestant #2	$1	$1	$100	$100	$1	$100	$1
Contestant #3	$1	$100	$1	$100	$1	$1	$100

When Contestant #1 says she cannot tell it rules out possibility 4 because if Contestant #1 saw a $100 bill on the back of Contestant #2 and Contestant #3, then she would immediately know that all three remaining bills were $1 bills and that she would have to have one of them pinned to her back. Next, when Contestant #2 says that she cannot tell either, that rules out two more of the possibilities. First, it rules out possibility 7, because if Contestant #2 saw two $100 bills on the backs of Contestant #1 and Contestant #3, then she would likewise know that only $1 bills remained and that she would have to have one of them. Second, it also rules out possibility 2 because *IF* Contestant #2 were to see a $100 bill on the back of Contestant #3 when Contestant #1 said she could not tell, then Contestant #2 would know that she had a $1 on her own back, which is why Contestant #1 could not determine the denomination of the bill on her own back. Thus, we are left with possibilities 1, 3, 5, and 6—and all of them require that Contestant #3 has a $1 bill pinned to her back! Try it!

Nowhere in the three premises does it explicitly state that Roger Maris hit 61 home runs in a single season. The first maintains that *either* he or Babe Ruth accomplished the feat, but it does not specify which one. The second statement maintains a conditional stating that if Henry Aaron was not the one to do it, then neither was Babe Ruth. The third asserts that Henry Aaron did not in fact hit 61 home runs. By themselves, these statements do not tell us *who* of the two disjuncts hit the 61 home runs. And we can't apply a disjunctive argument because none of the premises is a negation of either of the disjuncts in premise 1.

At this point it would be much easier to examine this argument by symbolizing it. First, we'll symbolize the premises and then list them:

1. M ▼ R   Conclusion: M
2. ~A ⇒ ~R
3. ~A
_____

We listed the conclusion on the upper right-hand side to remind us that it is the statement we are trying to derive. Since we can keep recombining statements we need to have a "destination statement" or *goal statement*. When we reach that goal statement, we have proven our conclusion.

Now, for our "rules" of combination, we can use the argument forms of the last chapter. We can also use the rules for logical equivalence we discussed at the beginning of this chapter. However, there are several other rules that do not ordinarily occur in simple arguments but are nevertheless of help in trying to derive conclusions from the set of premises. We now consider them.

Combination. The **combination** argument form associated with the conjunction is represented by the act of forming the conjunction itself. It occurs when we take two statements that we know (or assume) to be true and combine them into a single conjunction. The following argument is an example of combination:

> Eggs have a high cholesterol content.
> Cream has a high cholesterol content.
> _____
> Therefore: Eggs have a high cholesterol content, and so does cream.

or more simply

> Therefore: Both eggs and cream are high in cholesterol.

We can symbolize this argument as:

> 1. E
> 2. C
> _____
> Therefore: E & C (or) C & E

In fact, we can combine as many premises as we like, provided that we group them in twos with parentheses or brackets. So if we wanted to add ice cream to our list our conclusion would look like this:

> (C & E) & I

When we combine statements with ampersands, we are not asserting any relationship of dependence between the truth of the statements (as we were with the arrows). We are simply putting the statements together in one compound statement.

Simplification. **Simplification** is the opposite of combination. It occurs when we already have a conjunction and want to assert the truth of one of the conjuncts. The following argument is an example of simplification:

> Eggs have a high cholesterol content and so does ice cream.
> _____
> Therefore: Ice cream has a high cholesterol content.

Symbolized this argument looks like this:

> 1. E & I
> ─────────
> Therefore: I

Simplification can even work in the case of complex statements with more than one connective. But be careful about how the statements are grouped. For instance, the following argument is valid:

> Eggs are high in cholesterol, and if I eat ice cream I gain weight.
> ───
> Therefore: Eggs are high in cholesterol.

This argument would be correctly symbolized by

> 1. E & (I ⇒ W)
> ──────────────
> Therefore: E

But it would *not* be valid to say that the conclusion of this argument was I, since I is part of the conditional. Similarly, the following argument is *invalid* because it attempts to simplify a statement that is really not a conjunction:

> Whenever I eat bacon and eggs, I break out in a rash.
> ───
> Therefore: Whenever I eat eggs, I break out in a rash. (invalid)

This would be symbolized as

> 1. (E & B) ⇒ R
> ──────────────
> Therefore: E ⇒ R (invalid).

It would also be invalid to conclude simply E from this last argument.

Addition. This argument form rests on the fact that in a disjunction one of the disjuncts may be false. If we begin a simple argument with a statement that we know (or assume) to be true, we can form a true disjunction by simply "adding" a wedge and *any other statement.* Even if the statement added turns out to be false, the disjunction itself has to be true since the first disjunct is already true. It will also help to remember the "truth table" for the disjunction: The only time a disjunction is false is when *both* disjuncts are false. For instance, if I already know that "Paris is the capital of France," I also know that "Either Paris or Marseilles is the capital of France" or even "Either Paris or Berlin is the capital of France." In argument form, **addition** would look like this:

Paris is the capital of France.
_____

Therefore: Either Paris or Berlin is the capital of France.

or symbolically:

1. P
_____

Therefore: P ▼ B

This argument form can appear to be illegitimate and you may wonder how you can add an obviously false statement and get a result that is nevertheless true. But this argument form makes sense if you remember that you are not trying to say that the second statement *is* true, but merely that one or the other is. Since we already know that the first statement is true, then so is the resulting disjunction.

We next try to find the shortest logical "path" to the conclusion. This is how we might do it in the case of our argument concluding Roger Maris hit 61 home runs. By putting together Lines 2 and 3 and involving the rule of *modus ponens* (see the last chapter), we can produce a Line 4 that looks like this:

4. ~R

Then by combining our new Line 4 with Line 1 and applying the disjunctive argument, we can derive Line 5:

5. M

But M was our conclusion. So Line 5 is the last line we need to derive. It's the conclusion, and we've proven logically that *if* the argument's premises are true, then so is the conclusion (as well as Line 4). Taken as a whole, the argument would look like this:

1. M ▼ R   Conclusion: M
2. ~A ⇒ ~R
3. ~A
_____

4. ~R   Lines 2 & 3, *modus ponens*
5. M   Lines 4 & 1, disjunctive argument

On the left-hand side, we list the lines we combined to derive the conclusion we have drawn. Thus Line 4 was derived from Lines 2 and 3 using *modus ponens*. (From now on we'll abbreviate.)

But this is not the only possible way of deriving the conclusion, even if it is the shortest. There are other logical paths to the same conclusion. For instance, someone might have chosen to "translate" Line 1 to its logical equivalent using DeMorgan's law (DM) and place that on Line 5 (perhaps because she did not notice the possibility of reaching the conclusion on the next step). In that case our new Line 5 would look like this:

(Alternate) Line 5. ~(~M & ~R) Line 1, DM

Then Line 6 could be derived from combining Lines 4 and 5 and applying the rule for the conjunctive argument:

(Alternate) Line 6.   M Lines 4, 5 CA

The CA stands for *conjunctive argument.* The alternate argument would look like this:

1. M ▼ R   Conclusion: M
2. ~A ⇒ ~R
3. ~A
_____
4. ~R   Lines 2 & 3, *modus ponens*
5. ~(~M & ~R)   Line 1, DM
6. M   Lines 4 & 5, conjunctive argument

You might get some practice by trying other methods of reaching the same conclusion. Copy the premises down to the solid line (which indicates the end of the premises and the beginning of our deductions) and then try to derive the conclusion.

SUMMARY

A useful tool for Step 6 of the Technique is the truth table. A truth table can establish the logical equivalence of statements. Truth tables are also capable of testing an argument for validity. When using a truth table, we look at the possible combinations of truth values of all of the variables, and then solve for the truth values of the premises as well as the conclusion. If it turns out that there are no lines in which all of the premises yield a truth value of true while the conclusion is false, then the argument is valid. This is because it was shown that the truth of the premises guarantees the truth of the conclusion. If there is at least one line on which all of the premises yield a truth value of true while the conclusion yields a value of false, then the argument is invalid.

We also studied methods for "translating" complex statements governed by a given logical connective into statements with other logical connectives. Doing this requires negating the elements according to the rules spelled out in the chapter and encapsulated in the conversion pyramid of Figure 10.1.

Also included in this chapter was a discussion of the derivation of statements from arguments. To accomplish this we employed the valid argument forms of Chapters 6, 7, 8 and 9 and introduced three new rules including combination, simplification, and addition.

EXERCISES

A   LEVEL

Short Answers

C 1. What is a valid deductive argument?

C 2. What is a truth table and how can it be used?

C 3. Name a way, other than a truth table, for demonstrating that a conclusion logically follows from a set of premises.

True or False

* 4. _F_ A truth table shows that the argument symbolized is valid when there is a line on the table on which all the premises and the conclusion are true.

* 5. _T_ A truth table with four variables would require 16 lines to list all of the possible truth values.

* 6. _T_ By using a truth table, we can show that an argument is either valid or invalid.

* 7. _T_ A logical derivation can be used to demonstrate that an argument is valid or invalid.

* 8. _F_ *Combination* is the name of the rule by which two statements known to be true are joined in a disjunction.

* 9. _T_ *Addition* is the name of the rule by which a disjunction is formed from a statement already known to be true.

*10. _F_ *Simplification* is the rule by which a disjunction is simplified into one of its component disjuncts.

B   LEVEL

Use truth tables to determine whether or not the following arguments are valid:

C 1. If Rob goes to the party, then Sheila will not go. Sheila is not going. Therefore, Rob will.

   2. Whenever I wash my car it rains. I'm washing my car. Therefore, it will rain.

C 3. If women live longer than men, then Sheila will live longer than Rob. Women do live longer than men. Therefore, Sheila will live longer than Rob.

   4. Death results in either annihilation or paradise. If the result of death is annihilation, then death is not an evil. If death results in Paradise, then death is not an evil. Therefore, death is not an evil.

C 5. If the Blue Jays win the pennant, then part of the World Series will be played in a domed stadium. But if the Twins win the pennant, then part of the World Series will be played in a domed stadium. So either way, part of the World Series will be played in a domed stadium.

   6. Hitler to the Austrian government in 1938: "If you hold a plebiscite on unification with Germany, Germany will invade Austria." The plebiscite was not held. Germany invaded anyway. (Did Hitler break his word?)

7. The auto dealer says that I can't get both an automatic shift and power steering. If I get power steering, then I also must get cruise-control. But I don't want cruise control. So I guess I'll have to get the power steering.

8. I can't afford both power steering and cruise control. I also can't afford both cruise control and power windows. But I really want those power windows. So I guess I can afford neither power steering nor cruise control.

9. If you major in philosophy, you'll have to do a lot of thinking. If you major in engineering, you'll have to do a lot of math. I know that you'd prefer not to spend your time thinking or doing a lot of Math. Therefore, I advise you to major in something else.

10. The new manager of the radio station said that the new format should be based around either heavy metal or oldies rock. If they go to a heavy metal format, they'll alienate the older listeners, but if they choose to play oldies rock, they'll lose the younger crowd. The station owner doesn't want to lose either group. So he told the station manager to choose neither heavy metal nor oldies rock.

Derive the following conclusions from the premises. State the rules used in each step.

11. $A \Rightarrow B$, $B \Rightarrow C$, ~C.   Therefore: ~A

12. ~(P & Q), P, $R \Rightarrow Q$.   Therefore: ~R

13. $R \Rightarrow S$, R ▼ T, ~T.   Therefore: S

14. Z ▼ X, $X \Rightarrow Y$, $Z \Rightarrow Y$, $Y \Rightarrow N$.   Therefore: N

Isolate the conclusion of the following arguments. Then determine whether the conclusion can be derived from the premises. If the conclusion cannot be derived from the premises, state which logical fallacy may have been involved.

15. Whenever it rains, the streets get wet. Whenever the streets get wet, they get slippery. It is raining. Therefore, the streets are slippery.

16. Phil and Lisa will not both go to the concert. Phil is going to the concert. If Jane goes to the concert, then Lisa will go. Therefore, Jane will not go to the concert.

17. Whenever it rains, the streets get wet. Whenever the streets get wet, they get slippery. The streets are not slippery. Therefore they are not wet.

18. We can have either onions or anchovies on our pizza. But we can't have anchovies (since I don't like them). If we have onions, then we should also have olives. So, it looks like we'll be having olives as well as onions on our pizza.

C   LEVEL

Symbolize each of the following arguments. Then decide whether they are valid or invalid using first, a truth table, and second, a formal proof. (Some of these exercises come from those at the end of Chapter 9. When this is the case, the number in parentheses at the beginning of the passage indicates its number in Chapter 9. The material in parentheses is explanatory and may be ignored for purposes of this exercise.)

1. (1) "Always assume that students will cheat. If you have designed your course in such a way that cheating can occur, you can be sure that it will."
—Memo to teachers from Academic Integrity Board

(Reprinted courtesy of Theodore Arrington.)

(Since Professor Spacey reads the newspapers while his students take examinations) cheating can occur in his classes. Therefore cheating does occur in his classes.

2. (2) "Always assume that students will cheat. If you have designed your course in such a way that cheating can occur, you can be sure that it will."

—Memo to teachers from Academic Integrity Board

(Reprinted courtesy of Theodore Arrington.)

Professor Killjoy found two students cheating on one of her examinations. Thus she must have designed her course in such a way as to allow cheating to occur.

3. (3) In *The Jaguar Smile,* Salman Rushdie concluded that Nicaragua was not a "Marxist-style government" by making the following claim:

". . . if Nicaragua was a Soviet-style state, I was a monkey's uncle." Since Mr. Rushdie is obviously not a monkey's uncle, Nicaragua is not a Soviet-style state.

(From *The Jaguar Smile* by Salman Rushdie. Copyright © 1987 by Salman Rushdie. Used by permission of Viking Penguin, a division of Penguin Books USA Inc.)

4. (4) Socrates argument about death in *The Apology* can be paraphrased as follows:

Death is either annihilation or a journey to a heavenly reward. If it is annihilation, then there is no pain involved. If there is no pain involved, then death must be a good thing. But if death is a journey to a heavenly reward, then we can converse with famous people who have died in the past. If we can converse with famous dead people, then death is also a good thing. Therefore, death must be a good thing.

(Reprinted courtesy of Princeton University Press.)

5. (5) "That which you fear, you are fighting, and fighting always weakens you. Fear makes you impotent and makes higher levels inaccessible."

—From Dr. Wayne Dyer's self-help book *Real Magic*

(Reprinted courtesy of HarperCollins Publishers.)

Therefore fear makes higher levels inaccessible.

6. (6) "If both apelike and manlike wildmen do exist, it seems that the strongest evidence comes from recent or near-recent sightings and descriptions. To turn the discussion on its head for one moment, it is easy to see that the assumption that they do *not* exist rests on the belief that our world is so thoroughly explored . . . that no unclassified creatures will be discovered. It is equally easy to demonstrate how ill-founded this assumption is." (The author then goes on to demonstrate why this assumption is "ill-founded.")

—Myra Shackley in *Still Living: Yeti, Sasquatch and the Neanderthal Enigma*

(Copyright © 1983 Thomas and Hudson Ltd. Reprinted by permission of the publisher.)

7. (9) The argument concerning the discovery of Adam and Eve's skeletons in Colorado can be paraphrased as follows:

The male skeleton is missing a rib. If the skeleton were Adam's, it would be missing a rib. Therefore, the skeleton must be the skeleton of Adam.

—*Weekly World News*

(Reprinted courtesy of Weekly World News.)

8. (10) "If I discuss the singer (a person named "Orion"), who has since disappeared, it might look as though I'm involved in a scam . . . . If I don't bring up the singer Orion, then it is assumed that I'm covering up something. Either way I can be made to look devious."
—Gail Brewer-Giorgio commenting in the book *Is Elvis Alive?*
(Reprinted courtesy of Tudor Publishing Company.)

9. (11) "Every time I put a line in the water I said a Hail Mary, and every time I said a Hail Mary I caught a fish." Thus every time Fredo puts a line in the water, he catches a fish.
—the character "Fredo" in the movie *The Godfather Part 2* confiding to his nephew the secret of his success as a fisherman.

10. (16) "Ron Fielder arrived next . . . . Today, he was in an uncharacteristic bad mood, because the previous night a transit cop had issued him a summons for playing his radio too loud on the subway. Hanging up his coat, he told Rose Mary the story, and said, 'It *couldn't* have been too loud. I was sleeping while it was playing.'"
—Related by Susan Orlean in *The New Yorker*
(Reprinted by permission; © 1992 Susan Orlean. Originally in *The New Yorker*.)

CASE STUDY

Derivations and the Technique

The previous two case studies were designed to show how the Technique could be applied to displaying, analyzing, and assessing the structure of most argument forms. Now we need to show how the Technique can apply to specific practical problems such as those found on standardized tests where knowledge of the equivalence of different statement forms can be extremely helpful. Of course, the range of applications is significantly broader than that, but at least a couple of examples may help indicate how wide that scope can be.

Here is an example of a typical question or problem:

Conditions are getting out of hand here. Unless Doris goes, then Hubert must go. But she will not go if he stays. So, both of them will have to go.
Question: What is the main flaw in this reasoning?
A. The first claim, that conditions are getting out of hand is irrelevant.
B. A possible course of action is overlooked.
C. It is assumed that staying is the same thing as not going.
D. The conclusion refers to a possibility that is not explicitly referred to in any one of the premises.
E. We have insufficient information about the conditions.

Which one of these five answers seems to be the best one? We could symbolize each one of the simple statements in order to see what conclusions have to follow from them. Accordingly, let:

C = Conditions are getting out of hand here.
D = Doris goes.
H = Hubert goes.

The argument then would be diagrammed:

1. A   Given
2. ~D $\Rightarrow$ H   Given
3. ~H $\Rightarrow$ ~D   Given
_____

So, 4. D & H   Conclusion to be proven

To examine the relationships between these four statements, we can take a look at the logical equivalences of each of the statements, particularly statements 2 and 3, since they are the complex premises. Statement 2, "if Doris does not go, then Hubert must go," is the conditional statement form logically equivalent to the disjunctive statement form, "either Doris goes or Hubert must go." Statement 3, "if Hubert does not go then Doris will not go," is the conditional statement form logically equivalent to the disjunctive statement form, "either Hubert goes or Doris does not go." From this vantage, the conclusion that both of them have to go does not follow from the premises because it is possible that Hubert goes and Doris does not. In other words, a crucial alternative or possible course of action has been overlooked. This was answer B above.

Another way of deriving the same answer from this problem is to note that statement 2 says ~D $\Rightarrow$ H, and statement 3 says ~H $\Rightarrow$ ~D. This latter statement (statement 3) is logically equivalent to D $\Rightarrow$ H. Thus, statement 2 says if Doris does not go, then Hubert must go; and statement 3 says that if Doris goes, Hubert must go anyway. So, the conclusion is that in either case, whether Doris goes or not, Hubert must go. But, Doris does not have to go. Therefore, a possible option has not been considered: Hubert going and Doris not going. Again, answer B proves to be the best answer of the five that are given.

Try a second example:

> *A person who does not exercise will not be healthy, and a person who is not healthy will not live a successful life.*
> *Question: It logically follows that*
> *A. People should exercise.*
> *B. People should live successful lives.*
> *C. People who exercise live successful lives.*
> *D. People who exercise are healthy.*
> *E. People who live successful lives exercise.*

In this example we are given two premises and told that a conclusion is missing, but deductively follows from them. We can let:

E = A person exercises

H = A person is healthy.

S = A person lives a successful life.

The premises are then represented symbolically:

$$\text{~}E \Rightarrow \text{~}H$$

and

$$\text{~}H \Rightarrow \text{~}S$$

We can see by our Chain Argument Rule that the missing conclusion must be

$$\text{~}E \Rightarrow \text{~}S$$

But, from our rules for equivalence we can also see that premise 1 is logically equivalent to $H \Rightarrow E$; that Premise 2 is equivalent to $S \Rightarrow H$; and that the conclusion is equivalent to $S \Rightarrow E$. Thus, we can look back at the possible answers and see that answers A and B do not necessarily follow for two reasons: One, they are simple statements that cannot be derived from either of the two complex statements; and, two, they both contain the word "should," which makes them different statements from the ones that are given. Thus, they go beyond anything contained in the premises. Answer C, $(E \Rightarrow S)$, is not entailed by our premises although it *looks* similar to the derived conclusion, except for the important difference that it is missing the negation signs. The same is true of answer D: it is represented $E \Rightarrow H$ and it *looks* a lot like the first premise, which is $\text{~}E \Rightarrow \text{~}H$, except again the important negation signs are missing. Answer E is represented $S \Rightarrow E$ and is an exact match for the logical equivalent to the conclusion we saw above. So, E is the correct answer.

Suppose we continued with this problem and added a second question:

Which of the following statements must also be true?
A. Either a person exercises or they are not healthy.
B. Either a person does not exercise or they are healthy.
C. A person cannot both exercise and not be healthy.
D. A person cannot both be healthy and not exercise.
E. Only healthy people exercise.

If we symbolically represent each of the possible answers, we get:

A. $E \blacktriangledown \text{~}H$ B $\text{~}E \blacktriangledown H$ C. $\text{~}(E \,\&\, \text{~}H)$ D. $\text{~}(H \,\&\, \text{~}E)$ E. $E \Rightarrow H$

Since the given premises and the derived conclusion are already in hypothetical or conditional form, let us put each one of the possible answers in that same statement form and check to see which ones, if any, match.

- A. E ▼ ~H is logically equivalent to ~E ⟹ ~H (which matches our first premise and so is correct.)
- B. ~E ▼ H is logically equivalent to E ⟹ H (which does not match either premise or the derived conclusion, so it is incorrect.)
- C. ~(E & ~H) is logically equivalent to ~E ▼ ~(~H), which is ~E ▼ H, which is E ⟹ H (which we just saw in the case of answer B to be incorrect.)
- D. ~(H & ~E) is logically equivalent to ~H ▼ ~(~E), which is ~H ▼ E (which is logically equivalent to answer A, so it is also correct.)
- E. E ⟹ H was already in conditional form and shown to be incorrect in the cases of answers B and C.

So, only Answers A and D are correct answers.

Let us add a dimension to this kind of problem by posing a third question relating to the initial set of conditions that were given:

> Suppose each one of the following statements is true. Which one or ones of them would severely damage the given argument?
> (i) I know people who exercise but who are not healthy.
> (ii) I know people who live successful lives but who are not healthy.
> (iii) I know people who live successful lives but who do not exercise.

Answer (i) says there are people who exercise but who are not healthy, while premise 1 says that people who do not exercise are not healthy, but it doesn't guarantee that everybody who does exercise is healthy. So, answer (i) is not really damaging to the argument. Answer (ii) says that there are people who live successful lives who are not healthy. But, premise 2 says that everybody who lives a successful life is healthy, so answer (ii) directly contradicts this premise and would be very damaging to the truth of the premises if it were true. Answer (iii) says that there are people who live successful lives but who do not exercise. But our missing conclusion says that everyone who lives a successful life exercises, so answer (iii) directly contradicts that conclusion and would completely destroy the truth of the conclusion (and also imply that one or both of the premises had to be false). So, the correct answer would be that *both* (ii) and (iii) are severely damaging to the given argument.

11

STATEMENT FORMS: CONTRARIES, CONTRADICTIONS, AND TAUTOLOGIES

step five

Are there any fallacies?

▼

step six

What is the argument's structure?

▼

step seven

What other conclusions can be drawn?

▼

step eight

Do you agree or disagree with the conclusion?

If people don't want
to come out to the ballpark,
nobody's going to stop them.
—Yogi Berra (1959)

An aphorism never coincides
with the truth:
it is either a half-truth or
one-and-a-half truths.
—Karl Kraus (1930)

KEY TERMS

Contingent statement - A statement that under some truth conditions is a true statement and under other truth conditions is a false statement. All simple statements are contingent statements.

Contradiction - The conjunction of two statements related in such a way that exactly one must be true and the other must be false. The column under a contradiction in a truth table yields all lines with the value "false."

Contrary statements - Two statements which cannot both be true at the same time but which may be simultaneously false.

Inconsistent statements - A pair of statements which cannot be true at the same time. The two species of inconsistent statements are contrary statements and contradictory statements.

Tautology - A disjunction of a statement and its negation; it is always true. Its column in a truth table yields every line with a value of "true."

Another element in our assessment of arguments is the recognition of certain statement types. To better assess arguments, as we are asked to do in Steps 6, 7, and 8 of the Technique, we must become familiar with the complex statement forms known as *contraries, contradictions, tautologies,* and *contingent statements.* (Although contingent statements can also be simple as well as complex statements.)

Some pairs of statements cannot both be true at the same time. When a pair of statements cannot both be simultaneously true, they are said to be *inconsistent* with one another. Ralph Waldo Emerson once stated that "A foolish consistency is the hobgoblin of small minds. . . ." Nevertheless **inconsistent statements** can often be a problem when they occur in arguments. If we accept inconsistencies in our own reasoning, we can be sure that we believe in at least one false claim. Since it is not usually to our benefit to believe claims that we know to be false, it is important to determine where these inconsistencies lie and to root out those which are false. By the same token, finding inconsistencies in an opponent's argument can often be the basis for an effective counterargument. Since at least one of the two inconsistent claims must be false, we can often force an opponent to admit that one of her or his premises is false.

Having discussed the problems associated with inconsistent statements, we next consider statements known as tautologies. Because of their propositional form, they are statements that always turn out to be true. Finally, we briefly consider contingent statements, which are sometimes true and sometimes false.

There are two types of inconsistent statements, contraries and contradictories. Two statements are contrary to one another if it is impossible for them both to be true at the same time. They are contradictory to one another when they cannot both be true *and* cannot both be false.

11.1 CONTRARIES

Statements are said to be contrary to one another when they cannot both be true at the same time. To determine this about a pair of statements, you usually have to know a good deal about the content of each. For instance, you can determine that the following two statements are **contrary statements** only if you are aware of the fact that only one person at a time can be president of the United States:

> Bill Clinton is president of the United States.
> Hillary Rodham-Clinton is president of the United States.

These two statements cannot both be true, and in fact they *may* even both turn out to be false. This can be seen more readily by replacing the first of these two statements:

> Cheshire Clinton is president of the United States.
> Hillary Rodham-Clinton is president of the United States.

We can symbolize the fact that two statements are contrary by using the symbolization for *not both*. If we designate the two statements from our last example as C and H we can show that they are contraries by writing:

~(C & H)

which we can translate back into English as saying that "It is not the case that both C and H are true." Again this leaves open the possibility that they both may be false (which in fact they are).

Contrary statements can cause problems in two ways. The first has to do with the possibility of having contrary beliefs. The second arises when you consider the possibility of trying to follow contrary orders or instructions. When questioning our own beliefs, or the professed beliefs of others, it is worthwhile to look for contrary beliefs. This is important when you consider that our moral decisions are often made on the basis of principles in which we strongly believe. Contrary beliefs will often allow us to conclude anything we like from our principles. A student once began a paper with the following two lines:

> I am totally opposed to all killing of human beings by other human beings

and

> I am thoroughly in favor of capital punishment.

Can a person really have two opposing beliefs such as these? Well it's obvious that someone can *say* he has two opposing beliefs. That's exactly what the student did in the paper. But beliefs are more than statements filed away in our minds. If someone *really* believes something, he is ready to act on the basis of that belief. If someone regularly eats a lot of red meat, we're not going to let them get away with saying "I believe in vegetarianism." In the case of the student's opinion on capital punishment, the difficulty might arise if he were to serve on a jury deciding the fate of a convicted murderer. If he believes in the first statement, he'd be unwilling to vote for capital punishment. It would be at this point that these contrary beliefs would be "put to the test," and which principle he chose would at this point have a great bearing on another person's life.

Another problem arises when contrary statements are issued as orders or instructions. There are cases when it is really true to say that a person *can't* do both one and the other. This is particularly frustrating when another person is giving the instructions and he does not realize that his instructions are contraries. Thus the owner of a car dealership might be issuing contrary instructions to her sales staff by saying both

> Sell at least seven new cars today

and

> Catch up on all of your paperwork today.

In this example it might be the time factor that causes the two statements to be seen as contrary.

A more obvious example of contrary statements can be imagined in the case of driving a car while following the instructions of one of your passengers. Imagine you're coming to an intersection where you are faced with the options of turning left or right or continuing straight ahead. If your navigator tells you

> "At the next intersection go straight"

immediately followed by

"At the next intersection make a right turn"

you're going to have to find out which instruction is the correct one. You can't go *both* straight *and* to the right. You can only do one of these things. So you have to determine which course to take. Either you ask for clarification or maybe just guess. And of course there's still another option—making a left turn, which is an instance of how both of the contrary statements can turn out to be false.

The detection of contraries is useful in two ways. In the first place, we can detect when our own principles or ideas are contraries, and adjust them accordingly. A student can believe in not killing human beings *or* in capital punishment, but not *really* in both. If we want to be intellectually honest with ourselves, we have to make choices. A person cannot believe *everything*.

When criticizing another person's argument, it is also useful to point out inconsistencies. Telling someone else that her beliefs are inconsistent might not end the argument. But you will be in a position to force your opponent to *choose* one of the conflicting statements and disagree with the other. Finally, by recognizing that two instructions may be inconsistent with one another, we perhaps may be able to get a boss or parent to recognize the conflict. Claiming that the two are contraries is a good excuse for not doing both (although it may not be accepted as such).

EXERCISES

 A   LEVEL

Short Answers

1. When is a pair of statements said to be contrary to one another?
2. How does one symbolize a pair of contrary statements?
3. Why is it undesirable to hold inconsistent beliefs?
4. Name at least one benefit of being able to identify inconsistent statements.

True or False

* 5. ___T___ Inconsistent propositional statements are determined by the same rules as categorical inconsistencies.
* 6. ___T___ Contrary statements can both be false.
* 7. ___F___ Contrary statements may both turn out to be true.
* 8. ___F___ It is sometimes reasonable for a person to believe statements that are inconsistent with one another.
* 9. ___T___ The formal proposition ~(A & B) expresses the fact that the statements represented by A and B are contrary to one another.
*10. ___T___ Contradictory statements cannot both be true at the same time and cannot both be false at the same time either. So, when one is true, the other must be false.

B   LEVEL

State whether the following pairs of statements are contrary to one another. If you find that they are contrary to one another, be sure to state your reasons.

1. (a) I believe in God.
(b) I believe in the Devil.

2. (a) Brenda's favorite color is yellow.
(b) Brenda's favorite color is blue.

3. (a) St. Paul is the capital of Minnesota.
(b) Minneapolis is the capital of Minnesota.

4. (a) Sam Nunn is a senator from Georgia.
(b) Jimmy Carter is a senator from Georgia.

5. (a) It's raining.
(b) It's not raining.

6. (a) Karl Marx did not believe in an afterlife.
(b) Karl Marx believed in an afterlife.

7. (a) Peter enjoys listening to jazz.
(b) Peter enjoys listening to classical music.

8. (a) Barbara enjoys listening to rap music.
(b) Barbara hates listening to rap music.

9. (a) All Republicans are conservative.
(b) Some Republicans are not conservative.

10. (a) No Democrats are conservative.
(b) Senator Sam Nunn is a conservative Democrat.

C   LEVEL

Listen to a debate on a serious news analysis program. First try to find the inconsistencies in the individual positions advanced by the debaters. Then go on to list the statements made by one debater that are inconsistent with those of another. Finally, try to determine if there is any way that the inconsistencies among the debaters might be resolved to their mutual satisfaction.

11.2 CONTRADICTIONS

There is a particular form of inconsistency that can be recognized by a statement's *form* alone. In these cases the content doesn't matter. We saw that a pair of contrary statements could not both be true, but that they could both be false. Two statements are said to be contradictory when they cannot both be true *and* they cannot both be false. This results in the fact that exactly one of the statements *must* be true, while the other *must* be false. The most common form of the contradiction occurs when we have a situation where a statement and its direct denial are simultaneously asserted. The following is an example of a pair of contradictory statements in which one is the direct denial of the other:

Lisa is twenty years old.
Lisa is not twenty years old.

Not only must one of these sentences turn out to be true, but the other must turn out to be false precise-ly *because* the other is true. If we know that the statement "Lisa is twenty years old" is true, the statement "Lisa is not twenty years old" must for that reason be false. This leads to the most common form taken by a pair of contradictory statements—one is the negation of the other. This reciprocal relationship between the truth and falsity of contradictory statements can be demonstrated with a truth table:

L	L	~L
T	T	F
F	F	T

which shows that whenever L is true, ~L is false, and whenever L is false, ~L is true.

Now if we know this, then we also know that any attempt to bring these two statements together in a conjunction is going to produce a situation where the conjunction *has* to be false. Since either conjunct being false makes the entire conjunction false, this conjunction would *always* be false:

L & ~L

When contradictory statements are conjoined, the resulting statement is known simply as a **contradiction.** It is a statement that "speaks against itself" by asserting that one and the same statement is and is not true. A contradiction must therefore always be false. Again a truth table will demonstrate this:

L	~L	L & ~L
T	F	F
F	T	F

Every line under the column for the conjunction L & ~L is marked "false." This demonstrates that there is no possible way for a contradiction ever to be true—and we determined this simply by the form of the statement itself. It really doesn't matter what the L stands for. The fact that it is conjoined to its negation ~L makes the conjunction a contradiction. The following are also examples of contradictions:

S & ~S
P & ~P
(A ▼ B) & ~(A ▼ B)

while these are not:

S & ~R
~S & ~P
(A ▼ B) & ~(~A ▼ B)

SPORTING CONTRADICTIONS?

In a clever piece of journalism, Kenny Shoulder writes in "He Slud Home" for *TV Guide* the following jewels from sportscasting:

> New York Yankee commentator, Jerry Coleman was quoted as saying, "Mantle slides in with a stand-up double."
> And, veteran broadcaster, Ralph Kiner, New York Mets' announcer on WOR-9 since 1962 commented, "All of the Mets' road wins against Los Angeles this year have been at Dodger Stadium."
> We should not forget to mention Yogi Berra's now-famous, "It ain't over, 'till it's over."

Coleman's comment is an outright contradiction: if Mantle slid into second base, then it cannot be a "stand-up double," and if he had a stand-up double, then he could not have slid into second base. Perhaps, Coleman's colorful remark was meant to say tersely that Mantle slid into second base, but he actually had enough time for the hit to have been a stand-up double?

Kiner's comment about the Mets amounts to a tautology if it is true that all of the regular season games between the Mets and the Dodgers were played in either Shea Stadium (home games for the Mets) or in Dodger Stadium (road games for the Mets.) In other words, all of the road wins for the Mets over the Dodgers were road wins for the Mets over the Dodgers.

Finally, Yogi Berra's wry remark has to be a tautology also. The statement, "It's not over, 'till it's over," literally means that "If it's not over, then it's not over," which is logically equivalent to the tautology, "Either it's over, or it's not over." Try it!

(From Kenneth Shoulder, "He Slud Home," TV Guide, March 20, 1993, p. 16.)

Because the second conjunct looks exactly like the first, except for the presence of a tilde before the second, it is easy to see why these statements are contradictions. But often a contradiction is not so obvious. The statement $(\sim A \Rightarrow B)\ \&\ \sim(A \blacktriangledown B)$ is a contradiction. We can determine this by constructing a truth table and recalling the fact that *a statement is a contradiction if every line of its truth table turns out to be false:*

A	B	$(\sim A \Rightarrow B)$	&	$\sim(A \blacktriangledown B)$
T	T	T	F	F
T	F	T	F	F
F	T	T	F	F
F	F	F	F	T

While it is obviously worthwhile to ferret out the contradictions in our own beliefs, it is also useful in the course of an argument to point out the inconsistencies of your opponent. In the case of premises that are merely contrary (but not contradictory) this involves the practical task of pointing out where the inconsistencies lie. For instance, a person who made the contrary claims that Bill Clinton *and* Hillary Rodham-Clinton were both president of the United States could be reminded that since only one person is president at a time, only one of the statements could possibly be true. Contraries such as this one require you to look at the content of the statements in order to determine which can consistently be held.

In the case of contradictions, however, it is a question of form, and not content. Most people, of course, do not come right out and state contradictions. Contradictions are sometimes "hidden" within a set of premises and become apparent only when we attempt to discover them. To discover a lurking contradiction, it will be useful to first symbolize the premises, and then to use them to try to derive a contradiction. Consider, for example, the following argument:

> **Sales manager:** You want to make more money, right? If you want to make more money, you'll have to sell more. And if you want to sell more, you'll have to be much nicer to your customers. But you can't be nice to your customers. If you are nice, they'll take advantage of you.

If there's any conclusion at all to this argument, it's for the salespeople to start doing a better job. But if you take the sales manager's statements as a set of premises you'll find that they contain a hidden contradiction. We'll let the following letters stand for the statements of this argument:

> M = You want more money.
> S = You have to sell more.
> N = You have to be nicer to your customers.
> A = Your customers will take advantage of you.

This allows us to set up our premises as follows:

> 1. M
> 2. M $\Rightarrow$ S
> 3. S $\Rightarrow$ N
> 4. ~N
> 5. N $\Rightarrow$ A
> _____

To prove that this leads to a contradiction, we'll use our rules to try and prove this. The easiest way is to apply *modus tollens* to Lines 3 and 4:

> 6. ~S Lines 3 & 4, *modus tollens*

We can apply *modus tollens* again using Lines 2 and 6:

> 7. ~M Lines 2 & 6, *modus tollens*

Since in this case we're looking for a contradiction, we see that we can derive one by conjoining Lines 1 and 7 with the rule for combinations.

8. M & ~M

So we see that there *is* a contradiction inherent in the preceding argument. We've derived it on Line 8. By translating it back into ordinary language, we find that the sales manager assumes *both* that we want to make money *and* that we don't want to make money. If we put it all together, our proof looks like this:

1. M
2. M ⇒ S
3. S ⇒ N
4. ~N
5. N ⇒ A
_____

6. ~S   Lines 3 & 4, *modus tollens*
7. ~M   Lines 2 & 6, *modus tollens*
8. M & ~M   Lines 1 & 7, combination

You should notice that Line 5 was not used in deriving the contradiction; nor does it even tend to support the sales manager's conclusion. As we saw in Part 1 of this book, in most real-life arguments you tend to encounter these "free-floating" premises. When you confront a contradiction, you're put in the position of having to make a choice. Using our previous example, you can't turn left and not turn left at the same time. You either do or you don't.

CONTRADICTIONS IN THE MARKETPLACE?

Next time you are out purchasing some "non-alcoholic" beer, take a moment to read the label. Chances are you are going to be surprised to discover that "non-alcoholic beer" contains less than 1% (sometimes even 0.5%) alcohol. If that is the case, how can they call it "non-alcoholic"? And, what's worse, isn't that a little dangerous for recovering alcoholics who think they are getting the taste without any of the actual alcohol?

The packaging does seem to contain an outright contradiction: This bottle contains no alcohol and it is not the case that this bottle contains no alcohol. Or, put another way, to the question is there or isn't there any alcohol in this bottle, the answer is, "Yes, there is some, and, no, there is not any." Can you explain how this might have occurred?

EXERCISES

 A   LEVEL

Short Answers

 1. What is a contradiction?
 2. Explain the difference between contrary and contradictory statements.
 3. How can a truth table be used to determine that a pair of statements is contradictory?
 4. How can one prove that there is a contradiction within a set of premises through the use of a logical derivation?

True or False

 * 5. _T___ When all of the lines of a truth table for a given statement turn out to be false, the statement is a contradiction.
 * 6. _F___ In a contradiction, at least one of the component statements must be true while the other may be true or false.
 * 7. _F___ The statement symbolized (Z ⇒ R) & ~(R ⇒ Z) is a contradiction.
 * 8. _F___ The statements symbolized (B & ~C) ▼ ~(B & ~C) is a contradiction.
 * 9. _F___ Two statements cannot be contradictory and inconsistent at the same time.
 *10. _F___ "It is raining" and "it is sunny" are contradictory statements.

B   LEVEL

State whether the following pairs of statements are contradictory, or merely inconsistent:

 1. (a) It's raining.
    (b) It's not raining.
 2. (a) It's raining.
    (b) There's not a cloud in the sky.
 3. (a) Donna and Peter are going to the party.
    (b) Donna's going to the party, but Peter isn't.
 4. (a) Donna and Peter are going to the party.
    (b) Neither Donna nor Peter is going to the party.
 5. (a) You can have either a dog or cat as a pet.
    (b) You can have neither a dog nor a cat.
 6. (a) Turn left at the next intersection.
    (b) Turn right at the next intersection.
 7. (a) This elevator is going up.
    (b) This elevator is going down.

8. (a) You can have a pet.
    (b) You can't have a dog.
*9. (a) All Republicans are conservative.
    (b) Some Republicans are not conservative.
10. (a) All Republicans are conservative.
    (b) Senator Cohen is a Republican, but not a conservative.

Determine whether the following arguments contain contradictions. First translate its premises into symbolic form, and then try to derive a contradiction. (No conclusions have been listed since we are looking only for inconsistent premises here.)

*11. Whenever it rains, the streets get wet. The streets are not both wet and slippery. The streets are slippery. It is raining.

12. Either Lucy or Joe will go to the party. If Pam doesn't attend the party, then neither will Lucy. Pam is attending the party. Joe will not attend.

*13. I enjoy listening to either Beethoven or Bach. When I listen to Bach, I feel very logical. Whenever I hear Beethoven I feel very majestic. Right now I feel very logical. And I'm listening to Beethoven.

14. I do not enjoy listening to both Beethoven and Ives on the same day. I'm listening to Beethoven right now. If I don't listen to Ives today, then I won't have time for dinner. But I do have time for dinner.

C LEVEL

In the course of a week, try to find as many contradictions as you can from public as well as personal sources. Be sure to state what the contradiction is, and why only one statement must be true. Finally, determine which of the contradictories *is* in fact the true statement (although this may not always be possible).

11.3 TAUTOLOGIES AND CONTINGENT STATEMENTS

Just as a contradiction must always be false because of its form, so must a **tautology** be always true. And like the contradiction, this has nothing at all to do with the contents of the tautological statement, but only with its form. Remember that simple statements always have two possible truth values. But the truth value of the complex statement depends on those of the components. Sometimes the form of the complex statement ensures that the statement will always be true, regardless of the content. The usual form taken by a tautology is that of a disjunction of a statement and its negation. For instance, the following are all tautologies:

A ▼ ~A
B ▼ ~B
(C & D) ▼ ~(C & D)
(F ⇒ G) ▼ ~(F ⇒ G)

Notice that in each case the negated disjunct looks *exactly* like the affirmative one with the exception of the tilde. What a tautology is basically saying is that any given statement is either true or it is not true (false). When we looked at the contradiction we saw that any statement and its negation could not both be true. A tautology says that either a statement or its negation *must* be true. A tautology does not depend on the meaning or content of the terms involved. This results in part from our truth table for the disjunction. Remember the fact that a disjunction is true whenever either disjunct is true. Since one disjunct is the negation of the other, one of them has to be true. So on every line of the truth table for disjunctions we get a true result:

A ~A	A ▼ ~A
T F	T
F T	T

So it doesn't really matter what A *means*—A ▼ ~A must *always* be true.

But a tautology need not always take the form of a disjunction. Any complex statement that yields all true truth values are tautologies. The *negation* of a contradiction is a tautology, as are the following:

~(A & ~A)

B ⇒ B

(C & ~C) ▼ ~(C & ~C)

Contingent Statements

So in order to test a statement to determine whether or not it is a tautology, simply construct a truth table. The statement is a tautology when *all* of the possible truth value lines have values of T. If all the values are *false* then it's a contradiction. But what of the more usual case where some truth values are true and others false? This is, after all, the most common form of complex statement. This type of statement is known as a **contingent statement.** Its truth value depends on the truth values of its component statements and varies accordingly. Consider, for instance, the statement "Jill and Lisa will not both go to the same party." We'll symbolize this statement

~(L & J)

and then test it on a truth table. We get as a result:

L J	~(L & J)
T T	F
T F	T
F T	T
F F	T

So the statement ~(L & J) is sometimes true, and sometimes false. (It would be false, for instance, if both Lisa and Jill were to attend the party. We read this from Line 1.)

SUMMARY

Another element of Step 6 of the Technique is the familiarity with certain complex statement forms. In this chapter we discussed particular types of statements, some distinguished by their *contents,* the others by their *forms. Contrary statements* were said to be those that, because of their meaning (or content), could not both be true at the same time. A type of inconsistency is also exhibited on the formal level in the case of *contradictions.* These are statements that are inconsistent because one is the negation of the other. Contradictions must always be false. There are, however, statements that must always be *true* and these are known as *tautologies.* Tautologies are true statements which really tell us nothing because they have to be true regardless of their content.

Finally, the most common form of statement is the *contingent statement.* These are statements that under some truth conditions turn out to be true and under other conditions turn out to be false. The column under a contingent statement in a truth table contains at least one line marked true and at least one line marked false.

EXERCISES

A   LEVEL

Short Answers

1. What is a *tautology?*
2. Under what conditions is a tautology true?
3. State the difference between a contradiction and a tautology.
4. What is a *contingent statement?*
5. How does a tautology differ from a contingent statement?

True or False

6. ___F___ A tautology is always true because of its content.
7. ___T___ A contingent statement is sometimes true and sometimes false.
8. ___T___ The column of a truth table under a tautology yields a value of "true" on all of its lines.
9. ___T___ A contradiction is never true.
10. ___F___ The most common form of statement in use in everyday reasoning is the tautology.

B   LEVEL

Use truth tables to determine whether the following statements are contradictions, tautologies, or contingent statements:

1. Either it's raining or it's not.

2. If you don't go, then you don't go.

(* 3. Whenever it rains, it either rains or snows.

4. If Peter goes to the party, then Mary will either go or not go.

(* 5. If it's both raining and not raining, then it is either snowing or not snowing.

6. If I followed your instructions, then I'd both have to turn left at the next light and not turn left at the next light.

(* 7. Whenever I get hungry, I'm not hungry.

8. Diane either has a dog or doesn't have a dog, if we're talking about the same Diane.

State whether the following are contradictions, tautologies, or contingent statements:

(9. All bachelors are unmarried.

10. Betty is either married or unmarried.

(11. A carpenter is a person who works with wood.

12. That man must be a carpenter because he is building something out of wood.

(13. To be eligible to vote in the United States, you must be at least eighteen years of age.

14. If Rita likes Beethoven, then Rita likes Beethoven.

(15. If Paul likes Beethoven, then he likes classical music.

16. Joanne likes either Beethoven or Bach.

(17. Stealing is wrong.

18. Stealing is either right or wrong.

C   LEVEL

Look through several news analysis magazines for articles that contain arguments. Try to discover as many contrary sets of statements, contradictions, and tautologies as you can. In each case, do you believe that the author was aware of the type of statement being made? If so, what do you think his or her point was in using that particular type of statement?

CASE STUDY

Chromatic Fantasy, and Feud

(Selected excerpt from *Godel, Escher, Bach: An Eternal Golden Braid,* by Douglas R. Hofstadter.
Copyright © 1979 by Basic Books, Inc. Reprinted by permission of Basic Books, a division of HarperCollins Publishers, Inc.)

To balance the discussion of tautologies, contraries, and contradictions take a look at the interesting discussion created by Hofstadter concerning the nature of contradictions. Watch how the Tortoise uses normal, ordinary language and words in non-normal ways when it suits his purposes. Is he really contradicting himself or not? What makes you think he is or is not?

"Chromatic Fantasy, and Feud"

Having had a splendid dip in the pond, the Tortoise is just crawling out and shaking himself dry, when who but Achilles walks by.

Tortoise: Ho there, Achilles. I was just thinking of you as I splashed around in the pond.

Achilles: Isn't that curious? I was just thinking of you, too, while I meandered through the meadows. They're so green at this time of year. . .

Tortoise: You think so? It reminds me of a thought I was hoping to share with you. Would you like to hear it?

Achilles: Oh, I would be delighted. That is, I would be delighted as long as you're not going to try to snare me in one of your wicked traps of logic, Mr. T.

Tortoise: Wicked traps? Oh, you do me wrong. Would I do anything wicked? I'm a peaceful soul, bothering nobody and leading a gentle, herbivorous life. And my thoughts merely drift among the oddities and quirks of how things are (as I see them). I, humble observer of phenomena, plod along and puff my silly words into the air rather unspectacularly, I am afraid. But to reassure you about my intentions, I was only planning to speak of my Tortoise-shell today, and as you know, those things have nothing—nothing whatsoever—to do with logic!

Achilles: Your words DO reassure me, Mr. T. And, in fact, my curiosity is quite piqued. I would certainly like to listen to what you have to say, even if it is unspectacular.

Tortoise: Let's see. . . how shall I begin? Hmm. . .What strikes you most about my shell, Achilles?

Achilles: It looks wonderfully clean!

Tortoise: Thank you. I just went swimming and washed off several layers of dirt which had accumulated last century. Now you can see how green my shell is.

Achilles: Such a good healthy green shell, it's nice to see it shining in the sun.

Tortoise: Green? It's not green.

Achilles: Well, didn't you just tell me your shell was green?

Tortoise: I did.

Achilles: Then, we agree: it is green.

Tortoise: No, it isn't green.

Achilles: Oh, I understand your game. You're hinting to me that what you say isn't necessarily true; that Tortoises play with language; that your statements and reality don't necessarily match; that—

Tortoise: I certainly am not. Tortoises treat words as sacred; Tortoises revere accuracy.

Achilles: Well, then, why did you say that your shell is green, and that it is not green also?

Tortoise: I never said such a thing; but I wish I had.

Achilles: You would have liked to say that?

Tortoise: Not a bit. I regret saying it, and disagree wholeheartedly with it.

Achilles: That certainly contradicts what you said before!

Tortoise: Contradicts? Contradicts? I never contradict myself. It's not part of Tortoise-nature.

Achilles: Well, I've caught you this time, you slippery fellow, you. Caught you in a full-fledged contradiction.

Tortoise:	Yes, I guess you did.
Achilles:	There you go again! Now you're contradicting yourself more and more! You are so steeped in contraction it's impossible to argue with you!
Tortoise:	Not really. I argue with myself without any trouble at all. Perhaps the problem is with you. I would venture a guess that maybe you're the one who's contradictory, but you're so trapped in your own tangled web that you can't see how inconsistent you're being.
Achilles:	What an insulting suggestion! I'm going to show you that you're the contradictory one, and there are no two ways about it.
Tortoise:	Well, if it's so, your task ought to be cut out for you. What could be easier than to point out a contradiction? Go ahead—try it out.
Achilles:	Hmm. . . Now I hardly know where to begin. Oh. . . I know. You first said that (1) your shell is green, and then you went on to say that (2) your shell is not green. What more can I say?
Tortoise:	Just kindly point out the contradiction. Quit beating around the bush.
Achilles:	But—but—but. . .Oh, now I begin to see. (Sometimes I am so slow-witted!) It must be that you and I differ as to what constitutes a contradiction. That's the trouble. Well, let me make myself very clear: a contradiction occurs when somebody says one thing and denies it at the same time.
Tortoise:	A neat trick. I'd like to see it done. Probably ventriloquists would excel at contradictions, speaking out of both sides of their mouth, as it were. But I'm not a ventriloquist.
Achilles:	Well, what I actually meant is just that somebody can say one thing and deny it all within one single sentence! It doesn't literally have to be in the same instant.
Tortoise:	Well, you didn't give ONE sentence. You gave TWO.
Achilles:	Yes—two sentences that contradict each other!
Tortoise:	I am sad to see the tangled structure of your thoughts becoming so exposed, Achilles. First you told me that a contradiction is something which occurs in a single sentence. Then you told me that you found a contradiction in a pair of sentences I uttered. Frankly, it's just as I said. Your own system of thought is so delusional that you manage to avoid seeing how inconsistent it is. From the outside, however, it's plain as day.
Achilles:	Sometimes I get so confused by your diversionary tactics that I can't quite tell if we're arguing about something utterly petty, or something deep and profound!
Tortoise:	I assure you, Tortoises don't spend their time on the petty. Hence it's the latter.
Achilles:	I am very reassured. Thank you. Now I have had a moment to reflect, and I see the necessary logical step to convince you that you contradicted yourself.
Tortoise:	Good, good. I hope it's an easy step, an indisputable one.
Achilles:	It certainly is. Even you will agree with it. The idea is that since you believed sentence 1 ("My shell is green"), AND you believed sentence 2 ("My shell is not green"), you would believe one compound sentence in which both were combined, wouldn't you?
Tortoise:	Of course. It would only be reasonable . . . providing just that the manner of combination is universally acceptable. But, I'm sure that we'll agree on that.
Achilles:	Yes, and then I'll have you! The combination I propose is—

Tortoise:	But we must be careful in combining sentences. For instance, you'd grant that "Politicians lie" is true, wouldn't you?
Achilles:	Who could deny it?
Tortoise:	Good. Likewise, "Cast-iron sinks" is a valid utterance, isn't it?
Achilles:	Indubitably.
Tortoise:	Then, putting them together, we get "Politicians lie in cast-iron sinks." Now that's not the case, is it?
Achilles:	Now wait a minute . . . "Politicians lie in cast-iron sinks?" Well, no, but—
Tortoise:	So, you see, combining the two true sentences in one is not a safe policy, is it?
Achilles:	But you—you combined the two—in such a silly way!
Tortoise:	Silly? What have you got to object to in the way I combined them? Would you have me do otherwise?
Achilles:	You should have used the word "and," not "in."
Tortoise:	I should have? You mean, if YOU'D had YOUR way, I should have.
Achilles:	No—it's the LOGICAL thing to do. It's got nothing to do with me personally.
Tortoise:	This is where you always lose me, when you resort to your Logic and its high-sounding Principles. None of that for me today, please.
Achilles:	Oh, Mr. Tortoise, don't put me through all this agony. You know very well that that's what "and" means! It's harmless to combine two true sentences with "and"!
Tortoise:	"Harmless," my eye! What gall! This is certainly a pernicious plot to entrap a poor, innocent, bumbling Tortoise in a fatal contradiction. If it were so harmless, why would you be trying so bloody hard to get me to do it! Eh?
Achilles:	You've left me speechless. You make me feel like a villain, where I really had only the most innocent of motivations.
Tortoise:	That's what everyone believes of himself . . .
Achilles:	Shame on me—trying to outwit you, to use words to snare you in a self-contradiction. I feel so rotten.
Tortoise:	And well you should. I know that you were trying to set me up. Your plan was to make me accept sentence 3, to wit: "My shell is green and my shell is not green." And such a blatant falsehood is repellent to the Tongue of a Tortoise.
Achilles:	Oh, I'm sorry I started all this.
Tortoise:	You needn't be sorry. My feelings aren't hurt. After all, I'm used to the unreasonable ways of the folk about me. I enjoy your company, Achilles, even if your thinking lacks clarity.
Achilles:	Yes . . . Well, I fear I am set in my ways, and will probably continue to err and err again, in my quest for Truth.
Tortoise:	Today's exchange may have served a little to right your course. Good day, Achilles.
Achilles:	Good day, Mr. T.

3
APPLICATIONS

You should now be at the point where you understand the Technique. In this next section, you will learn how to apply some of these methods to different situations. In this section you will learn some methods for solving logical puzzles and for answering the reasoning portions of standardized examinations. You will also learn methods for writing arguments that you construct. First, you will reconsider a range of arguments that by their nature, remain inductive. These will include analogies and metaphors, causal arguments, explanations, theories, hypotheses, and several other forms of scientific reasoning.

12

INDUCTIVE REASONING

step five

Are there any fallacies?

step six

What is the argument's structure?

step seven

What other conclusions can be drawn?

step eight

Do you agree or disagree with the conclusion?

Ez soshubble ez a
baskit er kittens.
—*Joel Chandler Harris*

A theory can be proved by experiments;
but no path leads from experiment
to the birth of a theory.
—*Albert Einstein (1941)*

KEY TERMS

Analogical argument - An argument in which an analogy is used in support of a conclusion.

Analogy - The comparison or contrast of two different objects, ideas, or situations.

Causal explanation - An explanation based on the relationship between physical causes and their effects.

Combined method - A combination of the methods of agreement and difference. It is useful when the method of difference should be employed but the surrounding circumstances cannot be varied. Also called the *indirect method of difference.*

Hypothesis - A prediction about a cause-and-effect relationship.

Illustrative or explanatory analogy - The clarification of a difficult or complex point by comparison with a simpler case.

Inductive argument - An argument that does not guarantee the truth of the conclusion, even if the premises are known to be true.

Intentional explanation - An explanation based on the *reason* an individual does something.

Method of agreement - The variation of the surrounding circumstances of a suspected cause.

Method of concomitant variation - The correlation of varying degrees of a cause with varying degrees of the effect.

Method of difference - The variation of the suspected cause.

Method of residues - The correlation of causes and effects with the resulting "residue" effects attributed to the "leftover" causes.

Mill's methods - Methods of inductive reasoning analyzed by the philosopher John Stuart Mill.

Speculative analogy - An analogy used to guide actions.

Theory - A set of concepts that gives one a structure by which to make observations and frame hypotheses.

When reasoning deductively, we can be assured that our conclusions must be true if our arguments are valid and our premises are true. The necessity of the conclusion comes about as a result of the fact that the information contained by the conclusion is already contained in the premises. But inductive reasoning does not allow the luxury of certainty. **Inductive arguments** are arguments that do not guarantee the truth of the conclusion, even if the premises are known to be true. When reasoning inductively, we can never be completely certain that our conclusion is true even when our premises are all true and our argument is structurally reliable. In this type of reasoning, the information contained in the conclusion is *not* contained in the premises. Remember, the conclusion goes beyond what is contained in the premises.

But inductive reasoning is not the same as simply guessing. When we reason inductively, we evaluate the information we do possess and determine what is most probably true. The most common instrument of inductive reasoning is the analogy. After examining analogies, we will look at the forms of inductive reasoning as explained by the nineteenth-century philosopher John Stuart Mill.

12.1   ANALOGIES AND METAPHORS

An **analogy** is the comparison or contrast of two different objects, ideas or situations. Analogies are used in three ways that are relevant to critical thinking. They may be illustrative, speculative, or argumentative.

An **illustrative or explanatory analogy** is the clarification of a difficult or complex point by comparison with a simpler case. Chemistry teachers, for instance, often explain atoms by comparing them to the solar system, the sun representing the nucleus and the planets signifying the electrons. Parents of former years relied on the activities of "the birds and the bees" to explain human reproduction to their children.

A **speculative analogy** is one used to guide our actions. When a business person compares life to a "football game," for instance, he decides to approach things in a tough and resolute way. The fear of "another Pearl Harbor" has guided American foreign policy for more than half a century. For a scientist, a speculative analogy might suggest a line of experimentation. Czechoslovakian chemist Kekule provides a good example. Exhausted from unsuccessful attempts to discover the molecular configuration of benzene, the scientist lay before his hearth one evening watching his fire. Musing on the flames, he thought that they resembled serpents curling around to bite their own tails. Unable to get the benzene problem out of his thoughts, he finally connected the two. Rather than having a linear configuration, as he had been assuming, the molecule curled back around into a ring. The next day he began scientific testing of some of the consequences of this comparison. His comparison proved to be a good one. Note that the context of discovery may be quite different from the context of justification.

An **analogical argument** is one in which an analogy is used in support of a conclusion. Analogical arguments are inductive because they involve premises that state similarities between the object, idea, or situation in question and its analogue. These similarities are usually not under dispute. Further premises of an analogical argument go on to note further properties of the analogue. Although these properties may be obviously and indisputably present in the analogue, their presence in the original would at least be open to question. These arguments conclude that the property found in the analogue must therefore be present in the original. Former President Bush's comparison of Saddam Hussein to Adolph Hitler was a successful attempt to persuade the populace that war with Iraq was necessary. After all, Hitler had invaded a country,

LIFE'S A BEACH . . .OR A CUP OF TEA

In his book, *Lila,* Robert Pirsig has his main character, Phaedrus, try to explain why he kept his thoughts on little slips of paper:

> Now the main purpose of those slips was not to help him remember anything. It was to help him forget it. That sounded contradictory but the purpose was to keep his head empty, to put all his ideas of the past four years on the pilot berth where he didn't have to think of them. That was what he wanted.
>
> There's an old analogy to a cup of tea. If you want to drink new tea you have to get rid of the old tea that's in your cup, otherwise your cup just overflows and you get a wet mess. Your head is like that cup. It has a limited capacity and if you want to learn something about the world you should keep your head empty in order to learn it. It's very easy to spend your whole life swishing old tea around in your cup thinking it's great stuff because you never really tried anything new, because you could never get it in, because the old stuff prevented its entry because you were so sure the old stuff was so good, because you never really tried anything new . . . on and on in an endless circular pattern."

Here, Pirsig is offering a beautiful example of the illustrative use of analogies. His is not an argument by analogy *per se,* but rather an analogy that is used to reinforce an explanation. In other words, he is not saying that because the empty tea cup is capable of holding new tea that therefore his empty mind is capable of holding new ideas. Instead, he is employing the metaphor of the empty tea cup for the reader to draw parallels to what happens in his or her own thinking when their minds are "empty" and receptive to new ideas as opposed to what happens when the mind is already cluttered by the contents of a conceptual framework that will not allow for new ideas.

(Reprinted with permission from Robert M. Pirsig, Lila: An Inquiry into Morals, *New York: Bantam Books, 1991, pp 22–23.)*

just like Hussein had done. We let Hitler go to o long unopposed. The resulting millions of deaths could have been avoided had Hitler been stopped when he was weak. Hussein is now weak and if we don't stop him now, he will wreak havoc like Hitler. (Note also that this analogy functions *speculatively* in perhaps inspiring combatants to fight more tenaciously.)

The persistent problem of analogical argumentation is the fact that no two objects, ideas, or situations are ever exactly alike. No matter how many properties of two things are identical, there are always others that cannot be. Even identical twins are individuals with different names, a different birth order, and different experiences. This is most often the way to refute an analogical argument. By showing that there is a significant difference between the original and the analogue, one can challenge the suggested similarity. Such an objection is often commonly expressed by the retort "That's like comparing apples and oranges," meaning that the two situations are different enough to preclude any useful comparison.

Evaluating Analogies

The appropriateness of an analogy is a matter of degree. No two things are completely alike and all things are similar in some sense. Nevertheless, several criteria exist for evaluating how good or bad a particular analogy might be. An *analogy* should meet the following requirements.

1. An *analogy* should be more familiar than the subject of comparison. If you are discussing World War I, for instance, it might be useful to compare it to a family quarrel (since many of the reigning monarchs were related to one another). But it would be counterproductive in the discussion of family quarrels to compare them to World War I.

2. An *analogy* should be enlightening, and should provide information or a perspective that is not apparent in the subject of comparison. Using our previous example, the idea of family quarrels does indeed provide a useful perspective for analyzing the outbreak of World War I.

3. An *analogy* should be one that does not prejudice the issue by choosing an analogue with obviously biased connotations. A comparison often made by opponents of abortion is that between the abortion controversy and the struggle for the abolition of slavery. This is an example of a biased analogy, because a vast majority of people would never seek to defend slavery. On the other hand, it has been shown that a majority of Americans favor legalized abortion.

4. Because they are guides to action, *speculative analogies* should also be evaluated on the basis of their consequences and rejected if those consequences fail to materialize regularly. If someone were to compare prison boot camps to military boot camps, for instance, on the basis of the success of the military, it might transpire that prison boot camps did not have the same success. In this case, the analogy should be dropped.

5. Analogical arguments should also observe a final criterion. Because they rely on standard argument forms, analogical arguments must be evaluated on the basis of their logical structures and rejected if found invalid.

Although there are some obviously "false" analogies, most of the time it is a matter of judgment and degree. The more of these criteria an analogy fails to meet, the less appropriate it will be.

Metaphors

Metaphors constitute a very special class of analogies. A metaphor is the use of a word or phrase to describe something to which it does not literally apply. For instance, we can refer to a driver "weaving" through traffic and understand that he is not sitting in his car and literally weaving anything but is constantly switching lanes. We can also refer to the "mouth" of a bottle or of a river or of a "turning point" in life.

But unlike most other analogies, a metaphor does not explicitly announce itself. With most analogies we begin with an explicit comparison and announce this by saying things like "This is just like that" and then go on to list reasons. But metaphors are less obvious because they come into the conversation unannounced. This in itself would not be a problem except for the fact that metaphors carry a lot more *connotative weight* than ordinary analogies. The connotations of a term, as we discussed in Chapter 4, are those aspects of a term that influence the overall way we "feel" about it. For instance the term *murderer* explicitly denotes an individual who kills another, but also possesses the connotation of wrongfulness and evil, whereas the term *killer* does not necessarily do so. Since they are not functioning as explicit comparisons, metaphors rely highly on their connotative aspect to make their points. This is what we mean by their *connotative weight.*

Because of their ability to influence our feelings and attitudes, metaphors are very highly regarded in fields such as literature, poetry, and song writing. Dr. Martin Luther King's famous "I Have a Dream" speech instilled the hope and belief in many that social justice is possible. In effect, a metaphor gives us a new way of seeing things. It's not just a matter of point-by-point comparison. Metaphors are therefore much more difficult to refute. Their connotations tend to "fan out" into connotations of the connotations as the metaphor is internalized. A good example of this is the "clockwork universe." This was first invoked to explain the philosophy of the scientist Galileo. He compared the atoms in the universe to the parts of a clock. It was a metaphor that was immediately useful to science because it implied that future events could be predicted given enough knowledge of the present. (If I know how the clock works and what it reads now, I can tell you what it will read in three hours.) But the connotations of living in a clockwork universe became a problem when people began to realize that this meant that we as human beings were totally predictable and that our actions were not freely chosen.

EXERCISES

A   LEVEL

Short Answers

* 1. What is the difference between inductive and deductive reasoning?
* 2. What is an analogy?
* 3. What is a metaphor?
* 4. What is a speculative analogy?
* 5. How does a speculative analogy differ from an illustrative analogy?

True or False

* 6. _____ A metaphor relies more on the connotations of a term than does an analogy.
* 7. _____ Good analogies employ terms of comparison more familiar than those of the subject matter.
* 8. _____ Analogical arguments are usually worthless or fallacious.
* 9. _____ Analogies and metaphors are usually biased.
*10. _____ Speculative analogies should be evaluated on the basis of their consequences.

B   LEVEL

Evaluate the following analogies and metaphors:
* 1. Doing business is like playing a game of football.

2. A woman needs a man like a fish needs a bicycle.

* 3. An argument by analogy is like a rented tuxedo: It never quite fits.

4. Logic is like playing the piano because the more you practice, the more proficient you become.

* 5. Comparing a baseball team to a basketball team is like comparing apples and oranges.

6. Owning a pet is a lot like having a child.

* 7. Karl Marx believed that anyone who was a salaried employee of anyone else was a "wage slave."

8. According to former President Bush, Saddam Hussein was very much like Adolph Hitler.

* 9. Because they're usually the center of attention of a room, a television functions much the same way that fireplaces did a hundred years ago.

10. War is hell.

*11. The eyes are the windows of the soul.

12. The president of the United States is the head of the nation.

*13. Business is a rat race.

14. Cigarettes are coffin nails.

*15. (Difficult) "[James Joyce] once told me that writing a book is very much like writing music. I disputed that and asked 'How could you write a chord?' He said, 'Oh, it's so simple. Suppose I write in Chapter One about a man who has kidney disease, and sometime later in the book about a person who eats kidneys, and still later about someone who gets a kick in the kidneys. Then you have a chord.' I immediately understood that." (unattributed, in *The New Yorker,* 1992)

C   **LEVEL**

1. Find a chapter of a novel or a short story that employs metaphors. Evaluate the metaphors you find on the basis of their connotations and their relevance to the story. Be sure to note which emotions, if any, are intended to be aroused by the metaphor.

2. Analogies are often employed in the reporting of sports events. Watch a sporting event on television or listen to one on the radio and evaluate the analogies employed by the announcers on the basis of the rules laid out in this chapter.

12.2 MILL'S METHODS

The nineteenth-century British philosopher John Stuart Mill believed that there were four basic methods of inductive reasoning. (There are actually five if you count the "combined method.") Following these methods provides us with an approach much less susceptible to error than simple analogical reasoning. Nevertheless, it should be remembered that these methods are *inductive* and might lead to false conclusions even when scrupulously followed.

Before beginning our discussion of the individual methods, we should point out that Mill sees his methods as capable of isolating either causes or effects. The concept of cause and effect is one we ordinarily use in a variety of ways. It may be to find the solution to a problem or to assess a person's guilt or innocence. In some cases of problem-solving we attempt to find the cause of the situation. In others it is the effect that is at issue. **Mill's Methods** can be of help in either case.

The first of the four methods is called the **method of agreement.** This method is particularly useful when we are limited to *observation* and get little or no chance to experiment. This method is employed when we notice that a certain phenomenon or event is always accompanied by another constant element. If, for instance, Susan breaks out in a rash whenever she eats pizza, cheese danishes, and grilled-cheese sandwiches, she might use the method of agreement to conclude that she has an allergy to cheese. Similarly, if David causes a short circuit every time he plugs in his electric shaver, he might conclude that the shaver is causing the circuit breaker to trip.

The point of the method of agreement is that one particular element seems to be present whenever the phenomenon occurs. But this method can easily be misapplied, so it is important that as many observations as possible be made. For instance, in the case of Susan's allergy, she noticed that she ate cheese prior to every breakout of her rash. But she may not have noticed that in each case cited above she also ate flour (in the form of dough). For the method of agreement to be most effective she should have tried to vary every circumstance but the one in question. Once the cheese became suspect, she might have tried to eat cheese in other dishes and in other forms that did not contain dough, or tomato sauce, or sugar. She might even have tested her hypothesis by eating plain cheese to judge its effects.

So the method of agreement begins with a set of observations in which a single element is found to be present. Once this element is noticed it becomes the *hypothesis* or more simply the *suspect*. To test this suspected cause or effect, we then go on to observe other situations where the suspected cause or effect is present, but where the surrounding circumstances differ as much as possible. The more variety there is in the surrounding circumstances, the smaller the chance that we will mistakenly focus on the wrong suspect. Susan may never have discovered the cause of her allergy if she restricted her observations to her reaction to different types of pizza.

But no matter how hard we try to isolate the suspected cause or effect of a situation from a set of observations, we may overlook something that was present in all cases but of which we were unaware. In Susan's case, it is possible that all cheese contains some salt as a preservative and it was really the salt that was causing her allergic reaction. To minimize this type of mistake, Mill invokes a second method.

Mill's second method of inductive reasoning is known as the **method of difference.** Unlike the method of agreement, this method is more suitable to experimental manipulation. It also can help to confirm (or refute) a conclusion arrived at by the method of agreement. If the method of agreement keeps the suspected cause constant while varying the circumstances, the second method tests the results of keeping the circumstances constant while varying the suspected cause or effect.

A situation often encountered provides a good example. David plugs in his electric shaver (as he does every morning) and finds that it doesn't work. He wonders whether something is wrong with his shaver or with the electrical outlet. To employ the method of difference here, he must first make a guess at the suspected cause. Assume that be believes the shaver has worn out. (It's a fairly old one and it's already lasted longer than he has expected.) So his hypothesis is that the shaver is burned out, and the problem is not with the outlet. To test this hypothesis he takes another appliance (say, a hair dryer) that he knows is working and plugs it into the same outlet. If the hair dryer works, he knows that the outlet is not at fault and the problem must be with his shaver. The circumstances (the outlet and the flow of electricity) have remained constant. What has changed (the "difference") is that in the first case the shaver was present. In the second instant it was not (the hair dryer was substituted).

We can see by this example why the method of agreement may have been misleading. Suppose that David noticed that his shaver did not work. Instead of employing the method of difference, suppose that he had chosen the method of agreement. Rather than trying the hair dryer in the same outlet, he went around his house plugging the shaver into various unused outlets. By the method of agreement, he may have concluded that since the shaver did not work in all cases (that is, in all instances the experiments "agreed") that therefore the shaver was not working. But the problem here is that he may have neglected to notice that perhaps *none* of the outlets had any electricity flowing through them. Perhaps the circuit breakers controlling these outlets caused them all to shut off. The method of agreement would not have allowed David to notice this possibility. By employing the method of difference, however, he would immediately have suspected the outlet had the hair dryer failed to work.

Similarly, Susan could have tested her allergy to the cheese on the pizza by employing the method of difference. Instead of sampling different types of cheese (the method of agreement) she might have asked the cook to make her a pizza with everything *but* the cheese. If she still had an allergic reaction, this employment of the method of difference would have led her to suspect that another ingredient was causing her distress. If the reaction did not occur in the absence of the cheese, she could have rightly concluded that the cheese (or one of its components) was the cause of her problem.

While the method of difference should be employed to confirm the conclusions reached by the method of agreement, this may not always be possible. In such cases Mill suggests that we use the **combined method** of agreement and difference. He also refers to this method as the *indirect method of difference.* If a scientist, for instance, were to discover a cure for AIDS, she could not employ the method of difference directly. To do so would require that all of the circumstances remain the same while the drug was present *and* when it was not. But every human being varies greatly from every other in terms of chemical makeup. Once the scientist gave the cure to a subject, she could not "un-give" the drug. Either the subject takes the drug or he does not. And if the scientist were to give the same drug to a different subject, the chemical and metabolic circumstances would be different enough that we could not really say that the circumstances remained constant.

To overcome this problem, the scientist would test her discovery by giving the drug to a large number of patients. She might then compare the results to a similar number of patients who had not received the drug. (Perhaps they had been given placebos or sugar pills to rule out any psychological effects.) While the circumstances had not remained exactly the same in both cases, they were similar enough to admit of a comparison. By selecting large enough groups, the scientist would be allowed to test her cure "indirectly" by the method of difference. In fact, this is exactly why most testing done today on living subjects requires the existence of a "control group." The method is said to be combined in that it employs the method of agreement within both groups, and the method of difference in the contrast between two groups.

The **method of residues** is more appropriate to the carefully controlled experimentation of the laboratory than it is for everyday life. It is employed in a situation where we may have accounted for the causes of all the observed effects, but in which there is a "leftover" effect that remains unexplained. In such cases, the isolation of a causal element that had not been previously accounted for becomes paired with the unexplained effect.

Such a situation occurred when Einstein's general theory of relativity predicted that light from the sun could be observed bending around the moon during a solar eclipse. Classical physics, prior to Einstein, had assumed that light would not be attracted by gravitational fields. Hence, light emitted from the sun would not be "bent" when traveling past the moon. When the light from the solar eclipse of 1919 was measured, it was found to bend at precisely the angle predicted by Einstein's theory. The effect of gravity on light rays was the "residue" effect for which classical physics had provided no explanation. (Although the bending had been noticed before, it was thought to be due to errors in measurement, or else blamed on the imprecision of the measuring devices.)

The fourth and final method cited by Mill is the **method of concomitant variation.** This method is used when we cannot employ the method of difference because there are no available instances where the cause in question is absent. Unless you are on a space shuttle, for instance, you can't escape the force of the earth's gravity. In these cases we notice the effect we are studying varies with a particular cause. Although we cannot use the method of difference to get rid of that cause completely, we may be able to experiment by varying that cause and noticing its effects. A teacher might notice, for instance, the effort of classroom temperature on students' test performance. While he could not employ the method of difference to rid the classroom entirely of heat, it might be possible to vary the temperature to see what effect it might have on the average grade. Similarly, a scientist might test the effect of background noise on a patient's blood pressure by varying the pitch or the loudness.

Note that with the method of concomitant variation the effect need not always be in a one-to-one ratio with the cause. A small variation in one might produce a large variation in the other. It may require a large amount of testing to determine the exact correlation between the two to determine the precise mathematical relationships.

While Mill believes that these four methods (five if you count the combined method) exhaust all the possibilities of inductive reasoning, he does not claim that these methods are foolproof. Nevertheless, they provide a much greater possibility of reaching a true conclusion than mere guessing.

Before going on to look at some of the inductive fallacies that can occur with the employment of these methods, we ought to note that since the time during which Mill wrote his book, mathematicians, scientists, and philosophers have developed more precise statistical methods for arriving at inductive conclusions. The advent of the computer in the mid-twentieth century has enabled even greater sophistication in the employment of inductive reasoning. Yet these developments are simply elaborations of Mill's methods. The great discoveries of science follow the same lines of reasoning as everyday problem-solving—and both scientific as well as everyday reasoning are subject to the same mistakes. Mill's methods are summarized in Table 12-1.

Several fallacies are associated with inductive reasoning. Unlike the formal fallacies, however, the inductive fallacies leave some room for disagreement in particular cases. This is because inductive reasoning is essentially based on *comparisons.* It allows us to compare things we know well with things with which we are less familiar. While analogies and metaphors stress the similarities between the known and the unknown, Mill's methods require us to pay attention to the differences as well. The problems arise because no matter how alike two situations may be, there must always be *some* difference. No two situations are ever completely alike.

But when we use inductive reasoning, there is a tendency to focus on the similarities and to neglect the differences. Because there are some points of comparison between the two situations, it is easy to forget that not all points of the comparison will hold. Consider the following fallacies.

TABLE 12-1
SUMMARY OF MILL'S METHODS

The methods of agreement and difference, and the combined method can be summarized by noting the change, or lack of change in the hypothesis or the surrounding circumstances:

Method	Hypothesis or Suspected Cause or Effect	Surrounding Circumstances
Agreement	Remains the same	Varies
Difference	Present in one case, absent in the other	Remains the same
Combined	Present in first group, absent in second	Varies within each group

The methods of residues and concomitant variations can be summarized by noting which elements are correlated with one another:

Method	Correlation
Residues	Known causes correlated with known effects; "leftover" causes correlated with "leftover" effects
Concomitant	Variations in causes numerically correlated
Variation	With variations in effects

Hasty Generalization

This fallacy is one that often accompanies the method of agreement. It occurs when we have evidence that a few cases have a common feature and then go on to conclude that all or most cases of the same phenomenon have that feature. For instance, if we notice that many marriages wind up in divorce, we may hastily generalize to the conclusion that all or most marriages cannot survive. Or perhaps someone notices that all of the pet dogs she has encountered have fleas and goes on to conclude that all dogs have fleas.

The difficulty in identifying this fallacy arises when we try to determine just how many cases are required before a generalization can be legitimately made. The answer is going to vary in different cases. It will also be affected by the fact that no matter how many specific instances one has of a particular phenomenon, there is always the possibility that there are some contrary cases that we just have not run across. As the eighteenth-century philosopher David Hume pointed out, no generalization can ever be one hundred percent certain. No matter how many days the sun rises, there is always the possibility that it will fail to do so tomorrow.

To reduce the natural uncertainty of generalizations, scientists and mathematicians have developed laboratory and statistical methods to eliminate some of the haste. But even these methods have not completely eliminated mistakes. And if scientists in a laboratory are subject to these sorts of errors, we can expect that those of us who do our thinking outside of the laboratory will occasionally do likewise.

But this should not stop us from reasoning inductively. It should, however, make us somewhat more careful when we do generalize and to avoid the haste with which we come to certain conclusions. When dealing with human beings, such hasty generalizations can lead us to an unfair assessment of other individuals and in extreme cases to racial, ethnic, or religious prejudice.

As mentioned earlier, there are no clear-cut rules as to when we have generalized too hastily. But there are some things that we can watch for. For instance, we might ask ourselves whether or not there are other examples that we could examine which might present a counterexample to our generalization. To ignore those instances is to be guilty of a mind as closed as the churchman who refused to look through Galileo's telescope because he was afraid that Galileo was right and that there really were rings around the planet Saturn. Keeping an open mind can help us avoid many mistakes.

Another thing to keep in mind is the number of examples we have chosen compared with the total number of instances of the phenomenon in question. If someone concludes that all people of Chinese ancestry like to ride bicycles when he has met only three, he would do well to remember that there are currently more than one billion people in the world who fit the category. On the other hand, if we have never met a dog who didn't like meat, and we have run across a good number of dogs in our lifetime, we can safely conclude that at least *most* dogs like meat.

This brings us to a third point. When speaking in general terms, it is much more intellectually honest to employ the term *most* rather than *all*. Doing so doesn't mean that we are employing a "weasler" allowing us to save face if we turn out to be wrong. Rather, we are indicating that despite the evidence we have amassed, we are open to the fact that there are some cases that may contradict our conclusion. We are also acknowledging the fact that we are using *inductive* rather then formal reasoning and that the truth of our premises in no way guarantees the truth of our conclusions.

Accident

Another fallacy that can arise with inductive reasoning is one that is pretty much the opposite of hasty generalization. It occurs when we have concluded that *most* examples of a given phenomenon have a common feature and then go on to assert that because a particular instance is a case of the phenomenon, it must also possess that feature. Consider the example about dogs mentioned earlier. Having concluded that most dogs enjoy eating red meat we may be led to erroneously conclude that a particular dog with which we are acquainted will also enjoy eating red meat. Yet it is possible that our generalization is true, while the particular dog in question is a notable exception. It is worthwhile to remember that with this type of argument, as with all inductive reasoning, the conclusion is by no means guaranteed. When we are talking about the characteristics of a group of individuals or a group of things, we almost *never* mean to assign the characteristics of the group to *all* of the members of that group. Not all players in the National Basketball Association are tall, and although most cats enjoy an occasional saucer of milk, there are some that do not.

EXERCISES

A   LEVEL

Short Answers

* **1.** Describe Mill's method of agreement.
* **2.** What is meant by Mill's method of difference?
* **3.** What does Mill mean by the method of concomitant variation?
* **4.** Briefly describe the method of residues.
* **5.** How does the fallacy of hasty generalization exhibit "bad" inductive reasoning?
* **6.** What is the fallacy of accident?

True or False

* **7.** _____Mill's methods are essentially sophisticated versions of comparative reasoning.
* **8.** _____The method of residues states that whatever is left over after all of the premises of an argument have been verified must be false statements.
* **9.** _____The fallacy of Hasty Generalization is often committed as a misapplication of the method of agreement.
* **10.** _____"Most Americans are patriotic and Jim is an American so he must be patriotic" is an example of the fallacy of accident.

B   LEVEL

For each of the following problems, determine which of Mill's methods would be most appropriate to its solution. Be sure to propose a strategy for discovering the answer.

* **1.** Determining whether or not a car battery is dead.
  2. Ascertaining which appliance is causing an electrical circuit breaker to shut off.
* **3.** Finding the best temperature to set a thermostat at to promote the growth and flowering of houseplants.
  4. Determining how much sugar to add to an incomplete recipe. (Assume you know everything except the amount of sugar to add.)
* **5.** The relationship between how fast you jog and how far you can go.
  6. Which food is causing an allergic reaction.
* **7.** The effects of phases of the moon on crime in a given community.
  8. The relationship between poverty and crime.
* **9.** How cholesterol relates to heart disease.
  10. The success of an advertising campaign played to different television markets across the country.

C   LEVEL

The following are examples of the application of inductive reasoning taken from various articles. For each of the following, state which of Mill's methods is being applied. Also suggest any shortcomings of the stated approach.

1. There are several studies showing a link between increased milk intake and lowered cholesterol. The latest evidence comes from a study conducted by researchers at Pennsylvania State University, published this year in the *Journal of the American College of Nutrition* (Vol. 11, no. 1):

   > During a one-week baseline period, researchers measured the cholesterol, blood pressure and triglycerides of 64 people, ages 21 to 73. The researchers then asked these people to add a quart of solids-fortified skim milk to their daily diets. Researchers continued to take the same measurements during the remaining eight weeks of the milk-supplementation experiment. Results of the comparison among the people whose cholesterol started at or above 190 milligrams per deciliter. . ., cholesterol levels dropped dramatically, by 6.6 percent at the end of the eight weeks. Overall, for the entire group, cholesterol levels dropped 5.7 percent.
   >
   > —George L. Blackburn, M.D., Ph.D. in *Prevention* Magazine
   >
   > (Reprinted by permission of *Prevention.* Copyright © 1992 Rodale Press, Inc. All rights reserved.)

2. I was introduced to the idea of a global environmental threat as a young student when one of my college professors was the first person in the world to monitor carbon dioxide (CO_2) in the atmosphere. Roger Revelle had, through sheer persistence, convinced the world scientific community to include as part of the International Geophysical Year (1957–58) his plan for regularly sampling CO_2 concentrations in the atmosphere. His colleague C. D. Keeling actually took the measurements from the top of the Mauna Loa volcano in Hawaii. In the middle 1960s Revelle shared with the students in his undergraduate course on population the dramatic results of the first eight years of measurements: The concentrations of CO_2 were increasing rapidly each year. . . . Professor Revelle explained that higher levels of CO_2 would create what he called the greenhouse effect, which would cause the earth to grow warmer. The implications of his words were startling: we were looking at only eight years of information, but if this trend continued, human civilization would be forcing a profound and disruptive change in the entire global climate.

   —Senator Albert Gore in *Earth in the Balance*

   (Reprinted with permission from Albert Gore, *Earth in the Balance,* New York: Houghton Mifflin Company, 1992.)

3. As the various mental faculties gradually developed themselves the brain would almost certainly become larger. No one, I presume, doubts that the large proportion which the size of man's brain bears to his body, compared to the same proportion in the gorilla or orang, is closely connected with his higher mental powers. We meet with closely analogous facts with insects, for in ants the

cerebral ganglia are of extraordinary dimensions, and in all the Hymenoptera these ganglia are many times larger than in the less intelligent orders, such as beetles.

—Charles Darwin in *The Descent of Man*

4. It was established from an enormous body of statistics, taken during 1853, that the unmarried men throughout France, between the ages of twenty and eighty, die in a much larger proportion than the married: for instance, out of every 1000 unmarried men, between the ages of twenty and thirty, 11.3 annually died whilst of the married, only 6.5 died. A similar law was proved to hold, during the years 1863 and 1864, with the entire population above the age of twenty in Scotland: for instance, out of every 1000 unmarried men, between the ages of twenty and thirty, 14.97 annually died, whilst of the married only 7.24 died, that is less than half. Dr. Stark remarks on this, "Bachelorhood is more destructive to life than the most unwholesome trades, or than residence in an unwholesome house or district where there has never been the most distant attempt at sanitary improvement." He considers that the lessened mortality is the direct result of "marriage, and the more regular domestic habits which attend that state."

—Charles Darwin in *The Descent of Man*

5. The idea that chemical signals can affect gene activity dates to the early days of embryology. When researchers cut pieces of tissue from one part of an embryonic frog and placed them at another site, the transplanted tissue would sometimes grow into a form appropriate to its initial location—resulting, for example, in a frog with a misplaced limb. But if an embryo was manipulated early enough, it would recover and produce a normal animal. Such results suggested that undetected signals could affect subsequent gene expression.

—Tim Beardsley, *Scientific American,* August 1991.

(Reprinted with permission from Tim Beardsley, "Smart Genes," *Scientific American,* August 1991, Vol. 265, No. 2, p. 88.)

12.3 HYPOTHESES AND THEORIES

Scientific reasoning has come a long way since the time of John Stuart Mill. Statistical methods for evaluating data and the refinement of experimental procedures to ensure unbiased results have allowed science to come as far as it has in the past century. Yet much of scientific method is still based on the hypothesis-experimentation model with which Mill was familiar.

But the method of hypothesis-experimentation is not at all peculiar to science. It becomes relevant in almost all cases of problem-solving. Even though statistical data and laboratory methods are not readily available to most of us, a correct application of this type of reasoning can help us to avoid many errors.

Hypotheses

Hypotheses are suppositions or assumptions about what may be the case. A scientist hypothesizes about natural processes. In solving everyday problems, we hypothesize when we conjecture about a possible solution. Hypotheses are not created in a vacuum, but in the context of situations in which they arise. The context includes the scientist's or problem-solver's experiences. A professional mechanic has a much better chance of solving an automotive problem than an amateur.

Hypotheses in themselves, however, can never solve the problems they address. Whether or not they are true can be determined *only* by testing them or putting them into practice. The image of the serpent biting its own tail suggested to Kekule the hypothesis of the benzene *ring*. But as we related in the story, it was still necessary for Kekule to *test* his hypotheses in the laboratory.

To derive a strategy for testing an individual hypothesis, it is important to remember that each hypothesis involves predictions. Consider the example of an automobile that will not start. One possible hypothesis for this failure is that the battery is too low on power to turn over the engine. This hypothesis involves the consequence that none of the car's accessories drawing power directly from the battery should exhibit full power. So one way to test this hypothesis is to tap on the horn. If it does not sound as loud or steady as usual, then the prediction has been verified. Another way to test this hypothesis would be to turn on the headlights and check their intensity.

Notice that we said in the previous paragraph that the horn not sounding or the lights not working would not *prove* that the battery was the problem. But it does lend *support* to that conclusion, and having *both* the horn and the lights fail lends stronger support to the conclusion than would be the case if only one or the other had not worked. But we can never obtain final and conclusive evidence that would guarantee our hypothesis is correct. Consider the fact that even if we replaced the battery with a new one and the automobile then starts, the possibility still exists that the low battery power was itself *caused* by a further problem in the electrical system. If even the newer battery runs itself out in a few days, the problem was not really "solved," it only seemed to be solved. This is, in fact, why scientists are so concerned with ensuring the objectivity of their methods. It is very easy to mistake an apparent solution for a genuine one. Basically, hypotheses can be evaluated according to the following criteria:

1. *Consistency with established claims:* Any hypothesis that is inconsistent with proven claims may be rejected prior to testing.
2. *Clarity:* The hypothesis should be unambiguous and its meaning clear.
3. *Relevant testing:* The tests or experiments designed to verify the hypothesis should be relevant and not establish claims that are only tangentially relevant to the hypothesis.
4. *Variety in testing:* The tests or experiments should include as broad a range as possible.
5. *A skeptical attitude:* Since most of us tend to favor our own ideas, it's a good thing when testing an hypothesis to remember that we can be wrong.

On this last point it might be good to remember the attitude of the escape artist Harry Houdini who desperately wanted to communicate with the spirit of his deceased mother. Despite his desire to believe that such communication was possible, he did his best to disprove any spiritual medium or advisor who claimed to be able to help him. Houdini wanted to believe, but he wanted to believe truthfully.

Theories

While most people tend to use the word *theory* to describe what we call a *hypothesis,* they are not actually the same thing. A **theory** is a set of concepts, hypotheses, and perspectives explaining a related group of phenomena. Theories *include* hypotheses, but are really much more. Darwin's theory of evolution, for instance, is not simply the hypothesis that humans and apes evolved from a common species. The theory includes concepts such as "natural selection" and "competition among species." These concepts are not so much hypotheses as they are terms we are meant to apply to our observations. The kinds of questions that we ask are defined by the concepts that we are using. For instance, someone accepting Darwin's theory might be tempted to ask the question "Is the extinction of the dodo bird a case of natural selection?" The same question would not even occur to someone professing to be a Creationist (i.e., someone who rejects Darwin's theory and accepts the biblical account of creation).

Theories, of course, also give us political perspectives and may affect the way we evaluate events. Marxist theorists, for instance, rely heavily on the concept of "domination." When they analyze any historical event, they tend to see it as the case of one group dominating (usually unfairly) another group. An individual with a more democratically oriented theory of government might view the matter without invoking the idea of domination at all.

The benefit of working through a particular theory is that it does give one a perspective and a set of conceptual tools that would be unavailable without it. Without a theoretical framework of some sort we would simply be confronted with a plethora of unrelated facts. A theory gives us a place to look for the relationships. As a result, the theory we hold determines to a great extent the possible hypotheses we can develop. A modern medical practitioner, for instance, would not hypothesize that a patient's illness was due to an "imbalance of bodily humors." This explanation would only occur to someone familiar with medieval European medical theory. Similarly the medievalist would not understand what the modern doctor meant by an "infection."

The danger with a theory is that it can become confining and continue to influence our thought when it has outlived its usefulness. Theories are slow to die. It is psychologically difficult to reject a long-held theory. The tenacity with which many individuals argue their religious and political theories are notable cases. In fact, it seems to be a widespread human phenomenon that most people have a need to get others to accept the theories they themselves hold.

Reasons and Causes

There are two basic ways of explaining how an event came about. One way is to cite the physical events that transpired. The other is to focus on the reasons individuals have for acting. Explanations that rely on the sequence of physical events and conditions and their effects are known as **causal explanations.** Those based on the reasons why agents act as they do are referred to as **intentional explanations.** Note that a large number of events can be explained both intentionally and causally. For instance, a causal explanation of how the channels on a TV set were changed would involve a description of the way the remote control worked, how it sent its signals to the set, and how the internal circuits responded. But if we want to know *why* Keri changed the channel, we'd be looking for the reasons that motivated her to pick up the remote control. Generally, causal explanations answer the question of "How did it happen?" or sometimes even "What happened?", while intentional explanations address the question "Why did it happen?"

Intentional Explanations When we ask for the reasons why a person did a certain thing, we are looking for the motives that person had for acting the way he did. If Joey builds a doghouse for his dog, he might do it to give his "companion animal" a shelter from the elements. Now it's not always the case that we must really be sure that we know what a person's motives are for acting. This sometimes includes even our own

I'VE GOT A THEORY ABOUT THAT . . .

On the television show *Northern Exposure,* one of the main characters, Holling, finds the skeletal remains of a bear named "Jesse." For a myriad of reasons, he and "Jesse" had been long-time foes with a healthy mutual respect. Now, Holling was upset. He began to look over the decayed carcass and observed that there was not a mark on any part nor damage to any bone. He tentatively concluded that "Jesse" had not been killed by another animal. He further observed that all the claws (save the one Holling had bitten off!) were intact, as was the skull. He further concluded that "Jesse" had not been killed by human beings, who then would have taken these valuable parts. He continues to note that there were no sutures on his skull, nor any visible signs of injury, thereby concluding that no accident had befallen his old enemy. Holling then stands up in apparent disbelief and draws the tentative conclusion that "Jesse" probably died of old age.

What we have here in a nutshell is a classic case of an hypothesis in the formation. From carefully drawn observations, certain possible outcomes are ruled out. This process continues until the available data have been exhausted. Then a final estimate or conclusion is drawn that would appear to account for all of the observations without stretching credibility.

(Courtesy of CBS)

motivations. Joey might "really" have built his doghouse to lessen his guilt over the dog's banishment to the backyard. But these are matters for psychologists to resolve. What is pertinent here is the fact that even if we do sometimes fool others and ourselves, we do explain our actions on the basis of reasons.

While the reason why a person does something is based on their intentions, it is not the case that we would have to "read their minds" in order to ascertain why they were acting. If Joey bakes a birthday cake for Keri, we see him present it to her with a smile, and we know that it is Keri's birthday, we can pretty well conclude that the reason he baked it was to help her celebrate her birthday. Observing enough of the circumstances and actions leading up to an event can furnish good inductive evidence for concluding that someone acted for a given "reason." This can be crucial when trying to determine a person's guilt or innocence, for instance, in a court of law. Whether a killing was an act of murder or of self-defense depends on the reasons for the action. Morally, whether an action is right or wrong also may depend upon the *reasons* for the actions. Contributing to charity because you believe in the cause is a lot different than contributing in order to reduce taxes.

A reason is distinct from a cause in that the person forming the intention to act has some degree of control over the actions. When a person does something for a reason, we hold her *responsible* for her actions. But sometimes we do things that really have no reason. This is often the case when we do something "by accident" and "not on purpose." Accidentally turning off the TV by dropping the remote on the off-button isn't really doing it "for a reason." Some philosophers go so far as to say that when a person acts in such an accidental way, he really isn't "acting" at all. But even if we accept these events as actions, we have to acknowledge the important differences in the motivations or reasons behind them.

THE DEVIL MADE ME DO IT!

Not everyone agrees where to draw the line between reasons and causes, or even if a line should be drawn at all. In his powerful portrait of defense attorney Clarence Darrow, biographer Irving Stone describes part of Darrow's gut-wrenching decision to defend young Leopold and Loeb in the infamous and controversial murder trial:

> *Crime, Its Cause and Treatment* was the most valuable and revolutionary book he [Darrow] had yet written; in it he had stated the essence of his belief: the machine that is every man is completely formed by the time it slips from its mother's womb, but once its inherent boundaries had been proscribed, the actual fate or pattern of this human machine was determined by the circumstances in which it found itself set up in the external world. Under this philosophy there was no room for free will: a man acted according to the equipment with which he had been endowed and in accordance with the surroundings into which he had been plunged. If, then, there was no free will, there could be no praise or blame; no man was alone responsible for his acts: his ancestors were responsible, and the state of society in which he lived was responsible, and to punish a man for having a brain, a spirit, a character, a set of action impulses that had been determined for him by powers beyond his control, was stupid, wasteful, cruel and barbaric. The papers were screaming that there was absolutely no reason for this fiendish murder by Loeb and Leopold, that it could be traced to no intelligible causes. Yet Darrow knew that there were thousands of tiny and intricate reasons behind the crime, all of them woven into the character and environment of the killers, and that the causes would be intelligible once the world could be made to understand all the contributing factors that had made these two human machines go haywire.

For Mr. Darrow the reasons *were* the causes and, conversely, the causes *were* the reasons. There was no distinction to be drawn between the two.

(Reprinted with permission from Irving Stone, Clarence Darrow for the Defense, *New York: Bantam Books 1958 [13th ed., 1967], p. 244.)*

Causal Explanations While causal explanations are different from intentional ones, they do not necessarily exclude one another. In fact, every intentional explanation can be re-described as a causal one when seen from another perspective. Thus Keri's punching the button on the remote control can be explained on the basis of her *reason* for doing it. Alternately, we can look at her action on the basis of the electrical events that led to the channel being changed.

But causal explanations cover much more ground than do intentional ones. This is due in part to the assumption that most people make that every event has to have a cause. Nothing "just happens." When we wish to discover the cause of an event or condition, we look for the event or condition that preceded it and "caused" it to come about. There is obviously some ambiguity about the word *cause*. This has led philosophers over the years to make some distinctions about types of causes.

To begin with, we need to remember that *causes* are not the same thing as either *necessary conditions* or *sufficient conditions*. Causes can sometimes be necessary conditions, but effects can also be necessary conditions. (If an effect is *necessarily* produced by a specified cause, it is a necessary condition of that cause.) And a cause may or may not be a sufficient condition of its effect. What type of condition (necessary or sufficient) a cause is for its effect is determined by the type of cause it is.

A *direct cause* is a physical cause that can be cited as the "only" cause of an event. A bowling ball knocking over a pin would be said to directly cause the pin to fall over. Direct causes are sufficient conditions for their effects: A bowling ball hitting a pin is a sufficient condition for the pin's falling over.

Contributory causes occur when an event depends on two or more causes to make it occur. When building a campfire, a person needs to produce both fuel and a source of fire. Both are necessary conditions of the campfire (since you couldn't have a campfire without either of them). Taken together, they do not even constitute a joint sufficient condition for the campfire, since there are other necessary conditions (such as an absence of rain).

It may seem that just about every event must have contributory causes. Even the bowling ball knocking down the pin requires the existence of gravity. But remember that when we are offering an explanation, we are, as the Philosopher Jagewon Kim says, "in a state of puzzlement, a kind of . . . predicament. A successful explanation will get us out of this state." Since an explanation therefore is meant to answer a question, it should be directed only at the questions that are actually at issue. No one questions the existence of gravity here on earth, but it could become a factor if, for instance, astronauts decided to go bowling on one of the space shuttles. So the kind of explanation we offer is always context dependent. And whether or not we cite something as a contributory or direct cause will depend on the context in which the questions are asked as well.

SUMMARY

In this chapter we examined various methods of inductive reasoning. Inductive reasoning was seen to differ from deductive reasoning primarily because inductive premises do not *guarantee* the conclusion in the same way that deductive arguments do.

Metaphors and analogies were seen to function through comparison. By pointing out the similarities in things and events, other similarities are said to follow. While analogies tend to function on the denotative level, with explicitly drawn comparisons, metaphors have more of a symbolic function and tend to operate on the connotative level. Analogies and metaphors can often be misleading when employed in arguments and are not usually very reliable in establishing true conclusions.

A more reliable method of inductive reasoning was introduced by the philosopher John Stuart Mill. His methods of inductive reasoning are intended to increase the accuracy of inductive conclusions. The *method of agreement* holds the suspected cause constant while varying the circumstances. The *method of difference*, on the other hand, holds the surrounding circumstances constant while observing the effects first with, then without the suspected cause. The *combined method of agreement and difference* (also known as the *indirect method of difference*) is useful in cases where one would like to employ the method of difference, but in which the surrounding circumstances cannot be held constant. The combined method employs two groups with similar, but not identical, circumstances: In one group the suspected cause is present, in the other it is not. The *method of residues* requires us to correlate known causes with known effects, and "leftover" causes with "leftover" effects. Finally, the *method of concomitant variation* is one in which mathematical relationships between various "amounts" of cause and effect are correlated.

Theories and hypotheses were seen as tools to aid our inductive reasoning. Theories like those of relativity and evolution give us a set of concepts for looking at the world. Hypotheses, on the other hand, make specific predictions about cause-and-effect relationships.

Finally, we made a distinction between intentional and causal explanations of events. Intentional explanations rely on a person's motives for performing some action, while causal explanations focus on the physical events leading to the event in question.

EXERCISES

 A   LEVEL

Short Answers

* **1.** The statement "The battery is probably dead" may be best classified as a hypothesis or theory?
* **2.** The statement "We can account for the different species through the idea of evolution" can be best classified as a hypothesis or theory?
* **3.** What is a causal explanation?
* **4.** What is an intentional explanation?
* **5.** What is the difference between a direct and contributory cause?
* **6.** Describe the difference between a theory and a hypothesis.

True or False

* **7.** _____ The contributory cause of an event is not in itself sufficient to bring that event about.
* **8.** _____ Intentional explanations can sometimes also include causal explanations.
* **9.** _____ Darwin's theory of evolution is really a hypothesis.
* **10.** _____ A direct cause of an event is also a necessary condition for that event to take place.

B   LEVEL

Reasons and Causes. State whether the following explanations are causal or intentional:
* **1.** John stepped off of a bus because it was his stop.
  2. Allison was pushed off the bus because it was crowded.
* **3.** Keri got to work late because she got stuck in traffic.

4. Joey came to work early because he wanted to catch up on some things he hadn't finished the day before.

* 5. The child was injured when she fell from her crib.

6. The dog dug a hole in the backyard to hide his bone.

* 7. Because of his training, the soldier was able to fight well in the battle.

8. Keri was in a bad mood because her supervisor was angry at her for coming to work late.

* 9. Joey hit the ball to right field because he saw that the right-fielder was playing very deep and he knew that he could hit the ball in front of her.

10. The ball did not travel as far as it normally would have because the bat cracked when it connected with the ball.

*11. A bigot is someone who judges other people by their racial or ethnic heritage, or by their religious beliefs.

12. The bank teller hit the alarm after fainting at the sight of the robber's gun.

*13. Former President Bush made war against Hussein because he wanted to liberate Kuwait.

14. Former President Bush initiated the war against Iraq because he was under the influence of the tranquilizer Halcion.

*15. The defendant got drunk because he wanted to forget his problems.

16. The defendant crashed into the plaintiff's car because he was intoxicated.

*17. The defendant was intoxicated because he is an alcoholic.

18. Allie bought a candy bar because she was hungry.

*19. John bought a candy bar because he was influenced by the advertisement.

20. Despite her reservations, Keri did the job because her boss had threatened to fire her if she didn't.

C   LEVEL

1. Find an article in a magazine explaining why a certain historical event took place. Then isolate the causal and intentional explanations offered in support of the author's conclusion.

2. Read an article in a scientific magazine or journal. Identify any hypotheses the author uses in support of his or her conclusion. Then try to isolate the elements of the theory which the author invokes.

CASE STUDY

Algorithms and Serendipity

A number of points make this case study particularly noteworthy. First, pay particular attention to the ways that forms of reasoning discussed in this chapter dovetail with the concepts of "paradigms", "exemplars", "algorithms", and "anomalies" portrayed by Dr. McDade. For instance, note how the concepts of exemplars and algorithms in scientific thinking rely upon metaphors and analogies. What do you perceive to be the relationships between paradigms and theories and hypotheses? At a deeper, self-referential level what do you take to be the implications of Dr. McDade's urging us as good thinkers to pay serious attention to anomalies when applied back to the Critical Technique itself?

Excerpts from "Algorithms and Serendipity"
by Dr. Joseph E. McDade, U.S. Centers for Disease Control
The Anderson Lecture
May 11–12, 1992
(Reprinted courtesy of Joseph E. McDade)

. . .The Anderson Lecture and other named lectures have special significance; they are times when the scientific community rededicates itself to the pursuit of excellence in science. This can be the only theme; certainly, then you will understand my insecurity as I attempt to provide the keynote for such an event.

Scientific excellence is manifested in many different ways, but ultimately it is measured by excellence in research. . . . Nothing has been more elusive than providing a formula that would ensure successful research. A superior intellect might help; barring that, hard work, dedication, and zeal would perhaps be useful. And a little luck certainly would not be unwelcome. But contrary to popular perception, most important discoveries really are not made solely by chance. Revolutionary discoveries are more likely to be made by the recognition, pursuit, and acceptance of significant anomalies. Certainly this is not novel thinking. Those of you familiar with Thomas Kuhn's book, *The Structure of Scientific Revolutions,* will recognize this statement as the central thesis of his classic monograph, published more than twenty years ago. Unfortunately, the corollary to Kuhn's hypothesis is that most of us fail to recognize meaningful anomalies when we see them. It is this theme that I wish to develop today.

Let me begin by briefly reviewing three basic concepts of Kuhn's hypothesis. First, there is the concept of the paradigm. Kuhn posits that fundamental paradigms evolve from time to time to explain an existing body of knowledge and to provide a framework for future experimentation. Centuries ago, for example, heliocentrisim and geocentrism were two opposing paradigms used to explain the movement of celestial bodies. . . . Paradigms are absolutely essential for scientific progress. The most successful paradigms are open-ended and leave all sorts of problems for its adherents to resolve. For example, ancient astronomers were attracted to heliocentrism because it answered questions that geocentrism could not. Heliocentrism also attracted followers because it promised new examples and ambiguities that required solution. In short, it promised a career of useful experiments that could be performed within the context of "normal" science.

Next, there is the concept of exemplars or algorithms. Paradigms are much more than theories. Kuhn concludes that paradigms invariably embrace, even connote, a specific approach to problem solving by following well documented exemplars. In physics a student quickly discovers that a laboratory exercise or problem is like one he or she has already solved and uses the exemplar to solve similar problems of greater and greater difficulty. The same approach carries over when the student begins to do research; experiments are performed using the same basic approach that one learned as a student. A similar situation exists in microbiology. Virtually every introductory microbiology course has a laboratory exercise that requires the student to identify an unknown microorganism by following an algorithm that has been carefully tested and verified over many years. Then, upon completion of the training, the newly minted microbiologist begins to ply his or her trade in the clinical setting, skillfully isolating and identifying various microorganisms that cause a given disease, to his or her, and presumably the patient's, great satisfaction.

The third component of Kuhn's hypothesis is the anomaly, defined here simply as any deviation from the expected natural order. Birds that can't fly is, of course, the classic example. Within the context of Kuhn's hypothesis, an anomalous observation is one that cannot be explained within the framework of an existing paradigm. Frequently, anomalies are ignored. This is not particularly surprising. At the very least anomalies cause us to repeat and refine our experiments; at the very worst, they could invalidate every experiment that we have ever performed. Anomalies in science can be a source of considerable anxiety and insecurity. Eventually, however, anomalies cannot be ignored; they point out the inadequacies of existing paradigms, pave the way for new ones, and further our progress and understanding.

The concepts of paradigms, algorithms, and anomalies are extremely useful in understanding the scientific process: paradigms provide a framework for research; algorithms provide both an approach and tools for verifying the paradigm and resolving some ambiguities. Anomalies, on the other hand, provide serious tests of a paradigm's fitness, and as I hope to demonstrate, are the least accepted member of this sacred scientific trinity.

13

STANDARIZED TESTS
AND LOGICAL PUZZLES

step one
What is the main claim?

step four
What is the meaning of the terms employed?

step two
Is there an argument?

step three
Are there any assumptions or implications?

step five
Are there any fallacies?

step six
What is the argument's structure?

step seven
What other conclusions can be drawn?

step eight
Do you agree or disagree with the conclusion?

There's a way to find out if
a man is honest—ask him.
If he says 'yes,' you know he
is crooked.
—Groucho Marx (1961)

He who says there
is no such thing as an honest man,
you may be sure
is himself a knave.
—Bishop George Berkeley (1746)

KEY TERMS

Liar's paradox problems - Logical puzzles or riddles the solution to which hinges upon discovering the truth value of particular statements within the puzzle.

Matrix problems - Logical puzzles that involve the use of grids or matrices to determine what is true and false of the individuals or things represented in the matrix.

Position problems - Logical puzzles that involve the spatial arrangement of people or things.

We are now ready to look at Step 7 of the Technique from a different perspective. This step involves the application of the Technique in the assessment of arguments where the conclusion is not stated. In such cases the conclusion must be drawn from the premises. When a detective examines evidence in a murder case, when a biological researcher attempts to solve a medical mystery, when a student attempts to answer questions on the reasoning portions of standardized tests, and when a puzzle fan attempts to solve logical puzzles, the conclusions are not present in the argument. They must be *discovered* or found. Chapter 13 shows how the previous steps in the Technique can help with the reasoning portions of standardized testing. It depicts the types of questions found on many standardized examinations and is followed by illustrated strategies for solving these problems. It also examines more informal puzzles to demonstrate the use of the Technique in more relaxed settings.

One of the most useful applications of critical thinking and logic is in the solution of logical puzzles. While the solution of logical puzzles presents an interesting and challenging pastime, facility with the methods of solving these puzzles is extremely useful in the area of standardized testing. The tests for admission to graduate and professional schools, e.g. law schools, business schools, and medical schools are increasingly reliant on the applicant's ability to engage in rational problem-solving. The Technique presented thus far in this book puts us in a very good position now to address the question of how certain logical puzzles may best be approached and solved. Three basic types of logical puzzles are addressed in this chapter.

1. Puzzles involving position diagrams
2. Puzzles employing matrices or grids
3. Puzzles based on the Liar's Paradox.

Our analysis of these puzzles and problems will employ many of the methods already learned, especially in the latter half of this book. What standardized tests often refer to as analytical reasoning is really a phase of thinking involving analysis, understanding, and inference of statements and relationships from a given set of conditions. Usually a scenario is presented in a terse form describing bits of information, sometimes apparently unrelated to one another. A set of rules is sometimes included as part of the description. Finally, a set of questions is posed asking the student to relate those bits of information. Note that the types of problems can vary greatly and novel sorts of puzzles and problems often arise. Nevertheless, the methods presented in this chapter should help to solve most of these problems and will suggest approaches to the newer types that are often included.

13.1   PUZZLES INVOLVING POSITION DIAGRAMS

Some of the problems or puzzles often encountered ask you to determine the organization or order of a situation from some fragmented data. This is called a **position problem.** You are then asked to draw inferences about the particular features or consequences of that situation. One approach taken is to try to visualize the situation mentally and then to answer the questions posed. But unless one has a photographic memory, this approach can lead to confusion and often to incorrect solutions. It is much more useful for you to draw diagrams expressing the relationships. For instance, if you are told that "Sarah sits to the right of Albert" you might simply jot down the relationship in spatial terms:

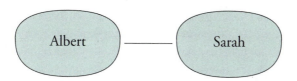

Simple Position Diagrams

Any positional inferences that you would need to draw are much more easily determined by schematizing such a relationship. In a more complicated example, you might be told that

1. Eight chairs are arranged around a circular seminar table.
2. One chair separates Betty from Elaine.
3. Betty sits directly opposite Ann.
4. Manny sits to Ann's left separating her from Elaine.
5. The instructor sits directly opposite Manny.
6. Fred sits next to the instructor and Peter sits next to Fred.
7. Phyllis sits directly opposite Peter

You would begin your diagram by drawing the eight chairs in a circular fashion. You then start with the information you already know, and then use it to determine the rest. Since we can begin anywhere on a circle and still preserve the relationship, we begin by placing Ann and Betty opposite each other:

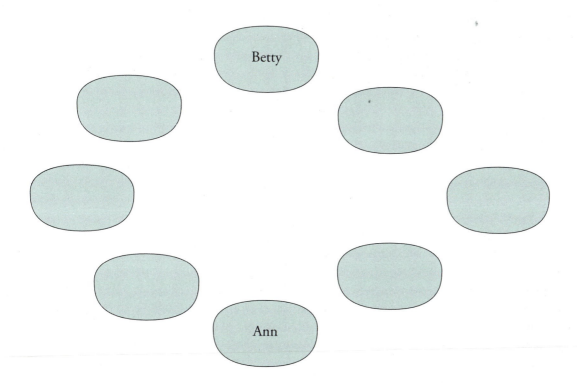

At this point we know that one chair separates Betty from Elaine, but we do not know whether to place Elaine to the left or right of Betty. This can be determined, however, by the other stipulation, namely, that Manny sits to the left of Ann and that Manny separates her from Elaine. We can therefore determine Elaine's position, and note that it is Manny who sits between her and Ann:

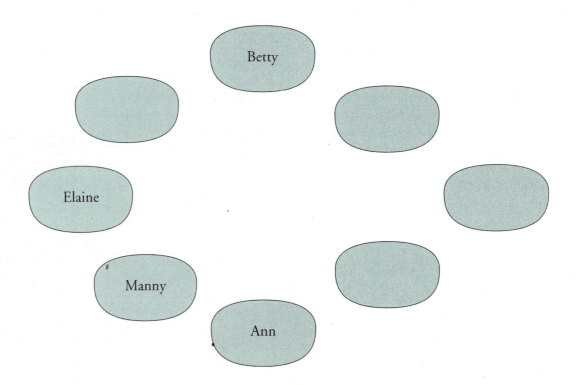

By the time we get to this point we would be able to answer a question such as "How many chairs away from Betty does Manny sit, and in what direction?" If more members of the seminar are mentioned, their positions can be determined by placing them in the appropriate parts of the circle. The trick is not necessarily to place the person in the order originally mentioned, but rather to establish first the relationships for which you have enough information. Then you can use this information to fill in the boxes for the relationships that are not immediately obvious. For instance, you would now be in a position to place the instructor in the seat directly opposite Manny, and answer the question "How many chairs separate Betty from the instructor?"

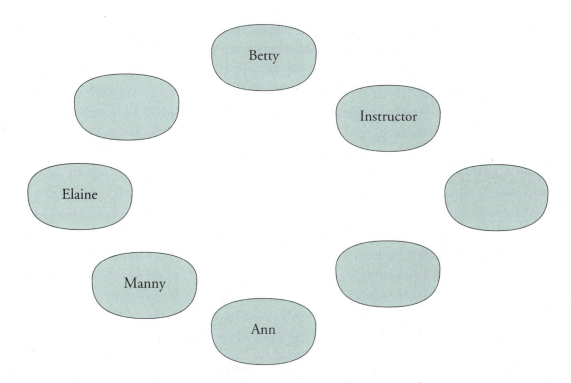

The diagram would now allow you to determine that the instructor sits to Betty's immediate left. We are now in a position to fill in the rest of the diagram:

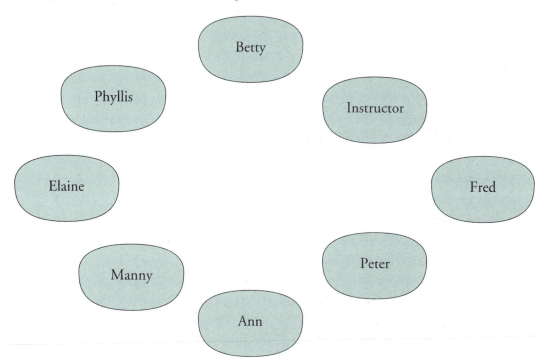

Having completed the diagram, we can now answer such questions as "Who is to the immediate right of Phyllis?" or "Who sits directly opposite Fred?" Just about any question asked about the seating arrangements can now be answered. Again, remember to establish the relationships that you are able to first, and then fill in the others on the basis of the ones you have already established.

Bilateral Relationships

Another type of relationship that often appears in these puzzles are bilateral relationships such as "older-younger" or "taller-shorter." These also can be solved with position diagrams. Consider the following relationships established among the members of a hypothetical basketball team:

1. George is taller than Kareem.
2. Harry is taller than George.
3. Isaiah is taller than Jalen.
4. Kareem is taller than Isaiah.
5. Larry is shorter than Jalen.
6. Magic is shorter than Larry.
7. No two players are exactly the same height.

As is often the case on standardized examinations, all of the members of the team have names starting with different letters. This means that we can shorten our work by diagramming only the first letter of each name of the players. We will establish each binary relationship first, placing the taller member of each pair on the top and the shorter on the bottom:

```
G    H    I    K    J    L
|    |    |    |    |    |
K    G    J    I    L    M
```

By combining these relationships with one diagram, we can establish the height relationships among the entire team. We do this by matching up the letters:

```
H
|
G
|
K
|
I
|
```

J
|
L
|
M

Having established the relationships among the entire team, it is now possible to go on to answer any question that might be posed. One word of warning here: It is not always the case that all of the relationships are established in the initial question. Often the questions that follow establish some of the links that were not present in the initial description. When this occurs, it is possible to draw partial diagrams, establishing those relationships that have been described. It is important to remember, however, not to make any assumptions about these relationships. If, for instance, it has been established that Mary is shorter than Caren and Caren is taller than Maggy, we do not know the height relationship between Mary and Maggy. Again, it will often be the case in standardized tests that the questions that follow will establish the required relationships. It is seldom, if ever, the case that a standardized examination will fail to provide the information needed for you to answer the questions asked. If, however, you feel that this is happening, do not waste any more time on the problem you are considering, but move directly on to something you can do. Get your confidence back. Then, if time remains, return to the perplexing problem after you have worked everything else and try to approach it with a fresh perspective.

Organizational Problems

Position diagrams are capable of representing many kinds of relationships in addition to spatial and bilateral ones: e.g., relationships in time, organizational ones, functional ones, relations of inclusion and exclusion. Consider the sample organizational problem below:

Al Brown, partner in the accounting firm of Earnest Whiners, must assemble an audit team for a client. His instructions are to use two experienced persons and two new associates to comprise the team. Seven persons in his department are available for the task:

1. Charles, Dave, Ed, and Frances are experienced.
2. Gina, Harry, and Ike are new associates.
3. Charles and Dave cannot work together.
4. Harry cannot work with Charles either.
5. Ed and Ike refuse to work together.

Questions

1. If Charles is put in charge of the audit team, the rest of the members MUST BE:
    (A)   Gina, Harry, and Ike
    (B)   Gina, Ike, and Frances
    (C)   Harry, Ed, and Frances
    (D)   Ike, Gina, and Dave
    (E)   Gina, Ike, and Ed

2. If Charles is not part of the audit team, but Harry is, which of the following *must be* true?

   (A)   Ed and Ike are on the team
   (B)   Frances and Gina are on the team
   (C)   Ed and Dave are on the team
   (D)   Gina or Ike is not on the team
   (E)   Dave or Frances is not on the team

3. Which of the following *has to be* true?

   (I)   Dave and Charles never work together.
   (II)   Frances and Ike never work together.
   (III) Dave and Frances always work together.
   (A)   I only
   (B)   II only
   (C)   I and II only
   (D)   II and III only
   (E)   I and III only

4. If Ike is included in the team, but Gina is not, then the other three members *must be*:

   (A)   Dave, Harry and Ed
   (B)   Dave, Harry, and Frances
   (C)   Ed, Gina, and Harry
   (D)   Harry, Ike, and Frances
   (E)   Charles, Dave, and Ed

5. Which of the following *must be* true?

   (I)   If Ed works, then Gina works.
   (II)   If Frances works, then Gina works.
   (III) If Gina works, then Ike works.
   (A) I   (B) II   (C) III   (D) I and II   (E) I and III

Before reading the answers and explanations, try working the problems on your own. In this way, you will get a feeling for the problem, and you will also be in a better position to compare your methods with the ones in the book, or with other solutions to the same problem or problem type. After all, the idea is for you to develop techniques that work for you. Whenever you discover strategies that make more sense to you, you should by all means use them.

Answers with Explanations

For this problem you may have charted the possible combinations that could occur, or you might have diagrammed the combinations that cannot work. A glance at the questions suggests that both could be helpful, provided that you don't waste time in formulating them. One technique for each of the two alternatives could be represented in Figure 13.1 and 13.2:

The problem could have been complicated had the initial conditions stated both the sets of auditors who could not work together and the sets who always work together. Still, we may recognize that there are some of the latter types of sets which are implied, but not stated. Now, to the specific questions:

FIGURE 13.1

POSSIBLE COMBINATIONS

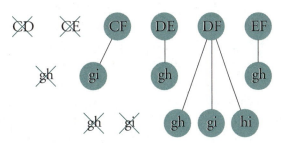

(So, the possible combinations are CFgi, DEgh, DFgh, DFgi, DFhi, and EFgh)

FIGURE 13.2

IMPOSSIBLE COMBINATIONS

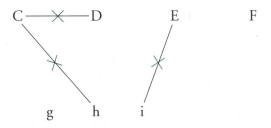

(Key for both figures: C = Charles, D = Dave, E = Ed, F = Frances, g = Gina, h = Harry, i = Ike)

1. We are given the rule of using two experienced auditors and two new ones. (We took that into account by using a capital letter to represent an experienced auditor, and a lower case letter to represent a new associate.) And, we are given that Charles is included in the team and is known to be experienced. The rest of the team then will have to include one more experienced person and two new ones. We can eliminate answer (A), since all three persons are new and we would fail to meet the 2E+2N (two experienced and two new persons) condition. Answer (C) can be ruled out too, because, counting Charles, the team would have three experienced auditors. Answer (D) cannot be correct either, for condition 3 tells us that Charles and Dave cannot work together, and this configuration includes both of them. Answer (E) also can be eliminated, since Ed and Ike would be members, and this violates the stipulated condition number 5.

So, by process of elimination, Answer (B) must be right. For test taking purposes, this would be sufficient; we could double check it quickly by referring to either one of the position diagrams we drew. Since, according to answer (B), the full team would consist of C,F,g, and i, two experienced persons and two novices, all of whom can work together, it is at least a possible combination. Referring back to Figure 13.1, whenever Charles is on the team, only one set of members would satisfy our criteria, and C,F,g,i is that set. Using Figure 13.2 on the other hand, since Charles cannot work with Harry, only two new associates are left that could be on the team. Since we *have to* have two new ones, Gina and Ike are *necessarily* on the team. And if Ike is necessarily on it, since he cannot work with Ed (condition 5), Dave and Frances are the only possible experienced auditors who could be team-members. But, Dave cannot work with Charles (condition 3), so Frances is the *only possible* person with experience who could be included. Hence, anytime Charles is picked for the team, Frances, Gina, and Ike *must be* the other members.

2. Now we are asked to determine the necessary consequences of Charles' being excluded from the team when Harry is included on it. Answer (A) cannot be correct, for it directly contradicts condition 5. Answer (B), that Frances and Gina are on the team, is trickier: both *could be* members of it, so the answer seems plausible. The key here lies in the emphasized word "must". So, while it is certainly possible that both Frances and Gina belong to the foursome, it is also possible that only one is included. Figures 13.1 and 13.2 show these possibilities. Since (B) doesn't *have to be* true, it is incorrect. Similarly, with (C), Ed and Dave *might* both be members of the A-team, but since they don't *have to be,* this response is incorrect.

The problem with answer (E) is that, while either Dave or Frances may not be on the team, there are two possible combinations of people that include both Dave and Frances (one with Gina and Harry, and one with Harry and Ike). So, (E) too, *may be* true, but it doesn't *have to be.* Only answer (D) MUST logically follow, for given that Harry is a team member, only one other new associate can be part of the group. Gina and Ike are the newcomers, one of whom *must be* included and one of whom *can not be.* That is, if Ike is on the team Gina cannot be; and if Gina is on the team, then Ike cannot be. Hence, either Gina or Ike is not on the team.

3. Again, the phrase, "HAS TO BE TRUE", is of crucial significance. This key should be quite simple for you, if you have already read Part Two; at any rate, terms signaling necessary conditions or combinations are employed to show that whatever reasons are given are supposed to guarantee irrevocably some particular conclusion. To tackle this particular problem then, a glance at the choice of answers suggests (a) the need to determine in the case of each one of the statements (i.e., I, II, and III) if it is a necessary consequence of the initial set of conditions, and (b) the need to jot down the numeral of each necessary inference found (for this is probably the most painful way to blow an answer).

Statement I *has to be true,* because it simply reiterates condition 3, that Charles and Dave cannot work together. Statement II, that Frances and Ike never work together, is incorrect under certain circumstances (look back at the diagrams if you need to do so). So, it doesn't *have to be true.* Statement III, that Dave and Frances always work together, has three counterinstances. So, it is definitely false. Since only statement I must be true, answer (A) is the correct one.

4. & 5. Practicum: The last two questions for the problem at hand call for the same basic operations tested by the first three. Try writing out your own answers to both questions with a complete justification or explanation of your conclusions. By all means, sketch a position diagram that will work best for you. If possible, compare your answers with those of others, so that (a) you can learn how to defend conclusions you think are correct, and (b) you can learn to spot gaps in the reasoning process (both your own and other persons) thereby becoming more alert to cognitive lapses.

Venn, Euler Diagram Problems Revisited

Venn diagrams, featured in Chapters Six and Seven, can be considered a kind of position diagram, especially if the relationship between the classes or sets is thought of in terms of inclusion and exclusion. Despite the fact that Venn Diagrams work well for depicting and assessing relations among three classes (particularly so in the case of syllogisms), this method loses its utility quickly as soon as the number of variables is increased. With two minor modifications to the method (which were part of a method devised by the Swiss mathematician, Leonhart Euler, and which predated that of Venn by a century), more variables or categories can be processed. From the chart in Figure 13.3 it can be seen that the changes occur only in the case of universal ("A" and "E") statements, i.e., "all" or "no" statements:

The differences seem negligible until one encounters problems similar to one which is contrived here. The Venn Diagrams will not work because there is no way to draw the overlapping relationships between five

FIGURE 13.3

A COMPARISON OF VENN AND EULER DIAGRAMS

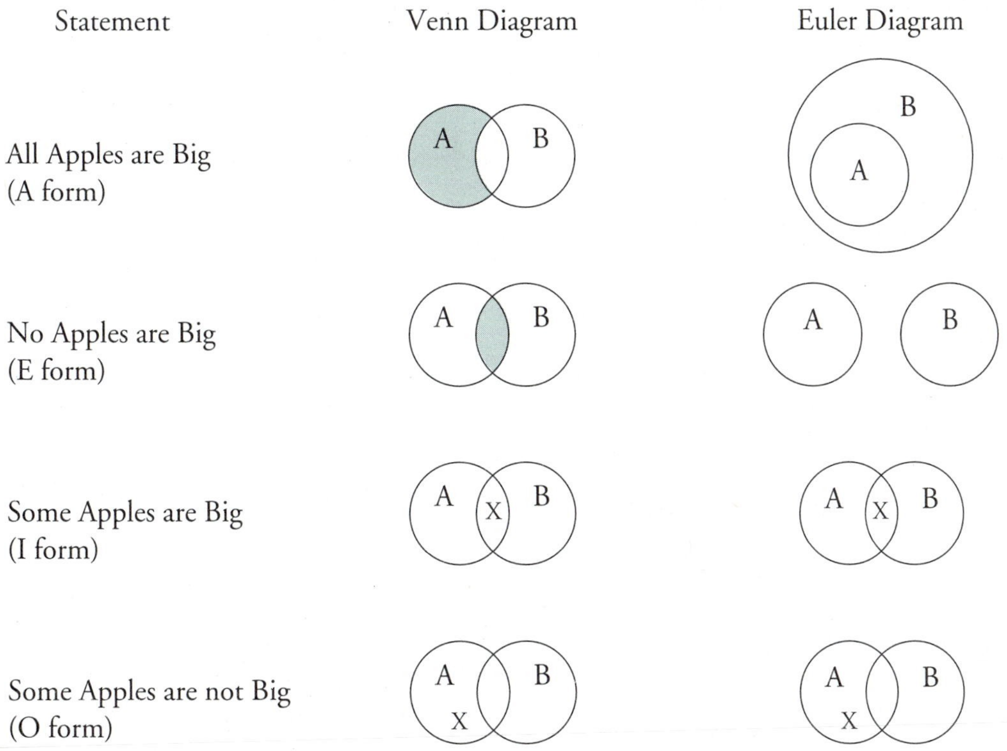

Statement	Venn Diagram	Euler Diagram
All Apples are Big (A form)		
No Apples are Big (E form)		
Some Apples are Big (I form)		
Some Apples are not Big (O form)		

classes on a two dimensional surface. Rather than come up with some "Rube Goldberg" invention to handle the task, the Euler Diagrams may do the job economically.

PROBLEM—GIVEN:

1. All T are O
2. All O are S
3. Some P are T
4. All P are O
5. No Q are S

QUESTIONS:

1. Which of the following MUST be true?
   (i) All T are S
   (ii) Some Q are O
   (iii) No O are Q
   (A) i only   (B) ii only   (C) iii only   (D) i and iii   (E) i, ii, and iii

2. Which of the following MUST be false?
   (i) All P are T
   (ii) No T are Q
   (A) i   (B) ii   (C) both i and ii   (D) either i or ii but not both   (E) neither i nor ii

Drawing the Euler Diagrams   A quick glance at the questions lets us know that the logically necessary consequences of the given data are being sought. That is, if the five given conditions are true, what else HAS TO BE TRUE too? The syllogism could be used to derive these inferences, but it would be quite cumbersome and time-consuming to work backwards in triads of statements and to determine which propositions to use. Taking Euler Diagrams as position diagrams, the illustrations in Figure 13.4 A-E provide a step by step drawing of each of the five given statements in the problem. As a rule of thumb, draw the universal statements first (i.e., the ones beginning with "All" or "No"); it will then be easier to know where to place the "X's" for the particular statements (i.e., the "some" statements).

Figure 13.4E is our position diagram at this stage. With an eye on the illustrations, turn to the questions.

Answers and Explanations

1. In this question we are asked whether any one or any combination of the three statements are necessary consequences of the original five conditions. Statement (i), that All T are S, is an elementary inference from conditions (1) and (2) showing up vividly with circle T being totally inside of circle S. Statement (ii), that Some Q are O, is necessarily false, since O is included in S and S is excluded from Q, and thus no Q are O. Statement (iii), No O are Q, must also be true: use the conclusion just generated (that No Q are O) and by immediate inference, its necessary truth can be seen. (If no African-Americans have ever been U.S. Presidents, then no U.S. Presidents have ever been African-Americans.) Since statements (i) and (iii) were the only ones that HAD TO BE TRUE, answer (D) must be the correct choice.

2. A shift from the necessary truth to the necessary falsity (or logical impossibility) of statements occurs in question two. It may be obvious now, but during pressured times we can easily become blinded by our suc-

FIGURE 13.4

EULER DIAGRAMS

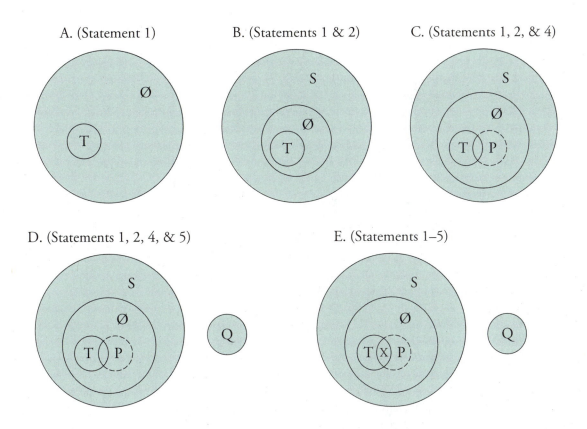

A. (Statement 1)   B. (Statements 1 & 2)   C. (Statements 1, 2, & 4)

D. (Statements 1, 2, 4, & 5)   E. (Statements 1–5)

cess in responding to the previous question, and continue in the present question to look for what HAS TO BE rather than what *cannot be* true. How about statement (i), that All P are T—is it a logical impossibility assuming the truth of the initial quintet? We know from Figure 13.4C that it is possible all P are T. The addition of condition (3) in Figure 13.4E tells us only that at least one P is T. Since the truth value of statement (i) cannot be determined with certainty, it doesn't HAVE TO BE false. So, it is not a correct response. According to statement (ii), no T are Q. Since all of circle T is included in circle S, and all of circle S is excluded from circle Q, no T could possibly be Q. Statement (ii) then is necessarily true; but the question asks for necessary falsity, so (ii) is not correct either. For this reason, answer (E), neither statement (i) nor statement (ii) *has to be* false, must be the correct choice.

Frequently, the later questions for this type of problem add new terms to the given conditions, which means that further additions will have to be made to the original diagram. These may be indicated by drawing dotted lines which can be erased as the problem continues and we are asked to return to the original set of conditions. A possible third question to this one, for instance, might be:

FIGURE 13.5

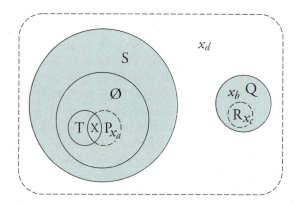

3. If "Some R are not T" is true, then which of the following *must be true?*

    (A)   Some R are not P
    (B)   No R are Q
    (C)   Some R are not Q
    (D)   Some S are not R
    (E)   none of the above

At this juncture we have to add to the diagram. How do we represent R? In order to cover the possibilities circle R could intersect all of the other variables. It may even encompass all of them, or it may be outside all of them. Begin as indicated in Figure 13.5, with a dotted or broken line, modifying as you need to for each of the statements to be checked. The idea is to try to show how each one *could* be false [since you were asked to show which one(s) *had to be* true].

Response (A) doesn't HAVE TO BE true, for we could put a provisional "X" or check in the area common to circle R and circle P, but outside of circle T. This is represented in Figure 13.5 by X_a. Likewise, answer (B) is not *necessarily* true, for we could have placed the check in the overlap of circle R and Q, indicating an R that isn't a T, but showing that "No R are Q" doesn't HAVE TO BE TRUE. (This configuration is represented by X_b.) In the case of answer (C), we could have drawn the circle of R's entirely inside the circle of Q's, in which case we would have R's that are not T's but not necessarily any R's that are not Q's. Here we might place an X_c inside of circle R or we could just use the X_b from the previous answer. Answer (D) does not HAVE TO BE TRUE either, for circle R could have been drawn so as to include all of circle S. (This would mean that All S are R, the direct contradiction of Some S are not R.) Answer (E), then, has to be the right one: none of the responses is a necessary conclusion from the new set of conditions.

Now that we have looked at some of the techniques for handling problems and puzzles that may be solved by pictorial representations and diagrams, it is time for you to try a few on your own.

EXERCISES

A   LEVEL

1. Why might it be better to diagram questions on relationships than to try to figure them out without a diagram? Under what conditions might it be better to forego the diagram?
2. Why is analytical reasoning found on standardized tests?
3. When you are drawing a position diagram, why would it be important to diagram the relationships in the order in which they occur? Can you think of any situations where this rule of thumb would not apply?
4. Would making assumptions be useful in answering analytical questions or creating position diagrams? Why or why not?
5. How should you handle standardized examination questions that do not provide all of the information needed to answer an analytical question?
6. When diagramming binary relationships, under what conditions would it be better to diagram each separate relation first and then combine them into a larger diagram? Under what conditions might it be better to draw the whole diagram as you proceed with each piece of information?

B   LEVEL

In order to practice the position diagramming techniques over a range of problems, try your hand at the ones below, and as you do, be sure to read the questions and problems carefully and draw a diagram or pictorial representation that makes sense to you any time you need to do so:

Questions 1–6 concern the following scenario:
1. Six friends—three boys (Ted, Fred, and Ned) and three girls (Jane, Laine, and Blaine)—are going to the movies.
2. All six sit in the same row which has only six seats.
3. No friends of the same sex sit next to each other.
4. Ted will not sit next to Laine.
5. Fred has friends on each side of him.
6. Laine sits between Fred and Ned, and next to each of them.
7. Blaine sits in the first seat and Ned sits in the last seat.

Question 1: It can be deduced from statements 1, 2, and 7 that
   (A) Laine sits next to Ned
   (B) Ned does not sit next to Ted

(C) Fred sits between two friends

(D) Jane sits next to Blaine

(E) None of the above

Question 2: It can be deduced from statements 1, 2, 6, and 7 that

I. Fred sits next to Jane

II. Ted doesn't sit next to Ned

(A) I only   (B) II only   (C) Both I and II   (D) Neither I nor II   (E) Either I or II but not both

Question 3: Which of the original statements can be deduced solely from statement 7?

(A) 1   (B) 3   (C) 4   (D) 5   (E) None of them

Question 4: Which of the following statements *must be true?*

(A) Blaine sits between Ted and Fred

(B) Ted sits next to Blaine and next to Jane

(C) Fred sits between Jane and Laine, but not next to either one

(D) Laine sits next to Fred, but not next to Ned

(E) Jane sits between Ted and Ned, and next to each

Question 5: Which of the following *must be* false?

(A) Ted sits next to Jane

(B) Blaine sits next to one friend only

(C) Laine sits next to Ted

(D) Fred sits next to Laine

(E) Laine sits between Blaine and Ned

Question 6: The friends could sit in which order?

(A) Blaine, Ted, Jane, Fred, Laine, Ned

(B) Blaine, Fred, Jane, Ted, Laine, Ned

(C) Ned, Laine, Ted, Jane, Fred, Blaine

(D) Ned, Ted, Laine, Fred, Jane, Blaine

(E) Fred, Laine, Ned, Blaine, Ted, Jane

Questions 7–10 test your powers of concentration in remembering relationships. Remember to read carefully and make notes as you need to.

GIVEN:

 1. Do, Re, Mi, and Fa are boys and girls.

 2. Do is Re's brother.

 3. Re is Mi's sister.

 4. Mi is Fa's brother.

Question 7: Which of the following HAS TO BE true?

I. Do is a boy

II. Fa is a girl

III. Mi is a boy

(A) I   (B) II   (C) III   (D) I and III   (E) II and III

Question 8: Which of the following *must be* false?

   I. Fa is Re's brother

   II. Do is Mi's brother

   (A) I   (B) II   (C) Both I and II   (D) Either I or II, but not both   (E) Neither I nor II

Question 9: Which of the following could be true?

   I. Fa is Re's sister

   II. Fa is Do's brother

   (A) I only   (B) II only   (C) Both I and II   (D) Either I or II, but not both   (E) Neither I nor II

Question 10: If Fa is a girl, then

   (A) Do is her brother

   (B) Re is her brother

   (C) Mi is her sister

   (D) Two of the above

   (E) None of the above

Questions 11–16 concern a group of eight friends going out to play volleyball under the following conditions:

Eight classmates—four girls: A, B, C, and D; and four boys: E, F, G, and H—are going to divide up into two volleyball teams of four persons each.

   (A) Team East and Team West each must have exactly four players.

   (B) D and H cannot be on the same team.

   (C) F and G have to be on the same team.

   (D) B has to be on Team West.

   (E) Each team must have at least one male and at least one female.

   (F) No team can have an equal number of males and females.

11. Which of the following represents a possible set of members for Team West?

   (A) A, B, D, and H

   (B) A, B, D, and E

   (C) B, D, F, and G

   (D) B, C, D, and G

   (E) A, F, G, and H

12. If A, D, and E are on Team East, the fourth member of that team must be

   (A) B

   (B) C

   (C) F

   (D) G

   (E) H

13. If D and F are on Team East, then Team West has to consist of

   (A) A, B, C, and H

   (B) A, B, C, and E

   (C) B, C, E, and G

(D) B, C, E, and H

(E) B, E, G, and H

14. If B and G are on the same team, all of the following have to be true, EXCEPT:

(A) D is on Team East.

(B) A and E are on the same team.

(C) G is on Team West.

(D) B and F are on the same team.

(E) C is on Team West.

15. If H is on Team West, which of the following pairs of classmates *cannot* be together on a team?

(A) F and H

(B) A and H

(C) C and F

(D) A and C

(E) D and E

16. Supposing Team East has A, F, G, and H as members and that Team West then has B, C, D, and E on its side: which of the following pairs of classmates may switch teams without violating any of the original conditions?

(A) A and D

(B) A and C

(C) E and G

(D) D and H

(E) A and B

Questions 17 through 22 concern family relations:

The following facts are known about a particular family:

(a) Senta is Benito's mother and Pedro's sister.

(b) Senta has fewer brothers than she has daughters.

(c) Benito has the same number of brothers as he has sisters.

(d) Diego, who is Benito's father and Senta's husband, had no brothers or sisters.

(e) Diego has many aunts and uncles, and all of them had children.

(f) Diego has more cousins than he has nephews and nieces.

(g) Members of the family never divorce or remarry and never marry their relatives. (Their family trees do fork!)

17. What is the smallest number of brothers that Benito could possibly have?

(A) 0

(B) 1

(C) 2

(D) 3

(E) 4

18. If Pedro has any children, they must be Benito's

(A) aunts and uncles

(B) nieces and nephews

(C) brothers and sisters

(D) grandparents

(E) cousins

19. Suppose Pedro were married. His wife would be Senta's

(A) mother-in-law

(B) daughter-in-law

(C) sister-in-law

(D) cousin

(E) sister

20. Suppose Senta has seven children. What is the greatest number of brothers that Pedro could have?

(A) 0

(B) 1

(C) 2

(D) 3

(E) 4

21. If Pedro has no children, then which of the following COULD BE true?

(I) Diego has more cousins than Pedro has nieces and nephews.

(II) Pedro has more nieces and nephews than Diego has cousins.

(III) Pedro has exactly the same number of nieces and nephews as Diego has cousins.

(A) I only

(B) II only

(C) III only

(D) I and III only

(E) I, II, and III

22. Return to the original set of conditions. Senta MUST HAVE

(I) an even number of children

(II) at least five children

(III) more sons than she has daughters

(A) I only

(B) II only

(C) III only

(D) I and II only

(E) II and III only

Questions 23 through 28 are concerned with the height relations between seven members of a basketball team. The coach and his trainer are taking the measurements and record the following data:

(a) George is taller than Harry.

(b) Harry is shorter than Isaiah.

(c) Isaiah is taller than Jalen.

(d) Kareem is taller than Isaiah.

(e) Larry is shorter than Jalen.

(f) Magic is shorter than Larry.

(g) No two players are exactly the same height.

23. If there are only two players taller than Jalen and Larry is shorter than George, only three players can be taller than which of the following?

(I) George

(II) Harry

(III) Isaiah

(IV) Magic

(A) I only

(B) III only

(C) I and II only

(D) III and IV only

(E) I, III, and IV only

24. Which of the following statements provides information which is unnecessary because it is already contained in the original seven statements?

(I) Harry is shorter than Kareem.

(II) Harry is shorter than Larry.

(III) Jalen is shorter than Kareem.

(A) I only

(B) II only

(C) III only

(D) I and III only

(E) II and III only

25. All of the following are *possible* height orders from tallest to shortest, *except* which one?

(A) George, Kareem, Isaiah, Jalen, Larry, Magic, Harry

(B) Kareem, George, Isaiah, Harry, Larry, Jalen, Magic

(C) Kareem, Isaiah, Jalen, George, Larry, Magic, Harry

(D) Kareem, Isaiah, Jalen, Larry, George, Magic, Harry

(E) Kareem, Isaiah, Jalen, Larry, Magic, George, Harry

26. If there are only two players taller than Isaiah, then which of the following statements *could be* true?

(I) George is taller than Kareem.

(II) Harry is taller than Larry.

(III) Kareem is taller than George.

(A) I only

(B) III only

(C) I and III only

(D) II and III only

(E) I, II, and III

27. Suppose Kareem is not the tallest. Then, which of the following statements *has to be* true?

(I) There are only two players taller than Isaiah.

(II) There are no more than five players taller than Larry.

(III) Magic has to be the shortest player.

(A) I only

(B) II only

(C) III only

(D) I and II only

(E) I, II, and III

28. Now suppose that only two players are taller than George. Then, which of the following statements *has to be* true?

(A) Kareem is definitely the tallest.

(B) Harry is definitely the shortest.

(C) Magic is definitely the shortest.

(D) Harry is taller than Magic.

(E) Jalen is taller than George.

Questions 29 through 34 pertain to the following scenario:

Cynthia, Debbie, Elaine, Frieda, and Glenda are top managers of an institution that requires them to schedule meetings which include only the five of them for the time frame beginning Monday the 20th and running through Sunday the 26th. At their meetings in order for any motion to pass, it must receive a positive vote from the majority of the members attending that meeting. Of course, each attendee is permitted only one vote per motion and there are no proxies for persons who cannot attend the meeting. Since they are busy executives, their schedules are subject to constant constraints. These they tell us are

(a) Cynthia cannot attend any meeting on a Monday.

(b) Debbie cannot attend any meeting on a Sunday.

(c) Elaine cannot attend any meeting on either a Saturday or on the 23rd of any month.

(d) Frieda cannot attend any meeting on a Sunday or a Monday.

(e) Cynthia and Debbie can only attend evening meetings.

(f) Glenda cannot attend any evening meeting at all.

29. At which one of the following times can Cynthia, Debbie, and Elaine attend a meeting together?

(A) Monday evening

(B) Tuesday afternoon

(C) Thursday evening

(D) Friday evening

(E) Sunday evening

30. Which of the following meeting times permits the greatest number of the group to attend?

(A) Wednesday evening

(B) Thursday afternoon

(C) Saturday evening

(D) Sunday afternoon

(E) Sunday evening

31. Which of the following meeting times would permit the fewest members of the group to be able to attend?

(A) Tuesday evening

(B) Thursday afternoon

(C) Friday afternoon

(D) Friday evening

(E) Saturday evening

32. At which one of the following times can both Cynthia and Frieda attend a meeting and also be sure that if they both vote for a motion that it will pass?

(A) Tuesday evening

(B) Wednesday evening

(C) Thursday evening

(D) Friday evening

(E) Sunday evening

33. At which one of the following times can both Debbie and Frieda attend a meeting and be sure that if they both vote for a motion then it will pass?

(A) Monday evening

(B) Tuesday afternoon

(C) Wednesday evening

(D) Thursday afternoon

(E) Thursday evening

34. During which of the following times can both Debbie and Cynthia attend a meeting and be sure that if they both vote in favor of a motion that it will pass?

(A) Tuesday evening and Thursday evening

(B) Thursday evening and Friday evening

(C) Thursday evening and Saturday evening

(D) Friday evening and Saturday evening

(E) Saturday evening and Sunday evening

Questions 35 through 40 involve the following scenario:

You have been asked to bake something for a sale and are given a recipe which has four dry ingredients (baking powder, cinnamon, flour, sugar—not necessarily in that order) and three wet ingredients (eggs, milk, oil—again, not necessarily in that order). The recipe also contains the following directions:

(a) Add ingredients one at a time.

(b) Milk must be added directly after the flour.

(c) Eggs must be added directly after the sugar.

(d) Cinnamon needs to be added any time after the milk.

(e) Add the oil last.

(f) A wet ingredient cannot be added directly after another wet ingredient.

35. Which of the following can be the order, from first to last, in which you add the ingredients of this recipe?

(A) baking powder, flour, milk, cinnamon, sugar, eggs, oil

(B) flour, milk, sugar, baking powder, eggs, cinnamon, oil

    (C) sugar, eggs, baking powder, cinnamon, flour, milk, oil

    (D) baking powder, sugar, eggs, flour, milk, cinnamon, oil

    (E) sugar, eggs, flour, milk, baking powder, oil, cinnamon

36. Of the seven ingredients, how many of them could be the first ingredient that you use to begin this recipe?

    (A) 1

    (B) 2

    (C) 3

    (D) 4

    (E) 5

37. Of the seven ingredients, how many of them could you add immediately before you add the cinnamon?

    (A) 1

    (B) 2

    (C) 3

    (D) 4

    (E) 5

38. Which of the following pairs of ingredients cannot be next to each other in the order of added ingredients?

    (A) flour, sugar

    (B) cinnamon, sugar

    (C) baking powder, sugar

    (D) baking powder, cinnamon

    (E) baking powder, flour

39. Suppose you choose to begin with sugar as your first ingredient. Then, which of the following cannot be the number 5, 6, and 7 ingredients that you add?

    (I) cinnamon, baking powder, oil

    (II) milk, baking powder, oil

    (III) milk, cinnamon, oil

    (A) I only

    (B) II only

    (C) III only

    (D) I and II only

    (E) I, II, and III

40. Which one of the following ingredients could you not use as the second ingredient?

    (A) baking powder

    (B) eggs

    (C) flour

    (D) milk

    (E) sugar

Questions 41–46 pertain to the following scenario:

You are on a trip to a city you have never before visited and discover the following information about one of the city's public parks: the park is exactly one hundred yards long on each side and is bounded on each side by three straight streets each of which runs into the other two streets. You also know:

(a) One of the streets runs due north and south and is called "City Limits Boulevard" because it also forms one of the boundaries of the city.

(b) The second street is only one hundred yards long and dead-ends into each of the other two streets. For this reason it is called "Dead End Way".

(c) The third street is called "Main Street" and it runs through the center of town and dead-ends into City Limits Boulevard.

(d) There are five ways to get into the park: two of them occur between the north and east corners of the park.

(e) There is a children's amusement ride which continues to run on a circular track through the park.

(f) There is an old World War II fighter plane on a pedestal in the middle of the park.

41. Which of the following statements *has to be* true?

   (A) Main Street and Dead End Way meet at the east corner of the park.
   (B) Main Street and City Limits Blvd. meet at the south corner of the park.
   (C) Dead End Way and City Limits Blvd. meet at the north corner of the park.
   (D) Dead End Way and City Limits Blvd. meet at the east corner of the park.
   (E) City Limits Blvd. and Main Street meet at the north corner of the park.

42. Which of the following statements *could be* true?

   (I) City Limits Blvd. and Dead End Way meet at the east corner of the park.
   (II) City Limits Blvd. and Main Street meet at the north corner of the park.
   (III) Main Street and Dead End Way meet at the north corner of the park.
   (IV) Main Street and Dead End Way meet at the south corner of the park.
   (A) I only
   (B) II only
   (C) II and III only
   (D) II and IV only
   (E) III and IV only

43. Suppose that three of the ways to get into and out of the park occur on City Limits Blvd. Which of the following have to be true?

   (I) There is at least one way into the park on Dead End Way.
   (II) There is at least one way into the park on Main Street.
   (III) There is no way in or out of the park on the south side.
   (IV) There is no way in or out of the park on the north side.
   (A) I only
   (B) III only
   (C) IV only

(D) I and III only

(E) II and III only

44. Which of the following statements *cannot possibly be* true?

(A) The WWII airplane is northwest of the center of town.

(B) The WWII airplane is directly east of the center of town.

(C) The WWII airplane is southwest from the center of town.

(D) The WWII airplane is farther north than the center of town.

(E) The WWII airplane is farther south than the center of town.

45. If City Limits Blvd. and Dead End Way meet at the south corner of the park and if the children's amusement ride always goes clockwise on the track, then the ride passes the streets in which order?

(I)   Dead End Way, then City Limits Blvd, then Main St.

(II) Main St., then City Limits Blvd., then Dead End Way

(III) Main St., then Dead End Way, then City Limits Blvd.

(IV) City Limits Blvd., then Main St., then Dead End Way

(V)   City Limits Blvd., then Dead End Way, then Main St.

(A) I and II only

(B) III and IV only

(C) I, III, and IV only

(D) II, IV, and V only

(E) III, IV, and V only

46. Suppose Main Street is a one-way street heading east and the other two streets are two-way streets. In this case, traffic could move around the park in which of the following patterns?

(I)   Main Street to Dead End Way to City Limits Blvd.

(II) Dead End Way to Main Street to City Limits Blvd.

(III) City Limits Blvd. to Main Street to Dead End Way

(IV) City Limits Blvd. to Dead End Way to Main Street

(A) I and III only

(B) II and III only

(C) II and IV only

(D) I, II, and III only

(E) I, III, and IV only

13.2 PROBLEMS EMPLOYING MATRICES OR GRIDS AND *THE LIAR'S PARADOX*

Closely related to problems employing position diagrams are **matrix problems**. A *matrix* is a grid of boxes. Along the top of the matrix, one set of variables is diagrammed, while along the side another set is stated. In these problems, information given sometimes appears to be pointless and irrelevant but is not. The solution process requires the ability to make inferences by eliminating possibilities. The inferences which are made frequently require the ability to supply missing premises of an obvious nature. (For instance, if you are told "Abe beat the baker in three straight sets of tennis," you are supposed to conclude that Abe is not the baker, since no one beats himself in tennis.) Here's an example:

> Mrs. Epson has four children, two boys (Able and Baker) and two girls (Charlie and Delta), who are in the first, second, third, and fourth grades, but not necessarily in that order. We also know:
> 1. The boys are in a grade lower than Charlie.
> 2. Able is in the third grade.
> 3. Delta is in either the lowest or highest grade.
>
> Questions:
> 1. What grade is Baker in?
>   A. First
>   B. Second
>   C. Third
>   D. Fourth
>   E. Cannot be determined
> 2. From the lowest to the highest grade, what is the order of Mrs. Epson's children?
>   A. Able, Baker, Charlie, Delta
>   B. Delta, Charlie, Able, Baker
>   C. Delta, Able, Baker, Charlie
>   D. Delta, Baker, Able, Charlie
>   E. Able, Delta, Baker, Charlie

To solve this problem we now construct our grid. Since the grade level of each person constitutes one of the variables, we can state the grades along the top of the grid. Along the side we list each of the possible names. We then proceed to put a T for true in any box that we can determine. Since each of the children is in only one grade, by putting a T in a box, we can then proceed to put an F for false in each of the other boxes in the line and column.

	First Grade	Second Grade	Third Grade	Fourth Grade
Able				
Baker				
Charlie				
Delta				

After reading condition 1, we can proceed to place an F in the blocks by Charlie's name for the first and second grades. Since we are told that the boys—there are two of them—are in grades lower than Charlie, she cannot be in the first or second grade. We could also put F's in the fourth-grade blocks next to Able's and Baker's names.

Condition 2 tells us that Able is in the third grade. To indicate this we place a T in the row by Able's name under the third-grade column. This enables us to put an F in every empty block in the row by Able's name, and an F in every empty block in the column under the third grade, for no one else could be in it, insofar as each one must occupy a different grade. At this stage of the drawing, there will be an F in each row by Charlie's name except in the fourth-grade column. We are justified then in putting a T here, which means we can also put an F in the fourth-grade block by Delta's name.

Condition 3 tells us that Delta is either in the first or fourth grade (or you could have eliminated the second- and third-grade blocks by her name). Since she cannot be in the fourth grade (since Charlie is), Delta must be in the first grade. This means that only one possibility is left for Baker: He must be in the second grade. The final matrix looks like this:

	First Grade	Second Grade	Third Grade	Fourth Grade
Able	F	F	(T)	F
Baker	F	(T)	F	F
Charlie	F	F	F	(T)
Delta	(T)	F	F	F

So we see that the answer to Question 1 has to be B. Baker is in the second grade. The answer to the second question therefore has to be D and the order of the grades is Delta, Baker, Able, Charlie.

Under actual test conditions, you should be prepared to use matrices such as this one. You should try to look ahead to the answers that follow before drawing the diagram, however. This is because you may have enough information to answer the questions without drawing the entire grid. Since the time allotted on an actual exam is limited, this would be a useful strategy.

Also it may be the case that more than two sets of variables are presented in a question. When this is the case, you should draw as many diagrams as are necessary to answer the question. In each case, be sure to use T's and F's to determine the answers, or any other symbols, say X's and O's, that make sense to you.

The Liar's Paradox

A number or riddles share the common trait of involving inferences from a set of given truth conditions. These puzzles test your ability to determine who is lying and who is telling the truth by statements they make or are made about them. While these sorts of problems are less frequently found on standardized examinations than are the matrix or position problems, they are useful in developing deductive skills.

The **liar's paradox** gets its name from the puzzling result that occurs if we ask the same question of two persons, one of whom always tells the truth and one of whom always lies. If the truth-teller were asked if she were telling the truth, she would respond by saying "Yes, because I am the truth-teller." But the liar will respond in the same way. While we cannot determine who the truth-teller is with only one question, by combining several statements attributed to each, we can determine who is who.

THIS IS A LIE

Describing the "Epimenides paradox" or "Liar's paradox," Douglas Hofstadter writes:

Epimenides was a Cretan who made one immortal statement: "All Cretans are liars." A sharper version of the statement is simply "I am lying"; or "This statement is false." It is that last version which I usually mean when I speak of the Epimenides paradox. It is a statement which rudely violates the usually assumed dichotomy of statements into true and false, because if you tentatively think it is true, then it immediately backfires on you and makes you think it is false. But once you've decided it is false, a similar backfiring returns you to the idea that it must be true. Try it!

(Selected excerpt from page 17 of Godel, Escher, Bach: An Eternal Golden Braid, *by Douglas R. Hofstadter. Copyright © 1979 by Basic Books, Inc. Reprinted by permission of Basic Books, a division of Harper-Collins Publishers, Inc.)*

Suppose that you are asking directions in an unfamiliar city. In this city, you also know that each of the residents either always tells the truth or always lies. (It is a point of civic pride.) You want to determine which one or ones to listen to. They make the following statements:

1. All three of us are liars.
2. No, only two of us are.
3. Wait, that's not true either.

Which should you listen to?

To solve this problem, consider the statements one at a time. To begin with, #1 must be lying, because if all three were in fact liars, then he would be telling the truth. And if he were telling the truth, then he must be a truth-teller. So, by saying that all three are liars, we know that #1 must be a liar. And since #1 is lying, then we also know that at least one of the others must be telling the truth (since it is a lie that all three are liars).

Then, when #2 claims that there are two liars, #3 says that that is not correct either. Since the statements made by #2 and #3 contradict one another, one of them must be lying and the other must be telling the truth. (Remember, if two statements contradict one another, exactly one must be true and the other must be false.) Now consider: If #2 were telling the truth, there must be two liars (since this is precisely what #2 is stating). But if # 3 is telling the truth, then there must also be two liars. (We have, after all, ascertained that #1 must be lying and if #3 is telling the truth, then #2 must be lying also.) So, either way, there must be two liars. But this is precisely what #2 is stating. So #2 *must* be the truth-teller. And it is #2 whom we should ask for directions.

So the correct approach to this type of problem is to examine the content of each of the three statements, and then to look at the possibility that the statement is true given what is being asserted about the remaining statements.

Sometimes these problems are presented in such a way that the number of true or false statements is presented as part of the problem. When this is the case, you can begin by looking for contradictions. Ask yourself the question "Which pairs of statements cannot both be true and cannot both be false?" The next problem illustrates how this approach can lead to a solution:

> Four people who had grown up in a small town applied for work with an industry that had just moved into town. Since the firm operated as a Defense Department contractor handling classified material and information, all applicants had to be thoroughly screened. The four people being screened were friends and were interviewed as a group by a personnel officer who determined that one of the four was a foreign agent, but he did not know *which* one. When he asked each of the applicants to make a statement about this piece of information, the responses were:
>
> Andrea: I am not the spy.
> Betty: Clovis is the spy.
> Clovis: Andrea is the spy.
> Doreen: Well, I'm no spy.
>
> A hidden polygraph/voice-verifier determined that three of the four statements were lies and only one was telling the truth. Who was telling the truth and who was the spy?

To begin with, note that the statements made by Andrea and Clovis are contradictory. One is telling the truth and the other must be lying. So either Andrea or Clovis is the truth-teller (since the problem specifies that there is only one truth-teller). But this also means that Betty and Doreen must be lying. Since Doreen is lying, and she claims that she is not the spy, she must be the spy. This further implies that Clovis is lying, since she claims that Andrea is the spy and we have already ascertained that Doreen is the spy. Finally, since Clovis's statement is a lie and it contradicts Andrea's statement, Andrea must be telling the truth. Therefore, Andrea is telling the truth, and Doreen is the spy.

Notice that in solving these problems, it is important to be on the lookout for contradictions. Once a contradiction has been discovered, the content of each of the contradictory statements can be applied to

A TRUE DILEMMA

Some liar's paradox puzzles present an insoluble dilemma. We have seen several variations on a theme in which a person who has just been convicted of a crime is offered a choice of capital punishments: death by fire or death by drowning. If the prisoner makes a true statement, then he will die by fire; if he makes a false statement, then he will die by drowning. After thinking for a minute, the prisoner says, "I will die by drowning." What is interesting about this perceptive statement? If the prisoner were to die by drowning, the statement would become true, but the death by drowning only follows a false statement, so the prisoner would have to die by fire. But if the prisoner dies by burning, then the statement would in fact be false, so he cannot die by fire either!

RIDDLE OF THE PRISONER'S DILEMMA

Another variation of the liar's paradox occurs in word problems such as the following:

An above-average intelligence prisoner serving a long-term sentence is confronted by her jailer and placed in a room where she is offered a choice. The room is rectangular in shape with identical doors at opposite ends of the room. One of the doors leads to instant death; the other, to immediate freedom. The prisoner is free to pick either door to exit the room. And, in order to help the perplexed prisoner, on two opposite walls of the room are two identical computers: one programmed to give only truthful responses and the other programmed to lie all of the time. The jailer explains to the prisoner that she may ask one and only one question of either one of the computers. Each computer is aware of the other computer and knows how the other computer will respond. What question should she ask? (Think about this one before looking up the answer.) There are probably several responses that could work. Here is a little diagram to help you visualize the scenario.

If you need a hint, remember that it will be helpful if your question concerns both (a) the door you need to pick and (b) the computer you are questioning.

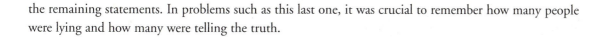

the remaining statements. In problems such as this last one, it was crucial to remember how many people were lying and how many were telling the truth.

SUMMARY

In this chapter we began our study of Step 7 of the Technique: the drawing of conclusions from arguments in which the conclusion must be discovered. We discussed three types of problems or puzzles, some of which appear on standardized examinations. The first type of problem discussed was that known as a position problem. *Position problems* involve the spatial arrangement of people or things. These problems are solved by drawing diagrams representing possible positions and then filling in the positions with the people or things known to inhabit them. From this initial information, other positions may be determined.

   Matrix problems involve the use of grids or matrices to determine what is true and false of the individuals or things represented in the matrix. In these problems it is assumed that only one box in each row and each column may be true and all the others must be false. Once it is found that one box in the matrix is "true" it can be determined that the remaining boxes in the row and column must contain values that are false. In such problems it is not always the case that the entire grid must be filled. How much of the grid is necessary to fill in is determined by the questions asked. To this end, it is useful to look ahead to the questions before filling in the matrix.

   Liar's paradox problems involve the supposition that some statements must be true and others false. It is often an assumption of these problems that the individuals imagined either always lie or always tell the truth. Other problems of this sort specify the number of true or false statements involved. The solution to this type of problem requires the comparison of statements and the search for contradictions among the statements.

EXERCISES

A   LEVEL

True or False

1. _____ A matrix diagram is useful for answering questions that cannot be answered with a position diagram.
2. _____ In a matrix diagram you should not use immediate inferences to help fill in the grid.
3. _____ Matrix diagrams employ the terms *true, false,* and *maybe* to determine which conditions have been fulfilled.
4. _____ Matrix diagrams are most useful in solving problems that employ two or more sets of variables.
5. _____ When using a matrix diagram on an examination, you should look ahead to the questions and possible answers before drawing the matrix.

6. _____ Liar's paradox problems require that we know who is telling the truth and who is lying before we begin to solve the problem.

7. _____ One variety of the liar's paradox does not specify how many truth-tellers and how many liars are involved in the solution.

8. _____ Liar's paradox problems can be solved only by employing a lie detector or polygraph.

9. _____ Spotting contradictions is often helpful in the solution of problems of the liar's paradox type.

10. _____ The solution to liar's paradox problems involves applying the content of statements made by the participants to the claims of the other participants.

B   LEVEL

Answer the following questions based on the information given for each set of questions. Be sure to draw a matrix or grid or at least a diagram that makes sense to you.

Questions 1 through 6 pertain to the following scenario:

Mr. Al, Mr. Fred, and Mr. Richard live in Bennington, Washington, and Memphis, but not necessarily in that order. They happen to be flying on a plane whose flight crew, coincidentally, are also named Al, Fred, and Richard. They are the pilot, the co-pilot, and the navigator; but, again, not necessarily in that order. We also know six pertinent facts:

(a) Mr. Richard lives in Memphis.

(b) Mr. Fred knows nothing about greeting cards, even though he is an artist.

(c) Al won the last three gin rummy games with the co-pilot.

(d) The flight passenger whose name is the same as the navigator's lives in Bennington.

(e) The navigator himself lives in Washington.

(f) The navigator's next door neighbor happens to be one of the passengers who has been in the greeting card business for 20 years.

1. Which passenger is from Bennington?

(A) Al

(B) Richard

(C) Fred

(D) Mr. Al

(E) Mr. Fred

2. Which is the passenger from Washington?

(A) Al

(B) Richard

(C) Fred

(D) Mr. Al

(E) Mr. Fred

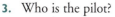

3. Who is the pilot?
   (A) Al
   (B) Richard
   (C) Fred
   (D) Mr. Al
   (E) Mr. Fred

4. Who is the co-pilot?
   (A) Al
   (B) Richard
   (C) Fred
   (D) Mr. Al
   (E) Mr. Richard

5. Who is the navigator?
   (A) Al
   (B) Richard
   (C) Fred
   (D) Mr. Richard
   (E) Mr. Fred

6. Which city is the pilot from?
   (A) Bennington
   (B) Washington
   (C) Memphis
   (D) Either (A) or (C)
   (E) Cannot be determined from information given

Questions 7 through 15 concern the following problem:

The National Collegiate Women's Basketball championship team boasts five starters: Angie, Beth, Caren, Deana, and Emily. They come from all parts of the world: Afghanistan, Brazil, Canada, Denmark, and Ethiopia, but not necessarily in that order. They are majoring in Art, Biology, Computer Science, Drama, and Economics; but, again, not necessarily in that order. Interestingly enough, none of these women comes from a country beginning with the same letter as her name, and her major begins with a different letter than either her name or the country from which she comes. The Biology major does not come from Canada. Beth is neither the Economics major nor the Art major; and she does not come from either Canada or Denmark. Deana's home is actually in Ethiopia, but she is neither the Art major nor the Biology major. Angie is not from Brazil. In fact, Emily is not from Brazil either; and Emily is not the Biology major or the Drama major.

7. Which of the women comes from Afghanistan?
   (A) Angie   (B) Beth   (C) Caren   (D) Deana   (E) Emily

8. Which of the women is the Art major?
   (A) Angie   (B) Beth   (C) Caren   (D) Deana   (E) Emily

9. Which of the women comes from Brazil?
   (A) Angie   (B) Beth   (C) Caren   (D) Deana   (E) Emily
10. Which of the women is the Biology major?
   (A) Angie   (B) Beth   (C) Caren   (D) Deana   (E) Emily
11. Which of the women comes from Canada?
   (A) Angie   (B) Beth   (C) Caren   (D) Deana   (E) Emily
12. Which of the women is the Computer Science major?
   (A) Angie   (B) Beth   (C) Caren   (D) Deana   (E) Emily
13. Which of the women is from Denmark?
   (A) Angie   (B) Beth   (C) Caren   (D) Deana   (E) Emily
14. Which of the women is the Drama major?
   (A) Angie   (B) Beth   (C) Caren   (D) Deana   (E) Emily
15. Which of the women is the Economics major?
   (A) Angie   (B) Beth   (C) Caren   (D) Deana   (E) Emily

Questions 16 through 25 pertain to the following puzzle:

ACME Industries (yes, them again) is offering a panel discussion complete with live TV coverage. You are to announce the seven panelists, only you seem to have misplaced your notecards. Here's all the information you can remember: the seven persons include ACME's CEO; ACME's President; ACME's Comptroller; ACME's General Counsel; ACME's Public Relations Director; ACME's Vice President in charge of Sales; and ACME's Vice President in charge of Marketing. So far, so good; but let's see—what were their names? One was Connor. Jackson was another. There were also Osgood, Samuels, Quincy, and Rhyno. The last one was . . . Deljoo, yes, that's the ticket. Their Alma Maters are Arizona State University, Brown University, University of Cincinnati, Duquesne, East Carolina State, Florida State, and Goddard College. But you need to match the right names with the correct title and Alma Mater. All you can remember in addition are the following pieces of information:

(1)   The comptroller must be both an MBA and a CPA.
(2)   The CEO, one of the VP's, and the other one named Connor are married. The rest are single.
(3)   The General Counsel is the only person with a doctorate in jurisprudence.
(4)   Osgood, Samuels, and Quincy, and the VP of Marketing have no advanced degree beyond the B. A.
(5)   The VP of Sales, the President, Osgood, and Deljoo meet every Tuesday for a power lunch.
(6)   Rhyno is the only J. D. or attorney in the group.
(7)   Jackson is the P. R. Director, but did not graduate from Cincinnati, FSU, or Goddard.
(8)   Samuels is married to Quincy's sister.
(9)   Deljoo received the MBA from Arizona State University.
(10)   The lawyer is an Ivy Leaguer (went to Brown).
(11)   The person who graduated from Duquesne has a sister who is married to the V. P. of Sales.
(12)   Neither the V. P. of Marketing nor Osgood went to Goddard.
(13)   The person who went to FSU used to be a V. P. before moving to the top of the corporate ladder.

16. Who is ACME's CEO?

(A) Connor   (B) Jackson   (C) Osgood   (D) Samuels   (E) Quincy

17. Who is ACME's President?

(A) Connor   (B) Jackson   (C) Osgood   (D) Samuels   (E) Quincy

18. Who went to Brown University?

(A) Jackson   (B) Osgood   (C) Quincy   (D) Rhyno   (E) Deljoo

19. Who went to Goddard College?

(A) Osgood   (B) Samuels   (C) Quincy   (D) The CEO (E) The Lawyer

20. Which one of the following is married?

(A) Jackson   (B) Osgood   (C) Quincy   (D) Rhyno   (E) Deljoo

21. Connor is actually:

(A) The CEO   (B) President   (C) Comptroller   (D) VP of Sales   (E) VP of Marketing

22. Which clues have redundant or superfluous information?

(A) Clues 4 and 12   (B) Clues 8 and 11   (C) Clues 2, 3, and 4   (D) None of the above

(E) All of the above

23. Where did the President go to school?

(A) Arizona State Univ.   (B) Univ. of Cincinnati   (C) Duquesne University   (D) East Carolina State Univ.   (E) Florida State Univ.

24. Where did Connor go to school?

(A) Arizona State   (B) Brown Univ.   (C) Univ. of Cincinnati   (D) FSU   (E) Goddard College

25. The person who went to Arizona State moved up in the company to become:

(A) CEO   (B) President   (C) Comptroller   (D) General Counsel   (E) PR Director

Solve the following problems by determining who is lying and who is telling the truth. Assume that each speaker either tells the truth all of the time or lies all of the time.

Questions 26 through 28 concern the following three persons:

Albert: "Two of the three of us are truth-tellers."

Beatrice: "No, only one of us is a truth-teller."

Clarissa: "That's right. Beatrice is telling the truth."

26. Albert is (A) a truth teller,   (B) a liar.

27. Beatrice is (A) a truth teller,   (B) a liar.

28. Clarissa is (A) a truth teller,   (B) a liar.

Questions 29 through 31 concern the following three people:

Ulysses: "All three of us are truth tellers."

Xerxes: "That's correct. All three of us are telling the truth."

Zooey: "Unfortunately, that is not true."

29. Ulysses is (A) a truth teller,   (B) a liar.

30. Xerxes is (A) a truth teller,   (B) a liar.

31. Zooey is (A) a truth teller,   (B) a liar

Questions 32 pertains to the following purely fictitious scenario:

A major sports celebrity was accused of committing a heinous crime. When Chief Inspector Petrovich was assigned the case, a number of wannabe famous persons came forth claiming to be eye-witnesses. Petrovich decided to interview the first five personally and here is what he heard:

Danster: "Don't trust Jimbo; he lies all the time."

Glennmeister: "Well, Maribeth is the one person I know you can trust."

Chien: "Actually, Jimbo is the one person you can trust."

Jimbo: "Wait; you can trust me and the Danster. We always tell the truth."

Maribeth: "Glennmeister's right; you can always trust me."

With unerring instinct and detective's intuition, Inspector Petrovich knew that four of his five witnesses were lying and would therefore be unreliable informants. This also meant that one and only one of the fivesome was telling the truth and might give him a break in the case.

32. Who is the truth teller?

(A) Danster (B) Glennmeister (C) Chien (D) Jimbo (E) Maribeth

LEVEL

The following question involves several variables. Use a matrix diagram to solve the puzzle and be sure to show all of your work.

I. A murder has been committed in the room diagrammed. Vivian, a soap-opera star, was murdered with poisoned cognac. There are four people remaining in the room, two seated in chairs

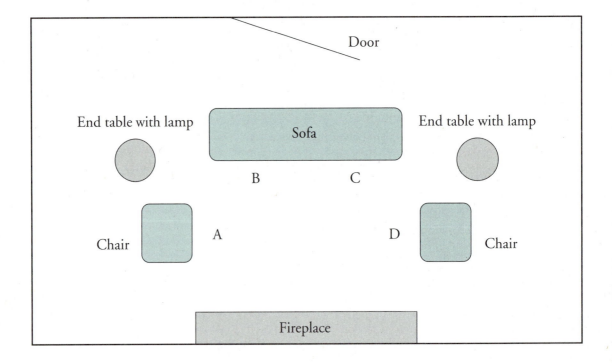

(shown as A and D in the diagram) and two others sitting on a sofa in front of a fireplace and between the two chairs (shown as B and C in the diagram). The foursome begins to discuss this serious matter because they realize that one of them must be the murderer. Their names are Mitchell, Glunn, Armstrong, and Sachs. By profession they are a general, a professor, an astronaut and a physician. We also know:

A. A waitress pours a shot of brandy for Armstrong and a beer for Glunn.

B. In the mirror over the fireplace, the general sees the door close behind the waitress who is leaving the room. He turns to speak to Sachs who is sitting on the sofa with him.

C. Both Mitchell and Sachs have no brothers or sisters.

D. The professor is a teetotaler (i.e., he does not drink alcohol).

E. Mitchell, who is sitting in one of the chairs, happens to be the astronaut's brother-in-law. The professor is next to Mitchell on Mitchell's left.

F. Suddenly, a hand sneakily drops something into Armstrong's brandy. It is the murderer. No one has left his seat and no one else is in the room.

What is the profession of each person, where is he sitting, and who is the murderer?

Solve the following liar's paradox problem:

2. On a sultry Fourth of July five friends were celebrating the release of their leader and mentor, Dr. John, from federal prison on that day. It is he and he alone who knows where the three million dollar heist has been hidden for the past ten years. But the party was only a few hours old when the doctor was found bludgeoned to death with a brass candlestick. Then, only four remained and one of the four had Dr. John's knowledge.

The police, however, had been keeping surveillance on the crew. Although they have discovered a great deal, they do not know who the murderer is. When the gang learned of this they decided to give themselves up—but only in order to confuse the detective investigating the case. They hoped she would be confused enough to botch her case. The foursome decided that each of them would make exactly four statements, of which three would be true and one false. But they are unaware that the police have monitored them and know of this decision. In ignorance of this bit of information, the four suspects make their statements:

Peter: **A.** Well, Quince was with me in the basement at the time.

        B. The candlestick is Shelby's.

        C. I didn't commit the murder.

        D. Rota didn't do it either.

Quince: **A.** I've never been in the basement.

        B. It's ironic that this is Independence Day.

        C. Everyone of us is covering up something.

        D. But I didn't do it.

Rota: **A.** Doc had to be murdered after the party started:

        B. Any one of us could have done it.

        C. I didn't do it.

        D. Quince is the guilty one.

Shelby: **A.** There were only five of us here.

B. Peter's wrong if he's implying that I did it.

C. I didn't do it.

D. That's not my candlestick.

CASE STUDY

The Mystery of Portia's Caskets

For persons who enjoy logical puzzles and word games, the market boasts of a number of highly original and intriguing books, magazines, pamphlets, that take off in quite an array of directions. Certainly one of the more prominent authors is Raymond Smullyan. We have included a small sample from his *What Is the Name of This Book?* Try to solve each one of the mysteries he presents *before* looking up the answers the back of the book. Note that for many of these riddles, there is more than one way to deduce the correct answer.

The Mystery of Portia's Caskets
by Raymond Smullyan
(Reprinted with permission From Raymond Smullyan, *What Is the Name of This Book?*,
10th ed., New York: Prentice Hall, 1978.)

A. The First Tale
_____

67a. _____

In Shakespeare's *Merchant of Venice* Portia had three caskets—gold, silver, and lead—inside one of which was Portia's portrait. The suitor was to choose one of the caskets, and if he was lucky enough (or wise enough) to choose the one with the portrait, then he could claim Portia as his bride. On the lid of each casket was an inscription to help the suitor choose wisely.

Now, suppose Portia wished to choose her husband not on the basis of virtue, but simply on the basis of intelligence. She had the following inscriptions put on the caskets

Gold	**Silver**	**Lead**
THE PORTRAIT IS IN THIS CASKET	THE PORTRAIT IS NOT IN THIS CASKET	THE PORTRAIT IS NOT IN THE GOLD CASKET

Portia explained to the suitor that of the three statements, at most one was true.

Which casket should the suitor choose?

67b. _____

Portia's suitor chose correctly, so they married and lived quite happily—at least for a while. Then, one day, Portia had the following thoughts: "Though my husband showed *some* intelligence in choosing the right casket, the problem wasn't really *that* difficult. Surely, I could have made the problem harder and gotten a *really* clever husband." So she forthwith divorced her husband and decided to get a cleverer one.

This time she had the following inscriptions put on the caskets:

Gold

THE PORTRAIT
IS NOT IN THE
SILVER CASKET

Silver

THE PORTRAIT
IS NOT IN
THIS CASKET

Lead

THE PORTRAIT
IS IN THIS
CASKET

Portia explained to the suitor that at least one of the three statements was true and that at least one of them was false.

Which casket contains the portrait?

Epilogue _____

As fate would have it, the first suitor turned out to be Portia's ex-husband. He was really quite bright enough to figure out this problem too. So they were remarried. The husband took Portia home, turned her over his knee, gave her a good sound spanking, and Portia never had any foolish ideas again.

B. The Second Tale _____

Portia and her husband did, as a matter of fact, live happily ever after. They had a daughter Portia II—henceforth to be called "Portia." When the young Portia grew to young womanhood, she was both clever and beautiful, just like her mommy. She also decided to select her husband by the casket method. The suitor had to pass *two* tests in order to win her.

68a. The First Test. _____

In this test each lid contained *two* statements, and Portia explained that no lid contained more than one false statement.

Gold

(1) THE PORTRAIT
IS NOT IN HERE

(2) THE ARTIST OF
THE PORTRAIT IS
FROM VENICE

Silver

(1) THE PORTRAIT
IS NOT IN THE
GOLD CASKET

(2) THE ARTIST OF
THE PORTRAIT IS
REALLY FROM
FLORENCE

Lead

(1) THE PORTRAIT
IS NOT IN HERE

(2) THE PORTRAIT
IS REALLY IN
THE SILVER
CASKET

Which casket contains the portrait?

68b. The Second Test. _____

If the suitor passed the first test, he was taken into another room in which there were three more caskets. Again each casket had two sentences inscribed on the lid. Portia explained that on one of the lids, both statements were true; on another, both statements were false; and on the third, one statement was true and one was false.

Gold

(1) THE PORTRAIT IS NOT IN THIS CASKET

(2) IT IS IN THE SILVER CASKET

Silver

(1) THE PORTRAIT IS NOT IN THE GOLD CASKET

(2) IT IS IN THE LEAD CASKET

Lead

(1) THE PORTRAIT IS NOT IN THIS CASKET

(2) IT IS IN THE GOLD CASKET

Which casket contains the portrait?

14

ARGUMENTATIVE WRITING

step one
What is the main claim?

step four
What is the meaning of the terms employed?

step two
Is there an argument?

step three
Are there any assumptions or implications?

step five
Are there any fallacies?

step six
What is the argument's structure?

step seven
What other conclusions can be drawn?

step eight
Do you agree or disagree with the conclusion?

Hang by your thumbs, everybody!

Write if you get work.

—*Bob and Ray radio show (1946)*

Three hours a day will produce

as much as a man ought to write.

—*Anthony Trollope (1870)*

KEY TERMS

Analogical argument - An argument based on an analogy or comparison between two things or states of affairs, one better known than the other.

Definitional argument - An argument seeking to establish the meaning of a term.

Moral argument - An argument that attempts to establish that something "ought" to be the case or that something is "right" or "wrong."

Statistical argument - An argument based on probability theory.

With this chapter, we have finally reached the point where the different elements of the Technique are brought together. Strictly speaking, they are brought together in Step 8. This step involves the application of the results of our previous studies. We have, so far, been engaged in the analysis of claims and arguments made by others. It is now time to apply the methods learned in this book creatively in the construction of valid and well-written arguments. It should be noted from the outset that the manner for constructing and presenting an argument depends largely on the audience for whom it is intended. A well-constructed letter to the editor may make for a poor essay written for a history class. The way that evidence is presented to a jury will differ from the way a chemist uses evidence to justify a hypothesis. However, all argumentative essays are similar in that good ones exhibit sound reasoning and clear presentation. We will begin by going through the seven previous steps of the Technique, and showing how they can be applied in the writing of a good argumentative essay.

Step 1: Determine the Main Claim When writing an argumentative essay, it is important to determine the main claim that you would like to advance. As we have seen, the major claim of an argument is its conclusion, and the supporting evidence is supplied by the premises. Many argumentative essays lack this essential ingredient, and it is often difficult to determine precisely which point the author is attempting to make. To accomplish this it is first necessary to determine the purpose for which we are writing or stating the argument. It is useful at this point to be able to state our conclusion in a single sentence. If it is difficult to summarize our claim in a single sentence, it may be because we are unclear in our own minds as to the point we are trying to make. An argument intended to justify the inclusion of gay individuals in the military might, for instance, be confused with an argument attempting to support the rights of gay people in general. Thus the broadness or narrowness of our conclusion should first be determined.

Step 2: Construct the Argument Once our conclusion has been determined and stated, the next step is to decide which evidence we would like to use in its support. The premises of the argument need to be decided. What kind of evidence are we going to use? The answer to this question depends on the type of argument that is being written. For instance, an essay written for a sociology class may require the use of statistical evidence. A letter to the editor, on the other hand, might rely more exclusively on anecdotal evidence. And it may even be the case that the premises used in support of the conclusion require subsidiary arguments to support them. This depends largely on whether the evidence is generally accepted by the audience being addressed. Support for gays in the military would require far more argumentation if the audience were a conservative church group than if it were attendees at a gay-rights rally.

Step 3: Detect Assumptions and Implications It is also important to determine whether or not any hidden assumptions are involved in our premises or conclusion. While the use of hidden assumptions may make for a more persuasive essay, their use is somewhat unfair. We need to allow our opponent the opportunity to respond to our claims. If any of the assumptions are hidden, this makes such a response impossible. But making our presuppositions explicit has the advantage of making our case more airtight, and it also helps prevent others from willfully distorting what we have omitted.

Step 4: Clarify Meaning Having determined the conclusion and premises of our argument, the next step would be to ensure that the meaning of the terms employed is clear, precise, and unambiguous. It is often the case that terms employed in arguments are too broad or vague to be of much use. An argument for the free-market system, for instance, might involve the use of the term *socialist* in a negative way. But what precisely is a socialist? For some people the term denotes something like *communism;* for others it is intended to mean anyone supporting any type of government intervention in the marketplace. A good argumentative essay will make the meaning of the terms clear. When necessary, stipulative definitions should be employed so that the audience understands precisely which terms are under discussion. Stipulative definitions should not be disguised as reportive definitions. When a definition is used to clarify the meaning of a term, it should be stated whether that definition is a generally accepted one.

Step 5: Search for Fallacies You should look over your argument to find any fallacious reasoning you may have employed. The employment of fallacious reasoning can often make you feel clever and provide you with a sense of creative satisfaction. But its use is not only unfair; when fallacies are used in an argument, that argument is more vulnerable to refutation. A fallacious argument is a weak argument and one that can be refuted by anyone with a knowledge of the fallacies involved.

Step 6: Determine the Argument's Structure This will depend largely on the type of evidence you employ. If the evidence is statistical, for instance, you should be careful to construct an argument based on reliable inductive reasoning. Should the argument be presented in the form of an analogy, you should take care to ensure that the points of comparison really are similar enough to make your point. A good deductive argument will lead the audience to accept the necessity of the conclusion, whereas an invalid argument will open the way to an easy refutation.

TO BE OR NOT TO BE—RATIONAL, THAT IS

Particularly when writing, but in just about every other phase of life as well, the question arises of when to be rational and when, not to be. Trying to be calm and rational when one is about to be mugged or shot may or may not be the best course of action to take. At times it is very difficult to determine just what would be the best thing to do, even after the fact and in retrospect. When, for example, Malcolm X offered his readers the choice of "the ballot or the bullet" he was partially faced with such a dilemma. At the first blush, such a "black-or-white" choice seems to be a classic case of our fallacy of Limited Options. A little closer inspection reveals that more is going on in this instance. By offering the so-called "choice" between giving black Americans and other minorities the right to vote versus the possibility of being shot to death, it almost seems as if Malcolm has traded the Limited Options fallacy for the Appeal to Fear fallacy. In point of fact what he may be doing is underscoring that the prejudiced attitude perpetuating the refusal to grant voting rights to blacks is inherently irrational. In other words, if these forces could not be reached rationally, they would have to be persuaded "irrationally" either by fallacy or by something perhaps more threatening. Would that make it a good argument? What about an effective argument?

Step 7: Draw Conclusions Having constructed and assessed your argument according to the six previous steps, it is now time for you to examine your argument to determine whether other conclusions may be drawn from the evidence you have presented. Perhaps your premises lead to more than one conclusion. You should ask yourself whether or not these conclusions are acceptable, given the main claim you were trying to make. If you are not satisfied with the other conclusions that can be drawn from your argument, you may have to adjust the premises accordingly. You have to be careful, though, not to delete or add any premises that would significantly weaken or invalidate the argument's support for your conclusion.

Step 8: Write Down Your Argument Instead of assessing the arguments offered by others, you are now in a position to write your essay defending your main claim. Although the form and content of the argument have been determined, you must now find a way of expressing your argument in essay form. Be sure to remember that your readers do not have the capability of reading your mind. Try to explain every premise as clearly as you can, and show the connections you are making between those premises.

It is important that your argument pay heed to all of the lessons learned in this book. By checking each element of the Technique, you will help to ensure that your argument will be both sound and fair. Several things can be done prior to the actual writing of the argument that may assist you in covering these points. What follows are a list of things you can do to reinforce your ability to write a good argumentative essay.

Draw a Preliminary Diagram

It is helpful to draw a rough diagram of the argument you are seeking to present. This should be done according to the method suggested in Step 3 of the Technique (Section 3.2). In the first place, drawing such a diagram will afford us a way of seeing just what the main reasons for our conclusion are. It may also tip us off as to which of our premises stand in need of further support and which are fairly self-sufficient or at least non-controversial in the particular context.

A diagram is also useful in that it will allow us to see at a glance just which evidence may be missing in support of our case. This is especially true if the argument we are presenting is long and involved. It is often difficult to assess the soundness of an argument presented in prose form.

Furthermore, a diagram or outline will provide a guide to the actual writing of the argument. It is often possible to lose sight of our argument's structure. When this occurs it is frequently the case that we go off on tangents and write about material that is not relevant to the point we are trying to make. An argument that sticks to the point and provides only relevant support is the most effective in persuading the audience of the conclusion's truth. In extreme cases the original conclusion might unintentionally be abandoned in favor of a point that was not even at issue. This diagram should be readily available when you are actually writing your argument and frequent references to it should be made during the course of its actual construction.

Rank the Evidence

Another useful tool in the writing of an argumentative essay is the ranking of the premises or evidence from the strongest to the weakest. This will enable you to determine which premises need the most support and which can do with less. The strongest piece of evidence is probably best placed where it will achieve its greatest effect on the audience. This is usually the first or last point to be made. For long and involved essays, the final point to be made will usually have the greatest effect.

When the premises are ranked according to their importance, it will help determine how much treatment each should receive. Suppose, for instance, that your conclusion is that people should not engage in bungee jumping. You might offer as evidence three premises: (1) it is a waste of time, (2) it is expensive, and (3) it is dangerous. It is not the case that each of these reasons should carry the same weight. More than likely, reason 3 is a much stronger and more important piece of evidence than the other two. If you were called on to justify your conclusion, you might mention the first two reasons and back them up with a few brief statements. But the bulk of your argument should center around reason 3. The more important reasons should be covered in much greater detail than those that are less important.

Determine Whether There Is a Need for Further Research

At this point, you should be able to determine which points need further substantiation. This may require going to a dictionary to clarify a definition. It might also be necessary to find factual support for your conclusion in the form of statistical or anecdotal evidence. The weak points of your argument may need to be reinforced. Although we may be convinced of the truth of our conclusion, our audience may require further evidence. Searching for such evidence may not always be a pleasant task, and we might even discover that some of our premises are in fact simply wrong. But a good argument requires the best support available. And personal conviction or fear of being wrong do not justify inadequate research.

Anticipate Possible Objections

As you reconsider your argument with a critical eye, you should try to determine what possible objections may be made to the claims you are seeking to advance. It would be easy to pick out weak objections or those that are only tangentially relevant. But ignoring the strongest objections can only lead to disaster. The advice often given to novice chess players is useful here. Anticipate that your opponent will make the "best possible move" to refute your argument. It is better to try to determine the main obstacles to your conclusion from the outset rather than to try to deal with them later. Look at your own reasoning with as critical and objective an attitude as you can. Ask yourself the most difficult and critical questions possible and you will be able to isolate the weakest links in your argument.

14.1 THE ARGUMENT'S FORMAT

Throughout the latter half of this book we have taken a look at a number of very different ways in which arguments can be structured. We did this in order to distinguish valid deductive arguments from invalid ones, and weak inductive arguments from strong ones. Just as each strand of the reasoning may fit a particular form, arguments as a whole tend to follow the same overall patterns. When writing an argumentative essay, the form we choose for it to take is very important. There are many forms from which we may choose. The one we finally choose depends on the type of essay we are writing. To a large extent it also depends on our own preferences. We will take a look at some of the more prominent forms and the conditions that would favor their use. We will also look at the circumstances that would make certain of these forms inappropriate.

"PC" TO THE RESCUE

In their *The Official Politically Correct Dictionary and Handbook,* Henry Beard and Christopher Cerf do a beautiful job of (1) sensitizing readers to the newly minted phrases that are nonoffensive and "politically correct" while (2) poking good-natured fun at taking the notion of "political correctness" to extremes. The book has many examples and it also contains a list of source notes. Here is an example of one definition garnered with the aid of the American Hyphen Society:

Borealocentrism: The implicit belief that the peoples and cultures of the Northern Hemisphere are superior to those of the Southern Hemisphere, characterized by the arbitrary placement of the North Pole at the "top" of the globe.

For example: a nonborealocentric globe would be characterized by having the South Pole at the "top."

(Reprinted with permission from Henry Beard and Christopher Cerf, The Official Politically Correct Dictionary and Handbook, *New York: Villard Books, 1992.)*

The Definitional Argument

On occasion you will be called on to write a **definitional argument.** A review of Step 4 of the Technique (covered in Section 4.2) can help in this regard. A definitional essay requires that you argue for a certain definition of a term that may or may not be currently accepted. Since the collapse of the communist system in many parts of the world, for instance, someone may wish to argue that the definition of *communism* has significantly changed, or perhaps that the definition *should be* changed. The first step in such an argument would be to establish why a currently acceptable definition is inadequate. To follow our example, if the current definition of *communism* were to be something like "it is a world movement that seeks to establish a socialist-like system of government throughout the world and is directed largely by the Soviet Union" we might want to argue that the definition is not currently very accurate. The first step, in this case, is to try to argue against the current definition. We might do this by first noting several facts that might serve as premises for the conclusion that "we need to change the definition." The evidence we might wish to use in support of this could note, for instance, that "there is no longer any Soviet Union." Another premise might be that it is by and large no longer a world movement.

As we have already seen, we would need to rank these two premises in order of importance. In this case it would seem that the notion that it is directed by the Soviet Union is a less important premise than the one that notes it is seen as a world movement. Such an argument would need to be established by citing facts that demonstrate the definition's inadequacy. Since it is generally known that the Soviet Union is no longer in existence as a political entity, the less important premise would be easiest to establish. It would require little, if any, research. The more important premise, however, might require more work. To prove that the movement is no longer a worldwide phenomenon we would have to look into the fate of various communist movements around the world. We might, for instance, cite the movement's fall in other nations such as Nicaragua and Eastern Europe. The support for this premise would require us to research political events during the past few years. Of course, the best source of research for this point would be recent news articles in magazines and newspapers as well as television and radio news reports.

Suppose that we have constructed this first stage of the argument; our next step would be to try to argue for a new definition. The new definition proposed might be, for instance, that "Communism is a discredited movement which sought the overthrow of capitalism." The next premise might therefore be that the movement is discredited. To establish this, we would use as one of our premises the conclusion of the first part of the argument. An additional premise might require research into the opinions of different authors who have pointed out that the movement no longer has the force that it once did. In this case opinion essays and editorials might serve as our evidence. Again, research is required to establish that this is the case. The most useful articles would be those written by former communists. After all, if communists themselves have changed their mind about the movement, we would have strong evidence that the argument has been discredited.

Anticipating objections to our new definition would be easy. For instance, it would be likely that a possible opponent would argue that "Well it doesn't matter that the Soviet Union has fallen. There is, after all, still a communist government in China and North Korea. The fact that it is no longer directed by the Soviet Union may be granted, but this is a small point. Furthermore, there are many people around the world who still believe in the establishment of communism." By anticipating such an objection, we would want to be sure that the ex-communists we have chosen are notable ones who carry much weight.

While the definition of communism might not strike you as very important in the overall scheme of things, definitional essays often have serious consequences. During the Reagan administration, for instance, schools were required under a federally funded program to provide a vegetable for school lunches. To cut down on expenses without changing the law, the administration decided simply to change the definition of "vegetable" to include vegetable products such as ketchup. Similarly, the definition of those who were eligible for federal money for help because they have the AIDS virus was subject to debate during the Bush administration. The HIV virus may *cause* AIDS, but a person with the virus does not actually develop the disease for some time. At any rate, the consequences of following one definition rather than another might be quite significant.

The Analogical Argument

Another common form of argument is one based on analogy. An **analogical argument** requires a comparison between two things, one of which is better understood than the point which is at issue. Be sure to consult Section 12.1 (which concerns one aspect of Step 6 of the Technique) when you attempt to construct such an argument. When constructing an analogical argument, the premises should involve the establishment of similarities between the two cases. While arguing for the inclusion of gays in the military, for instance, it was pointed out by many proponents that it was very much like the struggle to racially integrate the military in the late 1940s.

The structure of analogical arguments requires the establishment of the points of comparison. When it was pointed out that many soldiers would be uncomfortable with gays in the military it was argued that whites said they would be uncomfortable with blacks in the military when that was the issue but that such alleged discomfort did not diminish the capacity of the armed forces and that the inclusion of gays would produce the same results.

The objection to this argument was based on an attempt to show that the analogy was mistaken. Opponents argued that while race is a matter of birth, sexual orientation was a matter of choice, and further that it was a matter of morality. It was argued that a gay life-style was immoral and that therefore gays should be excluded on moral grounds. The rejoinder from the proponents was simply that a gay life-style was not a matter of choice nor morality at all.

So arguments that are structured as analogies revolve around the fact that the analogy chosen is or is not appropriate to the point at issue. Research is again required to establish these premises as true or not.

Moral Arguments

Moral arguments are those that argue for or against a certain course of action or state of affairs. The conclusion of such an argument consists of a statement that says that this is the way things ought or ought not to be. Moral arguments often use definitional and analogical arguments in support of their premises. But since the conclusion of a moral argument requires the term *ought* or one of its variations, it is important that moral arguments contain the term *ought* in at least one of the premises. Consider one of the arguments against legalized abortion. It is often argued that abortion is tantamount to legalized murder. Murder is wrong and is also illegal. Therefore abortion should also be illegal.

This argument against abortion contains elements of both analogical and definitional arguments. An opponent of this stance, for instance, might begin by arguing that *murder* has been incorrectly defined in a hidden premise. *Murder,* these individuals might argue, is a concept that applies only to "complete persons" and not to undeveloped fetuses. Furthermore, while abortion may in some way be "like" murder, it is not sufficiently similar to warrant a comparison. Finally, the *ought* in the conclusion of the abortion opponent's argument would seem to follow from the *ought* implied by the premise "murder is wrong." While few would argue against the premise that "murder is wrong," it could be more easily argued that the analogy and definitions implied by the premises do not lead to the *ought* implied by the conclusion.

Statistical Arguments

There is a common belief that "you can prove anything with statistics" and that from the same set of statistics you can often prove contradictory conclusions. Statistics is a branch of mathematics that has its own set of rules and requirements. Although we do not delve into statistical science here, **statistical arguments** should be subject to the dictates of Mill's methods. One should be on guard for inductive fallacies and avoid them when constructing such an argument. For instance, if one supports the conclusion that "all marriages will fail" with the statistic that "most marriages wind up in divorce" one will be guilty of the fallacy of Hasty Generalization. It is important to review the strictures of Mill's methods when constructing arguments of this form so as to avoid fallacious reasoning.

Finally, you should remember that no matter how good an argument you have constructed there is always room for opposition. Very few, if any, arguments go unchallenged. Also try to remember that the purpose of thinking critically is not simply to sharpen your argumentative skills. Keep an open mind. Despite our illusions, none of us is always right. To believe we are infallible is the surest way to close our minds to new thoughts and ideas. Critical thinking skills should not become a hindrance to your intellectual growth, but should enhance it. And never forget Hamlet's admonition to Horatio:

There are greater things in heaven and earth than are dreamt of in your philosophy.

SUMMARY

In this chapter we bring together the different aspects of the Technique in the construction of arguments. One should first establish the conclusion he or she wishes to argue (Step 1), and then determine which premises would support that conclusion (Step 2). In developing these premises, you should be on the lookout for logical assumptions and implications (Step 3) and unclear meanings (Step 4). You should also be on the lookout for both formal and informal fallacies (Step 5) and avoid them in the construction of the argument. Your argument's structure should next be evaluated (Step 6). A determination of which other conclusions may be drawn from your argument should next be assessed (Step 7). Finally, you should proceed to express your written argument in a clear and understandable way (Step 8).

It would be helpful to draw a diagram of the argument in order to get an overview of the argument and determine whether or not the general structure is a good one. It is also useful to rank the premises in the order of their importance for the purpose of determining which premises need the most support and which

SO CLEAN IT SQUEAKS

When writing argumentatively it is important to keep in mind the purpose behind and the context motivating the reasoning. If, for example, the context is a letter to the editor of a newspaper or magazine, one must tread a fine line between losing the spark of emotional fire generating the essay in the first place and running the risk of having some editor cut out most of the critical underpinning in favor of a snappy two line sound-bite. Put more curtly, if we try to sanitize our writing too much by purging it of any trace of fallacious appeal, we may look as ridiculous as the person who tried to change Lincoln's Gettysburg Address from "Four score and seven years ago our forefathers brought forth on this continent a new nation..." to "Eighty-seven years ago the U.S. was founded...."

To give a more recent example, when Dr. Martin Luther King, Jr., was arrested in Birmingham, he wrote in part of his "Letter from the Birmingham Jail":

> ...I cannot sit idly by in Atlanta and not be concerned about what happens in Birmingham. Injustice anywhere is a threat to justice everywhere. We are caught in a network of mutuality, inescapably tied in a garment of destiny. Whatever affects one directly affects all indirectly....

To be sure, there is a great deal of metaphorical and figurative language in the middle of this passage. Indeed, there are some powerful emotional appeals at play here. Technically, these might be considered logical fallacies. Yet, given the historical context, they actually show remarkable restraint and if anything, give evidence of the triumph of genius over some petty rules of logic. And, just as importantly, they are bolstered by good reasoning both before and after this particular context.

need less. At this point it can be determined where further research may be needed. It is also necessary to anticipate possible objections to the argument being constructed and to shore up the premises that might be attacked.

Arguments can be constructed on the basis of several formats. *Definitional arguments* support a definition for a given term. These arguments often require a preliminary argument against a currently accepted definition and then proceed to an argument establishing a new definition. *Analogical arguments* are constructed on the basis of an analogy or comparison between two cases. These arguments often proceed on the basis of establishing the adequacy of the comparison. *Moral arguments* seek to establish that something should be the case or that a course of action ought to be taken. They often contain subarguments of the analogical or definitional sort. Finally, *statistical arguments* are those that seek to establish a conclusion on the basis of statistical data. They should be subject to the strictures of Mill's methods and avoid the fallacies of inductive reasoning.

EXERCISES

 A   LEVEL

Short Answers
* **1.** What is the first thing that should be established in the construction of an argument?
* **2.** Which problems should one be on the lookout for in the statement of a conclusion?
* **3.** List several things that one should do in evaluating the premises and conclusion of an argument.
* **4.** What is the purpose of diagramming an argument before it is actually constructed?
* **5.** Why is it useful to rank the premises of an argument in the order of their importance?
* **6.** Why should one anticipate possible objections to an argument?
* **7.** What is a definitional argument?
* **8.** What is an analogical argument?
* **9.** Under what conditions does one employ a moral argument?
*10. What is a statistical argument? What should one be on the lookout for in the construction of such an argument?

 B   LEVEL

Determine which type of argument each of the following conclusions would most likely take. Then try to create possible premises to support them.
* **1.** A law should be passed to establish better gun control.
  2. National health care insurance would greatly benefit the economy.
* **3.** The term *liberal* is frequently misapplied.
  4. Intelligent people should vote for the Democratic candidate.

  * **5.** Television is like a drug.

    6. A certain Supreme Court decision is mistaken.

  * **7.** Most people believe in God.

    8. Abortion is murder.

  * **9.** Abortion is a woman's right.

  10. Bill Clinton's presidency is not very successful so far.

Short Answer/Multiple Choice

*__11.__ Rank the following claims from most specific to least specific:

(A) A lot of people believe that Elvis is still alive.

(B) Over ten percent of the people alive today think Elvis is still alive.

(C) 12.9% of Americans and another 420,000,000 people world-wide feel that Elvis is still alive.

(D) 26,954,500 Americans as well as 420,505,000 people from other countries believe that Elvis is still alive.

12. Rank the following pieces of evidence from strongest to weakest for the purpose of supporting the claim that "cigarette smokers should seriously consider breaking their habit."

(A) Cigarette smoking is a dirty, nasty habit.

(B) Cigarette smoking annoys or bothers a lot of people.

(C) Cigarette smoking has been shown to be dangerous to your health.

(D) Cigarette smoking actually costs a lot of money.

(E) Cigarette smoking can be very inconvenient for the smoker.

*__13.__ Rank the following claims in order of their relative strength from strongest to weakest:

(A) The Redskins will win the SuperBowl this year.

(B) Most sportswriters and coaches around the country feel that the Redskins will win the SuperBowl this year.

(C) If all of their key players remain healthy, the Redskins will probably win the SuperBowl this year.

(D) The Redskins have as good a chance as any team this year of winning the SuperBowl.

(E) The Redskins seem to be one of the strongest teams in professional football this year.

A number of standardized tests from areas as diverse as the Law School Aptitude Tests to the Graduate Record Examinations and Graduate Management Admissions Test utilize questions that ask the reader to pick out parallel forms of reasoning, or to identify which forms of reasoning most closely resemble a given line of reasoning. For each of the questions below, pick out the best answer and be ready to explain why you find it to be the best one.

14. "If Jason and Justin go to the party, then Marcie is not going to go. But, Marcie is going to the party. Therefore, either Jason or Justin is not going to the party." Which line of reasoning most closely resembles this train of thinking?

(A) Marcie must have some sort of problem with either Jason or Justin or both of them, because she would not go to the party if they decide to go.

(B) If your tires wear out in the next twelve months or you have a flat, then ACME will repair or replace them for free. But ACME did not repair or replace them for free, so they must not have worn out or gone flat.

(C) Whenever the price of grain goes up and inflation climbs significantly, then the commodity market shows favorable gains. However, the commodity market is not showing favorable gains, so either the price of grain has not gone up or inflation has not climbed significantly.

(D) Jason and Justin have gone to the last 5 parties together and each time Marcie has refused to go if they went. Therefore, she will refuse to go again this time if they both decide to go.

(E) If Aunt Bea and Uncle Will come to the city, then Marcie won't be able to go to the party anyway. But Aunt Bea and Uncle Will are not coming to the city, so Marcie will be able to go to the party if she wants.

*15. "Since there have been no major hurricanes in the South Caribbean in the past six years, the South Caribbean will not be hit by a major hurricane this year." Which form of reasoning most closely parallels this form of reasoning?

(A) Since all island groups that are prime sailing areas have not been hit by hurricanes in the past few years, there must be some major weather factor which is contributing to the abnormal weather patterns.

(B) Since most of the houses in New England are made of wood rather than brick, it must be a more plentiful natural resource than clay.

(C) Since the last six sailing vacations I took had wonderful weather, the next sailing vacation I take will probably have terrible weather.

(D) None of the politicians interviewed about the scandal so far has been willing to talk. So, the politicians we have not yet interviewed will not be willing to talk either.

(E) All of the Southern-based corporations have been advertising their wonderful winters, so the corporations in other parts of the world will start advertizing the strong points of their corporate headquarters.

16. "TV Sitcoms are mindless escape mechanisms; therefore, television is quite detrimental to the education of children." Which of the following arguments is most similar to this line of reasoning?

(A) Sculpture is a sight for sore eyes; so, the arts are quite beneficial to society's mental welfare.

(B) My brother is a bookie; therefore, he is selfish and does not care what happens to other people.

(C) Drugs are basically bad for people; therefore, high risk heart patients should not take aspirin.

(D) International terrorism is increasing annually; therefore, people do not care about human life as much as they used to do.

(E) Parasites are amazingly adaptable; therefore, Spanish Moss is one of the most versatile plants in the world.

*17. "Most philanthropic aviators are lefthanded. Dr. Aton is a philanthropic aviator. Therefore, Dr. Aton is probably lefthanded." Which one of the following lines of reasoning is most like the above argument?

(A) I do not know who wrote *For Whom the Bell Tolls.* I do know my next door neighbor. Therefore, my next door neighbor did not write *For Whom the Bell Tolls.*

(B) Just about every tall building has an elevator. The Washington Monument is a tall building. Therefore, The Washington Monument probably has an elevator.

(C) People who ring my doorbell during dinner are annoying. Salesmen always ring my doorbell during dinner. Therefore, salesmen ringing my doorbell are annoying.

(D) Very few sculptors achieve fame during their own lifetime. Fred is a sculptor. Therefore, Fred will probably not achieve fame during his own lifetime.

(E) Most people who go to the polls do so out of a sense of civic responsibility. Therefore, people who do not go to the polls must refrain from voting because of reasons of conscience.

18. "People will succeed in life if and only if they apply themselves diligently. Therefore, a person's applying herself diligently is a necessary condition for their succeeding in life." Which of the following lines of reasoning is closest in form to the preceding argument?

(A) City University uses only ACME computers. Since the computer is an ACME computer, it must be one of City University's computers.

(B) Whenever I am awake, I think I am awake. And, when I am asleep, I sometimes think I am awake. Therefore, I may be asleep right now, since I think I am awake.

(C) Big people and only big people can buy clothes at ACME's Big Shop. Since Tina is a small person, she cannot buy clothes at ACME's Big Shop.

(D) Ollie accompanies Fran when, and only when, Kukla cannot accompany Fran. It has to follow then, that Kukla's inability to accompany Fran is a necessary prerequisite for Ollie's accompanying Fran.

(E) It is stupid if, and only if, I cannot understand it. Therefore, intelligence is a necessary condition for understanding.

C   LEVEL

1. Write a clear concluding statement for five of the twelve following topics:
   (A) gun control
   (B) national health care insurance
   (C) reincarnation
   (D) a political candidate you particularly like (or dislike)
   (E) a movie, TV show, CD, tape, or concert
   (F) an ecological/environmental issue
   (G) educational reform
   (H) a Supreme Court decision
   (I) something pertaining to sexual relationships
   (J) "family values"
   (K) the notion of political correctness
   (L) professional athletes' salaries

2. What do you find to be the three most important reasons in support of each conclusion you reached?

3. What would you consider to be the two main lines of objection that could be raised against your conclusion?

4. How would you handle those objections?

5. Draw a diagram of the outline of the argument you have to this point.

The set of exercises below pertain to writing arguments in their entirety:

6. Construct an argument of your own in which you make use of the overall form of modus ponens or "affirming the antecedent." Either part, the antecedent or the consequent, of the main conditional statement may be complex or simple. Show in symbols or in simple language what that form is.

7. Construct an argument of your own in which you use the form of modus tollens or "denying the consequent." Again, either part of the main conditional statement may be simple or complex. Display in symbols or language the overall form of the argument.

8. Write a definitional essay in which you do one or more of the following:

    (A) Abstract a defining characteristic or set of characteristics which apply to a number of individual cases;

    (B) Use a "Paradigm Case" to show what defining traits pertain to a particular concept; or

    (C) Criticize a given definition according to its weaknesses, then stipulate what the definition should be and why.

9. Think of a possible scenario where the biconditional argument form would be the most appropriate form. Show that form in words or symbols.

10. Construct a chain argument that is at least four steps long. Again, show this argument in words or symbols.

11. Utilize an analogical argument form to argue for a conclusion in one of the following areas:

    (A) A morally sensitive issue (as to ethical rightness or wrongness of a particular course of action, or whether something should or should not be done).

    (B) A legal case (perhaps, as to how a pending case should be judged, based upon constitutional or other legal precedents).

    (C) An aesthetic judgment (as to the beauty or artistic merit of something, some work of art, or some artist's work).

Employing the methods developed in this chapter, write an argumentative essay on each of the following topics:

12. For or against capital punishment.

13. A letter to a graduate or professional school explaining why you should be admitted.

14. A comparison between alcohol and illegal drugs.

15. A definition of critical thinking.

More involved writing exercises: For each of the scenarios presented below follow the instructions appropriate to that question. Many of these exercises are designed to help you put together the skills developed throughout the text. They are also patterned after the kinds of writing sample questions that are found on graduate and professional school admission tests as well as the kinds of questions that some corporate and professional organizations require as writing samples.

16. A major U.S. pharmaceutical manufacturer has found that in packaging its most popular over the counter medicine, one million of its bottles supposedly containing the 500 milligram extra

strength pain reliever actually contain their "normal" strength, 200 milligram pain reliever. The "mistake" is not going to harm anyone; but the company recognizes that some action must be taken on their part. At the company's board meeting to discuss this incident several important policy directives are made clear:

(1) The company is concerned to maintain their strong public image of reliability, dependability, and integrity.

(2) The company is concerned to minimize its financial risks and costs.

(3) The company feels a strong loyalty to its shareholders and investors and wishes to maintain that trust.

(4) The company feels a strong sense of loyalty to its customers and wishes to keep their confidence and their business.

Two major proposals for dealing with this situation emerge at the board meeting:

A. Option One is for the company to handle the situation through its marketing department by utilizing already committed television and radio advertisement time to inform the public of the "packaging mistake." The commercials will feature some well-respected and trusted public figure who will explain how such errors commonly occur and that it could even redound to the consumer's benefit. The consumer may keep the regular strength medicine and send in the label from the "mistaken batches" and receive absolutely free a bottle of the extra-strength pain reliever. It is anticipated that advertising costs will be high and that the "rate of return" will be quite high.

B. Option Two is for the company to handle the situation through its distribution facilities by informing them of the appropriate batch and serial numbers of the "mistake bottles". These distributors in turn are to contact all of their retail facilities and have them post inconspicuous signs both where the pills are displayed and at the pharmacy counters. These signs are to guarantee the customer that if they have purchased a wrongly labeled bottle, their retailer will give them a new bottle of the correct kind, provided that they fill out form for the retailer which states their name, address, and phone number so that the manufacturer can send them something in appreciation for their cooperation. The cost of this option is expected to be less than half of Option One and the rate of return is calculated to be 45% of that figured in Option One.

Your job is to write a recommendation for one of these proposals over the other, or to come up with a plan that you can justify which incorporates parts of either proposal.

17. You have a brother who joined the U.S. Marine Corps four years ago and who has had a distinguished career and outstanding performance evaluations up until one month ago. He claims that it is time that he "came out of the closet" and he has admitted his sexual preference for males. Although he has had no "incidents" during his career in service, the Corps has asked him to resign and is willing to give him an honorable discharge if he does so. You have been in constant contact with him since this incident has achieved public notoriety.

Your job is to write a letter to your senator explaining how you think the United States military should handle such situations and what you feel should be the status of gay personnel in the militia. Be sure to support and justify whatever position you take.

CASE STUDY

Sample Student Argumentative Essays

Included below are three student essays on a variety of topics. The first is written to defend or maintain a point of view concerning the role of higher education in helping persons become better voters and citizens. That is its format. Its form relies chiefly on *modus ponens* (or affirming the antecedent). The second uses the format of recommending a particular course of action, namely, teaching sex education in grades seven through twelve. It relies on a slightly more complex form in which three types of premises need to be established: (1) a problem exists for some individual or group; (2) the range of possible solutions to the problem include PS_1, PS_2, . . . PS_n; and (3) the best possible solution is PS_2. The conclusion is then a variation of "That particular individual or group should implement PS_2." The third student essay relies more on the format we call an *evaluational essay,* which combines instrumental and consequential elements with fairness premises (or in this case, unfairness ones).

Essay 1: A College Education Can Help a Person Become a More Responsible Voter and Citizen by Melanie Pappas

Our world seems to become more complex and confusing by the day. It is difficult to keep up with, let alone understand, the barrage of information about politics, economics, legal and environmental issues that we encounter on a daily basis. If we are to be responsible for making decisions about the future of our communities and nation, then we must learn to sort out and understand relevant facts about these issues and make sound decisions about the validity of ideas. A college education can help us to accomplish this.

If a college education gives us knowledge, develops our thought processes and exposes us to differing points of view, then it can help us to become more responsible voters and citizens. Many feel that core liberal arts and business courses required by colleges and universities are of little practical use in the real world. But, one need only flip through a popular news magazine or watch a TV news broadcast to encounter numerous medical, legal, scientific, even mathematical concepts that are beyond the comprehension of the average high school student. Being able to read and understand information presented in the news media is vital to our being able to make informed decisions. College courses such as Psychology, Geography, History, Biology and Economics can provide the basic knowledge needed to comprehend the underlying facts of important issues that we face as citizens and voters.

Not only must we be able to comprehend information, we must also be able to evaluate and make judgments about what we hear and read. These skills can be developed during our college years as we learn to participate, think for ourselves and express ourselves, hopefully gaining confidence in our abilities to judge and evaluate. Finally, learning to understand the viewpoints of others is important in making responsible decisions about issues that affect everyone. The college experience offers to most of us the experience of a larger and more diverse population of ideas and opinions than we may have encountered in our secondary schools, communities or jobs. This can open our minds to different ways of seeing the world, to understanding that our own experiences shape our own realities so that we can hope to understand, or at least acknowledge, the realities or others.

It may be objected that general life experience can provide these abilities. This may often be true. But how long must we muddle along, learning and developing on our own to get to the same point to which a few years of thoughtfully planned, organized study can bring us? Of course formal education can only go so far in making us responsible voters and citizens. But the more we understand current events, the harder it is to just ignore our responsibilities to the world around us.

We can become more responsible in the decisions we make as voters and citizens by being able to read, understand and evaluate information we receive from the world around us, and being willing to accept that there are viable points of view besides our own. By developing our knowledge, judgment skills and understanding of others, a college education can be an effective means for accomplishing these goals.

Essay 2: For Sex Education by Darlene Gibbs
(Reprinted with thanks to Dr. Milton Snoeyenbos.)
The increase in pregnancies and cases of sexually transmitted disease among teenagers are serious problems for the individual, and American society. In this essay I argue that ignorance is partly the cause of these problems; accordingly, we can alleviate them by sex education. Of the various places where sex education could be taught, I argue that schools are the best place, in particular, grades seven through twelve. Sex education should be required during these grades. It should be integrated into the curriculum rather than simply being a required one-semester course.

Teenage pregnancies and cases of sexually transmitted diseases among teens are serious problems for the individuals as well as American society. I have heard that over a million teens become pregnant each year; the majority, unmarried. These pregnancies often result in abortion or an unwanted child, neither result being desirable. The unwanted child is all too often unloved, neglected, or abused. The mother of such children is frequently doomed to a life of welfare dependency; her children frequently repeat the dependent lifestyle. Cases of sexually transmitted diseases also seem to be increasing among teens. Almost any recent high school graduate knows some teen with a sexually transmitted disease; this used to be fairly rare. Five years ago the only teens with AIDS were those who required blood transfusions; today the media routinely report teenage AIDS victims. In addition to the victims' suffering, the social cost of AIDS is significant. Teenage pregnancy and sexually transmitted diseases are serious problems that we should try to resolve.

Although the sexual problems mentioned have no single cause, ignorance is a significant factor. A relatively high percentage of pregnant teens apparently do not fully understand how they became pregnant, and they certainly do not comprehend the full consequences of an unwanted pregnancy. And teens are often woefully underinformed about the causes and consequences of sexually transmitted diseases. I would guess that no more than one teen in five knows what genital herpes is or knows that once you have it you have it for life.

To provide information to young people, we need some form of sex education, a controversial topic, since many parents believe they alone have a right to instruct their children in such areas. To clarify the issue, we should distinguish two types of sex education. In one sense sex education can focus on just the facts of reproduction and disease prevention. In a broader sense, sex education covers moral as well as factual issues. I agree that morality is primarily a family issue upon which the schools should not intrude. On the other hand, students are individuals and have a right to factual information that has a significant impact on their future. It is clear that students minimally need to know the facts of reproduction and sexual disease prevention. So, the issue is where the students can best learn such facts. Of the three realistic options, school, home, and church, I shall argue that the factual aspect of sex education is best learned in schools. Teaching sex education in schools would enable more teens to know these important facts than teaching them in the home or church. If we require sex education in school (a claim for which I shall argue shortly), then almost all teens would be instructed. In contrast, only about 50% of families attend church regularly. Although many parents adequately instruct their children, many do not. Many simply say nothing out of ignorance or embarrassment. Of course, we could mail information to parents, but, apart from the expense, there is no guarantee it would be presented. Furthermore, teens are notoriously reluctant to listen to their parents.

In addition to breadth of coverage, the schools would convey more information more accurately than the home or church. The school system requires teacher certification; in sex education this helps ensure the instructors are competent and that the information will be conveyed. One can assume the principal will see to it that the sex education lesson plan will be followed strictly. The classroom is also conducive to learning. Students will feel free to ask questions they might not mention to their parent or minister. They also get the input of other students, which is valuable in learning. In contrast, the clergy are not trained to teach sexual facts, and the state could not require the clergy to be so trained. The likely result would be a lot of misinformation. Then, too, some clergy would probably distort the facts to fit their own religious assumptions. As for the parents, many do a good job; but, many parents, perhaps most, simply do not know the facts, and most are probably not good instructors.

To ensure coverage, sex education should be required in schools. The fact is that serious consequences often result from sexual ignorance, and the vast majority of youths are truly ignorant of these facts. Every teenager needs this information. Furthermore, teens have a right to this information, which is today vital to their survival and health. The best way to guarantee that they have this information is to require sex education. As an elective, students whose parents wanted to not take the course would probably never receive this important information. And students who didn't want the material could avoid it. But this information is important enough today to require schools to teach it.

Considerable controversy exists as to where in the curriculum sex education should be taught. Instead of arguing over whether it should be taught as a one-semester course at the grade, middle, or high school level, I suggest it is better to integrate the subject into the regular curriculum during grades seven through twelve. The problem with a one-semester course at the grade or middle school levels is that some of the information will not be comprehended, and some will subsequently be forgotten. At the high school level the course will be too late for some teens. Integrating the material would enable facts about puberty to be taught at the middle school level, and more complex facts would be taught later, say in a biology class. Integration over six grades would enable information to be continuously supplied to students, which would be better than a one-semester course at whatever level.

In conclusion, unwanted teenage pregnancies and sexually transmitted diseases are serious problems for teens, and are in part due to ignorance. To solve these problems we need a sex education program based in the schools, rather than just instruction in the home and church. Sex education should be required, not just an elective, and it should be integrated into the grades seven through twelve curriculum, rather than being required as a one-semester course.

Essay 3: The Death Penalty Is Unfair by Jorge Gonzalez
(reprinted with thanks to Professor Milton Snoeyenbos.)

We all know we have to tolerate some injustices in life, and we cannot condemn totally something that is a little bit unfair. However, something that is totally unfair is wrong. Capital punishment is totally unfair; there is nothing fair about it across the board. So, it is wrong.

In some cases we could tolerate some unfairness or harm if good results occurred at the end. But a harmful practice that is unnecessary is unfair. Execution is killing someone, which is certainly harmful, and it is unnecessary to protect the public. We can just lock up murderers and throw away the key. If the worry is escapees, build stronger walls. If the worry is pardons, don't pardon murderers.

Some say that fairness requires a balancing of the scales of justice. Murder tilts the scales, and supposedly only execution will rebalance them. However, fairness does not require a literal eye-for-an-eye. We do not rape the rapist or break the back of someone who caused another's back to break. That would be barbaric. Fairness requires an appropriate equivalent punishment, not exactly the same punishment.

Of course, murder is a particularly abhorrent crime, for the victim's life is gone. But it doesn't follow that society must execute a murderer to express its outrage or revulsion. That begs the whole point, which is: How severe should we punish murder to express our abhorrence of it? We can't just assume execution is the answer.

Another argument made for the death penalty is that justice requires that we place a high value on a human life and execution shows that society does value life by going to great lengths to protect it. But this is inconsistent; we don't show we value life by killing someone. So imprisonment shows we value life more than execution does. Also, when the state executes someone, everyone in that state has a hand in it. The executioner only incidentally pulls the switch. The state, and that means everyone, authorizes the killing. So we all devalue life. We all take part in the injustice.

The actual court practice involving a death penalty case cannot avoid being unfair. A first-degree murder determination rests on whether the act involved premeditation, which means an intent formed before the act was actually committed. But nobody sees someone else's intent. So the determination rests on something nobody can observe, which will lead to many courtroom errors. If a person is indeed guilty of murder, a finding of premeditation points him to the chair; lack of premeditation means jail. Since the line is based on something you cannot see, there will be many unfair errors here.

Some innocents will be executed, which will be totally unfair. This sort of situation can never be "balanced," since the life cannot be returned. To think you could pay the victim's family is a cruel joke, since the victim is the one owed compensation and he can never be compensated in any way.

The death penalty is undeniably unfair to blacks in America. We all know more blacks are executed than whites even though blacks constitute only one-tenth of the population. And we all know that when a black kills a white he has a much higher probability of getting the death penalty than when a white kills a white. Things may be improving, but the justice system is still far from fair in capital cases.

The death penalty is also unfair to society's poor. Rich people are not executed here. You cannot name one. You know from the news that those on death row are mainly poor. These are the very people who have already been treated unfairly by society. A large percentage of those executed are mentally retarded. Many are illiterate. Many have alcohol or drug problems. Their poverty means they cannot get top-notch legal representation. These people, those of us who needed help the most but were unfairly denied it, are our death penalty candidates. Capital punishment means those without the capital get the punishment.

APPENDIX OF VALID ARGUMENT FORMS

VALID SYLLOGISMS

e.g. All A is B
No B is C
No A is C

(1) Have exactly 3 class terms each used twice, with the same meaning both times.

(2) Have NO negative (E or O) Statements, or one negative premise and one negative conclusion.

(3) Have a middle term that is distributed at least once.

(4) Have any terms which are distributed in the conclusion also distributed in the premises.

(5) In case both premises are universal (A or E Form) and the conclusion is a particular (I or O Form), Must have at least one member known to exist in each of the 3 classes.

Simple Dilemma
Either R or S
If R, then W
If S, then W
W

CONDITIONAL ARGUMENT FORMS

Modus Ponens
If A, then B
A
B

Modus Tollens
If A, then B
Not B
Not A

Chain Argument
If A, then B
If B, then C
If A, then C

CONJUNCTIVE ARGUMENT FORMS

Not both A and B
A
Not B

DISJUNCTIVE ARGUMENT FORMS

Either A or B
Not A
B

Complex Dilemma
Either R or S
If R, then W
If S, then U
Either W or U

APPENDIX OF FALLACIES AND INVALID ARGUMENT FORMS

BY CONTENT

Fallacies of Irrelevant Premises
(Psychological)
Personal Attack
   Circumstantial
   Abusive
   Genetic Fallacy
   Blame/Praise by Association
   Poisoning the Well
   You Too Fallacy
Red Herring
Appeal to Fear
Appeal to Pity
Misuse of Humor
Appeal to Tradition (or Novelty)
Popular Appeals
Bandwagon Fallacy
Emotional Appeals
Misuse of Authority

(Grammatical)
Equivocation
Amphiboly
Composition
Division

Fallacies of Inadequate Premises

Hasty generalization
Accident
Argument from Ignorance
Begging the Question
   Assuming the Conclusion
   Circular Reasoning
   Definitional Hedge
   Weasel Words
Assuming the Cause
Assuming Existence
Fakey Precision
Faulty Analogy

Fallacies of Unfair Premises

Misrepresentative Generalization
Leading Question
Limited Options Fallacy
   Either-Or Fallacy
   False Dilemma
Straw Person Fallacy
Fallacious Extension
Slippery Slope
Misuse of Hypothesis
     (Contrary to Fact)
Fallacy of Stress

BY FORM

Faulty Linkage (Formal Fallacies)
Four Terms Fallacy
Faulty Exclusions Fallacy
Fallacy of the Undistributed
   Middle Term
Fallacy of Illicit Distribution
Existential Fallacy
Fallacy of Affirming the
   Consequent
Fallacy of Denying the Antecedent
Fallacy of Denying the Conjunct
Fallacy of Affirming the Disjunct
Broken Chain Fallacy

SOLUTIONS TO SELECTED EXERCISES

CHAPTER 1
ANSWERS TO EXERCISES ON PAGES 9–11

1. B
2. A
3. Answers A, B and D are all correct.
4. D
5. B is the preferable answer, although some might claim the other options are equally viable answers.
6. Premises or the premise set.
   Conclusion.
7. Hidden, unstated, tacit or implicit
8. Logical presupposition
9. Deductive
10. Inductive

1. That the defendant was innocent or guilty of the crime.
3. That the viewer should buy the toothpaste.
5. One should not smoke.
7. The child should abide by the moral of the story.
9. There is no "conclusion" to a concert.
11. Evidence in support of the defendant, e.g., witnesses, alibis, etc.
13. The needs of that particular charity and the good work they do.
15. That cheating is the only way to pass/that cheating is immoral.
17. Scientific data showing the lack of supporting conditions for intelligent life.

CHAPTER 2

ANSWERS TO EXERCISES ON PAGES 21–24

A LEVEL

1. A disagreement is a difference of opinion, attitude, or belief, while an argument is a line of reasoning composed of premises and a conclusion.
2. An interpretive disagreement is a dispute centering around the meaning of some thing or event, while a verbal disagreement involves the use of terms in two different ways, such that the parties to the dispute end up talking past one another.
3. Evaluative (probably moral, social, or political)
4. False
5. False
6. False
7. Evaluative (note the operative word, "better")
8. Factual
9. Interpretive
10. Interpretive
11. Evaluative
12. Evaluative—Moral
13. Evaluative—Practical
14. Evaluative
15. Evaluative—Moral
16. Evaluative
17. Evaluative—Practical, or Factual
18. Evaluative—Aesthetic
19. Factual
20. Interpretive

B LEVEL

1. Factual disagreement over who wrote the novel *The Outsider.*
3. Evaluative/Practical disagreement over the best way from Lake Nebagamon to Minneapolis. Also interpretive to the extent that Judy has a different meaning of "better."
5. Verbal disagreement: George is talking about consequences, while Jimmy is speaking of motives. There is an evaluative disagreement about the policy itself.
7. Mainly factual: Can the river be canoed by anyone or not? Evaluative disagreement over the experience needed to negotiate the Upper Gauley, possibly; or Interpretive if it concerns just what constitutes an "experienced open boat canoeist."
9. Verbal disagreement: Ellen is talking about eradicating the disease while Barbara is worried about the cost. It will probably become Evaluative very shortly.

ANSWERS TO EXERCISES ON PAGES 30-32

A   LEVEL

1. An argument is composed of statements, some of which are premises, while one is the conclusion.
2. A statement is a declarative utterance which can be seen as being either true or false. All statements are sentences. Some sentences are statements, but some are not. Sentences can also express commands, exclamations, questions, etc.
3. Arguments are lines of reasoning in which premises are used to support a conclusion which is not as well accepted as the premises. When one offers an explanation, the conclusion is already taken as accepted.
4. Therefore, thus, so
5. Because, since
6. True
7. False
8. False (While it is true all statements are sentences, not all sentences are statements.)
9. True (This is one of its functions.)
10. True

B   LEVEL

1. Probably an explanation.
   Conclusion: Dick and Debbie prefer meals low in saturated fats.
   Premise: Dick and Debbie are trying to control their cholesterol intake.
3. Conclusion: We should just get a rental movie.
   Premises: We spent all our money/We have only six dollars.
5. Explanation.
   Conclusion: Clinton won the election.
   Premise: He won back Democratic votes who had gone for Bush and Reagan.
7. This can be read as a rhetorical question which offers the argument:
   Premise: The Earth's temperature has risen.
   Conclusion: There is global warming.
9. Premise: We are sailing toward the pole star/The wind is off our starboard beam/The compass is pointing to 360 degrees.
   Conclusion: We are sailing a northern course.
11. Conclusion: Clinton needs a healthy third force in his campaign.
    Premises: Clinton needs Perot to keep the Southern States in play.
13. Conclusion: Arguments about reducing U.S. Forces in Europe are flawed.
    Premise: U.S. ignores events in Europe at its own peril.
15. Conclusion: Marcus has pledged $1 million to the Holocaust Museum.
    Premises: Six million people were exterminated/There are still people in the world who are savages.
    This one is also an explanation.

A   LEVEL

1. In a deductive argument the truth of the premises guarantees the truth of the conclusion, in an inductive argument there is no such guarantee.
2. Because in an inductive argument, the premises only point to a greater or lesser probability that the conclusion is true. The conclusion of an inductive argument is not contained in the premises.
3. There is no new information in the conclusion which is not already in the premises.
4. False
5. True
6. False

B   LEVEL

1. P-1: Every day that the traffic is reported to be congested I always take the subway to town.
   P-2: The traffic report is for another day of gridlock.
   _____
   C: I will take the subway to town today.
          Premise Indicator: "Since"

If you take P-1 as a statement about the past (in other words, "every day up until today") then the argument is Inductive since the conclusion goes beyond the premises to talk about today. However, P-1 is more likely a statement about "every day", past, present, and future, and hence, the argument is a Deductive piece of reasoning that looks something like

      P-1: If A (traffic is congested), then B (I take the subway)
      P-2: A (traffic is congested)
      _____
      C: B (I take the subway)

3. P-1: Anniece has taken her dry-cleaning to three of the twelve Acme Dry-Cleaning stores and has been dissatisfied with their work each time.
   _____
   C: Acme Dry-Cleaners must not do very high-quality work.
          Conclusion Indicator: "She has concluded that"

This one is an Inductive argument. She may have been unfortunate in the few times she took her clothing to those cleaners. It is also possible that the other nine out of twelve stores do outstanding quality work and never leave customers unsatisfied while the three she did visit normally do excellent work too.

5. P-1: I was on flight 108 from Salem to San Diego at the time.
   P-2: Nobody can be two places at once.
   _____
   C: I could not have been driving the car at that time.
          Indicator Word: "Because" indicates a premise.
                  "And" indicates another premise in this case.
          Extraneous Expression: "Your Honor"

This argument is intended to be Deductive. If it is true that I have an iron-clad alibi where I was at the time and if it is equally true that no no can be two places at the same time, then it must be true that I could not have been at a second place simultaneously.

7. P-1: Senator Snort said he would not enter the upcoming gubernatorial race unless the Democrats made him angry.

   P-2: So far no one has aroused his ire.

   _____

   C: Senator Snort doesn't plan on entering the race.

   Indicator Words: The first "So" is not used to indicate a conclusion, but a point in time (hence it is temporal, not logical).

   The second "So" indicates a conclusion.

There are at least two ways of looking at this example. First, the form of the argument is basically one in which someone is claiming:

   If X does not happen, then Y will not happen.

   (And) X is not happening.

   _____

   (So)   Y will not happen.

This is a Deductive Argument.

The second way of looking at the example is to notice that there is a difference between SAYING that you will not enter the race and NOT PLANNING to enter the race. Because of this, perhaps subtle, distinction, the conclusion may go beyond what is claimed in the premises and, hence, make this more of an Inductive or Non-Deductive Argument. We would favor looking at the example in the former way but would not quibble with the second reading.

9. P-1: They don't card anyone.

   P-2: They've got the best juke-box around.

   P-3: They've got the cheapest beer prices.

   _____

   C: Mack's is the best bar around.

This rather terse Argument is definitely Inductive. The "fact" that a bar does not "card" anyone or has the best juke-box around or the cheapest beer prices does not necessarily mean that it is the best bar around, unless one is underage or likes being with underaged drinkers or likes the particular music in the juke-box or prefers drinking cheaper beers or a host of other concerns.

CHAPTER 3
ANSWERS TO EXERCISES ON PAGES 47 THROUGH 50

1. An assumption is a statement assumed to be true.

2. An explicit assumption is stated, while an implicit assumption is not directly stated.

3. A hidden assumption is the same thing as an implicit assumption. An unstated conclusion is one that is not explicitly stated, but which, it is assumed, the hearer will understand; either way, it differs from a hidden assumption which is a missing premise.

4. An implication is either an unstated conclusion, or a conclusion which may be reached by analyzing the premises.

5. The idea that we should remain as unbiased as possible in making explicit the implicit assumptions and unstated conclusions of arguments.

6. False

7. True

8. True

9. False

10. True

B LEVEL

1. Conclusion: You must be a registered voter.
   Premise: You were asked to serve on the jury.
   Implicit Assumption: Only registered voters are asked to serve on a jury.

3. Conclusion: You wrecked the car.
   Premise: When you wreck the car, you get a stupid look on your face.
   Implicit Assumption: You have a stupid look on your face, and the only time you get that stupid look is when you wreck the car.

5. Conclusion: Your parents won't let you drive the car.
   Premise: I've seen you walking to school for the past week.
   Implicit Assumption: If you're walking to school, it must be because your parents won't let you drive the car.

7. Unstated Conclusion: You'll have to report your interest income on your tax return.
   Premises: Anyone who makes more than $400 in interest income has to report it on their tax return/You made more than three times that much last year.

9. Conclusion: John must have been behind the wheel.
   Premise: John was the only one in the car.
   Implicit Assumptions: Whenever you are the only person in a car, you must be behind the wheel.

C LEVEL

1. Answer (B). (C) is not a bad answer, but in the passage by the use of the term "best" the author assumes that there are at least three forms of adjustment and we have to link three or more with "many".

3. The correct answer here is (B). We are looking for what conclusion has to follow from the fact that 45% of all Americans are displeased with the shape of their nose. It does not have to mean that (I) many Americans wish they could have their noses fixed. They may be more afraid of the surgery or unable to afford the cost or a host of other concerns. It does mean that (II) many (at least 45%) of the Americans are dissatisfied with their facial characteristics because we are going to assume that in virtually all of these cases, the noses are part of the facial characteristics. Note that it does not necessarily mean that (III) Most (i.e., over 50%) of American adults are displeased with one of their physical attributes. To be sure, you would think that if 45% didn't like their noses that surely another 6% would be dissatisfied about something else, BUT NOT NECESSARILY from the data

given. Both (I) and (III) go beyond what is contained in the originally given statement. Only (II) does not.

5. Again we are looking for the logical implications which follow from a given statement or set of statements. In this case, if there are no fewer than three but no more than five people in this class who understand the nature of this problem, then there MUST BE either three or four or five people who understand it. (We are assuming that a half a person does not count; in other words that the whole person either understands it or does not.) Statement I—that four people in the class understand the problem—may be true, but it doesn't HAVE TO BE, since there could be three or five people in the class who understand it. So, even if the answer had been phrased "At least four people in class. . ." it would not necessarily have been true. Statement II is that there are more than two people in this class who understand the problem and since three, four, and five are all "more than two," this answer MUST BE true. Statement III is that there are more than three people in the class who understand the problem. Well, if there are four or five people who do then this answer is correct. But, if there are only three people who understand it, then the answer is incorrect for three is not "more than three." So, the correct answer is (B) Statement II only.

7. Note that in this example, the premises concern the preferences of English tea drinkers and the price of Earl Blue Tea relative to Lippy's Tea. The conclusion is that Americans should purchase Earl Blue too and that they will save (money?). As such, one obvious missing link between premises and conclusion is that American preferences are (or should be) the same as those of their English counterparts. Answer (B) then is the best answer. Answer (A), that a cheaper brand of tea must be better is not warranted by this argument. That is too strong. However, if the assumption were that a cheaper brand of tea is not significantly worse than a more expensive brand, it might have been a better answer. Answer (C), that Lippy's is a poor quality tea is clearly unwarranted also. Indeed, it may even be a superb brand of tea and that would not damage this argument a bit. Answer (D), that teas are all alike in quality, so people should buy the cheapest brand of tea, is an interesting argument, but it is not relevant to THIS particular line of reasoning. Neither premises nor conclusion address the quality of either brand of tea. Answer (E) is that Earl Blue is the best and cheapest brand of tea available. This is not even suggested in the premises or the conclusion. In fact, the only part of this statement related to the argument is that Earl Blue is cheaper than Lippy's and that is actually stated, not implied or assumed. So, (B) is the only correct answer here.

ANSWERS TO EXERCISES ON PAGES 55 AND 56

A   LEVEL

1. A <u>convergent argument</u> is one in which two or more premises each independently support the same conclusion.
2. A <u>divergent argument</u> is a line of reasoning in which one premise or piece of evidence supports two or more independent conclusions.
3. A <u>compound argument</u> is one in which two or more premises rely upon each other to support a conclusion when none of the premises would adequately do so by themselves. A <u>divergent argument</u> takes off to support two or more independent conclusions from the same premise or premise set.

4. A simple <u>convergent argument</u> might be expressed in the following words and diagrammed as below:

> P-1: You are yawning.
>
> P-2: You cannot keep your eyes open.
> _____
> C: You must be sleepy

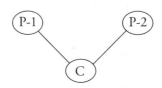

5. A simple <u>divergent argument</u> might be expressed in words as follows and diagrammed as shown below:

> P-1: I overslept.
> _____
> C-1: I am going to be late.
>
> C-2: I will not have time to clean up.

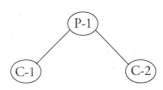

6. FALSE. Agreement or disagreement of the disputants has nothing to do with the form of the argument.

7. FALSE. Many arguments are linear or compound.

8. TRUE. In that way, each conclusion becomes a successive premise for the next conclusion (which then becomes a premise, until the last one.)

9. PROBABLY FALSE. Probably just as many arguments are convergent or compound as are linear. Moreover, we often reason by giving more than one piece of evidence for a conclusion.

10. TRUE. And we now have a key of representing this by making that line of implication darker than the other lines.

B   LEVEL

1. Statements: Dia-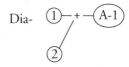
gram:

    1 = Ben is a Member of Congress.

    2 = Ben can send all of his official mail for free.

   A-1 = Members of Congress can send official mail for free.

3. Statements: Diagram:

    1 = Betty didn't invite Veronica to her party.

    2 = Betty and Veronica had just had a fight.

    3 = Betty and Veronica's husbands often get into
heated arguments when they are together.

        A-1 = Betty doesn't invite people she has been
fighting with to her party.

        A-2 = Betty doesn't invite people to her party when there's a good chance that they will fight.

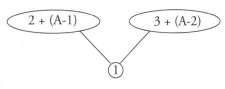

5. Statements:

    1 = I was late for the examination.

    2 = Professor Reed gave me an 'F'.

    3 = My grade point average is going to go way
down.

    4 = If my GPA goes way down, I'll lose my scholar-
ship and my parents will take away my car.

Diagram:

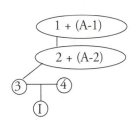

In this case Statements (1), (2), and (3) form a linear argument with each link being inductive. The link from (1) to (2) relies on the assumption (A-1) Being late for an examination is sufficient for Professor Reed to give someone an 'F'. (In other words, it was the lateness and not the performance on the exam that merited the grade.) The link from (2) to (3) relies on the assumption (A-2) Getting an 'F' grade will make my GPA go way down. The conclusion of this linear argument, Statement (3), when combined with Statement (4) deductively leads to the final conclusion which is implied but not actually stated, (I) = I will lose my scholarship and my parents will take away my car. Granted there is probably a line of reasoning in that statement itself—it makes a lot more sense to say that Because I will lose my scholarship, therefore my parent will take away my car than to say, Because my parents will take away my car, therefore I will lose my scholarship. But, because it is phrased the way it is, we will take it at face value for the moment. Notice also that Statement (4), for example, is what we call a Complex Statement. It actually is composed of three statements: (i) My GPA is going to go way down, (ii) I'll lose my scholarship, and (iii) my parents will take away my car. Within this complex statement are both a hypothetical or conditional statement {If (i), then [(ii) and (iii)]} and a conjunction {which is the [(ii) and (iii)] part}. We will see how to deal more effectively with Complex Statements as we refine the Technique further.

7. Statements:

    1 = The U.S. ought to try to make peace with Iraq.   Diagram:

    2 = Iraq is one of the most powerful nations in the region.

    3 = The U.S. (i.e., "we") should try to be on peaceful terms
with all influential nations.

    4 = The U.S. (i.e., "we") have lost enough lives already
trying to solve our differences through the use of force.

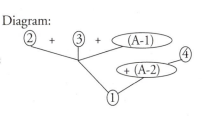

There appear to be two main parts to this line of reasoning. The first contains two premises, Statements (2) and (3) which together form a compound argument that is almost deductive. We need add only one small link between the two premises themselves, (A-1), "Any nation which is one of the most powerful in its region is an influential nation." If (2), (3), and (A-1) were all true, then the conclusion, (1), would have to be true too. The second part of the reasoning is inductive and is missing the unstated premise (A-2), "Whenever a country loses enough lives trying to solve its differences by force, then it ought to seek peace." It is a more difficult question to determine whether the first part of the reasoning is alleged to be of more importance than the second. We have represented both as being of equal importance, although a good case could be made for making the line between (2), (3), (A-1), and (1) darker than that between (4), (A-2), and (1).

9. Statements: Diagram:

① = If Senator Grams runs as the Republican nominee for President in '96, that will mean the conservative wing of the party has taken control.

② = If the conservative wing of the party takes control, then abortion will be a big issue.

③ = If the conservative wing of the party takes control, then gun-control will be a big issue.

④ = If abortion becomes the big issue, the Republicans will lose.

⑤ = If gun-control becomes the big issue, then the Republicans have a chance.

⑥ = If either (4) or (5), then it doesn't look very good for the Republicans in '96.

$$① + ② + ③ + ④ + ⑤$$
$$⑥$$

This example actually shows why we need a more sophisticated method for displaying the structure of complex arguments and complex statements as well. Given the method we have so far, Argument (9) is a compound argument with Statements (1) through (5) together providing deductive support for the conclusion which is Statement (6). The problem is that we do not yet have a way to show that this is an Invalid or bad line of reasoning. There really are no links left out. The reasoning simply looks like a kind of chain of hypothetical or conditional statements:

(1) If A, then B
(2) If B, then C
(3) If B, then D
(4) If C, then E
(5) If D, then F
(Assumed P) If (E or F), then not F
_____
So (6) not F

CHAPTER 4
ANSWERS TO EXERCISES ON PAGES 66 AND 67

A   LEVEL

1. Ambiguity is the confusion which results from the multiple meanings of a word or phrase.
2. Equivocation refers to the use of a crucial word or phrase in two or more distinctly different senses in one and the same context.
3. Words like this, that, here, there, whose and which.

4. Too much, too little, rarer, more well-done.
5. Lots, a whole bunch, a "bazillion"
6. True
7. False
8. True
9. True
10. False

B LEVEL

1. 'yes'
3. No quotes
5. . . . you don't know what 'you' means
7. No quotes or 'his name'
9. (a) 'The Greatest Show on Earth is playing at the big top'
   (b) "The sign," said The Greatest Show on Earth, "is playing at the big top."
11. Last Summer (may be referentially vague); a bunch of (is quantitatively vague).
13. men (vagueness by stress)
15. four letter word (could be referentially ambiguous—are we referring to the word 'love' or to something else.)
17. Stress on word 'tonight' (vagueness by stress)
19. hate (use—mention ambiguity)

ANSWERS TO EXERCISES ON PAGES 73 AND 74

A LEVEL

1. A reportive definition is an explanation of how a word or phrase is used in ordinary language or technical jargon.
2. A stipulative definition is an explanation of how a particular word or phrase will be used when that usage differs from the normal usage of that word.
3. Denotation is the actual set of objects, events or conditions to which a term refers. Connotation is the set of conditions for a term's use, including all the emotional flavoring which tinge its meaning.
4. By ostension, citing examples, complete inventory, synonym, and by connotation.
5. This refers to the scope of the meaning being ascribed to a word or phrase, it should not cover more or less than the term's denotation.
6. False
7. False
8. True
9. True
10. False

B   LEVEL

1. A reportive definition which is inadequate (plucked chickens also fit the definition)
3. A circular definition
5. Complete inventory
7. Ostensive Definition
9. A persuasive definition design to poison attitudes against "liberals."
11. Too narrow. Instructors teach adults as well as children. Too broad. People other than instructors (like parents) guide or teach children.
13. Totally negative description.
14. Irrelevant feature (the Broncos)
    Metaphorical (mile high city)
15. Metaphorical or figurative language
17. Both circular (repeating term being defined) and totally negative description (only telling what it is not).
19. Stipulative Definition
21. Too broad (money or currency are negotiable instruments too.) Maybe obscure (the definition is harder to understand than the word being defined.)
23. Stipulative Definition which cites an example.
25. Persuasive Definition calculated to influence attitudes against the SAT test. (It is probably true.)

CHAPTER 5
ANSWERS TO EXERCISES ON PAGES 87 THROUGH 89

A   LEVEL

1. Red Herring
2. The Bandwagon is a specific sort of Popular Appeal
3. Psychologically irrelevant premises occur when an appeal is made to the emotions. Grammatically irrelevant premises involve linguistic ambiguity.
4. False
5. False
6. True
7. False
8. False
9. True
10. False

B   LEVEL

1. Popular appeal
3. Personal Attack

5. Bandwagon
7. Emotional appeal ("degrading", "disgusting", "eyesores")
9. Bandwagon
11. Composition
13. Appeal to Pity
15. Appeal to Novelty
17. Amphiboly ("Christian Children's Hospital")
19. Poisoning the well ("even marginally informal voters know that.")
21. Misuse of Authority
23. Poisoning the well and emotional appeals.
25. Bandwagon
27. Red Herring (could be You Too also.)

ANSWERS TO EXERCISES ON PAGES 93 THROUGH 95

A LEVEL

1. Hasty generalization jumps to conclusions about the whole from insufficient evidence from the parts. In the fallacy of composition, one attributes qualities of the parts taken individually, to the whole.
2. Begging the question involves circular reasoning: one assumes the conclusion is true in order to prove it is true.
3. This assumes that because something is true as a rule, it is also true in every particular instance.
4. False
5. False
6. False
7. False
8. False
9. False
10. False

B LEVEL

1. Begging the question
3. Assuming the cause
5. Faulty analogy; could also be Accident
7. Assuming existence
9. Assuming the cause
11. Hasty generalization
13. Argument from ignorance
15. Assuming the cause

17. Accident
19. Argument from ignorance
21. Begging the question
23. Faulty Analogy

ANSWERS TO EXERCISES ON PAGES 99 THROUGH 102

A LEVEL

1. False
2. True
3. True
4. False
5. False
6. False
7. True
8. False
9. True
10. True

B LEVEL

1. Misuse of hypothesis contrary to fact
3. Slippery slope or Fallacious Extension
5. Leading question
7. Fallacy of Stress or Accent
9. Limited options
11. Leading question
13. Slippery slope (Fallacious Extension)
15. Fallacy of stress
17. Misrepresentative generalization (law students are not lawyers)
19. Limited options
21. Slippery slope (Fallacious Extension)
23. Fakey precision or Fallacy of stress
25. Limited Options (False Dilemma)
27. Personal attack (genetic fallacy)
29. Misuse of Authority, Begging the question, poisoning the well, and Bandwagon
31. Appeal to pity, plus Appeal to fear
33. Appeal to tradition, plus poisoning the well
35. Assuming the cause
37. You Too fallacy, Red Herring, and maybe Misuse of Humor

CHAPTER 6
ANSWERS TO EXERCISES ON PAGES 118 THROUGH 119

A   LEVEL

1. A Universal term is a class or set which has been quantified, usually by the words 'all' or 'no', to indicate that each and every member of that set has or lacks a particular trait.
2. A Particular term is a set or class in which only some of the members of that class are referred to.
3. A and I statements
4. E and O statements
5. "No"
6. "All" (or "Each" or "Every")
7. O-statements
8. At least one
9. The Predicate Term of the conclusion.
10. The term which occurs in each of the premises, but not in the conclusion.

B   LEVEL

1. A-Statement

Quantifier	Subject	Relationship	Predicate
All	{low-flying, high-speed aircraft}	Are	{planes which will have to use the city's alternative airport}

3. E-Statement

Quantifier	Subject	Relationship	Predicate
No	{person who has filed a tax extension}	Is	{person who is eligible for a tax return at this time}

5. I-Statement

Quantifier	Subject	Relationship	Predicate
Some	{recipe cards that she uses}	Are	{recipes that came from her grandmother's side of the family}

7. A-Statement

Quantifier	Subject	Relationship	Predicate
All	{Street lights in town}	Are	{things lit tonight}

It could also be as an I-Statement:

Quantifier	Subject	Relationship	Predicate
Some	{things lit tonight}	Are	{street lights in town]

9. I-Statement

Quantifier	Subject	Relationship	Predicate
Some	{students who were thought	Are	{people who showed

11. A-Statement

	to be too uninterested}		up for the rally}
Quantifier	Subject	Relationship	Predicate
All	{ones who ever had a heart that was not made of cast-iron}	Are	{ones who would be sorry for behaving that way}

13. Again, can be done several ways and will depend upon context:
A-Statement

Quantifier	Subject	Relationship	Predicate
All (of)	{these shoes}	Are	{things that are way too tight}

or I-Statement

Quantifier	Subject	Relationship	Predicate
Some	{shoes out of this particular bunch}	Are	{things that are way too tight}

15. Again, can be done in at least two ways and will depend upon context:
A-Statement

Quantifier	Subject	Relationship	Predicate
All	{ACME industries}	Is	{a company that does not make the strongest widgets in the business}

or E-Statement

Quantifier	Subject	Relationship	Predicate
No	{ACME industries}	Is	{a company that does make the strongest widgets in the business)

17. I-Statement

Quantifier	Subject	Relationship	Predicate
Some	{Sausage and Peppers}	Is	{a dish that is ready right now}

19. I-Statement

Quantifier	Subject	Relationship	Predicate
Some	{people I know}	Are	{people who attended the opening-day ceremonies at the stadium}

21. O-Statement

Quantifier	Subject	Relationship	Predicate
Some	{ones or people}	Are Not	{people who walk ten miles to school uphill in the snow anymore}

ANSWERS TO EXERCISES ON PAGES 131 AND 132:

A   LEVEL

1. A <u>categorical syllogism</u> is a two premise, one conclusion argument in which each of the statements is or has been recast in standard categorical form. A <u>valid categorical syllogism</u> is one in which the premises, if true, guarantee the truth of the conclusion.

2. (A) The Rule Method and (B) one of the Diagram Methods

3. No; because a universal statement does not necessarily guarantee that its classes have any members in them, whereas particular statements (the I- and O-Forms) do guarantee that there is at least one member of each class.

4. An <u>empty class</u> simply means a category that does not have any members in it. For example, the class of "people who can hold their breath for 15 minutes at a time" is probably an empty class.

5. When a term is <u>distributed</u> that means that for the statement form in question, reference is meant to apply to each and every member of that class. When a term is <u>undistributed</u> reference is meant to apply only to some of the members of that class, but not necessarily to all of them.

6. Negative statement forms (E- and O-Statements) have distributed predicates. Universal statement forms (A- and X-Statements) have distributed subjects.

7. The Faulty Exclusions Fallacy occurs in categorical syllogisms when there is only one negative statement or three negative statements or when both of the premises are negative (E- or O-Statements).

8. The Four Terms Fallacy is the mistake in syllogisms when more than three classes or categories occur.

9. The Fallacy of Illicit Distribution is the violation of Rule 3(B) in which a term is distributed in the conclusion but not in the premises. In effect the reasoning makes a leap from some of the members of that class in the premises to all of the members in the conclusion.

10. The Fallacy of the Undistributed Middle Term is a violation of Rule 3(A) in which the middle term, the one occurring in both of the premises and not in the conclusion, is not distributed in either premise.

11. The <u>Existential Fallacy</u> is a violation of the Corollary to Rule One, requiring that in syllogisms having two Universal (A- or E-Form) Statements in the premises and a Particular (I- or O-Form) Statement in the conclusion, one must examine each of the three classes to make sure that there is in fact in existence at least one member of the class. If any one of the classes is found to be empty or questionable, the Existential Fallacy is committed. If there are members of each class, the Rule is not violated.

12. <u>Proper names and singular terms</u> in Categorical Syllogisms are to be treated as class terms which have one and only one member (unless, of course, they are a conjunction of proper names). Usually, these terms are quantified by a Universal "All" or "No", because we are referring to the entirety of that individual.

B   LEVEL

1.
		D		U
P-1	A	All Economic Theories	are	Theories About Humans in Society

			U		U
P-2	I	Some Philosophical Theories		are	Theories About Humans in Society

			U		U
C	I	Some Philosophical Theories		are	Economic Theories

> **Mistake Box**
> Rule 1: ok
> Rule 2: ok
> Rule 3(A): X
> Rule 3(B): ok
> Cor: ok

Invalid Argument:
Undistributed Middle Term
(Theories About Human Beings in Society)

3.

			D		D
P-1:	E	No	Traffic Cops	are	One-Armed People

			U		D
P-2:	O	Some	V. P. Candidates	are not	One-Armed People

			U		D
C:	O	Some	V. P. Candidates	are not	Traffic Cops

> **Mistake Box**
> Rule 1: ok
> Rule 2: X
> Rule 3(A): ok
> Rule 3(B): ok
> Cor: ok

Invalid Argument
Faulty Exclusions:
Three E/O Statements
Violates Rule Two

5.

			D		U
P-1:	A	All	Multigrain Cereals	are	Important Fiber Sources

			U		D
P-2:	O	Some Kinds of Fruit		are not	Important Fiber Sources

			D		U
C:	A	All Multigrain Cereals		are	Kinds of Fruit

> **Mistake Box**
> Rule 1: ok (MGC's, IFS's, and Kinds of Fruit)
> Rule 2: X (only one E or O Statement)
> Rule 3A: ok (IFS is dist at least once)
> Rule 3B: ok (MGC is dist in Conc & in P-1)
> Cor: ok

Invalid Argument:
Faulty Exclusions,
(Only one E or O Statement in the argument)

7.

			U		U
P-1:	I	Some	ADs	are	LDs
			U		D
P-2:	O	Some	LDs	are not	PWHNHAA
			U		D
C:	O	Some	ADs	are not	PWHNHAA

Invalid Argument:
Undistributed Middle Term (Licensed Drivers is not distributed in either premise)

Mistake Box
Rule 1: ok (ADs, LDs, & PWHNHAA)
Rule 2: ok (one O in P-2; O in C)
Rule 3A: X (LDs is not dist)
Rule 3B: ok (PWHNHAA is dist in C and in P-2)
Cor: ok

9.

			D		D
P-1:	E	No	TTTG	are	TGFY
			D		D
P2:	E	No	TGFY	are	TTYL
			D		D
C:	E	No	TTTG	are	TTYL

Key: TTTG = Things That Taste Good
TGFY = Things (That Are) Good For You
TTYL = Things That You Like

Invalid Argument:
Faulty Exclusions—
Three E or O Statements

Mistake Box
Rule 1: ok (TTTG, TGFY, and TTYL)
Rule 2: XX (Three E or O Statements!)
Rule 3A: ok (Middle Term, TGFY, is dist in both premises.)
Rule 3B: ok (Both Terms are dist in C & P)
Cor: ok

11. First, put in standard form. Premise 1, "Not every Philosophy Course is a Skills Course," may be read as the negation ("NOT") of the A-Statement, All PC's are SC's. The direct opposite of an A-Statement is, not an E-Statement, but an O-Statement. So, P-1 should be expressed, "Some PC's are not SC's." Premise 2, "It is a Philosophy Course," is a categorical statement and as such is in A-Form: "All Logic Courses are Philosophy Courses." Finally, the Conclusion, "Logic is not a Skills Course," is actually an exclusion, saying that Logic is excluded from the class of Skills Courses. That is an E-Statement: "No Logic Course is a Skills Course."

The key for the classes then is   PC = Philosophy Course,
SC = Skills Course
LC = Logic course

			U		D
P-1:	O	Some	PC	is not	SC

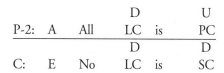
			D		U
P-2:	A	All	LC	is	PC

			D		D
C:	E	No	LC	is	SC

Invalid Argument:
Undistributed Middle Term—
The Class of "Philosophy Courses" is not distributed in either one of the premises.

> **Mistake Box**
> Rule 1: ok (L, S, and PD)
> Rule 2: ok (one O in P-1, E in Con)
> Rule 3A: X (M. T., PC, undist. twice!)
> Rule 3B: ok (Both terms are dist in C and also in the Prems.)
> Cor: ok

13. This one may be the subject of serious dispute. There are two distinct ways of doing it. First:

			D		D
P-1:	E	No	TS	is	PWWMFOTB

			D		U
P-2:	A	All	M	is	S

			D		D
C:	E	No	M	is	PWWMFOTB

Key: TS = True Scotsman
PWWMFOTB = People Who Would Make Fun Of The Bagpipes
M = Michael
S = Scotsman

Invalid Argument:
Four Terms Fallacy,
True Scotsmen, People Who Would Make Fun Of The Bagpipes, and Scotsmen

> **Mistake Box**
> Rule 1: X (Four Terms: TS, PWWMFOTB, M, and S, as per above key)
> Rule 2: ok (E in Prems & E in Conc)
> Rule 3A: ok (M. T. [TS] if any is dist)
> Rule 3B: ok (Both dist. in Conc & in P)
> Cor: ok

The problem here is that some people may want to say that the categories of Scotsmen and True Scotsmen are one and the same, making this a case of three classes or terms and, hence, a perfectly valid line of reasoning. For either side of this dispute the arguer should try to show (A) how the two classes of Scotsmen and True Scotsmen are in fact identical, that you could not find a member of one class who was not also a member of the other, and conversely, or (B) how the two classes of Scotsmen and True Scotsmen are actually different because you can find examples of people who are by birth of Scottish descent (and hence, Scotsmen), but who do not think or act like Scotsmen (and hence are not "True Scotsmen"—whatever that is.

15.

			D		U
P-1:	A	All	PWPTIBO	are	E

			D		U
P-2:	A	All	PWPTIOOBTO	are	A

			U		U
C:	I	Some	E	are	A

Key: PWPTIBO = People Who Put Their Interests Before Others
PWPTIOOBTO = People Who Put The Interests Of Others Before Their Own
E = Egoists   A = Altruists

Invalid Argument:
Four Terms Fallacy, They are (1) People Who Put Their Own Interests First, (2) Egoists, (3) People Who Put The Interests Of Others First, and (4) Altruists

Mistake Box
Rule 1: X (Four Terms: PWPITIBO, E, PWP-TIOOBTO, and A)
Rule 2: ok (No E or O Statements)
Rule 3A: There is no Middle Term
Rule 3B: ok (No dist. terms in Conc.)
Cor: ok (Both Prems are univ. & C is a particular, BUT each class is known to have at least one member)

17.

			D		D
P-1:	E	No	IS	are	GA
			D		D
P-2:	E	No	TAR	are	IS
			D		D
C:	E	No	TAR	are	GA

Key: IS = Invalid Syllogisms
GA = Good Arguments
TAR = True Act of Reasoning

Invalid Argument:
Faulty Exclusions, There are Three Negative Statements Which Violates Rule 2.

Mistake Box
Rule 1: ok (IS, GA, and TAR)
Rule 2: X (Three E statements)
Rule 3A: ok (IS is dist. twice)
Rule 3B: ok (both terms dist in conc. are distributed in prems)
Cor: ok (all are universal)

19.

			D		U
P-1:	A	All	TTAL	are	TWMSTM
			D		D
P-2:	E	No	YE	is	TWMSTM
			D		D
C:	E	No	YE	is	TTAL

Key: TTAL = Things That Are Logical
TWMSTM = Things Which Make Sense To Me
YE = Your Explanation

Valid Argument!
(All Rules Satisfied)
(This one may sound funny. What do you think is wrong with it? Hint: It is probably a content problem with one of the premises.)

Mistake Box
Rule 1: ok (exactly 3 terms)
Rule 2: ok (one E in P and one in C)
Rule 3A: ok (TWMSTM is dist once)
Rule 3B: ok (both terms are dist in C and also in the Prems)
Cor: ok (all statements are universals)

21.

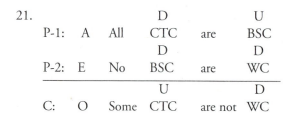

			D CTC	are	U BSC
P-1:	A	All	CTC	are	BSC
			D		D
P-2:	E	No	BSC	are	WC
			U		D
C:	O	Some	CTC	are not	WC

Key: CTC = Critical Thinking Courses
BSC = Basic Skills Courses
WC = Worthless Courses

Valid Argument:
All Rules Satisfied
(Including the Corollary)

Mistake Box
Rule 1: ok (CTC, BSC, and WC)
Rule 2: ok (One neg. in P-2; one in C)
Rule 3A: ok (M. T. Is BSC; dist. in P-2)
Rule 3B: ok (WC is dist in C; also in P)
Cor: (Both Prems are universals, conc is a Particular,
BUT, there are CTCs, BSCs, and WCs too, so OK.)

ANSWERS TO EXERCISES ON PAGES 141 THROUGH 143

A LEVEL

1. A Circle in a Venn Diagram represents a class or category. Think of it as the boundaries of a set whose members are all inside.

2. Venn Diagrams work best in displaying the relationship between three or fewer classes.

3. A portion of a Venn Diagram Circle is shaded in to show that there are no members in that particular part of the set.

4. The placement of an "X" in an area of a Venn Diagram indicates that there is at least one member known to exist in that region. For example, if there were two overlapping classes, marked S and P, and an "X" were drawn in that overlapping region, the "X" indicates that there is a least one S that is also a P (and, conversely, that there is at least one P that is also an S).

5. In a two-term Venn Diagram there are four areas which are represented.

   Let's use two overlapping circles to represent classes S and P.

   Area 1 = an S that is not a P
   Area 2 = an S that is a P (and a P that is an S)
   Area 3 = a P that is not an S
   Area 4 = something that is not an S or a P

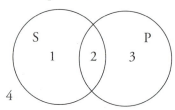

6. In a three-term Venn Diagram there are eight areas which are represented. (If you are in doubt see Figure 6.6 on page 135.)

7. False

8. True

9. False. It exists in one region or the other, but not necessarily in both.

10. True. But they will necessarily be invalid, because according to Rule One a VALID Syllogism has exactly three class terms.

 LEVEL

1. In order to facilitate working and understanding the diagram method of testing categorical syllogisms, we have included three diagrams for each problem to show the step-by-step process involved. The first diagram represents the drawing of the first universal premise in the argument. The second diagram represents BOTH of the premises diagrammed at the same time. This is how the finished product should look, because the conclusion should already be contained in the premises of a valid deductive argument. The third diagram represents what the conclusion *should look like*.

1.

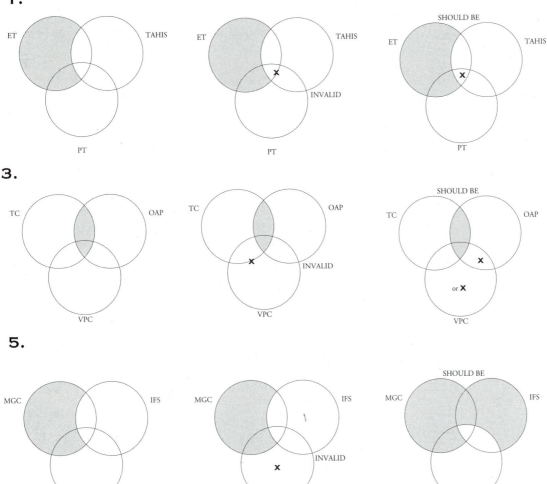

3.

5.

7.

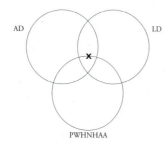

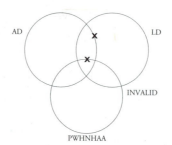

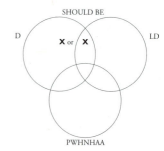

9.

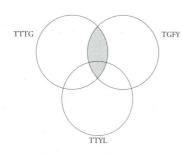

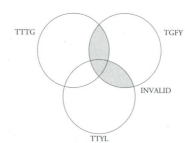

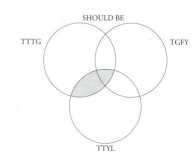

11.

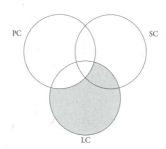

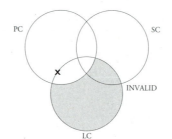

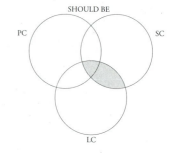

13.

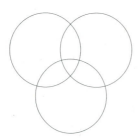

Four Terms—No Diagram
True Scotsmen
People Who Would Make Fun of the Bagpipes
Michael
Scotsmen

or

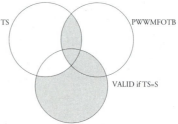

15. Four Terms—No Diagram
People Who Put Their Interests Before Others   Egoists
People Who Put The Interests of Others Before Their Own   Altruists

17.

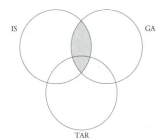 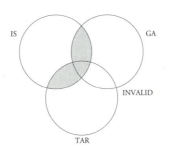 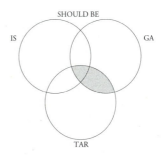

19.

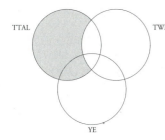 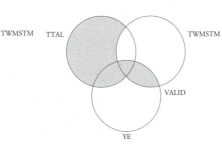 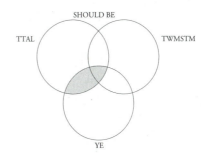

21.

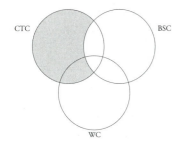 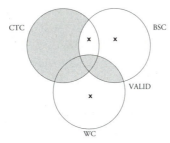 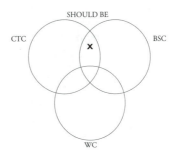

CHAPTER 7
ANSWERS TO EXERCISES ON PAGES 163 THROUGH 165

A   LEVEL

1. An <u>immediate inference</u> is the drawing of a necessary conclusion from a single premise. It is called "immediate" because there are no "mediating" terms, such as the middle term in a syllogism, needed to get from one point to the next.

2. The statement, "All P's are Q's," would not necessarily imply that "Some P's must be Q's" in the event that there were no such thing as either Ps or Q's (in other words that either P or Q or both were an empty class).

3. Whenever an E-Statement is known to be false, we know immediately that the I-Form of that statement must be true. We cannot immediately determine whether the A-Form or the O-Form of that statement is either true or false, but we do know that one of them must be true and the other has to be false.

4. If the O-Form is true, the A-Form of that same categorical statement must be False, because these two forms are always contradictory.

5. The immediate inference of <u>conversion</u> is the legitimate form of switching the subject and predicate classes of a categorical proposition. The E-Form and the I-Form Statements may be converted (have their subjects and predicates switched) without changing the Form of the Statement at all. The A-Statements may be converted but with two limitations: (1) they must be known to have at least one member of both the subject and the predicate class, and (2) they must be converted to I-Form Statements. (Just because All A's are B's does not necessarily mean that All B's are A's.) Finally, it must be remembered that the O-Form Statements may not be converted at all.

6. The E-Statement and the I-Statement Forms may be converted into the same statement forms—note that the distribution of each of their terms remains the same; that is, in the E-Form, the subject and predicate are both distributed (we are talking about all of the members of each class) and in the I-Statement, both subject and predicate are undistributed both times (since we are only referring to some of the members of each class).

7. The immediate inference known as <u>obversion</u> is the changing of a categorical statement from positive to negative to positive, with a corresponding change in the predicate class to its obverse or complementary class. All four of the categorical statement forms may be legitimately obverted.

8. As previously mentioned in Answer 7, any standard form categorical statement may be obverted. This is done by first changing the statement form from affirmative to negative to affirmative. There will be a corresponding change in the quantifier (unless we are dealing with the particular statement forms). The subject terms cannot be changed in any way. The predicate class is "obverted" by changing to its complementary class.

9. From an A-Statement to the E-Statement:

    E   No   Wizards   are   People Who Do Not Know Magic

10. It would remain an E-Statement with changed subject and predicate terms:

    E   No   People Who Know Magic   are   Wizards

B   LEVEL

1. A. True
   E. False
   I. True (as long as there were persons in attendance and persons carrying wallets.)
   O. False

3. I. True
    A. ?
    E. False
    O. ?

5. A. True
    E. False
    I. True   (As long as there are salespersons and people who meet their quotas.)
    O   False

Try Supposing that the Statement Forms in 6 Through 10 are false:

7. I. False
    A. False
    E. True
    O. True

9. A. False
    E. ?
    I. ?
    O. True

Converting:

11. E—Statement   D   D
                    No   Skydivers are Sculptors

13. I—Statement   U   U
                    Some Lovable Creatures are Kittens

15. Again, cannot be converted as an O-Statement. As in the previous example, if it were obverted then converted as an I-Statement, the result would be "Some people who do not love modern dance are people who love classical ballet."

17. Cannot be converted as an O-Statement. But, like number 15 above, this one could be converted AS AN I-STATEMENT (which would involve either retranslating or obverting first).
     I—Statement   U   U
     Some People Who Were Not Admitted Are People Who Came Late To The Theater

19. I—Statement   U   U
     Some Things That Are Good For A Number of Purposes are Handtools

Obverting:

                              D   D
21. A becomes E   No Doughnuts are Non-Tasty Treats
                              U   D
23. I becomes O   Some Articles of Clothing are not Non-Useless (Useful?) Things
                              D   D
25. A becomes E   No Scientific Experiment is an Unrepeatable Event
                              U   D
27. I becomes O   Some Children are not People Who Were Uncurious
                              D   U
29. E becomes A   All People Who Heard the Lecture are People Who Did Not
                                                Remain Unmoved

C   LEVEL

1.   Key: MB = Mortal Beings;   IMB = ImMortal Beings
          PB = Perfect Beings;   IPB = ImPerfect Beings
          HB = Human Beings;   NHB = NonHuman Beings

				D	U						D		D
A	All	MB	are	IPB		→	obverts to E	No MB	are	~~non IPB~~
E	No	HB	are	IMB		→	obverts to A	All HB	are	~~non IMB~~
A	All	PB	are	NHB		→	obverts to E	No PB	are	~~non NHB~~

A: D, MB, D U IPB
E: D No, D HB, D are, U IMB
A: D All, PB, D are, U NHB

┌─────────────────────────────────────┐   ┌──┐
│ **Mistake Box #1**   │   │ **Mistake Box #2**   │
│ Rule 1: X (6 Terms!)   │   →   │ Rule 1: ok (MB, PB, and HB)   │
│ Rule 2: X (only 1 E/O Stmt)   │   │ Rule 2: ok (one E in P; one in C)   │
│ Rule 3A: X (no Middle Term)   │   │ Rule 3A: ok (MT is MB; dist in P-1)   │
│ Rule 3B: X (no PB in prems)   │   │ Rule 3B: ok (both terms in C are dist in the │
│ Cor: ok   │   │   premises)   │
│   │   │ Cor: ok (all stmts are universals)   │
│   │   │ VALID ARGUMENT! Meets all Rules   │
└─────────────────────────────────────┘   └──┘

3.   Key: J = Joe   PWF401 = People Who Flunked the 401 Class
          PI402 = People in 402 Class   PWP401 = People Who Passed the 401 Class

		D		U						D		U
A	All PI402		are	PWP401	stays same	→	A	All	PI402		are	PWP401
E	No J	D is	PI402 D		stays the same	→	E	No J	D is	PI402 D		
A	All J	D is	PWF401 U		obverts to →	E	No J	D is	PWDNF401 D (=? PWP401) (D)

┌─────────────────────────────────────┐   ┌──┐
│ **Mistake Box #1**   │   │ **Mistake Box #2**   │
│ Rule 1: X (Four Terms)   │   →   │ Rule 1: ok (* See Below for Disc.)   │
│ Rule 2: X (Only one E Stmt)   │   │ Rule 2: ok (one in P; one in C)   │
│ Rule 3A: ok (PI402 is dist, twice)   │   │ Rule 3A: ok (PI402 is MT, is dist)   │
│ Rule 3B: ok (Joe is dist in C   │   │ Rule 3B: X (Now both terms in C are dist, │
│   & in P)   │   │   but PWP401 is undist in the premise)   │
│ Cor: ok (All are universal Stmts)   │   │ Cor: ok (All Ps and C are univs)   │
└─────────────────────────────────────┘   └──┘

INVALID ARGUMENT! Breaks Rules 1 & 2 → STILL INVALID ARGUMENT!
(Either it breaks Rule 3B as shown above or there are still 4 terms because "People Who Did Not Fail 401" is not exactly the same class as "People Who Passed 401".

*—For instance, there may be someone who did not take the class or who audited it. They would be included in the class of PWDNF401, but not in the class of PWP401.

5. Key: IFT = Inflammable Things   UST = Unsafe Things
       ST = Safe Things   NET = NonExplosive Things
       ET = Explosive Things   FT = Flammable Things

			D		U				D		D
P-1:	A	All	IFT	are	UST	obverts to →	E	No IFT	are	non X̶S̶T
			D		U				D		U
P-2:	A	All	ET	are	FT	stays same →	A	All ET	are	FT
			D		U				D		D
C:	A	All	ST	are	NET	obverts to →	E	No ST	are	non n̶o̶n ET

Mistake Box # 1
Rule 1: X (6 Terms—see above)
Rule 2: ok (all A-Statements)
Rule 3A: ok or No M.T.?
Rule 3B: ST is dist in Conc, not in P
Cor: ok (All are universals)

→

Mistake Box #2
Rule 1: ok or X (see below)
Rule 2: ok (One E in P-1, one in C)
Rule 3A: ok or No M.T. (see below)
Rule 3B: ok (both terms dist in C are dist in Premises)
Cor: ok (All are universals)

After obversion the argument appears to be "ok", except for the fact that there seem to be four terms. We have seen that "non-non-Explosive Things" is precisely the same class as "Explosive Things". And, "non-unSafe Things" is equivalent to "Safe Things". The problem appears to remain with Flammable Things and Inflammable Things. First, ask yourself: would you rather run into a truck with the label "Flammable Stuff On Board!" or one with the label "Inflammable Stuff On Board!"? Hopefully, you answered, "Neither!" If you look them up in an English dictionary, you will find that both classes have exactly the same meaning: "substances that will catch fire or burn". So there really are only three classes in this argument, and it is a VALID one.

ANSWERS TO EXERCISES ON PAGES 167 THROUGH 169

A   LEVEL

1. False. Either a Premise <u>or</u> a Conclusion may be left out of an enthymeme.
2. True. Often, that is why they are left out.
3. True. This is a very reliable way of determining exactly what is missing.
4. True. And, they have premises or conclusions which are not stated.
5. True.
6. True.
7. True, with an unstated conclusion that she must not be a good actress.
8. True. We are missing the obvious intermediary conclusion that Sam and Sally are persons.
9. False. It is an example of an invalid categorical syllogism. But no parts are missing.
10. False again.

B   LEVEL

1.   Given: (P-1) Andy is a Politician, and (C) He (Andy) is looking out for himself. What is missing is a (P-2) to the effect that Politicians always look out for themselves. To put this in standard form:

			D		U
(P-1)	A	All	Andy	is	a Politician

			D		U
(Missing P-2)	A	All	Politicians	are	People Who Look Out For Themselves

			D		U
(C)	A	All	Andy	is	A Person Who Is Looking Out For Themselves

> **Mistake Box**
> Rule 1: ok (3 terms—Andy, Politicians, People Who Look Out For Themselves)
> Rule 2: ok (All A-Statements)
> Rule 3A: ok (Middle Term, "Politicians", is distributed in P-2)
> Rule 3B: ok ("Andy" is distributed in the conclusion, and in P-1)
> Cor: ok (All Statements are Universals)

VALID ARGUMENT

3.   Given: (P-1) You just passed that trooper at 90 mph; (C) You are going to get a ticket. Missing here is a premise, (P-2), People Who Pass Troopers at 90 mph are People Who are Going to Get Tickets. This is one way of depicting the three classes (though there are other equally viable ones):

Y = You; PWPTA90 = People Who Pass Troopers At 90 MPH; PWAGTGT = People Who Are Going To Get A Ticket.

			D		U
(P-1):	A	All	Y	are	PWPTA90

			D		U
(Missing P-2):	A	All	PWPTA90	are	PWAGTGT

			D		U
(C):	A	All	Y	are	PWAGTGT

> **Mistake Box**
> Rule 1: ok (See 3 Cls above)
> Rule 2: ok (All A-Stmts)
> Rule 3A: ok (MT, PWPTA90 is dist in P-2)
> Rule 3B: ok (Y is dist in C and in P-1)
> Cor: ok (All Universals)

VALID ARGUMENT!

5.   Given: (P-1) Dr. K is not listed in the ERP; (C) Dr. K cannot be a reputable teacher. Missing is a premise which could be stated "None of those who are not listed in the ERP are reputable teachers" or "All Reputable Teachers are listed in the ERP." Our key will be DK = Dr. K; RT = Reputable Teachers; and TLIERP = Teachers Listed in the ERP.

			D		D
(P-1):	E	No	DK	is	TLIERP

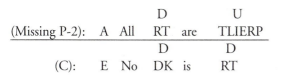

			D		U
(Missing P-2):	A	All	RT	are	TLIERP
			D		D
(C):	E	No	DK	is	RT

VALID ARGUMENT!

> **Mistake Box**
> Rule 1: ok (3 Terms Listed Above)
> Rule 2: ok (1 E in P; 1 in Conc.)
> Rule 3A: ok (TLIERP is dist in P-1)
> Rule 3B: ok (Both terms in Conc are dist, and also in Prem)
> Cor: ok (All Universals)

7. Given: (P-1) The "Journal" is an awful paper, and (P-2) That paper is not the "Journal". If it is being implied that (C) Therefore, that paper is not an awful paper, there may be a problem. The classes or terms are TJ = The "Journal", TP = That Paper, and AP = Awful Papers.

			D		U
(P-1):	A	All	TJ	is	AP
			D		D
(P-2):	E	No	TP	is	TJ
			D		D
(Missing C):	E	No	TP	is	AP

INVALID ARGUMENT! Illicit Distribution (of the term "Awful Papers"—in other words, there could be other awful papers besides the Journal)

> **Mistake Box**
> Rule 1: ok (3 Terms: TJ, TP, and AP)
> Rule 2: ok (one E in P and one in C)
> Rule 3A: ok (M.T., TJ, is dist twice)
> Rule 3B: X (TP is dist in C and in P2 But AP is dist in C, not in P-1)
> Cor: ok (all Statements are universal)

9. The conclusion is that it will rain today, based upon the evidence that I just washed my car. The missing premise that would guarantee this otherwise illogical conclusion is probably based upon the Fallacy of Assuming the Cause, but from a strictly formal point of view, it is that "whenever I wash my car, it rains." Putting the argument in standard categorical form, it looks like this—

			D	U
P-1:	A	All	Today is A Time I Just Washed My Car	

			D		U
P-2:	A	All	Times I Just Washed My Car Are Times It Will Rain [UNSTATED]	

			D	U
C:	A	All	Today is A Time It Will Rain	

VALID ARGUMENT: All Rules Satisfied; Missing a Premise as Noted Above Sorites:

> **Mistake Box**
> Rule 1: ok (Today, Times I Washed My Car, Times It Will Rain)
> Rule 2: ok (No E or O Statements at all)
> Rule 3A: ok (Middle Term is "Times I Washed My Car"; Distributed in P-2)
> Rule 3B: ok ("Today" is Distributed in Conc. and in P-1)
> Cor: ok (All statements are universals)

11.   All   Ronnie is a Lawyer
      All   Lawyers are People Who Argue Well
      All   Ronnie is a Person Who Argues Well (MISSING CONCLUSION)

      All   Ronnie is a Person Who Argues Well
      All   Ronnie is a Person Who Makes A Lot of Money
      All   People Who Argue Well Are People Who Make A Lot Of Money

Note: The First Argument with the missing conclusion is a valid line of reasoning. All of the Rules are met. The Second Argument, which begins by using the Missing Conclusion from the first argument is INVALID, because of the Fallacy of Illicit Distribution—People Who Argue Well is distributed in the conclusion but not in Premise 1. It is a kind of Hasty Generalization to assume that because Ronnie argues well and makes a lot of money that everyone who argues well makes a lot of money. Notice also that if the conclusion had been "So, Ronnie makes a lot of money," and the last statement, "Anyone who argues well makes a lot of money," the argument would have been a VALID one.

13.   All   Times It Rains Are Times The Streets Get Wet
      All   Times The Streets Get Wet Are Times More Accidents Occur
      All   Times It Rains Are Times More accidents Occur (Missing conclusion)

      VALID ARGUMENT

      All   Times It Rains Are Times More Accidents Occur (From Previous Conc.)
      All   Times More Accidents Occur Are Times the P. D. Has Much More Work
      All   Times It Rains Are Times The Police Department Has Much More Work

      VALID ARGUMENT

15.   All   Persons Watching Television Are Persons Having Deadened Imaginative Powers
      All   Peter Is A Person Having Deadened Imaginative Powers
      All   Peter Is A Person Who Watches Too Much Television

      INVALID ARGUMENT: At Least Two Problems Here—
      (A) Four terms fallacy: Persons Watching Television, Persons Having Deadened Imaginative Powers, Peter, and People Who Watch Too Much Television. Even if this were rewritten as three terms, it would still be
      (B) Fallacy of the undistributed middle term: The Class of Persons having Deadened Imaginative Powers is the Middle Term and It Is Undistributed Both Times

CHAPTER 8
ANSWERS TO EXERCISES ON PAGES 182 AND 183

A   LEVEL

1.   A conjunction is a "truth-functional connective" represented by the symbol "&", asserting that two claims are being put together as one compound claim in which both parts are true.

2.   A disjunction is a "truth-functional connective" represented by the symbol "▼", and asserting that two component claims are being put together as one complex claim in which at least one of the two components is true.

3. An <u>inclusive</u> disjunction is a complex "either-or" claim with two components such as <u>at least one</u> but possibly <u>both</u> statements are true. An <u>exclusive</u> disjunction is a complex "either-or" claim with two component statements, only <u>one</u> of which can be true.

4. The <u>truth value</u> of a statement is the artificial assignment of a value, either "true" or "false", to a statement in order to determine what consequences follow for the values of more complex statements or arguments.

5. Both conjuncts must be true.

6. Both disjuncts must be false. *false*

7. False (Both of them must be ~~true~~.)

8. True

9. True

10. True

11. False

12. False

13. False

14. True

15. False

16. True

B LEVEL

1. S ▼ T

~~3~~2. B & Y

5. F & B

7. (T ▼ F) = True

9. (F ▼ T) = True

ANSWERS TO EXERCISES ON PAGES 191 AND 192

A LEVEL

1. A <u>negation</u> is a "truth-functional connective" that does not really link anything but which changes the truth value of the statement or statement complex it modifies. It is symbolized by a tilde or "~".

2. A <u>conditional</u> statement is a complex claim expressing a hypothetical relationship between the truth values of its two component claims. It is a truth-functional relationship symbolized by an arrow or "⇒".

3. In a conditional statement neither the antecedent (the "IF" part) nor the consequent (the "THEN" part) is being asserted as categorically true, but rather the first condition is sufficient for us to know that the second condition is true, and the second condition is a necessary condition in the sense that if it, the consequent, were not true, then the antecedent could not be true either.

4. A hypothetical or conditional statement is false, just in case the antecedent is true and the consequent is false. For all other truth values of the antecedent and consequent, the complex statement (the conditional itself) is true.

5. True
6. False. (The antecedent _is_ false, but the consequent is not.)
7. False. (It is always the consequent of a conditional.)
8. False. (It is the antecedent—unless the condition turns out to be a <u>necessary and sufficient</u> one, as we shall see.)
9. False. (The phrase "only if" denotes a <u>necessary</u> condition.)
10. False. (Strictly speaking, it is not a "connector" at all. It serves as a truth-functional connective to change the truth value of the statement it modifies.)
11. True
12. False. The Statement, "Jim decided to accept the new job", is being asserted as true <u>independent</u> of other considerations, including the pay. (By the way, this is true if there are any job offers out there.)

B   LEVEL

1. $C \Rightarrow G$
3. $R \Rightarrow S$ (or, if S = you <u>do</u> smoke, then $[R \Rightarrow {\sim}S]$)
5. $M \Rightarrow L$
7. $H \Rightarrow E$
9. ${\sim}P \Rightarrow R$
11. $(T \Rightarrow F)$ = False
13. ${\sim}(T \,\&\, F) = {\sim}({\sim}) =$ True
15. $(F \Rightarrow F) =$ True

ANSWERS TO EXERCISES ON PAGES 196 THROUGH 198

A   LEVEL

1. A <u>biconditional</u> is also a "truth-functional connective"; in this case, a special form of the conditional in which each simple statement is both the necessary and the sufficient condition for the other. It is symbolized by the double arrow, "<——>".
2. A <u>necessary</u> condition is a <u>sine qua non,</u> a <u>prerequisite,</u> an <u>essential</u> condition, without which the antecedent of a conditional statement would be false. It is always the consequent of the complex hypothetical or conditional statement and symbolized to the right of the arrow, "$\Rightarrow$".
3. A <u>sufficient</u> condition is the antecedent or first half of a conditional or hypothetical statement. It is symbolized before or to the left of the arrow, "$\Rightarrow$", to show that it is <u>one</u> adequate way (not necessarily the <u>only</u> one) of insuring that the consequent must be true.
4. A conditional statement only asserts that the consequent is a necessary condition for the antecedent (or that the antecedent is a sufficient condition for the consequent) whereas in a <u>biconditional statement</u> each condition is both <u>sufficient</u> and <u>necessary</u> for the other condition. Put simply, if A is true, then B must be true too <u>AND</u> if A is false, then B must be false too. In a regular conditional statement, if A is true, B must be true too, but if A is false, B may be true or false.
5. TRUE.

6. FALSE. (Each has two components.)
7. FALSE. (It may only indicate a necessary condition.)
8. FALSE. (It would be "(V & N) $\Rightarrow$ L." It matters a great deal <u>where</u> the parentheses are put.)

B   LEVEL

1. D $\Rightarrow$ L
3. C $\Rightarrow$ E
5. ~J $\Rightarrow$ ~R
7. ~E $\Rightarrow$ ~J
9. M $\Rightarrow$ D
11. ~(~O & ~G)
13. (P ▼ R) & ~(P & R)
15. ~(C $\Rightarrow$ R)
17. [~(C ▼ P)] $\Rightarrow$ U
19. ~R & ~W
21. (G ▼ D) & P
23. (W ▼ F) & F
25. (P ▼ R) & (T ▼ L)
27. W $\Rightarrow$ F
29. C & (P $\Rightarrow$ S)
31. (L $\Rightarrow$ D) $\Rightarrow$ (C $\Rightarrow$ R)
33. ~D $\Rightarrow$ (P & R)
35. (A $\Rightarrow$ B) $\Rightarrow$ (C $\Rightarrow$ D)
37. P $\Rightarrow$ T
39. J $\Rightarrow$ V
41. Either yellow or blue is Lisa's favorite color.
43. If blue is Lisa's favorite color, then yellow is not Lisa's favorite color.
45. Blue is Lisa's favorite color, if and only if yellow is not Lisa's favorite color.
47. If I wash my car, then it is raining.
49. I am washing my car and it is raining.
51. It rains if and only if I wash my car.

CHAPTER 9
ANSWERS TO EXERCISES ON PAGES 211 THROUGH 213

A   LEVEL

1. A <u>Valid Argument</u> is a deductive line of reasoning in which if and only if all of the premises are true, the conclusions must be true too. An <u>Invalid Argument</u> is a line of reasoning put forward <u>as if</u> deductively the premises guaranteed the truth of the conclusion when in fact they do not do so. Because of a flaw in the structure of the reasoning in invalid arguments, the conclusion may turn out to be false even when all of the premises are true.

2. Yes. Because the Modus Ponens argument form is a valid one, in the case of an argument having this form and also having true premises, the conclusion must necessarily be true.

3. No. Because arguments having the form of denying the antecedent are invalid, even if the premises of such an argument form were true, the conclusion would not <u>have to be</u> true.

4. False. If one or more of the premises are false, the conclusion could be false too.

5. False. The conclusions of invalid argument forms may be true anyway, but for entirely different reasons, for example.

6. True

7. True

8. True

9. False It may be either true or false; the point is that an invalid argument form does not guarantee ANYTHING about the truth or falsity of the conclusion.

10. True

B   LEVEL

1. W ⇒ C   Valid:
    W   MODUS PONENS
    ―――
    C

3. ~E ⇒ I   Invalid:
    E (because S)   Denying the Antecedent
    ―――――――
    ~I

5. ~T ⇒ ~P   Valid:
    Y ⇒ ~T   Chain Argument
    ――――――
    Y ⇒ ~P

7. ~C ⇒ ~G   Valid:
    ~C   MODUS PONENS
    ―――
    ~G

9. ~T ⇒ ~P   Invalid:
    T   Denying The Antecedent
    ―――
    P

11. ~E ⇒ ~G   Valid:
    ~E   MODUS PONENS
    ―――
    ~G

13. V ⇒ (L & C)   Invalid: It is an inductive argument as it stands and it is fallacious. If the conclu-
    (L & C) ⇒ (P & I)   sion had been, "If we let the communists win in Vietnam, then Aus-
    (P & I) ⇒ A   tralia won't be far behind", the form would have been a valid one
    ―――――――――――――   (Chain Argument), although the content fallacy—Slippery Slope—
    S   would still remain.

15. E ⇒ S   Invalid:
    S   Affirming The Consequent
    ―――
    E

ANSWERS TO EXERCISES ON PAGES 218 THROUGH 223

A   LEVEL

1. A <u>Disjunctive Argument</u> is a valid form of reasoning which has the structure A ▼ B, ~A; therefore B.
    For example: Either Gore will write a sequel, or Hillary gets involved.
    <u>Gore is not going to write a sequel.</u>
    So: Hillary gets involved.

2. A <u>Conjunctive Argument</u> is a valid reasoning form having the structure:
    ~(A & B), A; therefore ~B.
    For example: The Bosnians and the Serbs cannot both win.
    <u>The Serbs win.</u>
    Therefore: The Bosnians cannot win.

3. In a <u>Disjunctive Argument</u> the reasoning is valid because if it is true both that (A) one of the two possibilities must be true, and (B) one of them turns out to be false, then (C) the other one HAS TO BE true [otherwise (A) was false]. Whereas in the argument forms which Affirm a Disjunct, when one of two possibilities must be true and one of the two turns out to be true, then we cannot draw any necessary inference about the truth or falsity of the other possibility.

4. <u>Conjunctive Arguments</u> are valid forms of reasoning that two things cannot both be true at the same time and that since one of them is true, the other one cannot possibly be true too. Arguments which Deny a Conjunct are invalid because the reasoning is that since two things cannot both be true at the same time and that since one of them is false, the other one must be true. The problem here is that it is possible that <u>neither</u> of the two possibilities is true.

5. A <u>Simple Dilemma</u> takes the form A ⇒ C, B ⇒ C, and A ▼ B; therefore C
    The conclusion of a simple dilemma is a simple statement (such as "C"), whereas the conclusion of a complex dilemma is a complex statement which is a disjunction, because the <u>Complex Dilemma</u> takes the form A ⇒ C, B ⇒ D, and A ▼ B; therefore C ▼ D.
    A Simple Dilemma might occur in reasoning such as this—
    If market conditions improve, then we will make money on this fund."
    If market conditions remain stable, we will make money on this fund."
    <u>Market conditions will either improve or remain stable.</u>
    So: We will make money on this fund.
    A Complex Dilemma might occur in reasoning such as this—
    If we utilize behavior modification, then we may have some undesirable side effects.
    If we utilize a Freudian approach, then we may reinforce unwanted neuroses.
    <u>We will utilize either behavior modification or a Freudian approach.</u>
    So: We may have either some undesirable side effects or reinforce unwanted neuroses.

6. False
7. True
8. False(Both contain disjunctions.)
9. True
10. False

B LEVEL

1. ~(C & S)   Valid:
    $\dfrac{C}{\text{~S}}$ Conjunctive Argument

3. ~(R & C)   Invalid:
    $\dfrac{\text{~C}}{R}$ Denying A Conjunct

5. ~(S & H)   Invalid:
    $\dfrac{\text{~H}}{S}$ Denying A Conjunct

7. L ▼ M   Valid:
    L ⇒ D   Simple Dilemma
    $\dfrac{M \Rightarrow D}{D}$

9. C ▼ T   Invalid:
    $\dfrac{T}{\text{~C}}$ Affirming A Disjunct

11. M ▼ L   Invalid:
    $\dfrac{L}{\text{~M}}$ Affirming A Disjunct

C LEVEL

1. D ⇒ C   Valid:
    $\dfrac{D}{C}$ Modus Ponens

3. N ⇒ M   Valid:
    $\dfrac{\text{~M (assumed)}}{\text{~N}}$ Modus Tollens

5. F ⇒ I   Valid:
    $\dfrac{I \Rightarrow W}{F \Rightarrow W}$ Chain Argument

7. DWI ⇒ F   Valid:
    $\dfrac{DWI}{F}$ Modus Ponens

9. C ⇒ (A & E)   Invalid:
    $\dfrac{(A \text{ \& } E)}{C}$ Affirming the Consequent

11. L ⇒ H   Valid:
     H ⇒ F   Chain Argument
     ‾‾‾‾‾   (Content Fallacy of Assuming the Cause)
     L ⇒ F

13. PC ⇒ Paid Dues Valid:
     PC   Modus Ponens
     ‾‾‾‾‾‾‾‾‾‾‾
     Paid Dues

15. H ⇒ R   Invalid:
     ~H   Denying the Antecedent
     ‾‾‾
     ~R

→ CHAPTER #10 ←

ANSWERS TO EXERCISES ON PAGES 236 THROUGH 238

 A   LEVEL

1. True
2. True
3. True
4. False. The inference is equally valid in both directions.
5. False. A ⇒ B is logically equivalent to ~(A & ~B).
6. False. "It's raining and the streets are wet" is logically equivalent to the statement "It is not the case that either it is not raining or the streets are not wet."
7. False. "It's raining and the streets are wet" is logically equivalent to "It is not the case that if it is raining then the streets are not wet."
8. False. (All of the lines must match up, including the false ones.)
9. False. It is logically equivalent to "It is not the case that neither Perot nor Bush lost the election of 1992."
10. True

 B   LEVEL

1.

A	B	~A	(~A & B)	(A ⇒ B)	(~A & B) ↔ (A ⇒ B)
T	T	F	F	T	F
T	F	F	F	F	T
F	T	T	T	T	T
F	F	T	F	T	F

They are NOT logically equivalent expressions.

3.

R	S	~R	~S	(R ⇒ ~S)	(~R ▼ ~S)	(R ⇒ ~S) ↔ (~R ▼ ~S)
T	T	F	F	F	F	T
T	F	F	T	T	T	T
F	T	T	F	T	T	T
F	F	T	T	T	T	T

These two expressions <u>are</u> logically equivalent.

5.

M	N	M $\Rightarrow$ N	~(M $\Rightarrow$ N)	(M & N)	~(M $\Rightarrow$ N) $\leftrightarrow$ (M & N)
T	T	T	F	T	F
T	F	F	T	F	F
F	T	T	F	F	T
F	F	T	F	F	T

They are <u>not</u> logically equivalent.

7.

(a) B $\Rightarrow$ F

(b) ~B $\Rightarrow$ ~F

B	F	~B	~F	(B $\Rightarrow$ F)	(~B $\Rightarrow$ ~F)	(B $\Rightarrow$ F) $\leftrightarrow$ (~B $\Rightarrow$ ~F)
T	T	F	F	T	T	T
T	F	F	T	F	T	F
F	T	T	F	T	F	F
F	F	T	T	T	T	T

They are <u>not</u> logically equivalent expressions.

9.

(a) ~L $\Rightarrow$ ~A

(b) L $\Rightarrow$ A

A	L	~A	~L	(~L $\Rightarrow$ ~A)	(L $\Rightarrow$ ~A)	(~L $\Rightarrow$ ~A) $\leftrightarrow$ (L $\Rightarrow$ A)
T	T	F	F	T	T	T
T	F	F	T	F	T	F
F	T	T	F	T	F	F
F	F	T	T	T	T	T

They are <u>not</u> logically equivalent expressions.

11.

(a) ~J $\Rightarrow$ L

(b) ~L $\Rightarrow$ J

~J	L	~L	J	~J $\Rightarrow$ L	~L $\Rightarrow$ ~J	(~J $\Rightarrow$ L) $\leftrightarrow$ (~L $\Rightarrow$ J)
T	T	F	F	T	T	T
T	F	T	F	F	F	T
F	T	F	T	T	T	T
F	F	T	T	T	T	T

The two statements <u>are</u> logically equivalent.

13.

(a) ~(B & T)

(B) ~B ▼ T

B	T	~B	~(B & T)	~B ▼ T	~(B & T) ↔ (~B ▼ T)
T	T	F	F T	T	F
T	F	F	T F	F	F
F	T	T	T F	T	T
F	F	T	T F	T	T

The two expressions are <u>not</u> logically equivalent.

15. ~A ⇒ B

17. ~(A ⇒ B)

19. S ▼ I = ~S ⇒ I (If you don't stop, I'll shoot.)

21. L ▼ ~J = ~L ⇒ ~J (If Lisa does not go to the concert, then Jill will not go.)

23. C ▼ L = ~C ⇒ L (If you don't take calculus to fulfill this requirement then you need to take logic to do so.)

25. P ▼ ~Q

27. ~(P ▼ ~Q)

29. ~B ▼ F (Either it does not break or we will fix it.)

31. O ▼ R (Either orange or red is Sara's favorite color.)

ANSWERS TO EXERCISES ON PAGES 248 THROUGH 251

A   LEVEL

1. A <u>Valid Deductive Argument</u> is a line of reasoning in which the truth of the premises would absolutely guarantee the truth of the conclusion, or, put more formally, it is one in which the conclusion must be true if and only if the premises are true.

2. A <u>Truth Table</u> is a method of assigning all possible truth values to the simple statements which comprise a complex statement in order to determine the truth values of that complex statement. Truth tables may be used to establish the logical equivalence between different statements, to determine the validity of arguments, to establish whether certain statement forms are tautologies, contradictions, or contingent statements, or even to solve certain kinds of logical puzzles and games.

3. To this point we have looked at several other methods: one, for example, are the Proofs and Derivations from the Rules found in Chapters Eight and Nine; another are the Rule Method and the Diagram Method for evaluating Categorical Syllogisms found in Chapters Six and Seven.

4. False. Validity is shown by constructing a truth table in which there are NO lines in which all of the premises are true and the conclusion is false.

5. True

6. True

7. True

8. False. It is the Rule by which two statements known to be true are joined together in a <u>conjunction.</u>

9. True

10. False. It is the Rule by which a <u>conjunction</u> is simplified into one of its component conjuncts.

B   LEVEL

1.

R ⇒ ~S
~S
———
R

R	~S	R ⇒ ~S	R
T	T	T	T
T	F	F	T
F	T	T	F
F	F	T	F

Line 3 shows an instance where both premises are true and the conclusion is false. Thus, the argument is INVALID.

3.

W ⇒ S
W
———
S

W	S	W ⇒ S	S
T	T	T	T
T	F	F	F
F	T	T	T
F	F	T	F

The argument is VALID: in all instances where premises are true (line 1), the conclusion is true too. And, anytime the conclusion is false (as in lines 2 and 4) at least one of the premises is false too.

5.

(a) B ⇒ W
(b) T ⇒ W
(c) B ▼ T
(d) W

B	T	W	(B ⇒ W)	(T ⇒ W)	(B ▼ T)	W
T	T	T	T	T	T	T
T	T	F	F	F	T	F
T	F	T	T	T	T	T
T	F	F	F	T	T	F
F	T	T	T	T	T	T
F	T	F	T	F	T	F
F	F	T	T	T	F	T
F	F	F	T	T	F	F

The argument is VALID. Whenever all the premises are true, the conclusion is true too (lines 1, 3, and 5); and in all instances in which the conclusion is false (lines 2, 4, 6, and 8) at least one of the premises is false.

7.

(a) ~(A & P)
(b) P ⇒ C
(c) ~C
(d) A

A	P	C	(A & P)	~(A & P)	(P⇒C)	~C	A
T	T	T	T	F	T	F	T
T	T	F	T	F	F	T	T
T	F	T	F	T	T	F	T
T	F	F	F	T	T	T	T
F	T	T	F	T	T	F	F
F	T	F	F	T	F	T	F
F	F	T	F	T	T	F	F
F	F	F	F	T	T	T	F

The argument is INVALID, because in line 8 of the table, all of the premises are true, but the conclusion is false.

9.

(a) P ⇒ T
(b) E ⇒ M
(c) ~T & ~M
(d) ~P & ~E

P	T	E	M	(P ⇒ T)	(E ⇒ M)	(~T & ~M)	(~P & ~E)
T	T	T	T	T	T	F	F
T	T	T	F	T	F	F	F
T	T	F	T	T	T	F	F
T	T	F	F	T	T	F	F
T	F	T	T	F	T	F	F
T	F	T	F	F	F	T	F
T	F	F	T	F	T	F	F
T	F	F	F	F	T	T	F
F	T	T	T	T	T	F	F
F	T	T	F	T	F	F	F
F	T	F	T	T	T	F	T
F	T	F	F	T	T	F	T
F	F	T	T	T	T	F	F
F	F	T	F	T	F	T	F
F	F	F	T	T	T	F	T
F	F	F	F	T	T	T	T

This argument is VALID: in all cases where the three premises are true (line 16), the conclusion is also true. And, in all instances where the conclusion is false (lines 1 through 10 and 13 and 14) at least one of the premises is also false.

11.

	(1) A ⇒ B	given
	(2) B ⇒ C	given
	(3) ~C	given
So,	(4) ~A	To Prove
	(5) ~B	Lines (2) and (3), Modus Tollens
	(6) ~A	Lines (1) and (5), Modus Tollens

13.

(1) R ⇒ S   given
(2) R ▼ T   given
(3) ~T   given; Therefore: S (To Prove)
(4) R   Lines (2) and (3), Disjunctive Argument
(5) S   Lines (1) and (4), Modus Ponens

15.

(1) R ⇒ W   given
(2) W ⇒ S   given
(3) R   given; Therefore: S (To Prove)
(4) W   Lines (1) and (3), Modus Ponens
(5) S   Lines (2) and (4), Modus Ponens

17.

(1) R ⇒ W   given
(2) W ⇒ S   given
(3) ~S   given; Therefore: ~W (To Prove)
(4) ~W   Lines (2) and (3), Modus Tollens

C LEVEL

1.

(1) D ⇒ C   given
(2) D   given; Therefore: C (To Prove)
(3) C   Lines (1) and (2), Modus Ponens

D	C	D ⇒ C	C
T	T	T	T
T	F	F	F
F	T	T	T
F	F	T	F

The argument is VALID: there are no instances where the conclusion is false and both of the premises are true. In case both of the premises are true (Line 1) the conclusion is also true.

3.

(1) N ⇒ M   given
(2) ~M   given; Therefore: ~N (To Prove)
(3) ~N   lines (1) and (2), Modus Tollens

N	M	N ⇒ M	~M	~N
T	T	T	F	F
T	F	F	T	F
F	T	T	F	T
F	F	T	T	T

The argument is VALID: In all cases where the conclusion is false (lines 1 and 2), at least one of the premises is false also. And, in all cases in which the premises are both true, the conclusion is also true (line 4).

5.

A = You Fear Something, B = You are Fighting Something, C = Something Weakens You, and
D = Higher Levels are Inaccessible

(1) A ⇒ B   given

(2) B ⇒ C   given

(3) C ⇒ D   given [If we take the indicator words at face the third premise could be read as
A ⇒ (C & D) or (A ⇒ C) & D.]

(4) A ⇒ D   (To Prove)

(5) A ⇒ C   lines 1 and 2, Chain Argument

(6) A ⇒ D   lines 5 and 3, Chain Argument

A	B	C	D	(A ⇒ B)	(B ⇒ C)	(C ⇒D)	(A ⇒ D)
T	T	T	T	T	T	T	T
T	T	T	F	T	T	F	F
T	T	F	T	T	F	T	T
T	T	F	F	T	F	T	F
T	F	T	T	F	T	T	T
T	F	T	F	F	T	F	F
T	F	F	T	F	T	T	T
T	F	F	F	F	T	T	F
F	T	T	T	T	T	T	T
F	T	T	F	T	T	F	T
F	T	F	T	T	F	T	T
F	T	F	F	T	F	T	T
F	F	T	T	T	T	T	T
F	F	T	F	T	T	F	T
F	F	F	T	T	T	T	T
F	F	F	F	T	T	T	T

The argument is VALID: In all cases where the three premises are true the conclusion is also true. And, anytime the conclusion is false, at least one of the premises is also false.

NOTE: Also, this way of construing the argument relies on the assumption that "something that weakens you makes you impotent."

7.

M = The Male skeleton is missing a rib. A = The skeleton is Adam's.

(1) M   given

(2) A ⇒ M   To Prove: A

Invalid: Fallacy of Affirming the Consequent

M	A	A ⇒ M	A
T	T	T	T
T	F	T	F
F	T	F	T
F	F	T	F

The argument is INVALID: In line 2, the conclusion is false, but both of the premises are true.

9.

(1) L ⇒ H   given

(2) H ⇒ F   given; To Prove: L ⇒ F

(3) L ⇒ F   Lines 1 and 2, Chain Argument

L	H	F	(L $\Rightarrow$ H)	(H $\Rightarrow$ F)	(L $\Rightarrow$ F)
T	T	T	T	T	T
T	T	F	T	F	F
T	F	T	F	T	T
T	F	F	F	T	F
F	T	T	T	T	T
F	T	F	T	F	T
F	F	T	T	T	T
F	F	F	T	T	T

The argument is VALID: in all cases where the premises are all true (Lines 1, 5, 7, and 8) the conclusion is also true. In all cases where the conclusion is false (Lines 2 and 4), at least one of the premises is also false.

CHAPTER 11
ANSWERS TO EXERCISES ON PAGES 260 AND 261

A   LEVEL

1. Two statements are said to be <u>contrary</u> when both of them cannot possibly be true at the same time, but both could conceivably be false at the same time.

2. ~(A & B) This says that both A and B cannot be true simultaneously. At least one of them, possibly both, have to be false.

3. There are a number of answers which could be given to this question:
   (A) Because <u>any</u> conclusion follows from inconsistent premises or beliefs, it would be possible to justify anything one wanted, which makes reasoning little more than a rubber stamp for whatever we were predisposed unreflectively to believe in the first place.
   (B) A second problematic area would be the upshot of trying to follow inconsistent orders or directions. Because obedience to one means disobedience to another, the only way to keep from violating contradictory instructions may be to do nothing (which may itself be another form of violating them).

4. Advantages of being able to spot inconsistent statements include
   (A) Being able to readjust our belief system and to grow with increased knowledge.
   (B) Being able to critically evaluate other people's reasoning so that you force them to reexamine and readjust their own lines of thinking and behavioral tendencies.
   (C) Being able to recognize when someone else is trying to sell you fallacious goods, so that you have good grounds for refusing to "buy" them.

5. Basically TRUE. At least from the large perspective, insofar as we are trying to determine if both claims can be simultaneously true and if they can be simultaneously false. As we get into details, inconsistent prepositional statements are determined either by truth tables or by the rules governing their usage, while categorical inconsistencies are determined by the Square of Opposition and the Rules for Immediate Inference (See Chapter Seven).

6. True. They just cannot be true simultaneously.

7. False

8. False. We may do it, but it is part of the meaning of "reasonable" in Western Logic that a statement and its contrary or contradiction cannot both be true at the same time.

9. True

10. True

B   LEVEL

1. It is possible to believe in both God and the Devil, especially when the two are not conceived as exactly contradictory to one another (e.g., as having exactly similar powers except one is all good and the other, all evil.) They are not contrary.
3. These two statements are <u>contrary,</u> if a state can have only one capital. Otherwise, they are not contrary, if we assume that Minnesota may have more than one capital.
5. These two are <u>contradictory</u> if they refer to the same place and time.
7. These may both be true. They are not contrary.
9. <u>Inconsistent</u> Statements. They contradict each other

C   LEVEL

1. For example, go back to Case Study Two on pages 36 through 38 and look at the clains made by Dennis Meadows and Lawrence Summers. Which ones of these are inconsistent?.

ANSWERS TO EXERCISES ON PAGES 266 AND 267

A   LEVEL

1. A logical <u>contradiction</u> is the conjunction of two statements related such that one must be true while the other is false and conversely, if the second is true, the first must be false. Such a conjunction shown in a truth table will result in all "false" values in the column under the conjunct.
2. Both contrary and contradictory pairs cannot be true simultaneously. However, contrary statement pairs <u>can</u> both be false (All chewing gum is sugarless/No chewing gum is sugarless), whereas contradictory statement pairs cannot both be false either. (If one is false, the other must necessarily be true.)
3. When the conjunction of those two statements is displayed in a truth table every line under that column will be "false".
4. One way is to derive a statement and its opposite or negation from the given set of premises. That statement and its contradiction may be simple (A & ~A) or complex [~(A ⇒ B) & (A ⇒ B)].
5. True
6. False. The second statement must necessarily be false if the first one is true.
7. False. A truth table will show that line 3 has a value of "true".
8. False. It would be a tautology.
9. False. All contradictory statements are also inconsistent insofar as one of the two has to be false.
10. False. This may generate some controversy, but most likely the disagreement will be verbal: if the statement "it is sunny" is exactly equivalent in meaning to "it is not raining", then the two statements will be seen as contradictory. On the other hand, because this can be seen as a matter of <u>content</u> rather than <u>form</u> some people will maintain that they have seen it raining when in fact the sun was still shining. Since both can be true, they are not even inconsistent.

B   LEVEL

1. Contradictory
3. Inconsistent
5. Contradictory
7. Inconsistent (It may not be moving at all.)
9. Contradictory

11. (1) R ⇒ W   given
    (2) ~(W & S)   given
    (3) S   given
    (4) R   given
    _____
    (5) ~W   Lines 2 and 3, Conjunctive Argument
    (6) ~R   Lines 1 and 5, Modus Tollens
    (7) R & ~R   Lines 4 and 6, Conjunction

13. (1) E ▼ A   given
    (2) A ⇒ L   given
    (3) E ⇒ M   given
    (4) L   given
    (5) E   given
    _____
    (6) M   Lines 3, 5 Modus Ponens

Not contradictory, perhaps she feels both logical and majestic while listening to Beethoven.

ANSWERS TO EXERCISES ON PAGES 269 AND 270

A   LEVEL

1. A <u>tautology</u> is a complex statement usually expressed as a disjunction of a statement and its negation such that a truth table column yields all "true" values.

2. Under any and all conditions, a tautology is true by virtue of its form alone and regardless of its content.

3. Actually, contradictions and tautologies are direct opposites insofar as one is a conjunction of two statements which is always false while the other is a disjunction of two statements which is always true. The tautology may be expressed as the denial of the contradiction and conversely, contradiction may be expressed as the denial of the tautology.

4. A <u>contingent statement</u> is one which yields a mixture of true and false values in a truth table. Basically, it is either a simple statement (they are all contingent statements) or a complex statement that under some truth conditions is true and under other conditions is false. We must look at the content of the statement to determine whether it is true or false.

5. A Tautology differs from a Contingent Statement in two important ways. First, all of the truth values for the tautology are "true", whereas they are not all true for a contingent statement. And, second, a tautology is determined by its form alone whereas a contingent statement is determined by its content.

6. False. (Because of its form.)

7. True. (Sort of: that is, its truth values may under certain conditions be true, but under other conditions be false.)

8. True.
9. True.
10. False. (The contingent statement is the most common.)

B   LEVEL

1.

R ▼ ~R — A Tautology

R	~R	(R ▼ ~R)
T	F	T
F	T	T

3

.

R ⟹ (R ▼ S) A Tautology

R	S	(R ▼ S)	R ⟹ (R ▼ S)
T	T	T	T
T	F	T	T
F	T	T	T
F	F	F	T

5.

(R & ~R) ⟹ (S ▼ ~S) A Tautology

R	S	(R & ~R)	(S ▼ ~S)	[(R & ~R) ⟹ (S ▼ ~S)]
T	T	F	T	T
T	F	F	T	T
F	T	F	T	T
F	F	F	T	T

7.

H ⟹ ~H   A Contingent Statement

H	~H	(H ⟹ ~H)
T	F	F
F	T	T

9. A Contingent Statement (which is true by definition)
11. A Contingent Statement
13. A Contingent Statement
15. A Tautology (R ⟹ R)
17. A Contingent Statement

CHAPTER 12
ANSWERS TO EXERCISES ON PAGES 281 AND 282

A LEVEL

1. <u>Inductive reasoning</u> is argumentation in which the conclusion goes beyond what is contained in the premises. Hence, the conclusion gives us new information. The premises may support this conclusion to a greater or lesser degree, but they can never guarantee it 100%. It would not be a contradiction to say all the premises are true, relevant, and fair, but that the conclusion might still be false. In the case of <u>deductive reasoning,</u> the argument is put forward as if the premises definitely guaranteed the truth of the conclusion all by themselves. No new information is needed because the conclusion is already contained in the premises (allegedly). In <u>valid</u> deductive arguments it would be an outright logical contradiction to maintain that the premises were true, but that the conclusion is false.

2. An <u>analogy</u> is a comparison of the similarities between two things, events, or ideas, usually for the purposes of illustration, speculation, or argumentation. Analogical reasoning is a form of logical inference based upon the assumption that if two things are alike in certain ways then they must be similar in other respects as well.

3. A <u>metaphor</u> is a figure of speech which may constitute a special class of analogies. Strictly speaking they are probably non-argumentative, because they consist of the use of a word or phrase to describe or modify something to which they do not literally apply. Still they may be persuasive because of the connotative force they carry.

4. A <u>speculative analogy</u> is an explicit comparison of one situation with another in order to instigate or guide actions. While it does more than merely illustrate similarities between two things or ideas, it stops short of actually putting forward the reasons or premises necessary to constitute an argument.

5. An <u>illustrative analogy</u> is the clarification of a more difficult or complex point by comparing it with something simpler or more well known. A <u>speculative analogy</u> does not merely seek to enlighten or explain, but to incite action or to direct behavioral tendencies and feelings.

6. True. (Ordinarily)

7. True

8. False. (Although they do not guarantee their conclusions, they are often the best form of reasoning available in the situation.)

9. Maybe True, but not necessarily (i.e., they do not have to be).

10. True

B LEVEL

1. Comparing the conduct of business with a football game is probably a <u>speculative analogy.</u> That is, it is doing more than merely illustrating information about doing business, but it is not trying to prove or establish a conclusion about business on this basis. If it incites one's employees to work harder, or to have a feeling of team spirit and camaraderie, perhaps it is effective for an employer. The problem here may be one of cultural bias: that is, people who do not grow up playing football or who do not like it may feel disenfranchised or slighted by this analogy as if business were not meant for them. Particularly women, Asians, physically challenged persons, to name a few may feel

as if they were being intentionally excluded. It also slights or biases the connotation of business as essentially a competitive, not a cooperative enterprise and also one which is insignificant or playful (like a game) and not of serious importance. Then, of course, we may have just performed overkill on an analogy that was not meant to be all that serious in the first place!

3. This one is a cute play on words but it does not explain or even illustrate very much. It is not an argument by analogy, nor is it speculative.

5. The comparison is one of those which is so time worn that it has probably outlived any utility it may have. If there is a conclusion to this, it is unstated and would probably be that baseball teams cannot be meaningfully compared to basketball teams. If so, we have not been given any real evidence to support such a claim other than the dysanalogy.

7. This one is actually a metaphor in which Marx has "poisoned the well" with the emotional appeal of the word "slave". It is calculated to have the effect of waking up salaried employees and wage earners into "realizing" that they are being exploited and enslaved. The fairness of such a metaphor would depend in part on how much actual evidence was given to support such a claim.

9. This is an illustrative analogy, not an argumentative or a speculative one. As such, it is helpful to a point, as long as we are mindful of some very key differences, such as family or personal interaction which centered around the fireplace but which is usually cut off by passive spectating around the television.

11. This is more of a literary metaphor. Perhaps it is illustrative, but it may also engender the Fallacy of Assuming Existence if it makes us uncritically believe in the existence of souls.

13. Perhaps this is a speculative analogy if it is meant to advise someone to be ruthless in their business endeavors. The use of the term 'rat', which generally has negative connotations, may make this analogy unduly biased. If the analogy is meant to be illustrative, then it may also cause negative impressions about business.

15. This is an illustrative analogy, meant to explain the author's style. It is helpful to those who understand what a musical chord is.

ANSWERS TO EXERCISES ON PAGES 288 THROUGH 290

A   LEVEL

1. The method of agreement asks us to vary the surrounding circumstances, while keeping the suspected cause or effect the same.

2. The method of difference requires us to vary the suspected cause, while we keep the surrounding conditions constant or the same.

3. The method of concomitant variation is one in which we match variations in the suspected cause with variations that occur in the effect.

4. The method of residues is one in which we first correlate known causes with known effects and then conclude that the remaining effects must be the result of the remaining causes.

5. Hasty generalization is a fallacy in which one draws a conclusion about an entire population or a different portion of it from an insufficient number of cases within that population.

6. In the fallacy of accident, one assumes that whatever quality is generally found to be true of a group must be present in each and every member of that group.

7. True
8. False
9. True
10. True (It would also be a Fallacy of the Undistributed Middle Term if analyzed as a Categorical Syllogism.)

B LEVEL

1. Method of Agreement: Try the horn, the lights, the radio, the lighter.
3. Method of Concomitant Variation: Experiment with various temperatures.
5. Method of Concomitant Variation: Correlate speed with distance.
7. Method of Concomitant Variation: Correlate crime rates with different phases of the moon.
9. Combined Method/Concomitant Variation: Establish "control groups", then vary the cholesterol intake.

ANSWERS TO EXERCISES ON PAGES 296 AND 297

A LEVEL

1. Hypothesis.
2. Hypothesis.
3. A causal explanation is one based on the physical relationship between causes and their effects.
4. An intentional explanation is based on the reasons one cites for performing an action.
5. A direct cause is said to be a sufficient cause for producing an effect. A contributory cause relies on other causes to produce the effect.
6. A hypothesis is a prediction about a cause and effect relationship. A theory is a set of concepts which provide a structure for making observations and framing hypotheses.
7. True
8. True
9. False
10. False

B LEVEL

1. Intentional
3. Causal
5. Causal
7. Causal
9. Intentional
11. Intentional
13. Intentional
15. Intentional
17. Causal
19. Intentional

CHAPTER 13

ANSWERS TO EXERCISES ON PAGES 315 THROUGH 325

A   LEVEL

1. One reason why a diagram might be helpful would be that it allows easy reference so that you may return to it again and again as needed when answering more than one question about a relationship or when answering long and protracted questions about the same relationship. On the other hand, if you are quick to visually imagine relationships or if they would require an inordinate amount of time to draw, you might be better off forgoing the diagram altogether.

2. Many standardized tests use analytical reasoning questions for several reasons:
    (a) they do have nice, neat, objective answers which can be justified;
    (b) they test different types of ability to conceptualize abstract relationships and to follow complex lines of reasoning;
    (c) they are not the kind of content questions which may be associated with a particular course of study or curriculum.

3. Usually, it is a good idea to diagram each set of relationships as they occur in the given part of the question, for each may in some way be dependent on the relationships that came before it. However, there are circumstances, for instance when a given piece of evidence makes no sense by itself until it is combined with a later piece of evidence, when this rule of thumb would not apply. Another example would be in the case of syllogistic reasoning; the universal premises should be diagrammed before the particular ones simply in order to make less work and save time.

4. Not only would making assumptions be helpful; sometimes they are absolutely necessary to the solution of a problem or puzzle.

5. First look to the questions that are going to be asked and then utilize the information to sketch out what relationships you can. After all, one of the answers may be "cannot be determined from the information given above".

6. Binary relationships may be diagrammed each as they occur and later combined, or combined from the outset. Which of the two procedures to take will depend upon how much information is given. For example, if you are given that A weighs more than B and that B weighs less than C, you cannot determine at this point whether A weighs more than C, less than C, or the same as C. You will have to await more information.

B   LEVEL

1. C
2. B
3. E (D looks like a great answer, but you need more information before you can draw this conclusion.)

4. B
5. C
6. A

7. D   Do = Male   All are brothers and sisters, if we assume that the relation-
8. E   Re = Female   ships are transitive.
9. D   Mi = Male
10. A   Fa = ?

11. B
12. B   A B C D   E F G H
13. A   D H
14. E   _____   _____   F + G
15. C   EAST   WEST   1–3 / 3–1
16. B

17. C
18. E
19. C
20. B (!)
21. E
22. E

23. A
24. D
25. B
26. E
27. D
28. A

29. D
30. A
31. B
32. C
33. E
34. C

35. D
36. C
37. C
38. A
39. B
40. A

41. A
42. C
43. E

44. B
45. C
46. A

ANSWERS TO EXERCISES ON PAGES 331 THROUGH 337

A LEVEL

1. True
2. False
3. Generally False (but could be true on occasion)
4. True(or more)
5. True
6. True
7. True
8. False
9. True
10. True

B LEVEL

1. E
2. D
3. A
4. B
5. C
6. E

7. B
8. E
9. C
10. A
11. E
12. D
13. A
14. B
15. C

16. C
17. E
18. D
19. B

20. B
21. E
22. A
23. C
24. C
25. C

26. B
27. B
28. B

29. B
30. B

31. A

32. A

C LEVEL

1. Dr. Mitchell is in seat A
   Professor Sachs is in seat B
   General Glunn is in seat C
   Astronaut Armstrong is in seat D
       Gen. Glunn is the murderer.
2. Peter is the murderer. Everything he says is true except C, his profession of innocence. Quince is telling the truth about everything except A, about never having been in the basement. Rota is telling the truth except in her statement D, where she accuses Quince. And, Shelby is telling the truth in three cases, A, B, and C; but, she is lying in her statement D where she denies that the candlestick is hers.

CHAPTER 14
ANSWERS TO EXERCISES ON PAGES 350 THROUGH 357

A LEVEL

1. The Conclusion or main point of the argument
2. To be able to state the conclusion as clearly, concisely, fairly, and adequately as possible in a single sentence.
3. Look for unstated assumptions and implications, clarify meaning, be alert to spot fallacies.
4. To get an overview of how the argument can be developed as well as to illuminate any structural flaws in the reasoning that may not be apparent otherwise.
5. To determine which premises need stronger or more stringent defenses.
6. This strengthens the reasoning by giving it more balance and by making it less susceptible to external attack.
7. A line of reasoning supporting a definition that is not currently accepted or which is controversial.

8. A line of reasoning comparing the point at issue with something better known or more simply understood in order to draw some conclusion about that point.

9. To argue that something is right or wrong; to argue for adopting a course of action; to pass judgment on something; to make a recommendation. . . .

10. Arguments that use laws of probability to establish their conclusions. Remember the warnings regarding Mill's Methods when evaluating them.

B LEVEL

1. Moral Argument
3. Definitional Argument
5. Analogical Argument
7. Statistical Argument
9. Moral Argument

11. D is most specific, followed by C, then B, and finally A
13. A appears to be the strongest, followed by B and C, then D, and finally E
15. D
17. B

Addition - The rule of combining a disjunct to a statement already known to be true.

Affirming a disjunct - An invalid argument of the form A ▼ B, A therefore ~B.

Affirming the consequent - An invalid argument of the form A ⇒ B, B therefore A.

Ambiguity - The confusion that results from the fact that a word or phrase has multiple, definite meanings and in which the intended meaning is not apparent.

Analogical argument - An argument in which an analogy is used in support of a conclusion.

Analogy - The comparison or contrast of two different objects, ideas, or situations.

Antecedent - The "if" part of a conditional statement. Symbolized, it is always placed to the left of the arrow.

Argument - A set of related claims in which one is said to follow from or be based on the others. The two types of claims in an argument are premises and conclusions.

Argument structure - How the premises of an argument are related to the conclusion.

Biconditional - Represented by a "⇔", a biconditional asserts that one component is true if and only if the other is true.

Broken chain - An invalid argument form in which the consequent of neither conditional premise is identical to the antecedent of the other. For instance, A ⇒ B, C ⇒ D therefore A ⇒ D.

Categorical logic - The study of arguments from the standpoint of the relationships between classes of entities or events.

Categorical statement - A premise or conclusion in a categorical argument and in which members of one class are said to be included in or excluded from another class.

Categorical syllogism - A two premise, one conclusion deductive argument in which all three of the statements are categorical in form.

Causal explanation - An explanation based on the relationship between physical causes and their effects.

Chain argument - A valid argument of the form A ⇒ B, B ⇒ C therefore A ⇒ C.

Claim - An assertion or statement capable of being assessed as true or false.

Combination - The joining of two statements into a single conjunction.

Combined method - A combination of the methods of agreement and difference. It is useful when the method of difference should be employed but the surrounding circumstances cannot be varied. Also called the *indirect method of difference.*

Complex dilemma - A valid argument of the form A ▼ B, A ⇒ C, B ⇒ D, therefore C ▼ D.

Compound argument - One in which two or more premises combine to imply the conclusion, but which do not do so independently.

Conclusion - The claim that is to be established or proven in an argument.

Conditional - Represented by a "⇒", a conditional or hypothetical statement asserts that if the first component (or antecedent) is true, then the second component (or consequent) is also true.

Conjunction - Represented by the symbol "&," a conjunction asserts that the two conjoined statements are both true.

Conjunctive argument - A valid argument of the form

~(A & B),A therefore ~B.

Connotation - The set of conditions for a term's use.

Consequent - The "then" part of a conditional statement. Symbolized, it is always placed to the right of the arrow.

Contingent statement - A statement that under some truth conditions is a true statement and under other truth conditions is a false statement. All simple statements are contingent statements.

Contradiction - The conjunction of two statements related in such a way that exactly one must be true and the other must be false. The column under a contradiction in a truth table yields all lines with the value "false."

Contradictions: - Two statements with the same subject and predicate, one of which must be true and the other false. Categorical contradictions are either A-Form versus O-Form or E-Form versus I-Form.

Contraries: - Two statements with similar subjects and predicates, one A-Form and the other E-Form, both of which cannot be true at the same time but which may both be false.

Contrary statements - Two statements which cannot both be true at the same time but which may be simultaneously false.

Convergent argument - One in which two or more independent claims or premises imply the conclusion.

Conversion: - Switching subject and predicate terms.

Critical technique - The eight-step method of critical thinking presented in this book.

Critical thinking - The ability to correctly validate or refute claims presented for our belief.

Definition - What a word means and the conditions governing how to use it.

Definitional argument - An argument seeking to establish the meaning of a term.

Denotation - The set of objects, events, or conditions to which a term is taken to refer.

Denying a conjunct - An invalid argument of the form ~(A & B), ~A therefore B.

Denying the antecedent - An invalid argument of the form A ⇒ B, ~A therefore ~B.

Derivation - This is the extraction of the conclusion from the premises according to the rules of logic.

Disagreement - A difference of opinion, attitude, or belief between two or more persons. or within one and the same person.

Disjunction - Represented by the symbol "▼," a disjunction asserts that one of the two component statements is true. If it is possible that both statements are true, the disjunction is said to be *inclusive*. If only one of the statements may be true, the disjunction is said to be *exclusive*.

Disjunctive argument - A valid argument of the form A ▼ B, ~A therefore B.

Distribution - That property of a class or term referring to the members of that class individually. A term is said to be distributed when reference applies to each and every member of that class. A term is said to be undistributed when reference does not necessarily apply to each and every member, but only to some.

Divergent argument - One in which a statement generates two or more independent conclusions or implications.

Enthymeme: - A syllogistic argument with a missing premise or a missing conclusion.

Equivocation - Occurs when a crucial word or phrase is used in two or more different senses in different contexts in an argument.

Evaluative disagreement - Difference in the assessment of the moral, aesthetic, or practical value of an event, object, or course of action.

Existential fallacy - The violation of Rule 4 of the Rule Method for testing the validity of categorical syllogisms and which holds that whenever both premises are universal statements (A- or E-Form) and the conclusion is a particular statement (I- or O-Form), all three of the terms or classes of the syllogism must be known to have at least one member for the syllogism to be valid.

Explanation - Usually a special kind of argument in which the conclusion is more familiar or better known than the premise or premises supporting it.

Explicit assumption - A claim that is actually stated and functions as the premise of an argument but which *is itself not supported by any further premises.* (An unsupported claim.)

Extraneous statement - A statement that is neither premise nor conclusion.

Factual disagreement - A dispute about a fact. May be settled by observation or experiment.

Fallacy - A mistake in the alleged connections between the premises and conclusion of an argument or within a premise.

Fallacy of faulty exclusions - The violation of Rule 2 of the Rule Method for testing the validity of categorical syllogisms and which holds that a valid categorical syllogism has either (A) no negative (that is, E- or O-Form) statements or (B) one negative statement in the conclusion and one negative statement in the premises.

Fallacy of illicit distribution - The violation of that part of Rule 3 of the Rule Method for testing the validity of categorical syllogisms and which holds that any term which is distributed in the conclusion must also be distributed in the premises.

Fallacy of inadequate premise - One in which the premise is relevant to the conclusion but actually provides insufficient support for that conclusion, or not as much as it claims to provide.

Fallacy of irrelevant premise - One in which the premise seems to support a conclusion but is in fact irrelevant to that conclusion.

Fallacy of the undistributed middle term - The violation of that part of Rule 3 of the Rule Method for testing the validity of categorical syllogisms and which holds that the Middle Term must be distributed at least once.

Fallacy of unfair premise - A fallacy which unfairly stresses a fact or misconstrues an opponent's claim or argument.

Formal equivalence - Statements are formally equivalent when they have the same truth values. This is also known as *logical equivalence.*

Formal reasoning - The assessment of arguments on the basis of their structure and without regard to the actual truth or falsity of the premises.

Grammatical ambiguity - Confusion resulting from faulty sentence construction that is open to two or more distinct interpretations and the context does not help clarify which one is meant.

Hidden assumption - An assumption in an argument that is not explicitly stated, but assumed to be true. A hidden assumption is also known as an *unstated premise,* or *logical presupposition.*

Hypothesis - A prediction about a cause-and-effect relationship.

Illustrative or explanatory analogy - The clarification of a difficult or complex point by comparison with a simpler case.

Immediate inference: - A conclusion drawn from a single statement.

Implication - A claim that follows from another claim such that, if the original claim is true, then the implication must also be true; also called an *unstated conclusion.*

Implicit assumption - An unstated claim functioning as the premise of an argument, sometimes known as an *unstated premise,* or logical presupposition.

Inconsistent statements - A pair of statements which cannot be true at the same time. The two species of inconsistent statements are contrary statements and contradictory statements.

Inductive argument - An argument that does not guarantee the truth of the conclusion, even if the premises are known to be true.

Intentional explanation - An explanation based on the *reason* an individual does something.

Interpretive disagreement - Conflict between different interpretations of the same set of facts.

Invalid arguments - Deductive arguments in which the conclusion is not necessarily true even if all the premises should turn out to be true.

Invalid deductive argument - An argument presented as a valid deductive argument, but due to a flaw in the argument's structure, it is possible for all of the premises to be true while the conclusion is nevertheless false.

Liar's paradox problems - Logical puzzles or riddles the solution to which hinges upon discovering the truth value of particular statements within the puzzle.

Linear argument - An argument in which the premises and conclusions can be arranged such that each claim implies the next.

Logical Connective - A term that connects statements together into a complex statement or that changes the truth value of a statement.

Matrix problems - Logical puzzles that involve the use of grids or matrices to determine what is true and false of the individuals or things represented in the matrix.

Meaning - What a word or phrase signifies, represents, or portends or how it is used in a particular context.

Mediate inference: - A conclusion (such as that of a syllogism) reached through the connection of two terms by a "mediate" or third term that bridges the gap between the other two terms.

Method of agreement - The variation of the surrounding circumstances of a suspected cause.

Method of concomitant variation - The correlation of varying degrees of a cause with varying degrees of the effect.

Method of difference - The variation of the suspected cause.

Method of residues - The correlation of causes and effects with the resulting "residue" effects attributed to the "leftover" causes.

Mill's methods - Methods of inductive reasoning analyzed by the philosopher John Stuart Mill.

Modus ponens - A valid argument of the form A $\Rightarrow$ B,

A therefore B.

Modus tollens - A valid argument of the form A ⇒ B, ~B therefore ~A.

Moral argument - An argument that attempts to establish that something "ought" to be the case or that something is "right" or "wrong."

Necessary condition - A condition that must be present for another to occur. It is symbolized as the consequent of a conditional.

Negation - Represented by a "~", a negation asserts that the following statement is *false*.

Obversion - Changing affirmative or positive statements to negative ones and negatives to positive or affirmative ones.

Position Problems - Logical puzzles that involve the spatial arrangement of people or things.

Premise - A claim offered in support of the conclusion.

Principle of fairness - The idea that one should be as fair as possible in assigning unstated premises or implications to the argument advanced by another.

Propositional logic - The study of relationships among specific assertions and denials and the assessment of the validity or invalidity of resulting argument forms.

Quantitative vagueness - Occurs when an expression is employed that refers to an indefinite amount of something.

Referential ambiguity - Occurs when a word or phrase can refer to two or more things, and it is not clear which of the two is intended.

Referential vagueness - Results from the use of a term that is not specific enough to indicate the conditions under which the term would apply.

Reportive definition - States how a term is actually used in normal language, or technically, or in the past.

Simple dilemma - A valid argument of the form A ▼ B, A ⇒ C, B ⇒ C therefore C.

Simplification - The assertion of one of a pair of conjuncts.

Sorites: - An argument composed of a string of categorical syllogisms, the conclusion of one becoming a premise for the next. Because sorites usually do not state the implied conclusions, they are examples of enthymemes.

Sound argument - A valid argument in which all of the premises are in fact true. The conclusion of a sound argument *must* be true.

Square of opposition: - A diagram showing the truth-relationships between different forms of categorical statements.

Speculative analogy - An analogy used to guide actions.

Statistical argument - An argument based on probability theory.

Stipulative definition - Specifies the precise meaning of how a term is going to be used in a specific context.

Strong inductive argument - One in which the truth of the premises establishes a relatively high degree of probability that the conclusion is also true.

Subalterns: - Two statements with the same subject and predicate, one of which is a universal statement (A-Form or E-Form), the other of which is a particular statement (I-Form or O-Form). If the universal statement is true and the class is known to contain at least one member, then the particular statement must also be true.

Subcontraries: - Two statements with the same subject and predicate, one I-Form and the other O-Form, which cannot both be false but may both be true.

Sufficient condition - A condition the presence of which is sufficient to conclude that another condition is also present. It is symbolized as the antecedent of a conditional.

Symbolic logic - The use of symbols to designate the logical connections between statements in order to assess the validity of arguments.

Tautology - A disjunction of a statement and its negation; it is always true. Its column in a truth table yields every line with a value of "true."

Term mention - A referral to the actual word or phrase itself—a term is mentioned when we talk about a term itself rather than using it.

Term use - The actual employment of a word or phrase in referring to a situation, event, or object.

Theory - A set of concepts that gives one a structure by which to make observations and frame hypotheses.

Truth table - A method for determining the truth value of complex statements. They can be used to establish whether or not two complex statements are logically equivalent. They can also be used to determine whether or not an argument is valid.

Truth value - Whether a statement is true or false.

Unstated conclusion - A conclusion not explicitly stated but usually thought to be inevitable given the con-

tent and structure of an argument. Also called a *logical implication.*

Unstated premise - A missing link in an inductive argument which connects the content of the premises with the content of the conclusion so as to turn the argument into a deductive one. Unstated premises are sometimes called logical or hidden assumptions or presuppositions.

Unsupported claim - A statement which functions as a premise in an argument but does not have another statement to act as a premise for it.

Vagueness by stress - The fact that the same set of words may be understood differently depending on how the words are stressed or accentuated.

Valid arguments - Deductive arguments in which if and only if all the premise all turn out to be true, does the conclusion *have* to be true.

Valid deductive argument - One that guarantees the truth of its conclusions. Another way of stating this is that if the premises of an argument are true, its conclusion *must* also be true.

Verbal disagreement - Results from different understandings of the meaning of a word or phrase.

Weak inductive argument - One in which the truth of the premises establishes a relatively low degree of probability that the conclusion is also true.